P9-DDG-367

Frontier

VOLUME TWO

DARWYN COOKE
WRITER AND ILLUSTRATOR

DAVE STEWART
COLORIST

JARED K. FLETCHER
LETTERER

Dan DiDio
VP-EXECUTIVE EDITOR

Mark Chiarello
EDITOR-ORIGINAL SERIES

Valerie D'Orazio
ASSISTANT EDITOR-ORIGINAL SERIES

Anton Kawasaki
EDITOR-COLLECTED EDITION

Robbin Brosterman
SENIOR ART DIRECTOR

Amie Brockway-Metcalf
ART DIRECTOR

Paul Levitz
PRESIDENT & PUBLISHER

Georg Brewer
VP-DESIGN & RETAIL PRODUCT DEVELOPMENT

Richard Bruning
SENIOR VP-CREATIVE DIRECTOR

Patrick Caldon
SENIOR VP-FINANCE & OPERATIONS

Chris Caramalis
VP-FINANCE

Terri Cunningham
VP-MANAGING EDITOR

Alison Gill
VP-MANUFACTURING

Rich Johnson
VP-BOOK TRADE SALES

Hank Kanalz
VP-GENERAL MANAGER, WILDSTORM

Lillian Laserson
SENIOR VP & GENERAL COUNSEL

Jim Lee
EDITORIAL DIRECTOR-WILDSTORM

David McKillips
VP-ADVERTISING & CUSTOM PUBLISHING

John Nee
VP-BUSINESS DEVELOPMENT

Gregory Noveck
SENIOR VP-CREATIVE AFFAIRS

Cheryl Rubin
SENIOR VP-BRAND MANAGEMENT

Bob Wayne
VP-SALES & MARKETING

DC: THE NEW FRONTIER VOLUME TWO

DC COMICS
1700 Broadway, New York, NY 10019
A Warner Bros. Entertainment Company

Printed in Canada. First Printing.
ISBN: 1-4012-0461-9

Cover painting and publication design
by Darwyn Cooke

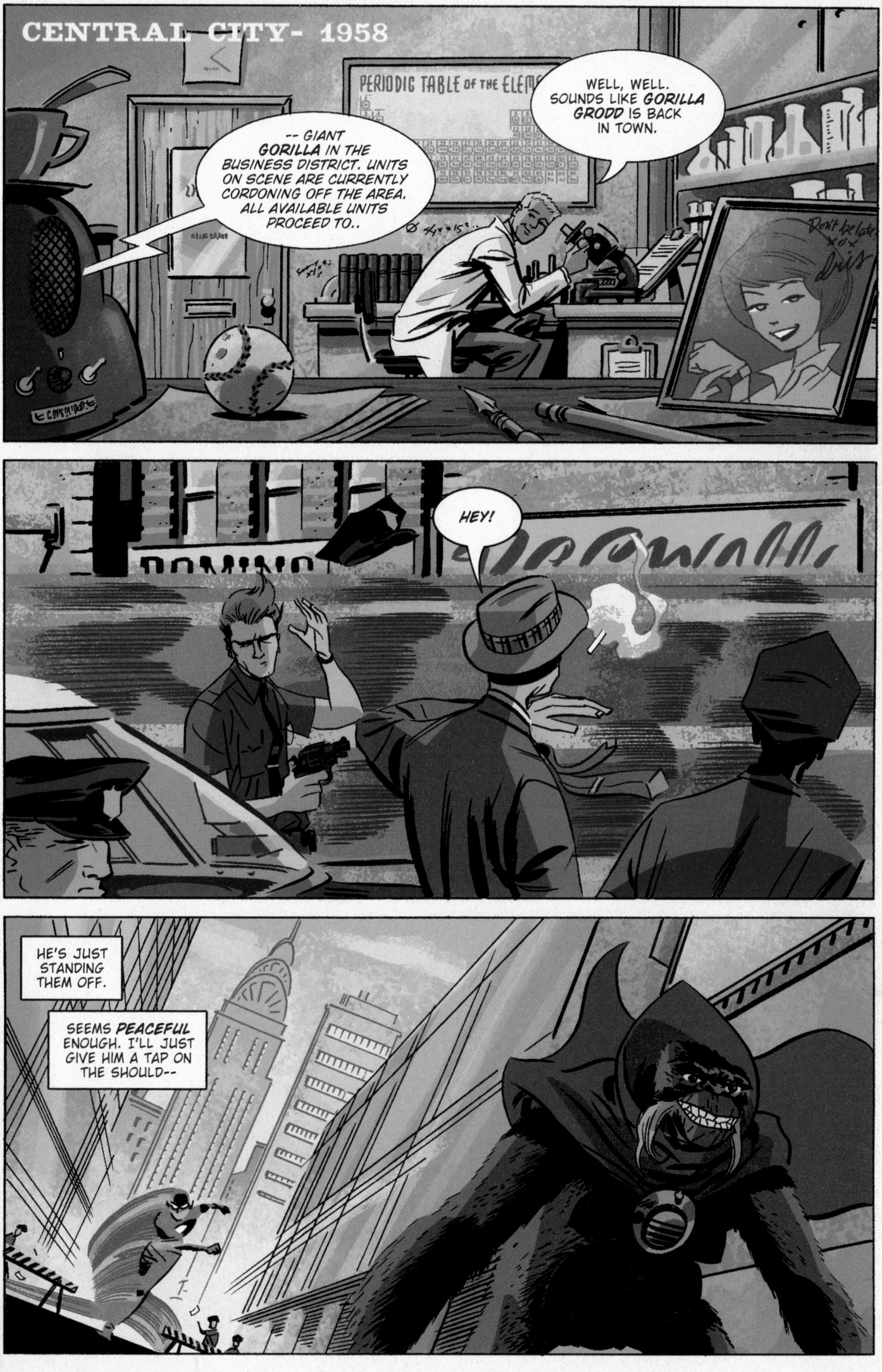
CENTRAL CITY- 1958
-- GIANT GORILLA IN THE BUSINESS DISTRICT. UNITS ON SCENE ARE CURRENTLY CORDONING OFF THE AREA. ALL AVAILABLE UNITS PROCEED TO..
WELL, WELL. SOUNDS LIKE GORILLA GRODD IS BACK IN TOWN.
PERIODIC TABLE OF THE ELEME
HEY!
HE'S JUST STANDING THEM OFF.
SEEMS PEACEFUL ENOUGH. I'LL JUST GIVE HIM A TAP ON THE SHOULD--

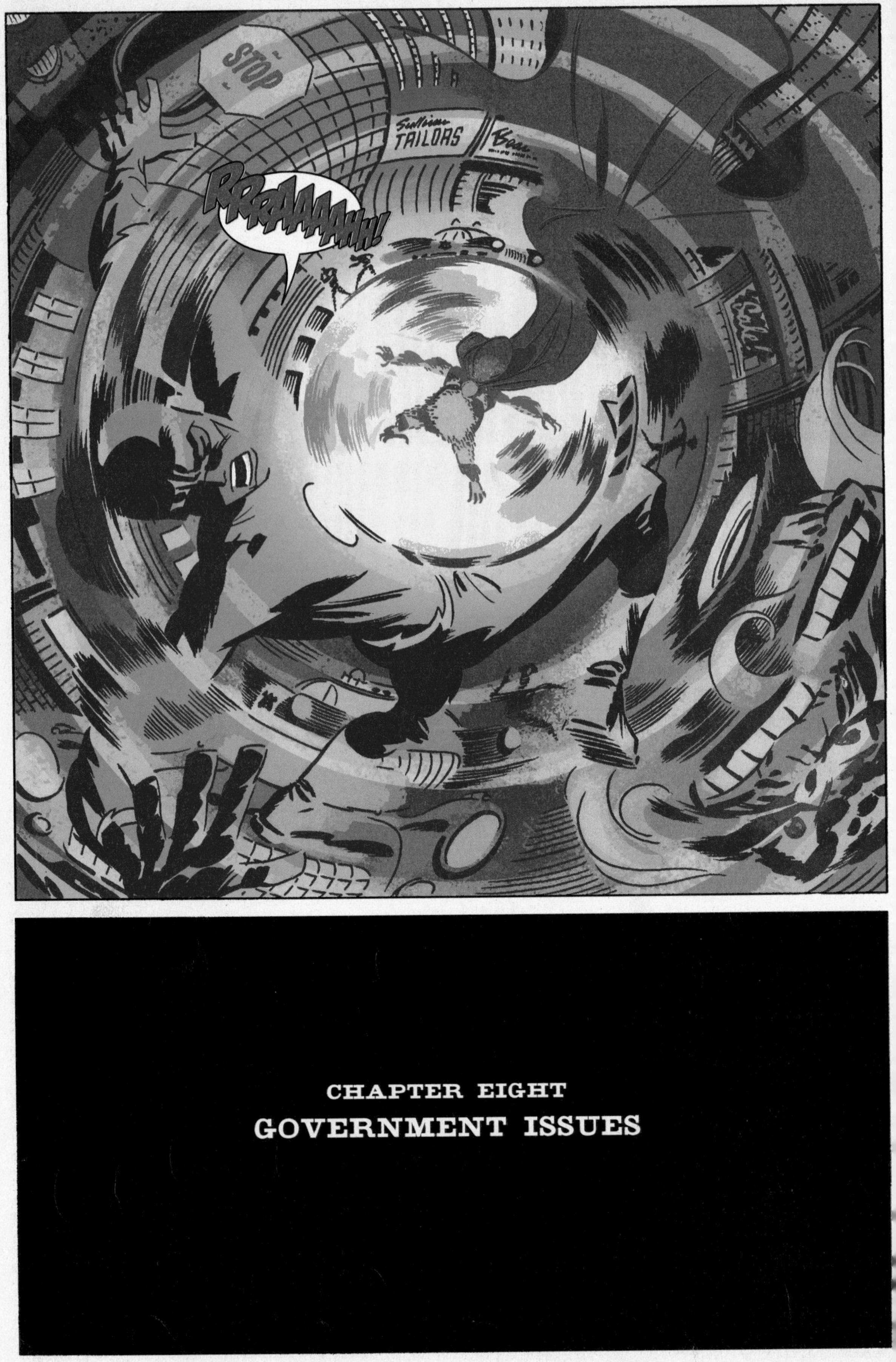
STOP
TAILORS
RRRAAAAAHH!

CHAPTER EIGHT

GOVERNMENT ISSUES

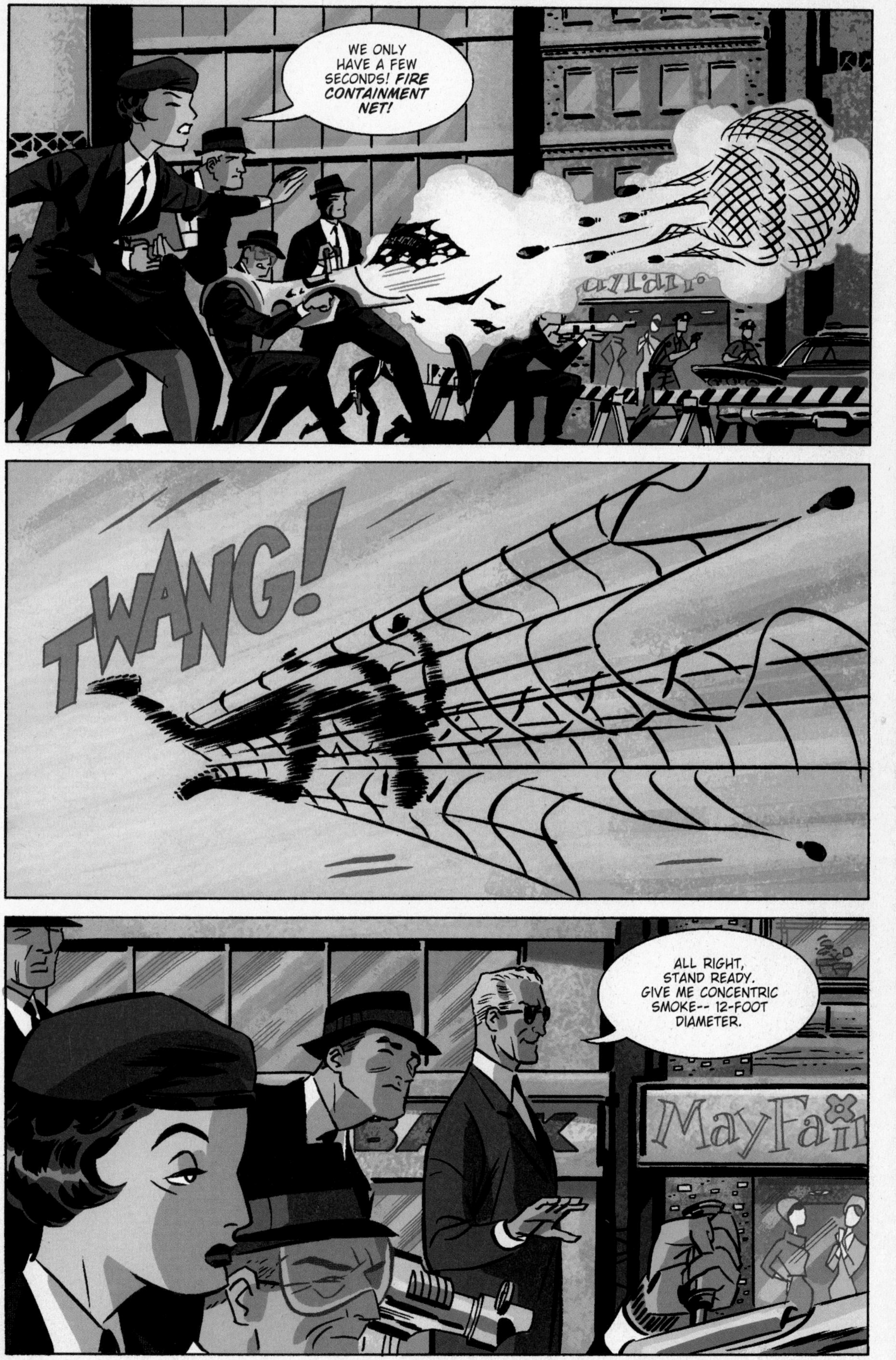
WE ONLY HAVE A FEW SECONDS! FIRE CONTAINMENT NET!
TWANG!
ALL RIGHT, STAND READY. GIVE ME CONCENTRIC SMOKE-- 12-FOOT DIAMETER.
MayFair

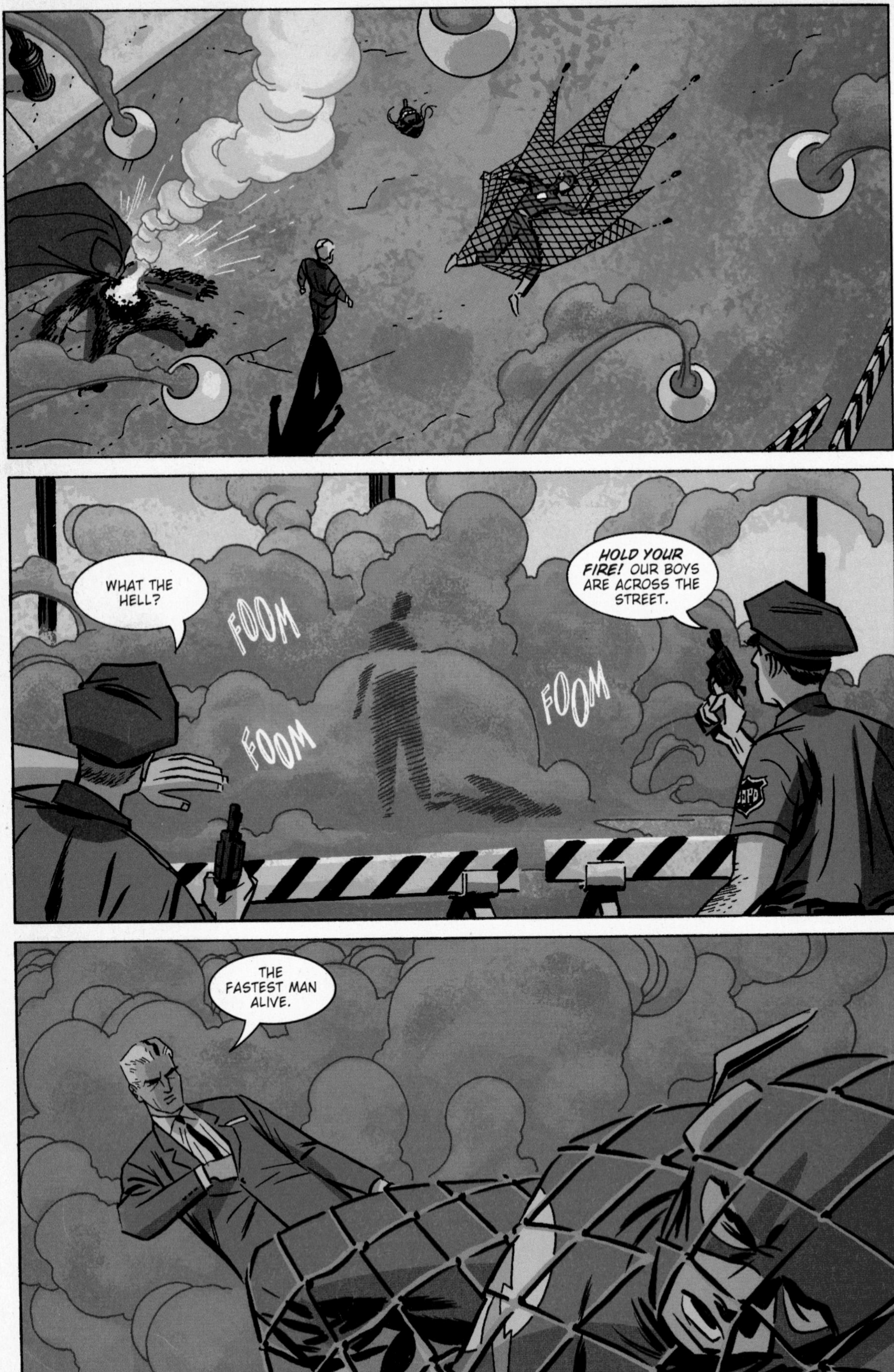
WHAT THE HELL?
HOLD YOUR FIRE! OUR BOYS ARE ACROSS THE STREET.
FOOM
FOOM
FOOM
THE FASTEST MAN ALIVE.

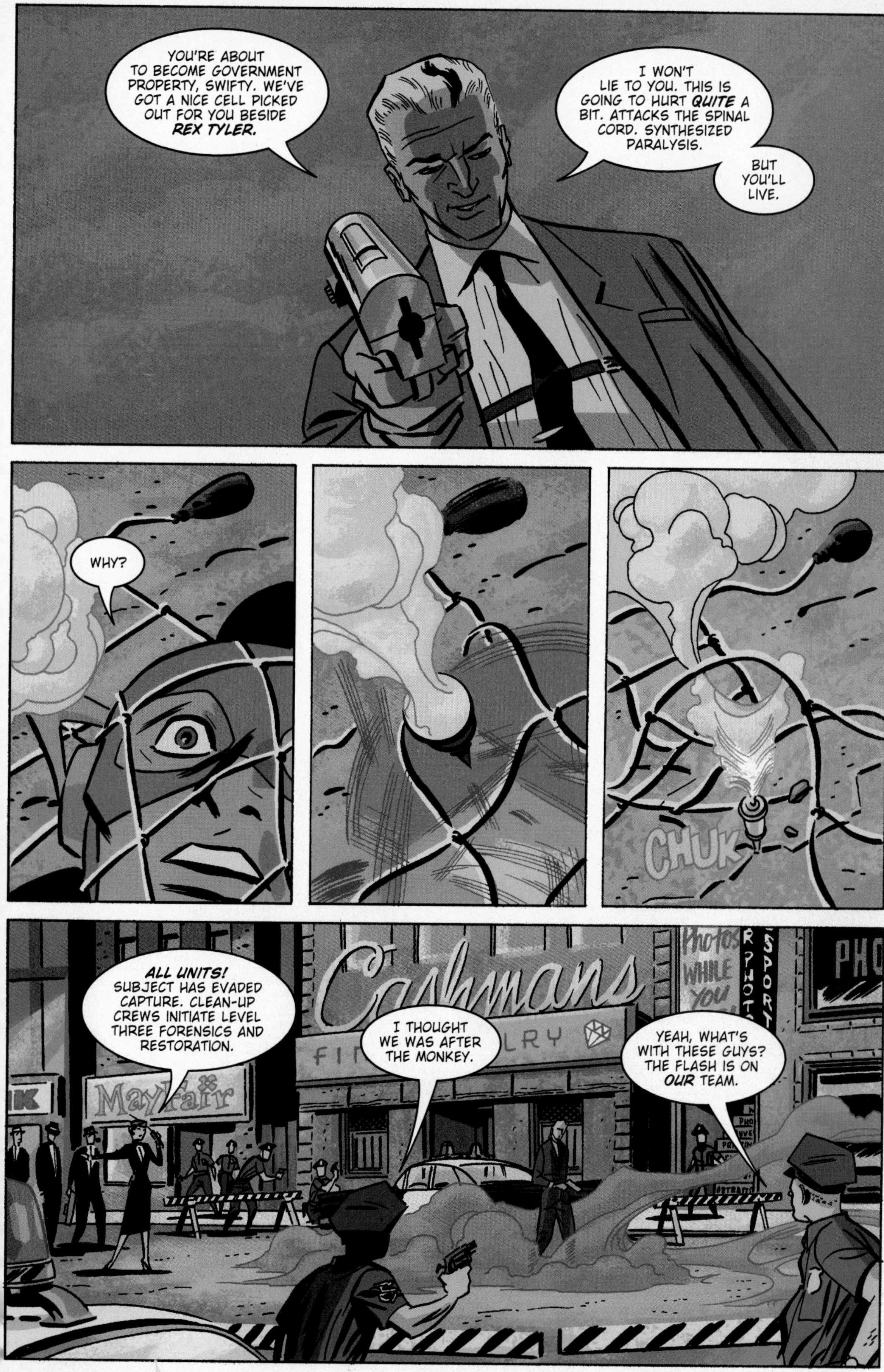
YOU'RE ABOUT TO BECOME GOVERNMENT PROPERTY, SWIFTY. WE'VE GOT A NICE CELL PICKED OUT FOR YOU BESIDE REX TYLER.
I WON'T LIE TO YOU. THIS IS GOING TO HURT QUITE A BIT. ATTACKS THE SPINAL CORD. SYNTHESIZED PARALYSIS.
BUT YOU'LL LIVE.
WHY?
CHUK
ALL UNITS! SUBJECT HAS EVADED CAPTURE. CLEAN-UP CREWS INITIATE LEVEL THREE FORENSICS AND RESTORATION.
I THOUGHT WE WAS AFTER THE MONKEY.
YEAH, WHAT'S WITH THESE GUYS? THE FLASH IS ON OUR TEAM.
Cashmans
MayFair
Photos WHILE YOU

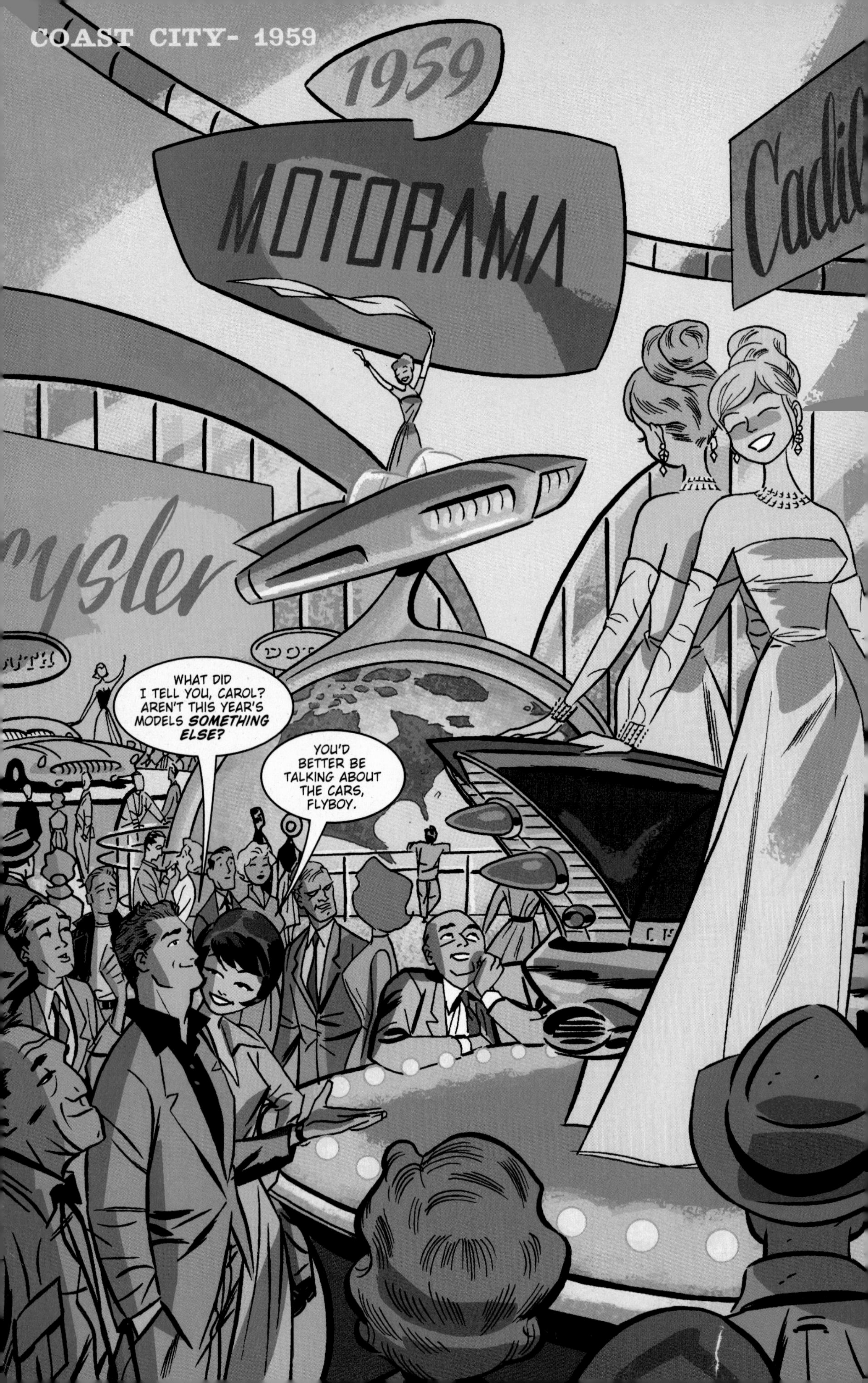
COAST CITY- 1959
1959
MOTORAMA
Cadil
ysler
WHAT DID I TELL YOU, CAROL? AREN'T THIS YEAR'S MODELS SOMETHING ELSE?
YOU'D BETTER BE TALKING ABOUT THE CARS, FLYBOY.

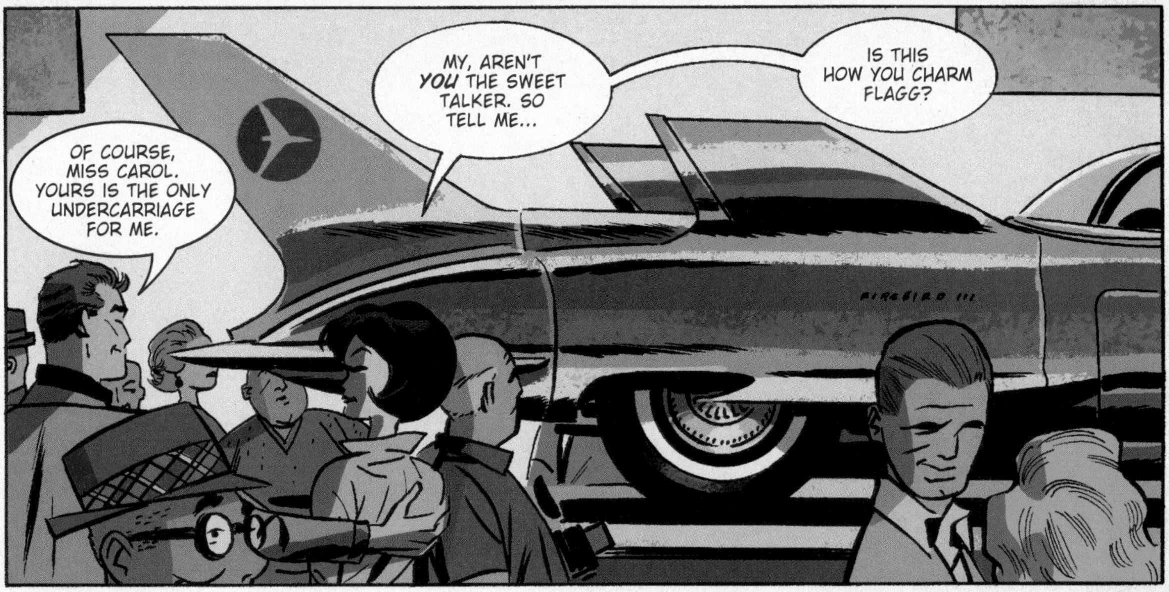
OF COURSE, MISS CAROL. YOURS IS THE ONLY UNDERCARRIAGE FOR ME.
MY, AREN'T YOU THE SWEET TALKER. SO TELL ME...
IS THIS HOW YOU CHARM FLAGG?

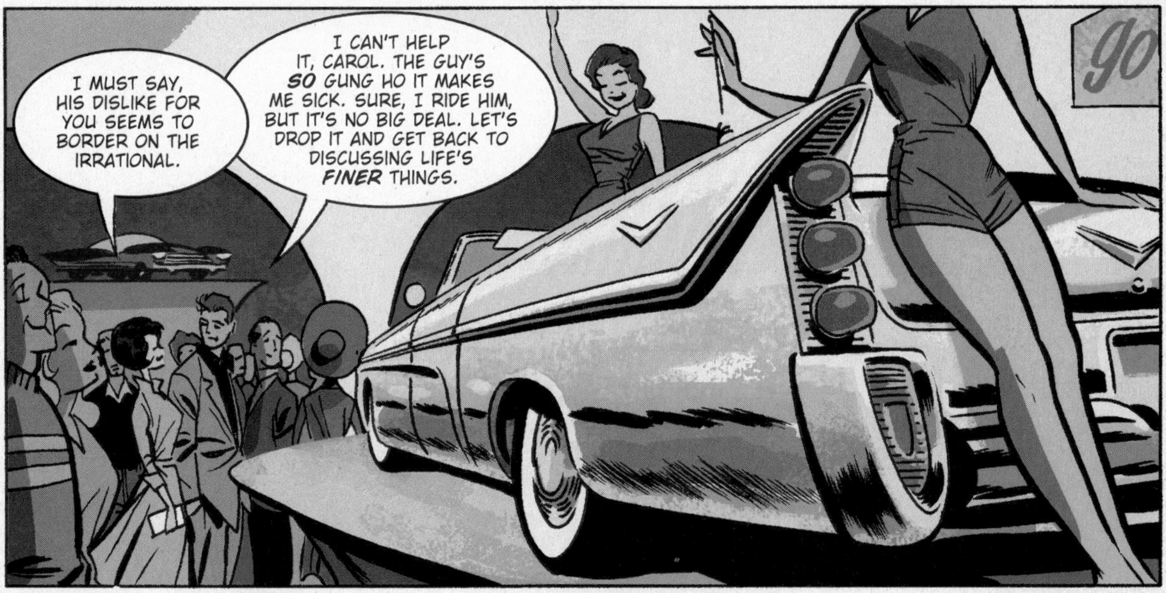
I MUST SAY, HIS DISLIKE FOR YOU SEEMS TO BORDER ON THE IRRATIONAL.
I CAN'T HELP IT, CAROL. THE GUY'S SO GUNG HO IT MAKES ME SICK. SURE, I RIDE HIM, BUT IT'S NO BIG DEAL. LET'S DROP IT AND GET BACK TO DISCUSSING LIFE'S FINER THINGS.

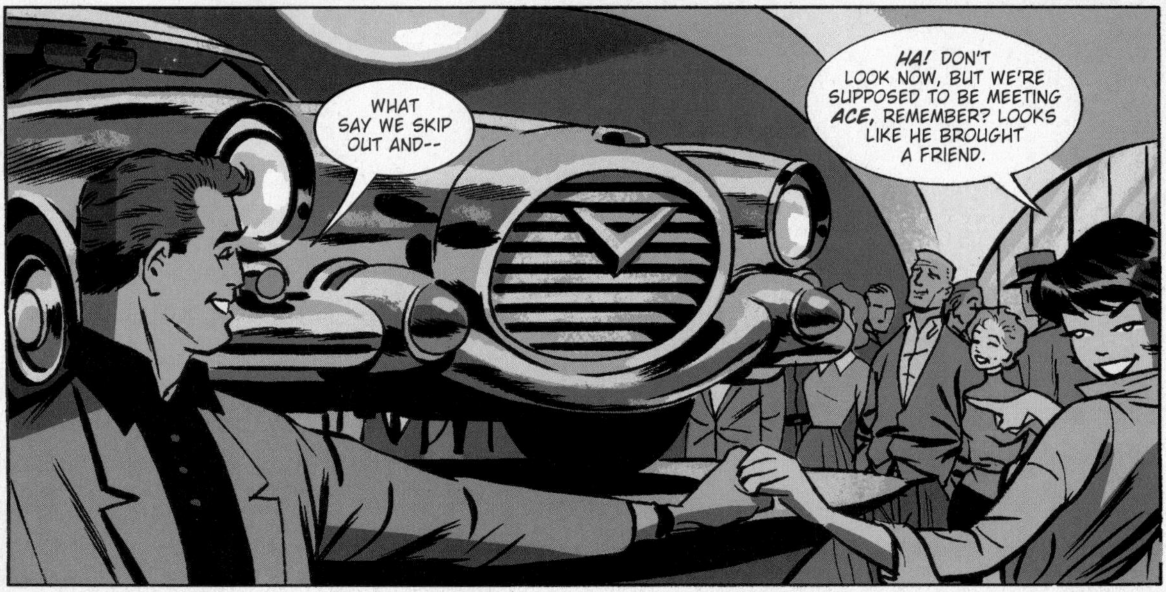
WHAT SAY WE SKIP OUT AND--
HA! DON'T LOOK NOW, BUT WE'RE SUPPOSED TO BE MEETING ACE, REMEMBER? LOOKS LIKE HE BROUGHT A FRIEND.

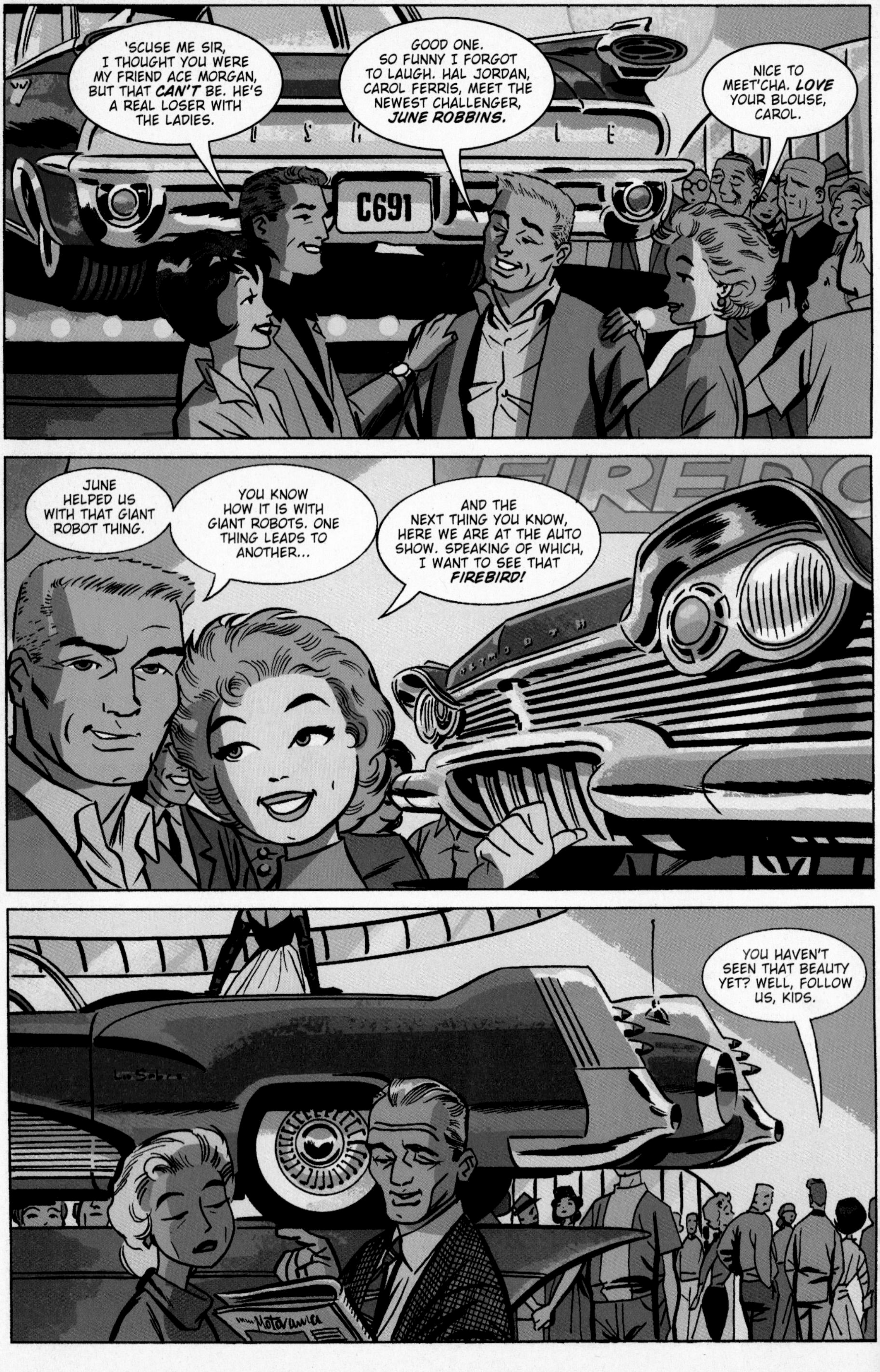
'SCUSE ME SIR, I THOUGHT YOU WERE MY FRIEND ACE MORGAN, BUT THAT CAN'T BE. HE'S A REAL LOSER WITH THE LADIES.
GOOD ONE. SO FUNNY I FORGOT TO LAUGH. HAL JORDAN, CAROL FERRIS, MEET THE NEWEST CHALLENGER, JUNE ROBBINS.
NICE TO MEET'CHA. LOVE YOUR BLOUSE, CAROL.
C691
JUNE HELPED US WITH THAT GIANT ROBOT THING.
YOU KNOW HOW IT IS WITH GIANT ROBOTS. ONE THING LEADS TO ANOTHER...
AND THE NEXT THING YOU KNOW, HERE WE ARE AT THE AUTO SHOW. SPEAKING OF WHICH, I WANT TO SEE THAT FIREBIRD!
YOU HAVEN'T SEEN THAT BEAUTY YET? WELL, FOLLOW US, KIDS.

CIVIL RIGHTS. IT HAS BECOME QUITE AN ISSUE IN AMERICA, AND FOR OBVIOUS REASONS, I TRY TO FOLLOW THE ISSUE CLOSELY.

Modern Day John Henry
Is this Southern vigilante a criminal or freedom fighter?
by Vicki Vale

Knoxville, Tennessee. 6 more members of the Ku Klux Klan were hospitalized last night for wounds suffered during an encounter with the vigilante known as "John Henry". This is the fifth such attack in as man's weeks. The appearance of John Henry has helped to further polarize an area that is already being torn apart by civil rights issues.

For years, it has been speculated that several areas of the South are controlled by the Klan. With members in every area of local and state politics and law enforcement, the Klan has been said to effectively block Federal civil initiatives. The rural areas outside the small town of Knoxville are no exception. As far back as the late 1800s, the KKK have controlled the region. Research to very few d Rights ab should get ic

one topic being discussed by both Black White in Knoxville. Everyone is talking about the vigilante known as John Henry Paul "lil Blue" Layne is a 27 year Man who lives in Willow Cr Knoxville. On the night of was hidden outside the for a meeting of the break up. He had three weeks record the

THIS JOHN HENRY, FOR EXAMPLE. A TRUE AMERICAN HERO, LIKE THE FATHERS OF THE REVOLUTION. HE FIGHTS ALONE FOR THE OPPRESSED, AGAINST AN EVIL THE REST OF THE COUNTRY IGNORES.

IF ONLY THERE WAS MORE MATERIAL AVAILABLE, BUT IT IS A SUBJECT THAT IS COVERED SOMEWHAT POORLY, CONSIDERING ITS IMPORTANCE.

MY INTEREST IN SUBJECTS LIKE RACISM AND UFO SIGHTINGS HAS MADE ME SOMETHING OF AN ECCENTRIC TO MY FELLOW OFFICERS. THEY KID ME QUITE A BIT...

...BUT I'VE BECOME THE PRECINCT'S RESIDENT EXPERT IN CRAZINESS.

HEY JOHN, HAVE WE GOT ONE FOR YOU!

NO DOUBT, JOHNNY BOY, THIS GUY IS ONE FOR YOUR WALL.

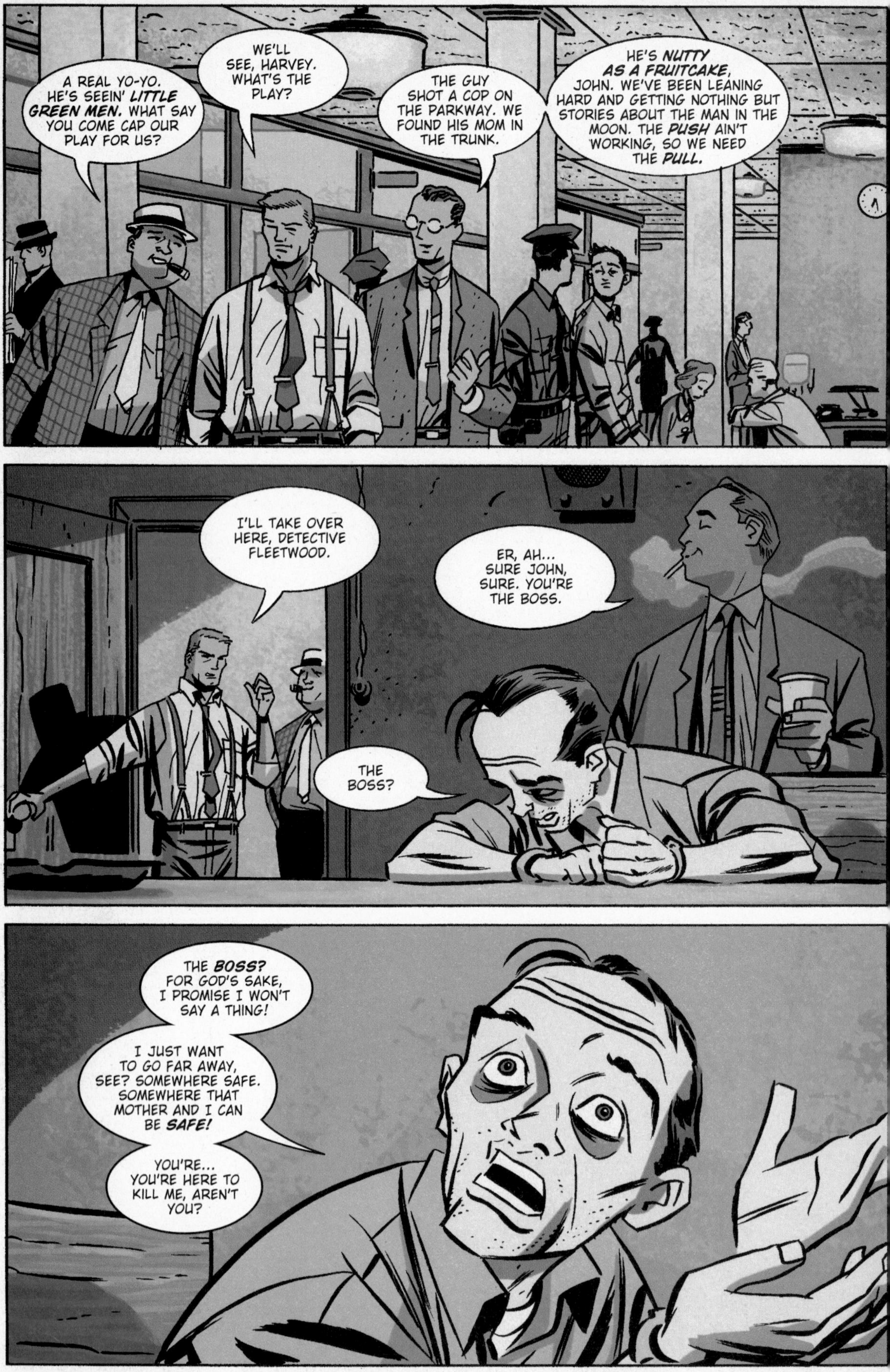
A REAL YO-YO. HE'S SEEIN' LITTLE GREEN MEN. WHAT SAY YOU COME CAP OUR PLAY FOR US?
WE'LL SEE, HARVEY. WHAT'S THE PLAY?
THE GUY SHOT A COP ON THE PARKWAY. WE FOUND HIS MOM IN THE TRUNK.
HE'S NUTTY AS A FRUITCAKE, JOHN. WE'VE BEEN LEANING HARD AND GETTING NOTHING BUT STORIES ABOUT THE MAN IN THE MOON. THE PUSH AIN'T WORKING, SO WE NEED THE PULL.
I'LL TAKE OVER HERE, DETECTIVE FLEETWOOD.
ER, AH... SURE JOHN, SURE. YOU'RE THE BOSS.
THE BOSS?
THE BOSS? FOR GOD'S SAKE, I PROMISE I WON'T SAY A THING!
I JUST WANT TO GO FAR AWAY, SEE? SOMEWHERE SAFE. SOMEWHERE THAT MOTHER AND I CAN BE SAFE!
YOU'RE... YOU'RE HERE TO KILL ME, AREN'T YOU?

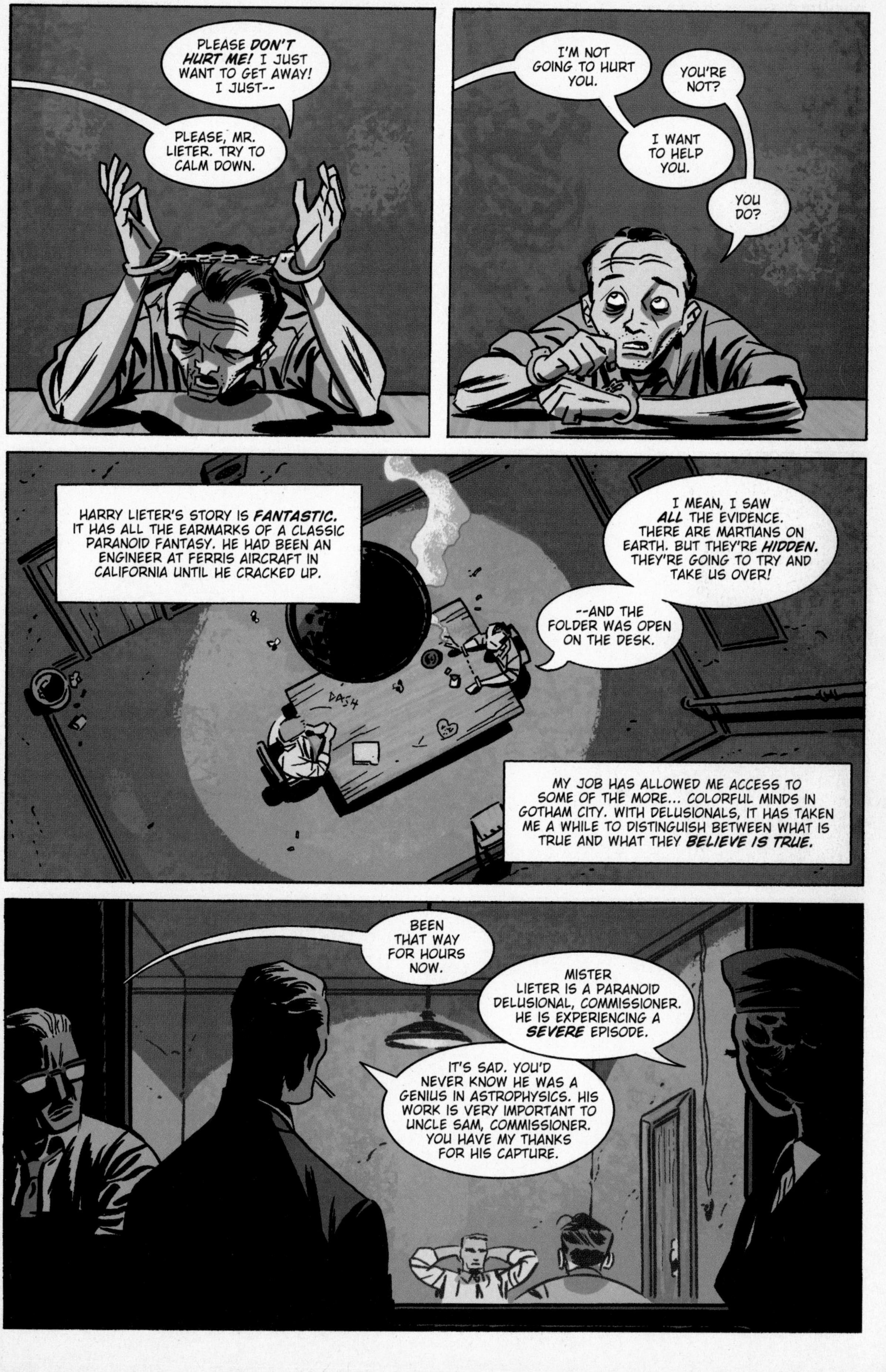
PLEASE DON'T HURT ME! I JUST WANT TO GET AWAY! I JUST--
PLEASE, MR. LIETER. TRY TO CALM DOWN.
I'M NOT GOING TO HURT YOU.
YOU'RE NOT?
I WANT TO HELP YOU.
YOU DO?
HARRY LIETER'S STORY IS FANTASTIC. IT HAS ALL THE EARMARKS OF A CLASSIC PARANOID FANTASY. HE HAD BEEN AN ENGINEER AT FERRIS AIRCRAFT IN CALIFORNIA UNTIL HE CRACKED UP.
I MEAN, I SAW ALL THE EVIDENCE. THERE ARE MARTIANS ON EARTH. BUT THEY'RE HIDDEN. THEY'RE GOING TO TRY AND TAKE US OVER!
--AND THE FOLDER WAS OPEN ON THE DESK.
DASH
MY JOB HAS ALLOWED ME ACCESS TO SOME OF THE MORE... COLORFUL MINDS IN GOTHAM CITY. WITH DELUSIONALS, IT HAS TAKEN ME A WHILE TO DISTINGUISH BETWEEN WHAT IS TRUE AND WHAT THEY BELIEVE IS TRUE.
BEEN THAT WAY FOR HOURS NOW.
MISTER LIETER IS A PARANOID DELUSIONAL, COMMISSIONER. HE IS EXPERIENCING A SEVERE EPISODE.
IT'S SAD. YOU'D NEVER KNOW HE WAS A GENIUS IN ASTROPHYSICS. HIS WORK IS VERY IMPORTANT TO UNCLE SAM, COMMISSIONER. YOU HAVE MY THANKS FOR HIS CAPTURE.

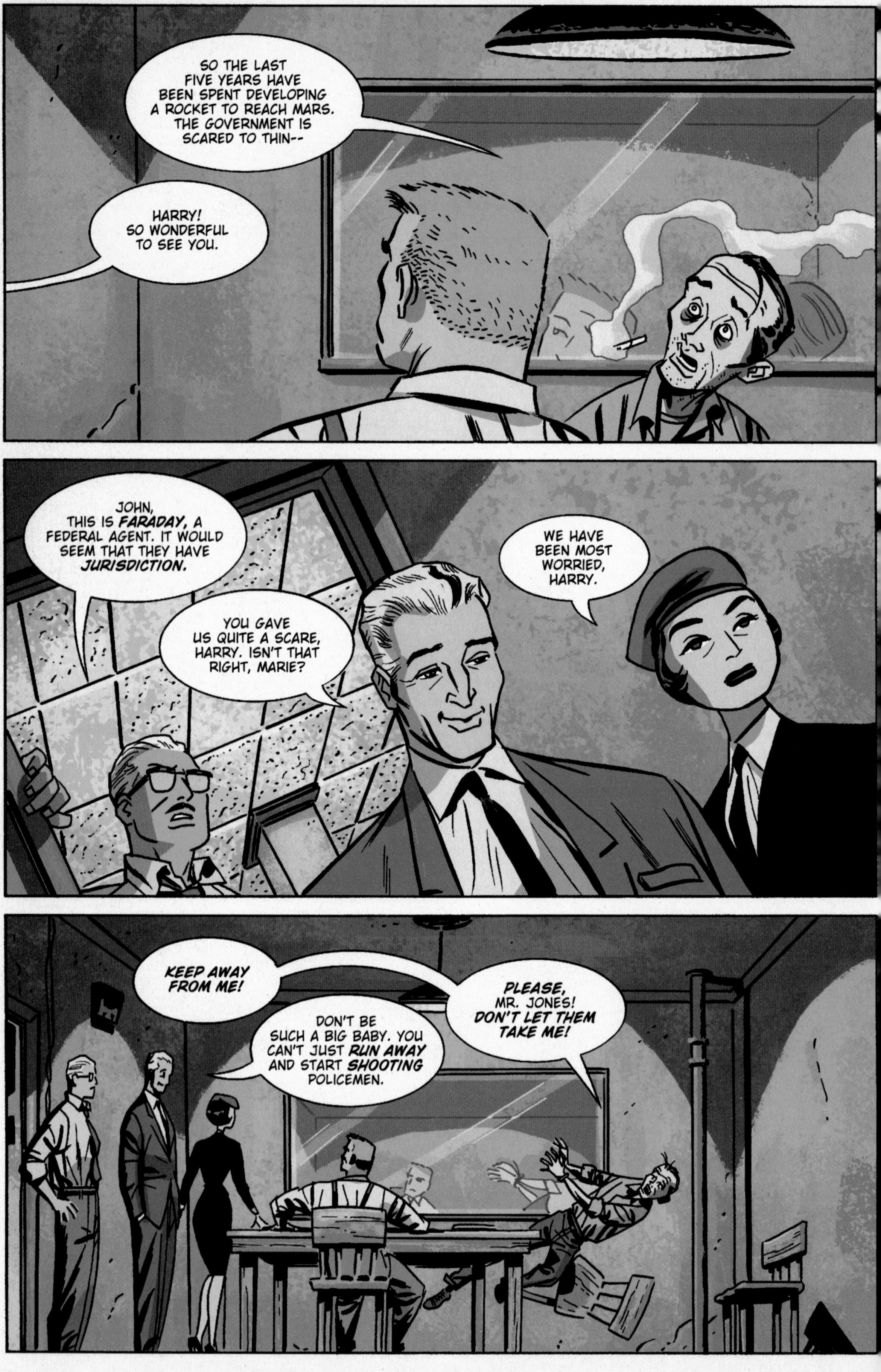
SO THE LAST FIVE YEARS HAVE BEEN SPENT DEVELOPING A ROCKET TO REACH MARS. THE GOVERNMENT IS SCARED TO THIN--
HARRY! SO WONDERFUL TO SEE YOU.
JOHN, THIS IS FARADAY, A FEDERAL AGENT. IT WOULD SEEM THAT THEY HAVE JURISDICTION.
YOU GAVE US QUITE A SCARE, HARRY. ISN'T THAT RIGHT, MARIE?
WE HAVE BEEN MOST WORRIED, HARRY.
KEEP AWAY FROM ME!
PLEASE, MR. JONES! DON'T LET THEM TAKE ME!
DON'T BE SUCH A BIG BABY. YOU CAN'T JUST RUN AWAY AND START SHOOTING POLICEMEN.

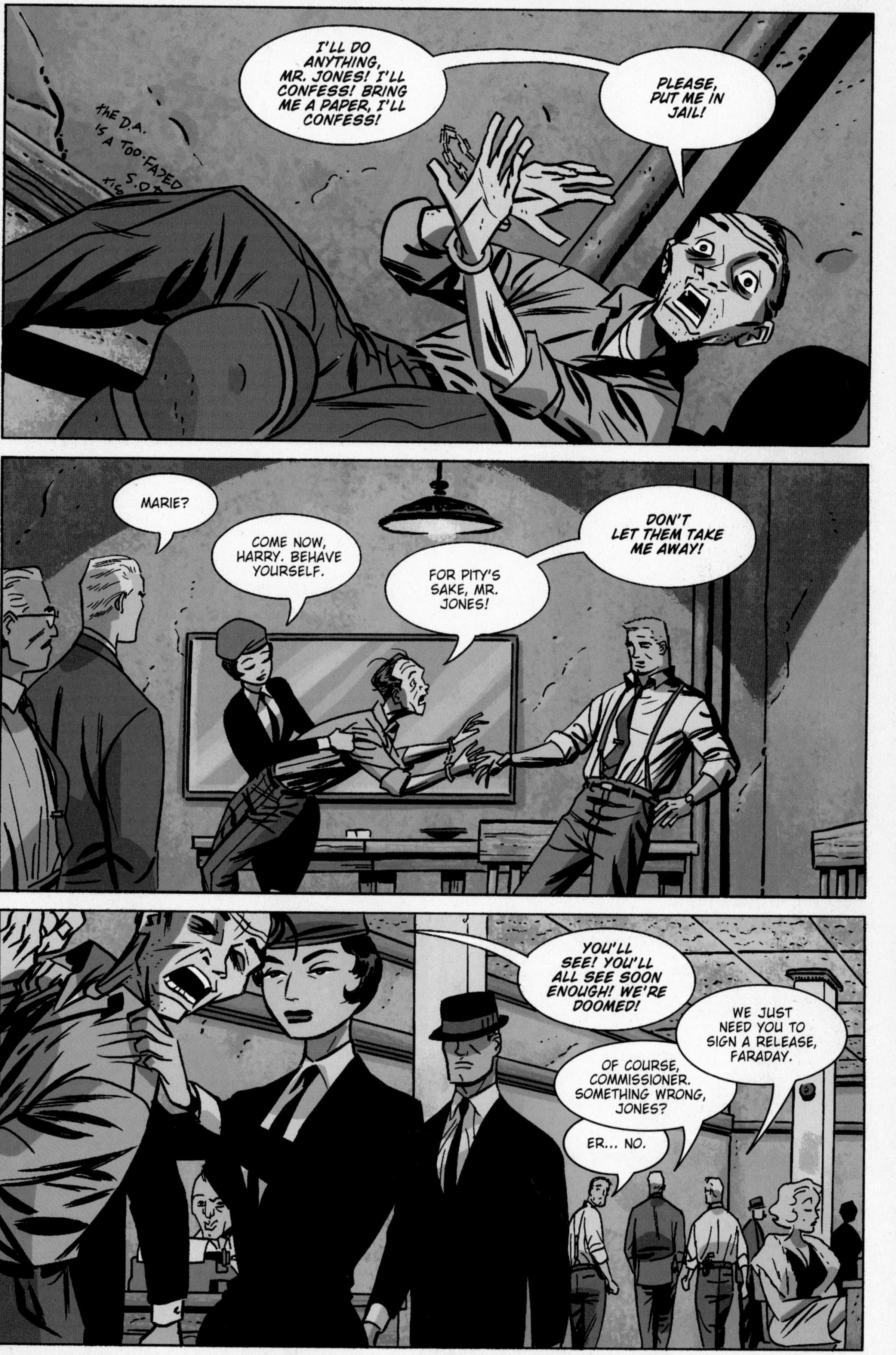
THE D.A. IS A TOO-FADED
I'LL DO ANYTHING, MR. JONES! I'LL CONFESS! BRING ME A PAPER, I'LL CONFESS!
PLEASE, PUT ME IN JAIL!
MARIE?
COME NOW, HARRY. BEHAVE YOURSELF.
FOR PITY'S SAKE, MR. JONES!
DON'T LET THEM TAKE ME AWAY!
YOU'LL SEE! YOU'LL ALL SEE SOON ENOUGH! WE'RE DOOMED!
WE JUST NEED YOU TO SIGN A RELEASE, FARADAY.
OF COURSE, COMMISSIONER. SOMETHING WRONG, JONES?
ER... NO.

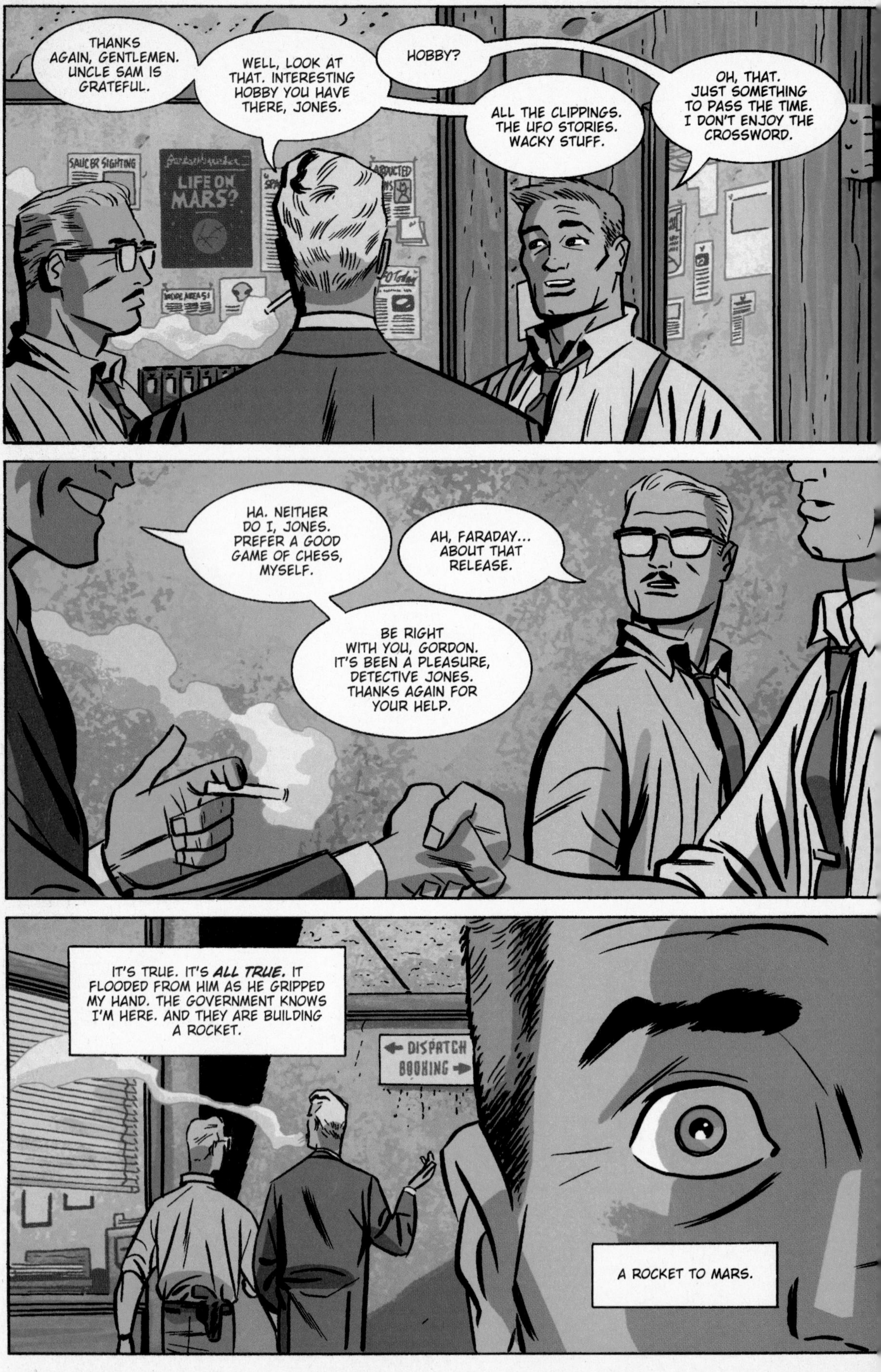
THANKS AGAIN, GENTLEMEN. UNCLE SAM IS GRATEFUL.
WELL, LOOK AT THAT. INTERESTING HOBBY YOU HAVE THERE, JONES.
HOBBY?
ALL THE CLIPPINGS. THE UFO STORIES. WACKY STUFF.
OH, THAT. JUST SOMETHING TO PASS THE TIME. I DON'T ENJOY THE CROSSWORD.
SAUCER SIGHTING
LIFE ON MARS?
HA. NEITHER DO I, JONES. PREFER A GOOD GAME OF CHESS, MYSELF.
AH, FARADAY... ABOUT THAT RELEASE.
BE RIGHT WITH YOU, GORDON. IT'S BEEN A PLEASURE, DETECTIVE JONES. THANKS AGAIN FOR YOUR HELP.
IT'S TRUE. IT'S ALL TRUE. IT FLOODED FROM HIM AS HE GRIPPED MY HAND. THE GOVERNMENT KNOWS I'M HERE. AND THEY ARE BUILDING A ROCKET.
← DISPATCH
BOOKING →
A ROCKET TO MARS.

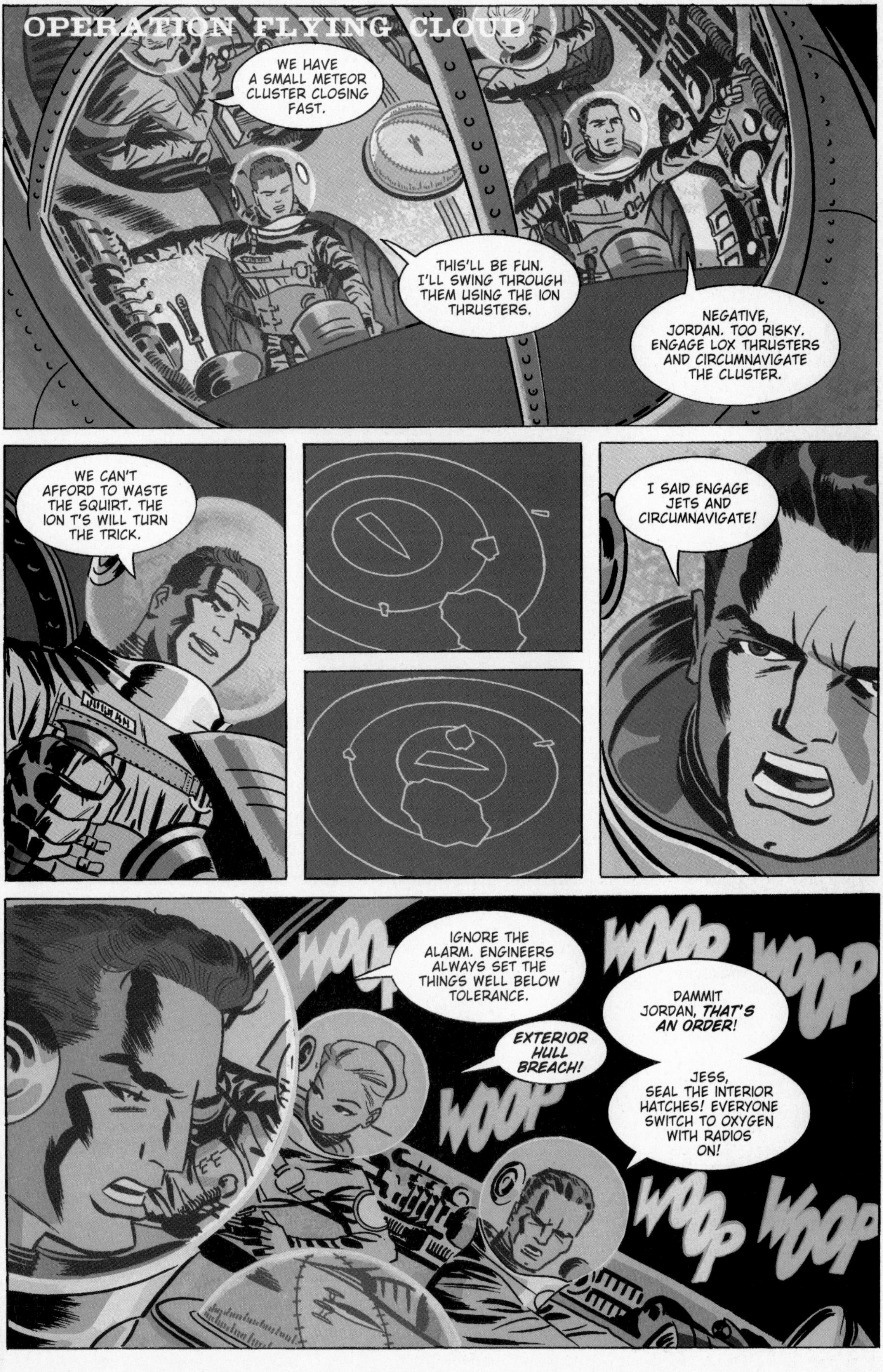

OPERATION FLYING CLOUD
WE HAVE A SMALL METEOR CLUSTER CLOSING FAST.
THIS'LL BE FUN. I'LL SWING THROUGH THEM USING THE ION THRUSTERS.
NEGATIVE, JORDAN. TOO RISKY. ENGAGE LOX THRUSTERS AND CIRCUMNAVIGATE THE CLUSTER.
WE CAN'T AFFORD TO WASTE THE SQUIRT. THE ION T'S WILL TURN THE TRICK.
I SAID ENGAGE JETS AND CIRCUMNAVIGATE!
WOOP WOOP WOOP
IGNORE THE ALARM. ENGINEERS ALWAYS SET THE THINGS WELL BELOW TOLERANCE.
DAMMIT JORDAN, *THAT'S AN ORDER*!
EXTERIOR HULL BREACH!
WOOP
JESS, SEAL THE INTERIOR HATCHES! EVERYONE SWITCH TO OXYGEN WITH RADIOS ON!
WOOP WOOP

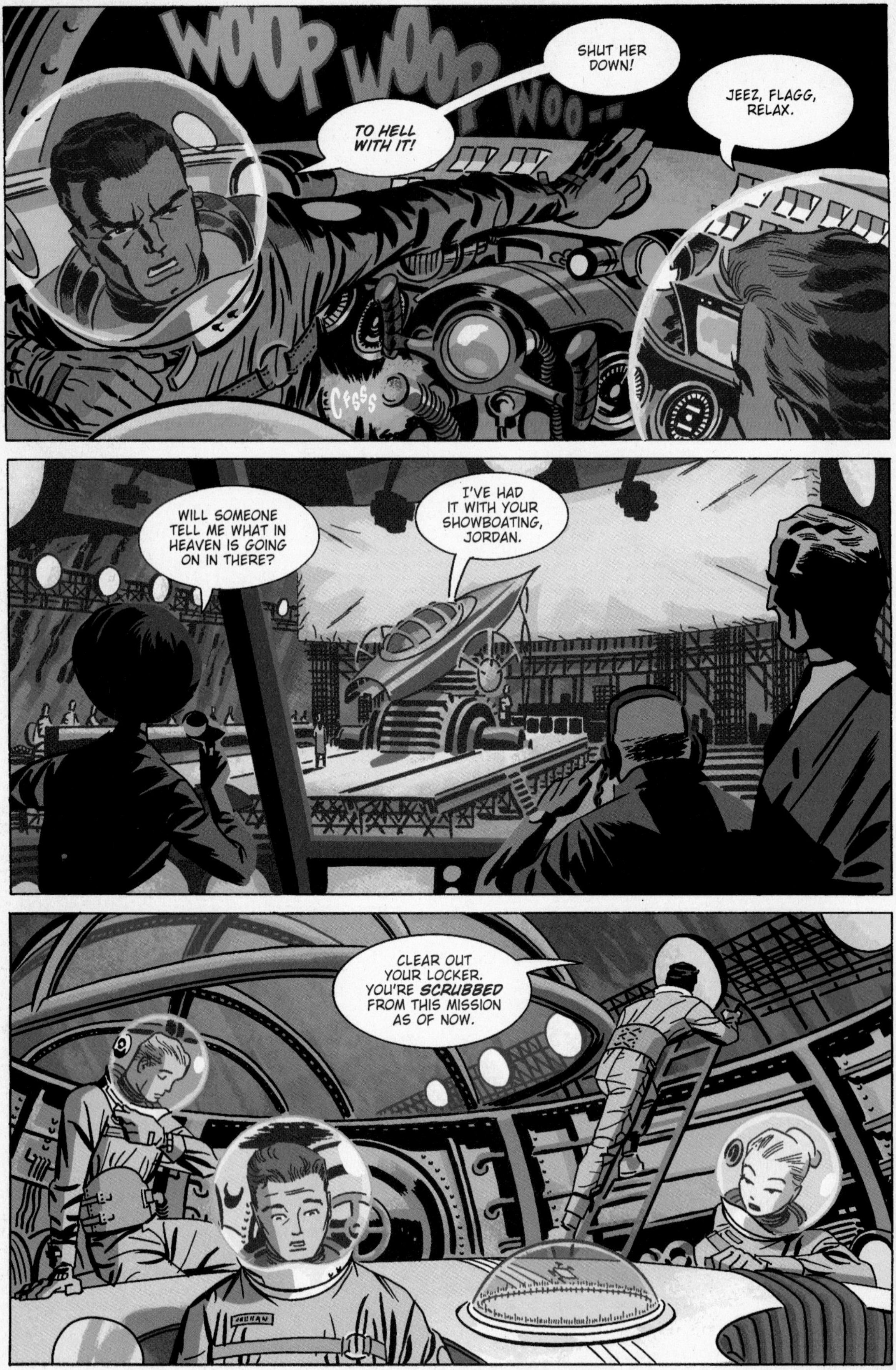
WOOP WOOP WOO--
TO HELL WITH IT!
SHUT HER DOWN!
JEEZ, FLAGG, RELAX.
CFSSS
WILL SOMEONE TELL ME WHAT IN HEAVEN IS GOING ON IN THERE?
I'VE HAD IT WITH YOUR SHOWBOATING, JORDAN.
CLEAR OUT YOUR LOCKER. YOU'RE *SCRUBBED* FROM THIS MISSION AS OF NOW.
JORDAN

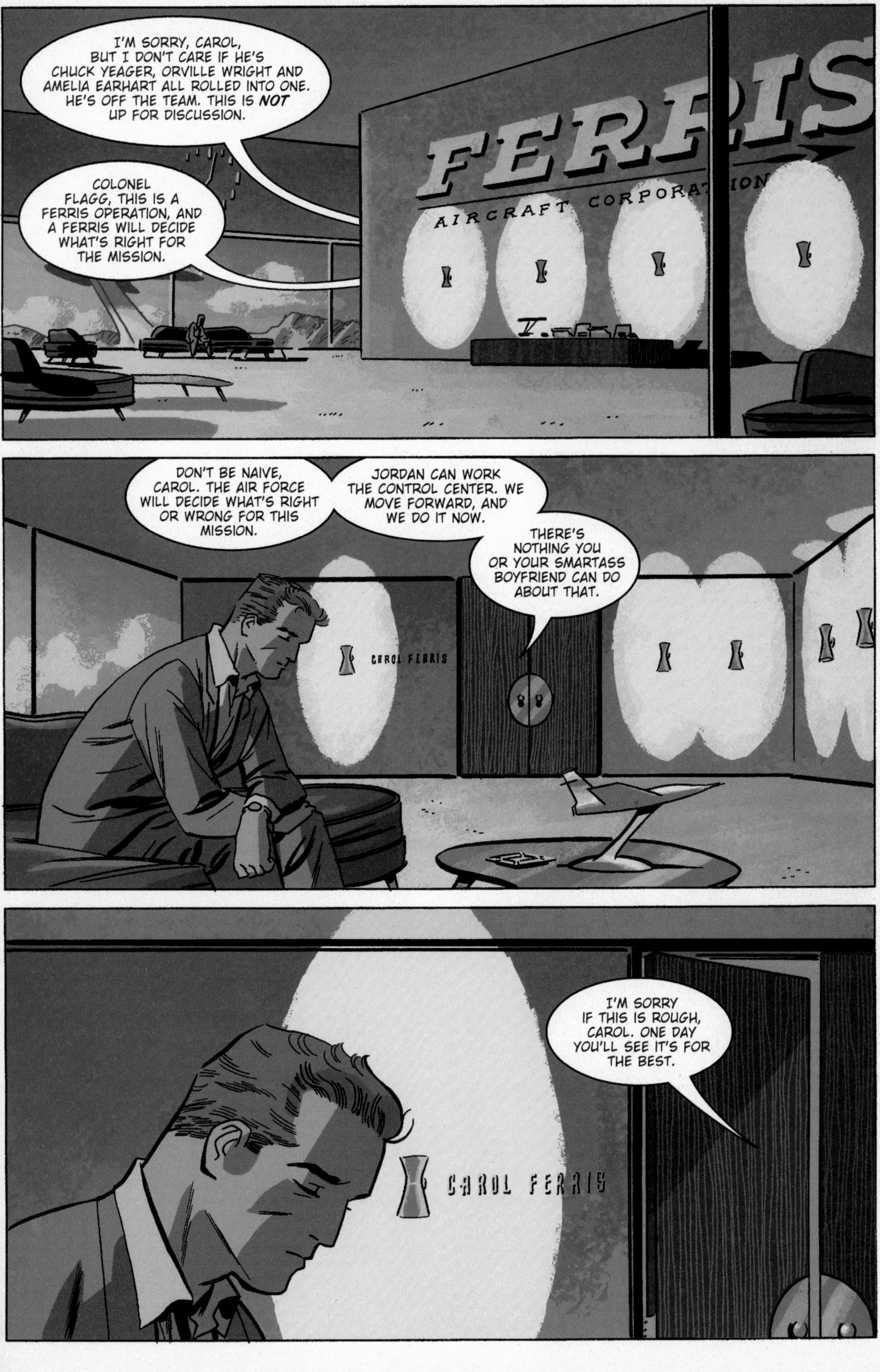
I'M SORRY, CAROL, BUT I DON'T CARE IF HE'S CHUCK YEAGER, ORVILLE WRIGHT AND AMELIA EARHART ALL ROLLED INTO ONE. HE'S OFF THE TEAM. THIS IS NOT UP FOR DISCUSSION.
COLONEL FLAGG, THIS IS A FERRIS OPERATION, AND A FERRIS WILL DECIDE WHAT'S RIGHT FOR THE MISSION.
FERRIS
AIRCRAFT CORPORATION
DON'T BE NAIVE, CAROL. THE AIR FORCE WILL DECIDE WHAT'S RIGHT OR WRONG FOR THIS MISSION.
JORDAN CAN WORK THE CONTROL CENTER. WE MOVE FORWARD, AND WE DO IT NOW.
THERE'S NOTHING YOU OR YOUR SMARTASS BOYFRIEND CAN DO ABOUT THAT.
CAROL FERRIS
I'M SORRY IF THIS IS ROUGH, CAROL. ONE DAY YOU'LL SEE IT'S FOR THE BEST.
CAROL FERRIS

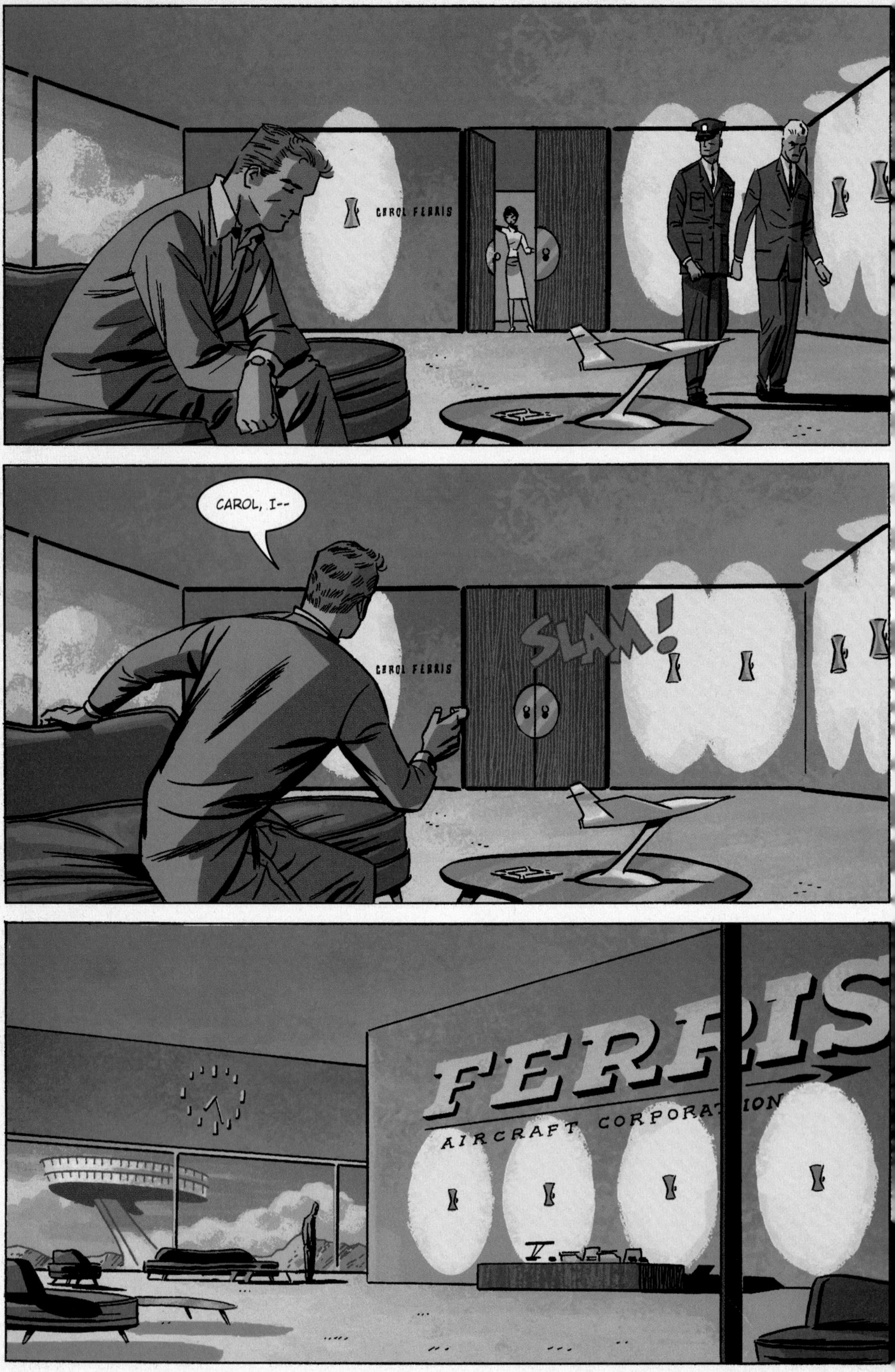
CAROL FERRIS
CAROL, I--
CAROL FERRIS
SLAM!
FERRIS
AIRCRAFT CORPORATION

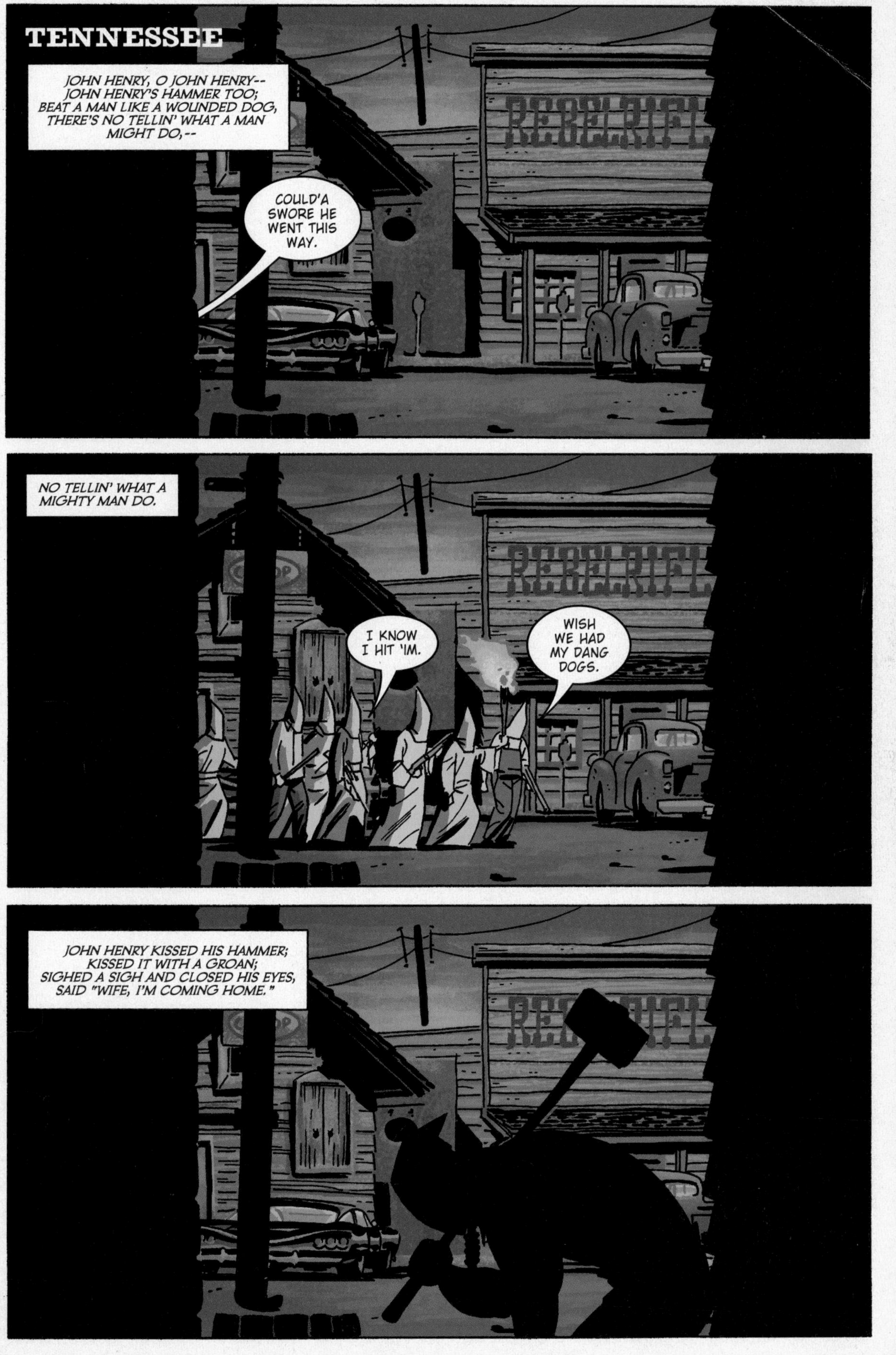
TENNESSEE
JOHN HENRY, O JOHN HENRY-- JOHN HENRY'S HAMMER TOO; BEAT A MAN LIKE A WOUNDED DOG, THERE'S NO TELLIN' WHAT A MAN MIGHT DO,--
COULD'A SWORE HE WENT THIS WAY.
REBELRIFL
NO TELLIN' WHAT A MIGHTY MAN DO.
I KNOW I HIT 'IM.
WISH WE HAD MY DANG DOGS.
JOHN HENRY KISSED HIS HAMMER; KISSED IT WITH A GROAN; SIGHED A SIGH AND CLOSED HIS EYES, SAID "WIFE, I'M COMING HOME."

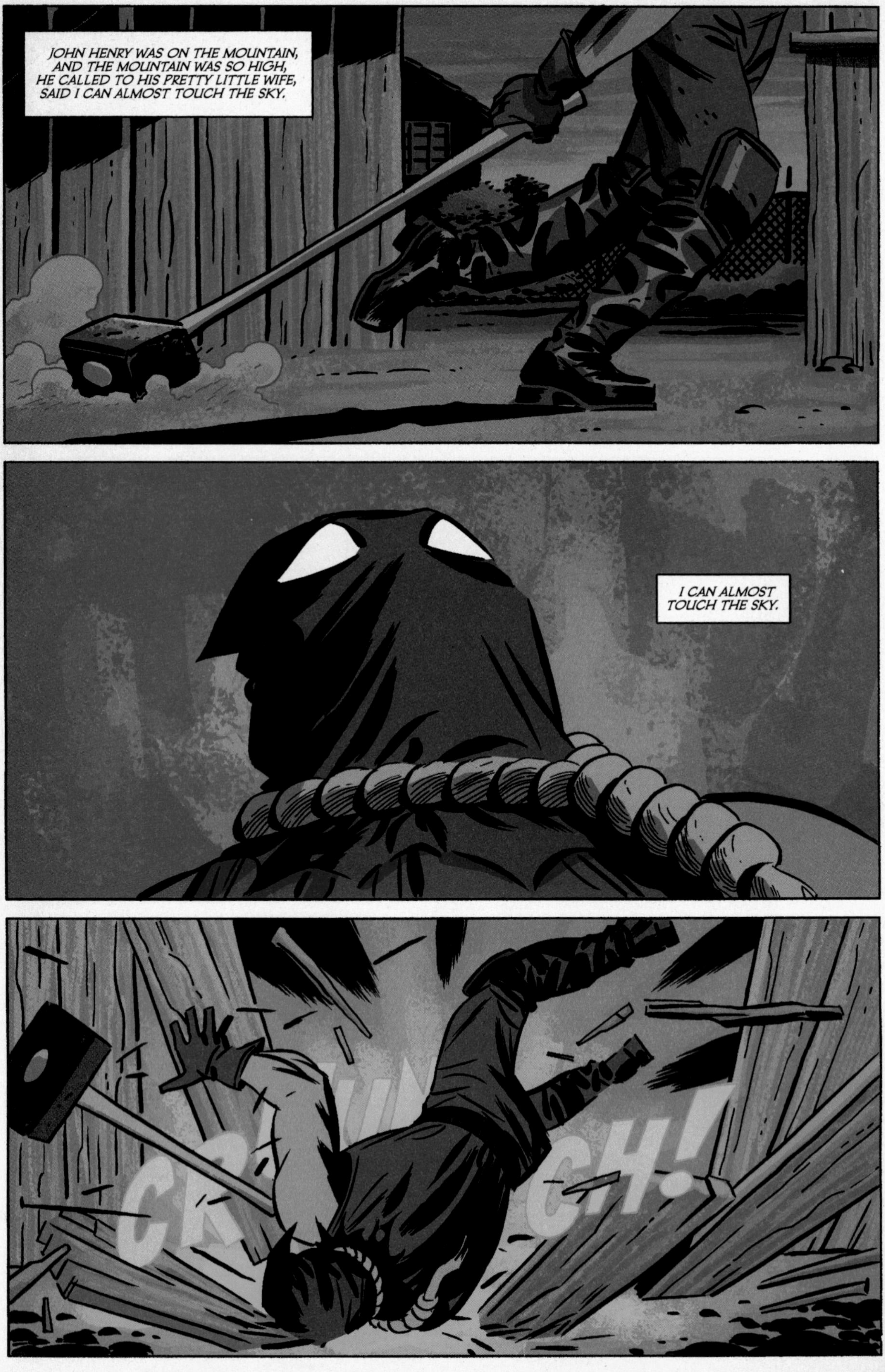
JOHN HENRY WAS ON THE MOUNTAIN, AND THE MOUNTAIN WAS SO HIGH, HE CALLED TO HIS PRETTY LITTLE WIFE, SAID I CAN ALMOST TOUCH THE SKY.
I CAN ALMOST TOUCH THE SKY.
CR UN CH!

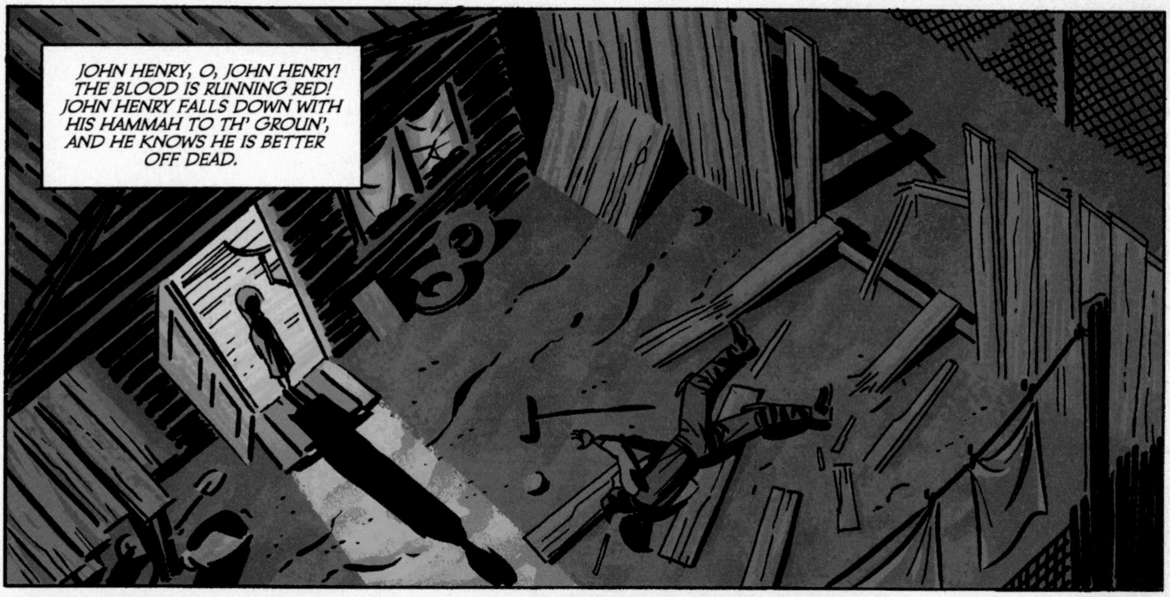
JOHN HENRY, O, JOHN HENRY! THE BLOOD IS RUNNING RED! JOHN HENRY FALLS DOWN WITH HIS HAMMAH TO TH' GROUN', AND HE KNOWS HE IS BETTER OFF DEAD.

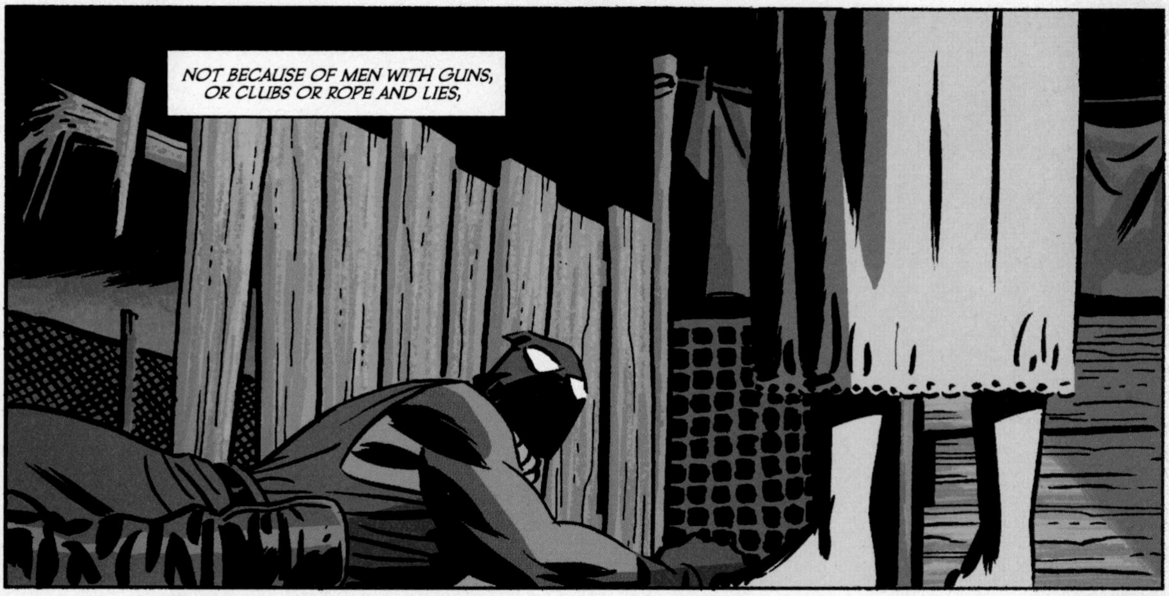
NOT BECAUSE OF MEN WITH GUNS, OR CLUBS OR ROPE AND LIES,

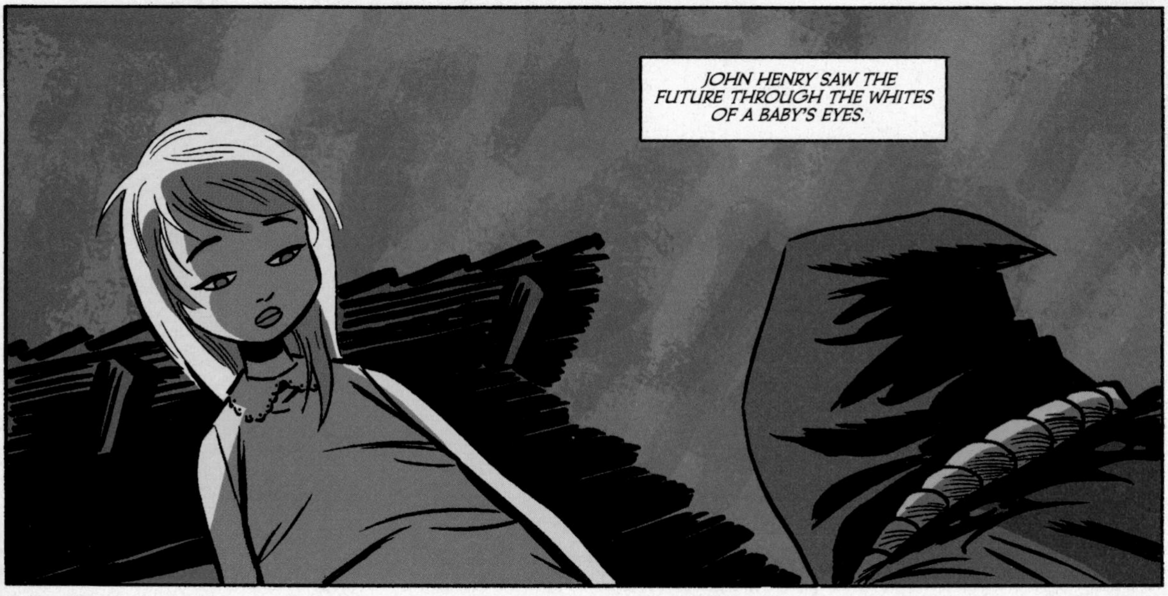
JOHN HENRY SAW THE FUTURE THROUGH THE WHITES OF A BABY'S EYES.

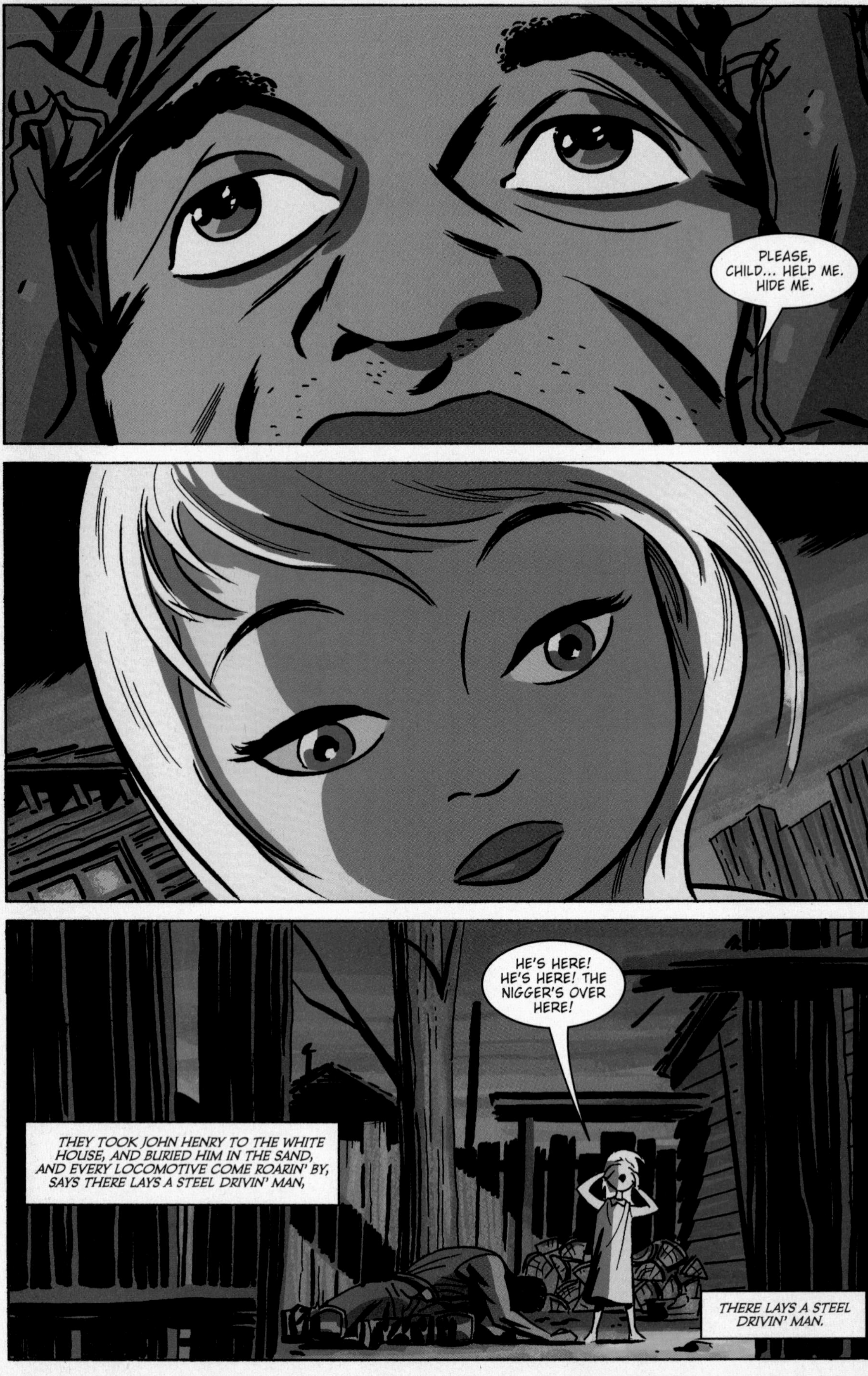
PLEASE, CHILD... HELP ME. HIDE ME.
HE'S HERE! HE'S HERE! THE NIGGER'S OVER HERE!
THEY TOOK JOHN HENRY TO THE WHITE HOUSE, AND BURIED HIM IN THE SAND, AND EVERY LOCOMOTIVE COME ROARIN' BY, SAYS THERE LAYS A STEEL DRIVIN' MAN,
THERE LAYS A STEEL DRIVIN' MAN.

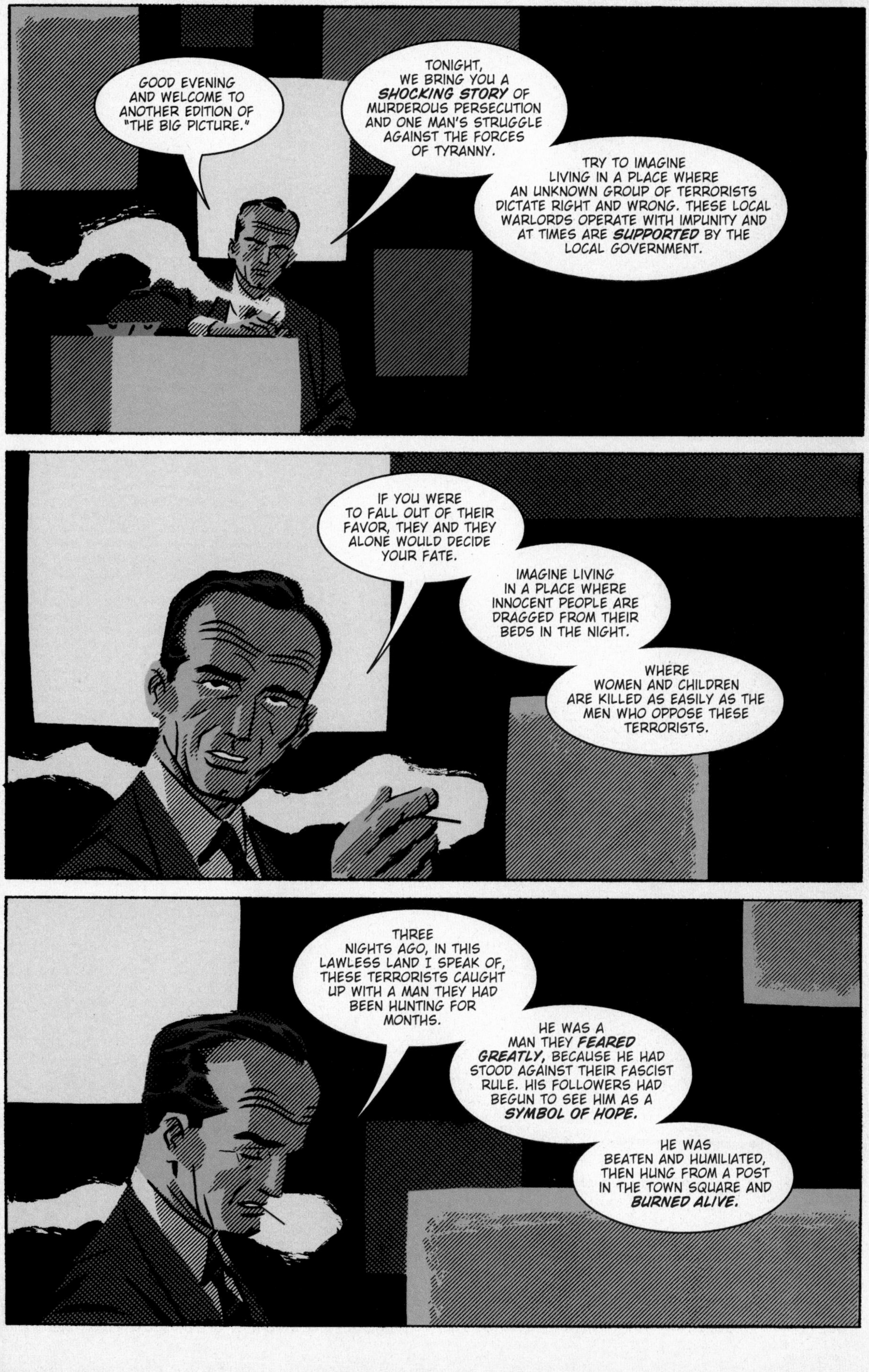
GOOD EVENING AND WELCOME TO ANOTHER EDITION OF "THE BIG PICTURE."
TONIGHT, WE BRING YOU A SHOCKING STORY OF MURDEROUS PERSECUTION AND ONE MAN'S STRUGGLE AGAINST THE FORCES OF TYRANNY.
TRY TO IMAGINE LIVING IN A PLACE WHERE AN UNKNOWN GROUP OF TERRORISTS DICTATE RIGHT AND WRONG. THESE LOCAL WARLORDS OPERATE WITH IMPUNITY AND AT TIMES ARE SUPPORTED BY THE LOCAL GOVERNMENT.
IF YOU WERE TO FALL OUT OF THEIR FAVOR, THEY AND THEY ALONE WOULD DECIDE YOUR FATE.
IMAGINE LIVING IN A PLACE WHERE INNOCENT PEOPLE ARE DRAGGED FROM THEIR BEDS IN THE NIGHT.
WHERE WOMEN AND CHILDREN ARE KILLED AS EASILY AS THE MEN WHO OPPOSE THESE TERRORISTS.
THREE NIGHTS AGO, IN THIS LAWLESS LAND I SPEAK OF, THESE TERRORISTS CAUGHT UP WITH A MAN THEY HAD BEEN HUNTING FOR MONTHS.
HE WAS A MAN THEY FEARED GREATLY, BECAUSE HE HAD STOOD AGAINST THEIR FASCIST RULE. HIS FOLLOWERS HAD BEGUN TO SEE HIM AS A SYMBOL OF HOPE.
HE WAS BEATEN AND HUMILIATED, THEN HUNG FROM A POST IN THE TOWN SQUARE AND BURNED ALIVE.

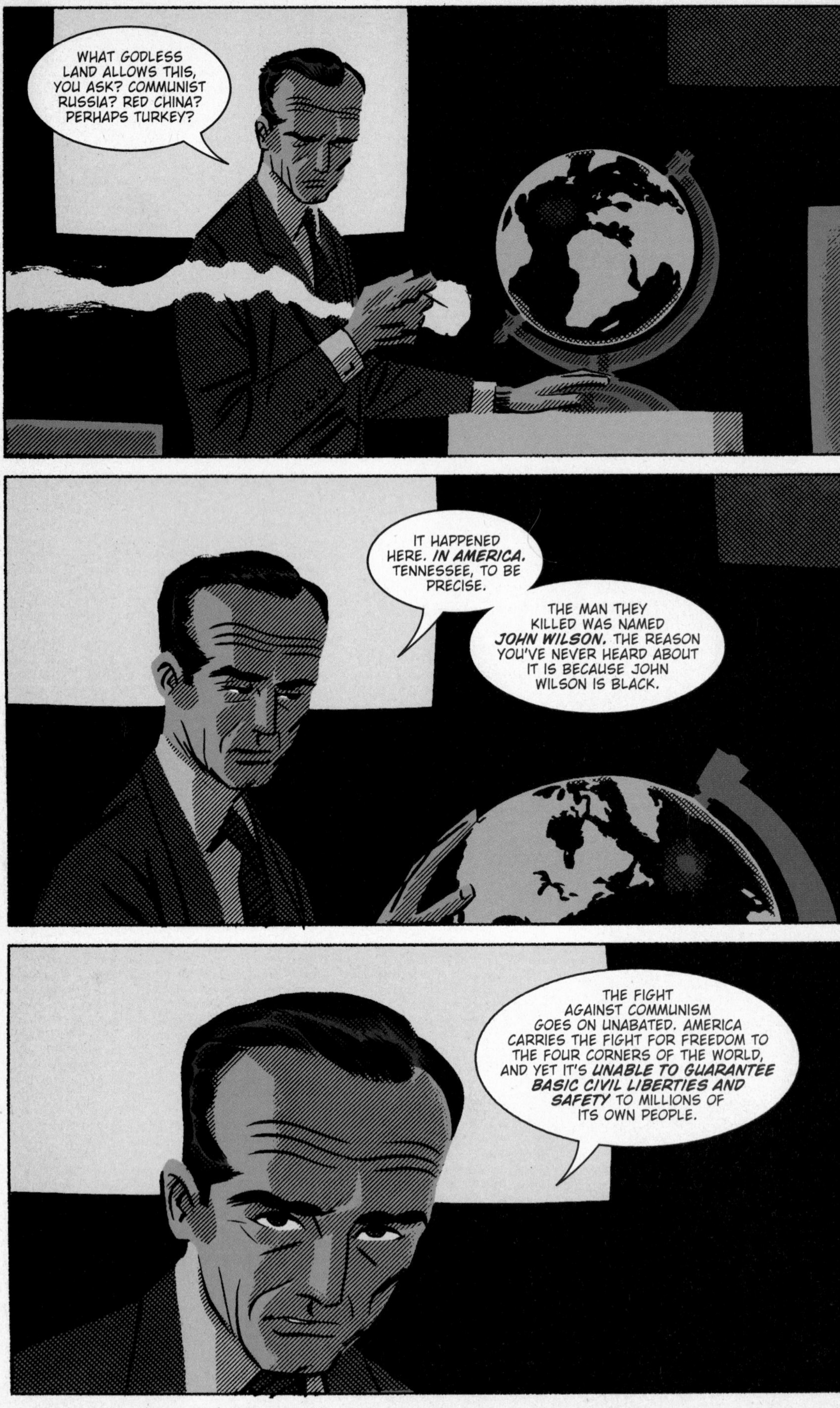
WHAT GODLESS LAND ALLOWS THIS, YOU ASK? COMMUNIST RUSSIA? RED CHINA? PERHAPS TURKEY?
IT HAPPENED HERE. IN AMERICA. TENNESSEE, TO BE PRECISE.
THE MAN THEY KILLED WAS NAMED JOHN WILSON. THE REASON YOU'VE NEVER HEARD ABOUT IT IS BECAUSE JOHN WILSON IS BLACK.
THE FIGHT AGAINST COMMUNISM GOES ON UNABATED. AMERICA CARRIES THE FIGHT FOR FREEDOM TO THE FOUR CORNERS OF THE WORLD, AND YET IT'S UNABLE TO GUARANTEE BASIC CIVIL LIBERTIES AND SAFETY TO MILLIONS OF ITS OWN PEOPLE.

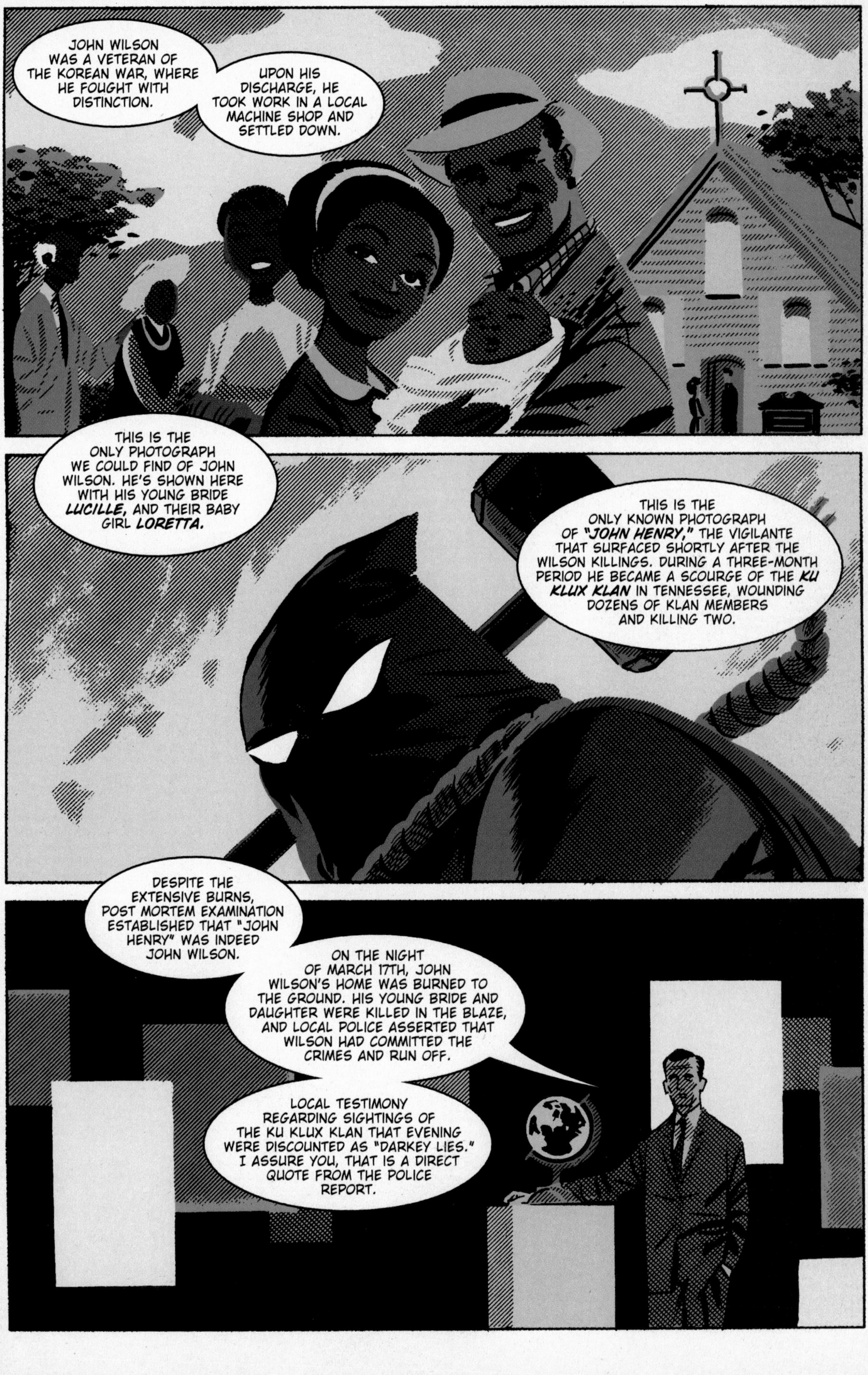
JOHN WILSON WAS A VETERAN OF THE KOREAN WAR, WHERE HE FOUGHT WITH DISTINCTION.
UPON HIS DISCHARGE, HE TOOK WORK IN A LOCAL MACHINE SHOP AND SETTLED DOWN.
THIS IS THE ONLY PHOTOGRAPH WE COULD FIND OF JOHN WILSON. HE'S SHOWN HERE WITH HIS YOUNG BRIDE ***LUCILLE,*** AND THEIR BABY GIRL ***LORETTA.***
THIS IS THE ONLY KNOWN PHOTOGRAPH OF ***"JOHN HENRY,"*** THE VIGILANTE THAT SURFACED SHORTLY AFTER THE WILSON KILLINGS. DURING A THREE-MONTH PERIOD HE BECAME A SCOURGE OF THE ***KU KLUX KLAN*** IN TENNESSEE, WOUNDING DOZENS OF KLAN MEMBERS AND KILLING TWO.
DESPITE THE EXTENSIVE BURNS, POST MORTEM EXAMINATION ESTABLISHED THAT "JOHN HENRY" WAS INDEED JOHN WILSON.
ON THE NIGHT OF MARCH 17TH, JOHN WILSON'S HOME WAS BURNED TO THE GROUND. HIS YOUNG BRIDE AND DAUGHTER WERE KILLED IN THE BLAZE, AND LOCAL POLICE ASSERTED THAT WILSON HAD COMMITTED THE CRIMES AND RUN OFF.
LOCAL TESTIMONY REGARDING SIGHTINGS OF THE KU KLUX KLAN THAT EVENING WERE DISCOUNTED AS "DARKEY LIES." I ASSURE YOU, THAT IS A DIRECT QUOTE FROM THE POLICE REPORT.

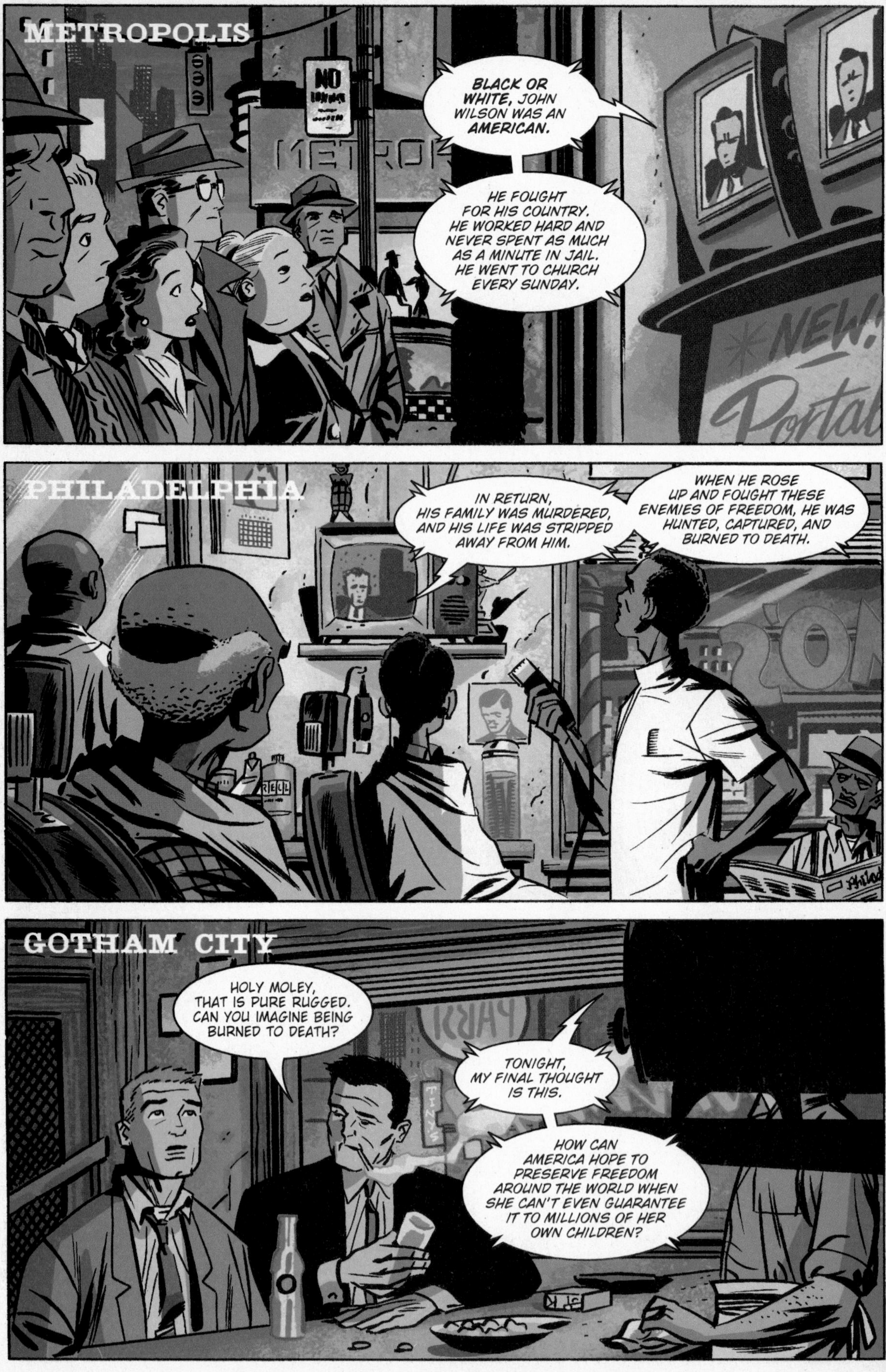
METROPOLIS
BLACK OR WHITE, JOHN WILSON WAS AN AMERICAN.
HE FOUGHT FOR HIS COUNTRY. HE WORKED HARD AND NEVER SPENT AS MUCH AS A MINUTE IN JAIL. HE WENT TO CHURCH EVERY SUNDAY.
NO
METRO
NEW!
Portal
PHILADELPHIA
IN RETURN, HIS FAMILY WAS MURDERED, AND HIS LIFE WAS STRIPPED AWAY FROM HIM.
WHEN HE ROSE UP AND FOUGHT THESE ENEMIES OF FREEDOM, HE WAS HUNTED, CAPTURED, AND BURNED TO DEATH.
GOTHAM CITY
HOLY MOLEY, THAT IS PURE RUGGED. CAN YOU IMAGINE BEING BURNED TO DEATH?
TONIGHT, MY FINAL THOUGHT IS THIS.
HOW CAN AMERICA HOPE TO PRESERVE FREEDOM AROUND THE WORLD WHEN SHE CAN'T EVEN GUARANTEE IT TO MILLIONS OF HER OWN CHILDREN?

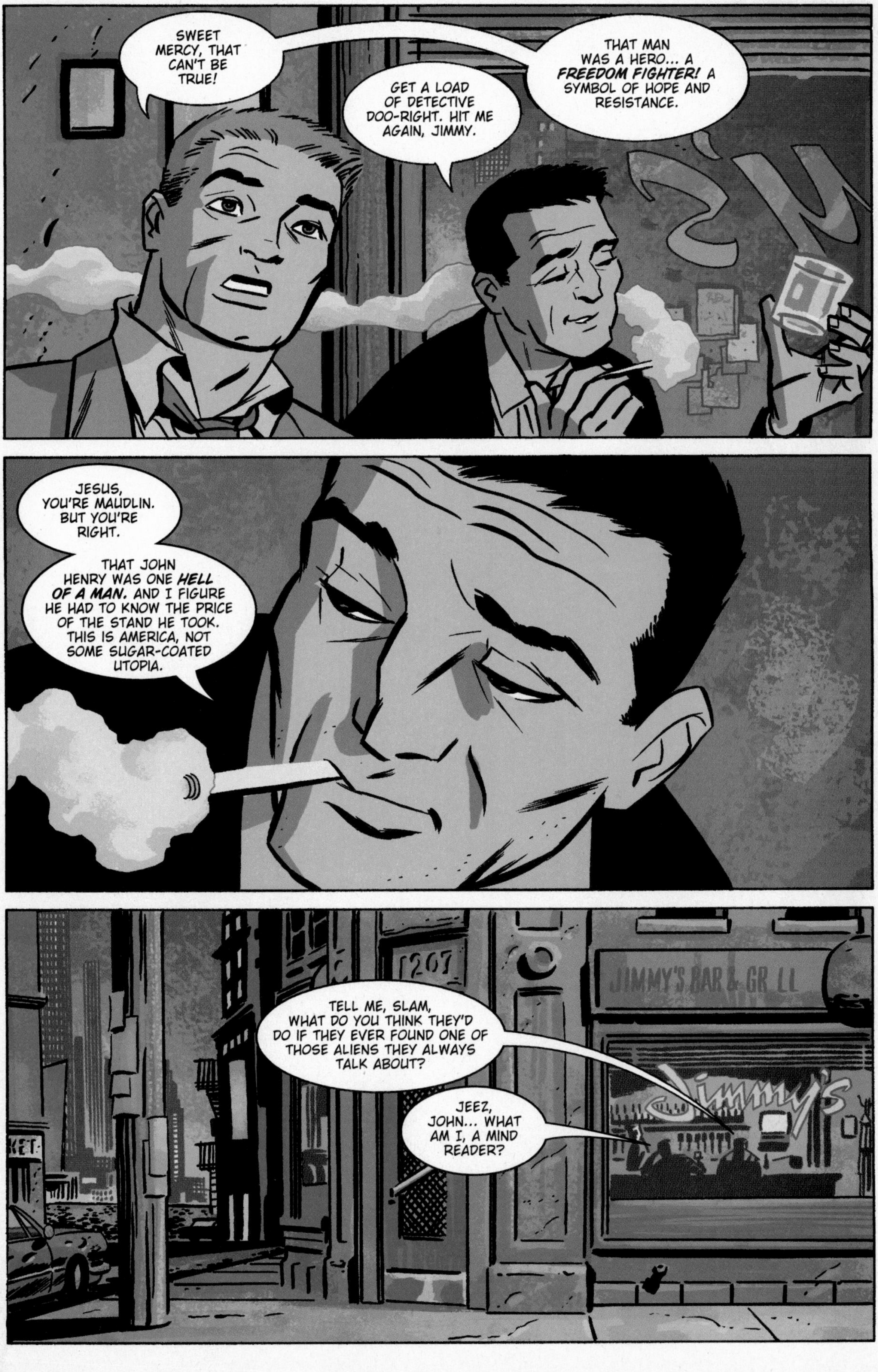
SWEET MERCY, THAT CAN'T BE TRUE!
THAT MAN WAS A HERO... A FREEDOM FIGHTER! A SYMBOL OF HOPE AND RESISTANCE.
GET A LOAD OF DETECTIVE DOO-RIGHT. HIT ME AGAIN, JIMMY.
JESUS, YOU'RE MAUDLIN. BUT YOU'RE RIGHT.
THAT JOHN HENRY WAS ONE HELL OF A MAN. AND I FIGURE HE HAD TO KNOW THE PRICE OF THE STAND HE TOOK. THIS IS AMERICA, NOT SOME SUGAR-COATED UTOPIA.
1207
JIMMY'S BAR & GR LL
Jimmy's
TELL ME, SLAM, WHAT DO YOU THINK THEY'D DO IF THEY EVER FOUND ONE OF THOSE ALIENS THEY ALWAYS TALK ABOUT?
JEEZ, JOHN... WHAT AM I, A MIND READER?

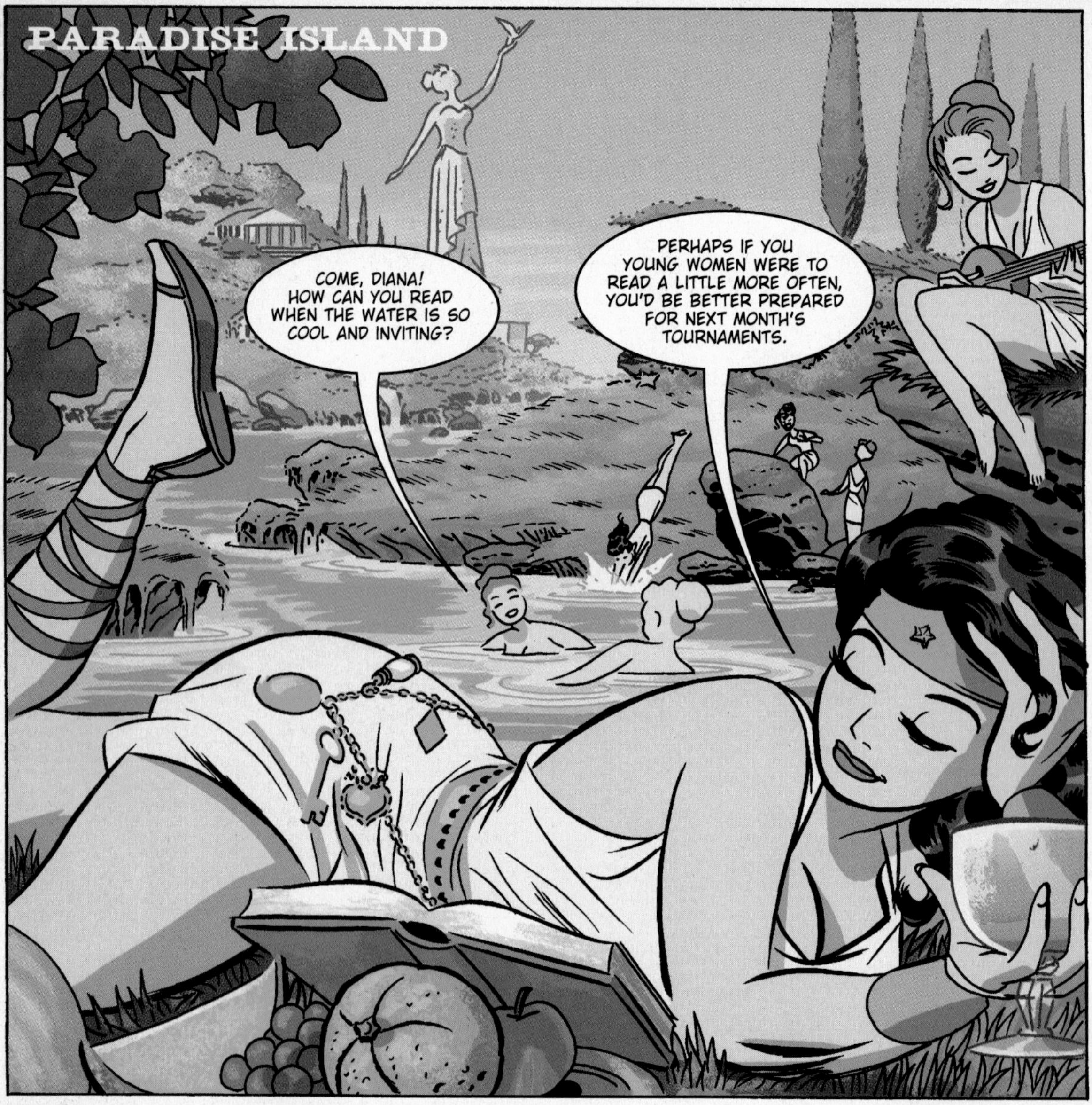
PARADISE ISLAND
COME, DIANA! HOW CAN YOU READ WHEN THE WATER IS SO COOL AND INVITING?
PERHAPS IF YOU YOUNG WOMEN WERE TO READ A LITTLE MORE OFTEN, YOU'D BE BETTER PREPARED FOR NEXT MONTH'S TOURNAMENTS.

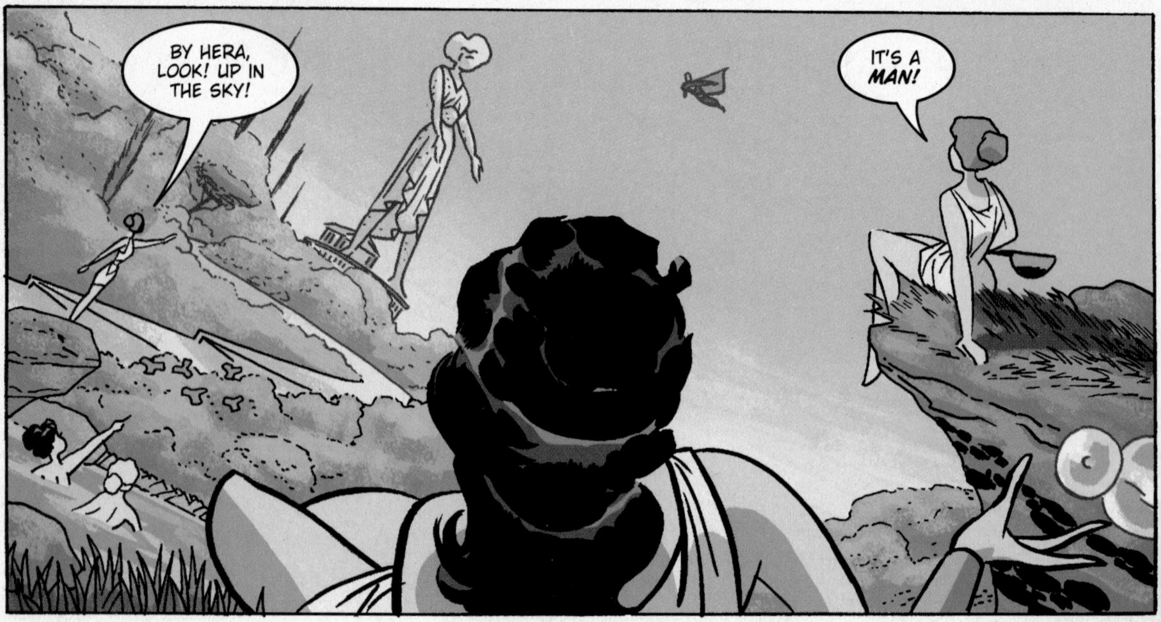
BY HERA, LOOK! UP IN THE SKY!
IT'S A *MAN!*

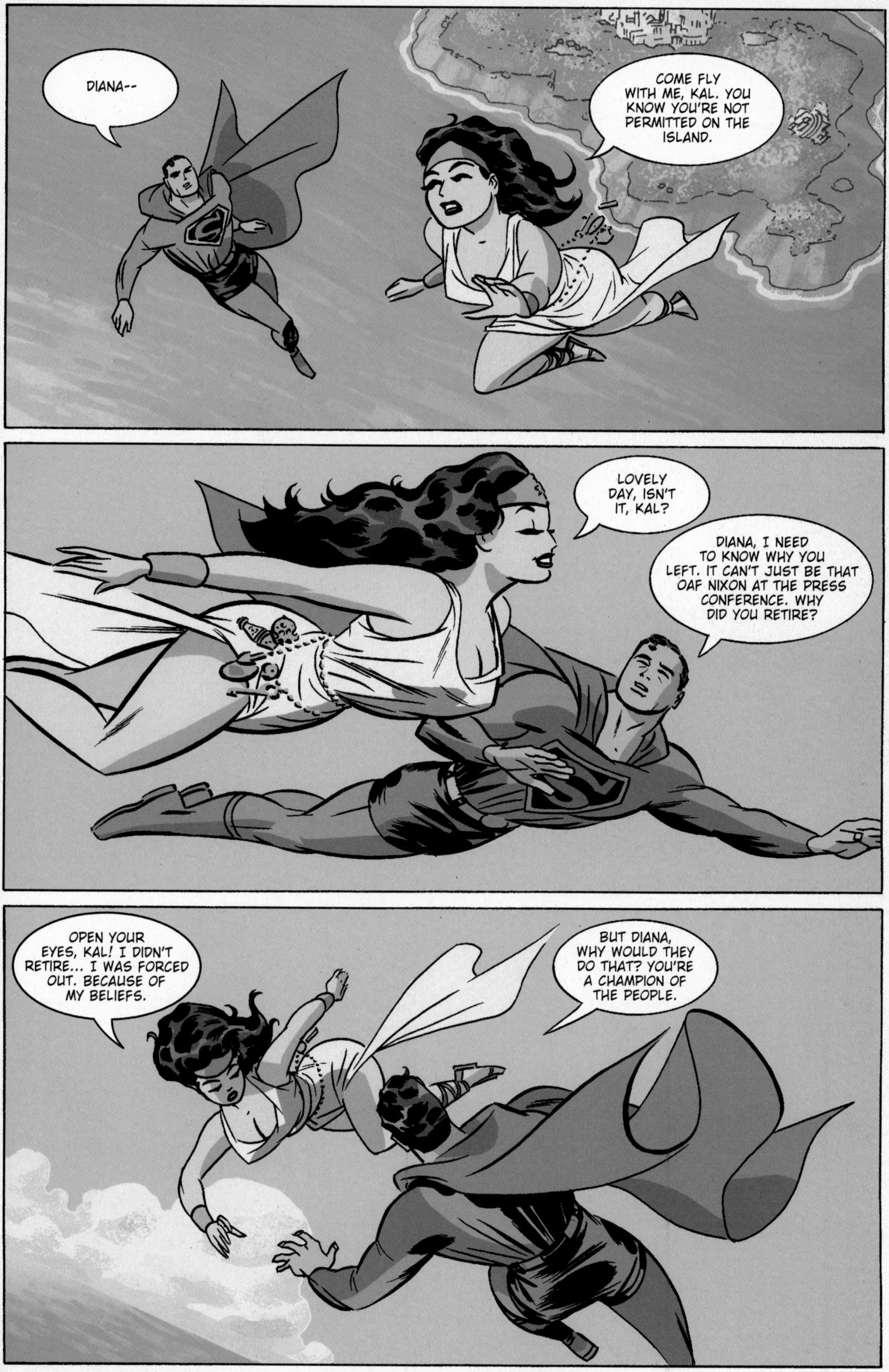
DIANA--
COME FLY WITH ME, KAL. YOU KNOW YOU'RE NOT PERMITTED ON THE ISLAND.
LOVELY DAY, ISN'T IT, KAL?
DIANA, I NEED TO KNOW WHY YOU LEFT. IT CAN'T JUST BE THAT OAF NIXON AT THE PRESS CONFERENCE. WHY DID YOU RETIRE?
OPEN YOUR EYES, KAL! I DIDN'T RETIRE... I WAS FORCED OUT. BECAUSE OF MY BELIEFS.
BUT DIANA, WHY WOULD THEY DO THAT? YOU'RE A CHAMPION OF THE PEOPLE.

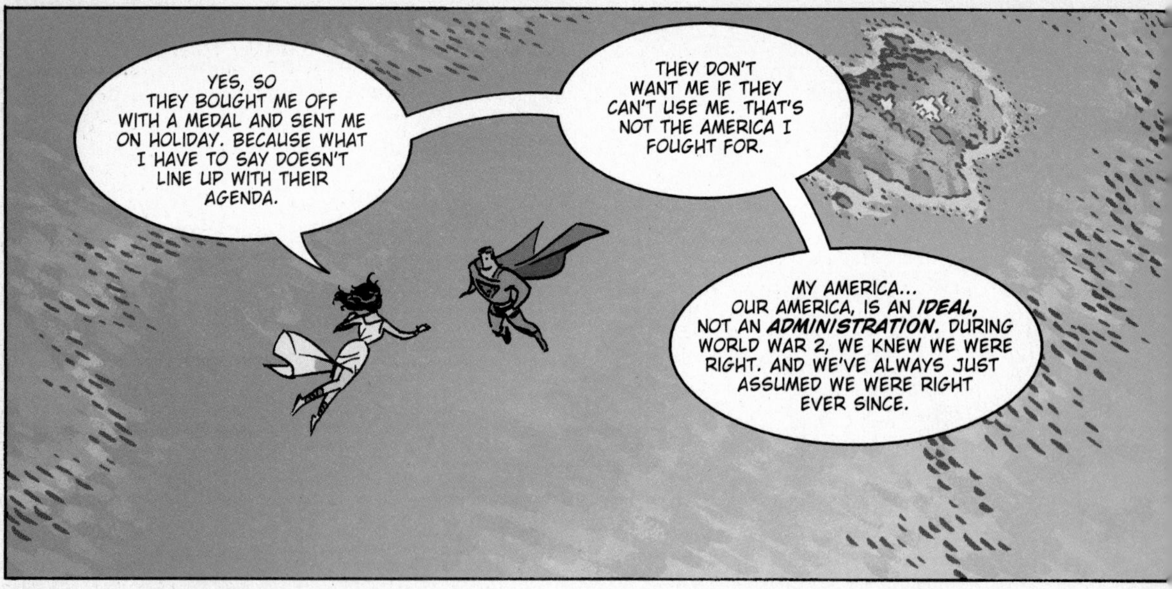
YES, SO THEY BOUGHT ME OFF WITH A MEDAL AND SENT ME ON HOLIDAY. BECAUSE WHAT I HAVE TO SAY DOESN'T LINE UP WITH THEIR AGENDA.
THEY DON'T WANT ME IF THEY CAN'T USE ME. THAT'S NOT THE AMERICA I FOUGHT FOR.
MY AMERICA... OUR AMERICA, IS AN *IDEAL,* NOT AN *ADMINISTRATION.* DURING WORLD WAR 2, WE KNEW WE WERE RIGHT. AND WE'VE ALWAYS JUST ASSUMED WE WERE RIGHT EVER SINCE.

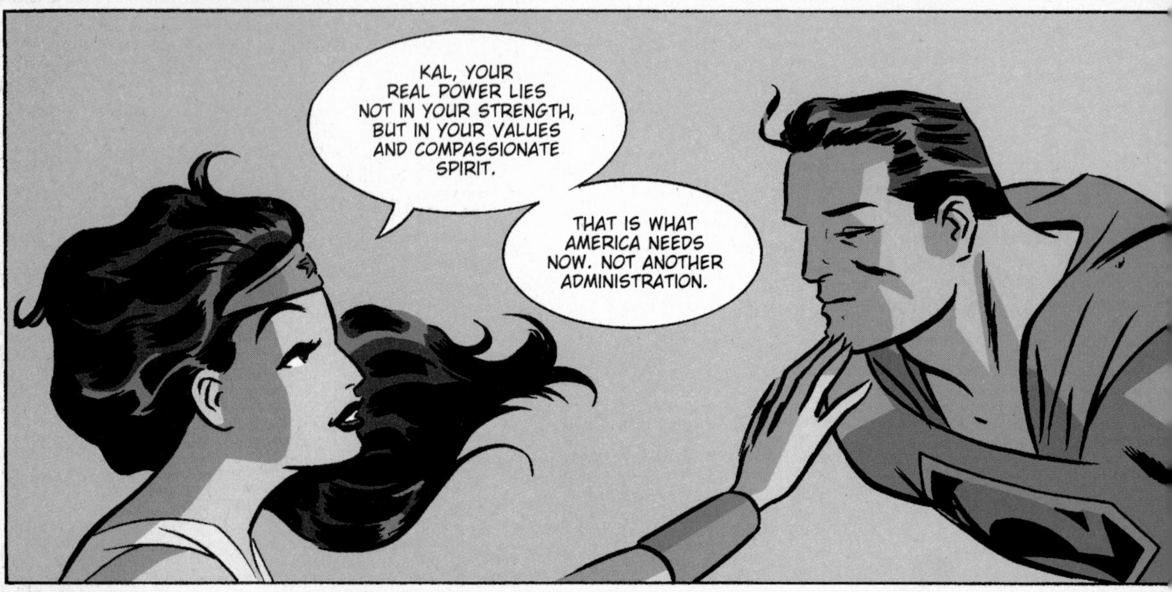
KAL, YOUR REAL POWER LIES NOT IN YOUR STRENGTH, BUT IN YOUR VALUES AND COMPASSIONATE SPIRIT.
THAT IS WHAT AMERICA NEEDS NOW. NOT ANOTHER ADMINISTRATION.

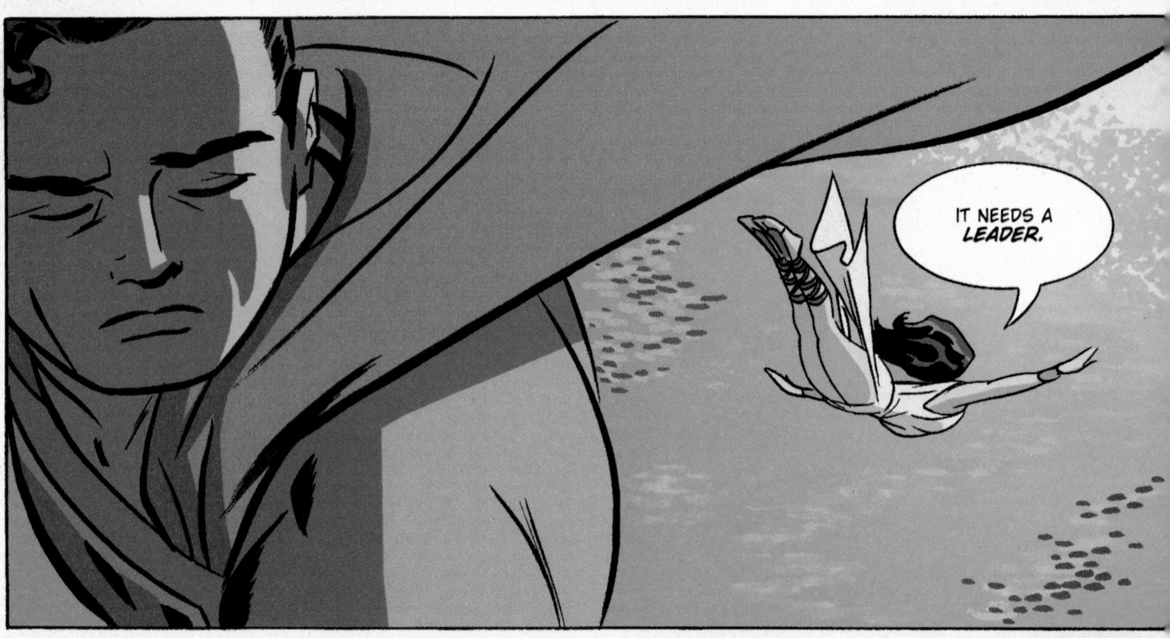
IT NEEDS A *LEADER.*

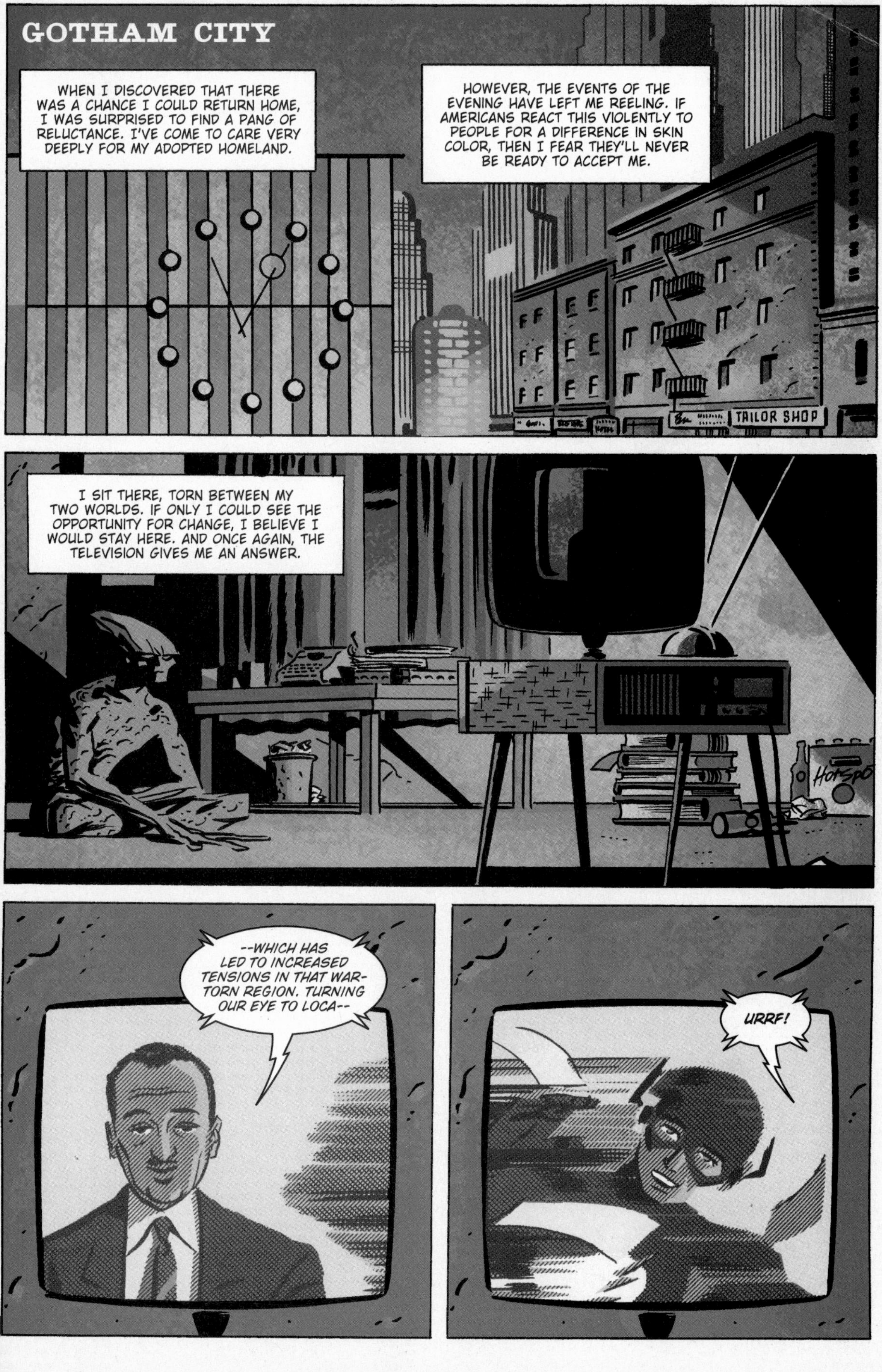
GOTHAM CITY
WHEN I DISCOVERED THAT THERE WAS A CHANCE I COULD RETURN HOME, I WAS SURPRISED TO FIND A PANG OF RELUCTANCE. I'VE COME TO CARE VERY DEEPLY FOR MY ADOPTED HOMELAND.
HOWEVER, THE EVENTS OF THE EVENING HAVE LEFT ME REELING. IF AMERICANS REACT THIS VIOLENTLY TO PEOPLE FOR A DIFFERENCE IN SKIN COLOR, THEN I FEAR THEY'LL NEVER BE READY TO ACCEPT ME.
TAILOR SHOP
I SIT THERE, TORN BETWEEN MY TWO WORLDS. IF ONLY I COULD SEE THE OPPORTUNITY FOR CHANGE, I BELIEVE I WOULD STAY HERE. AND ONCE AGAIN, THE TELEVISION GIVES ME AN ANSWER.
--WHICH HAS LED TO INCREASED TENSIONS IN THAT WAR-TORN REGION. TURNING OUR EYE TO LOCA--
URRF!

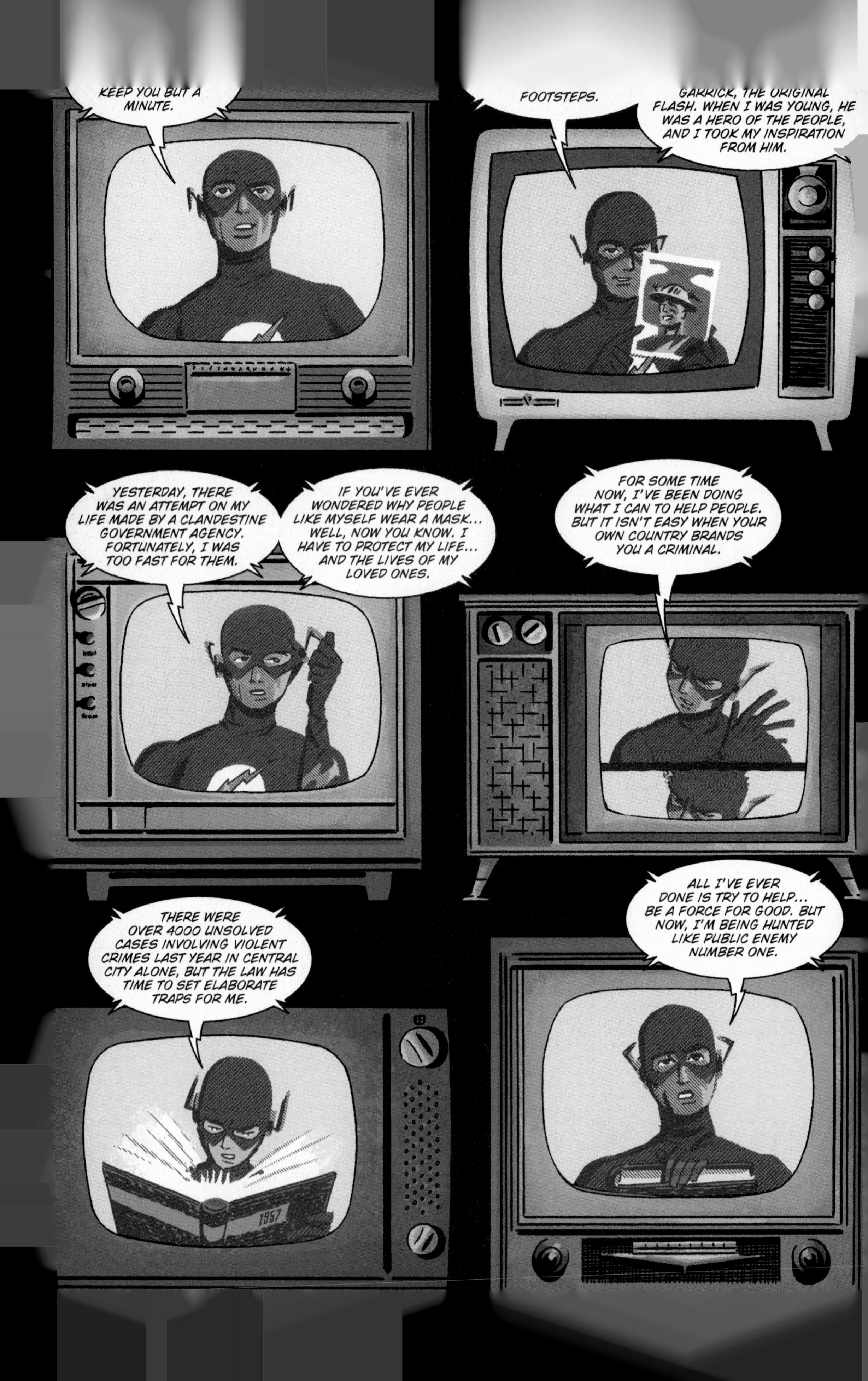
KEEP YOU BUT A MINUTE.
FOOTSTEPS.
GARRICK, THE ORIGINAL FLASH. WHEN I WAS YOUNG, HE WAS A HERO OF THE PEOPLE, AND I TOOK MY INSPIRATION FROM HIM.
YESTERDAY, THERE WAS AN ATTEMPT ON MY LIFE MADE BY A CLANDESTINE GOVERNMENT AGENCY. FORTUNATELY, I WAS TOO FAST FOR THEM.
IF YOU'VE EVER WONDERED WHY PEOPLE LIKE MYSELF WEAR A MASK... WELL, NOW YOU KNOW. I HAVE TO PROTECT MY LIFE... AND THE LIVES OF MY LOVED ONES.
FOR SOME TIME NOW, I'VE BEEN DOING WHAT I CAN TO HELP PEOPLE. BUT IT ISN'T EASY WHEN YOUR OWN COUNTRY BRANDS YOU A CRIMINAL.
THERE WERE OVER 4000 UNSOLVED CASES INVOLVING VIOLENT CRIMES LAST YEAR IN CENTRAL CITY ALONE, BUT THE LAW HAS TIME TO SET ELABORATE TRAPS FOR ME.
1957
ALL I'VE EVER DONE IS TRY TO HELP... BE A FORCE FOR GOOD. BUT NOW, I'M BEING HUNTED LIKE PUBLIC ENEMY NUMBER ONE.

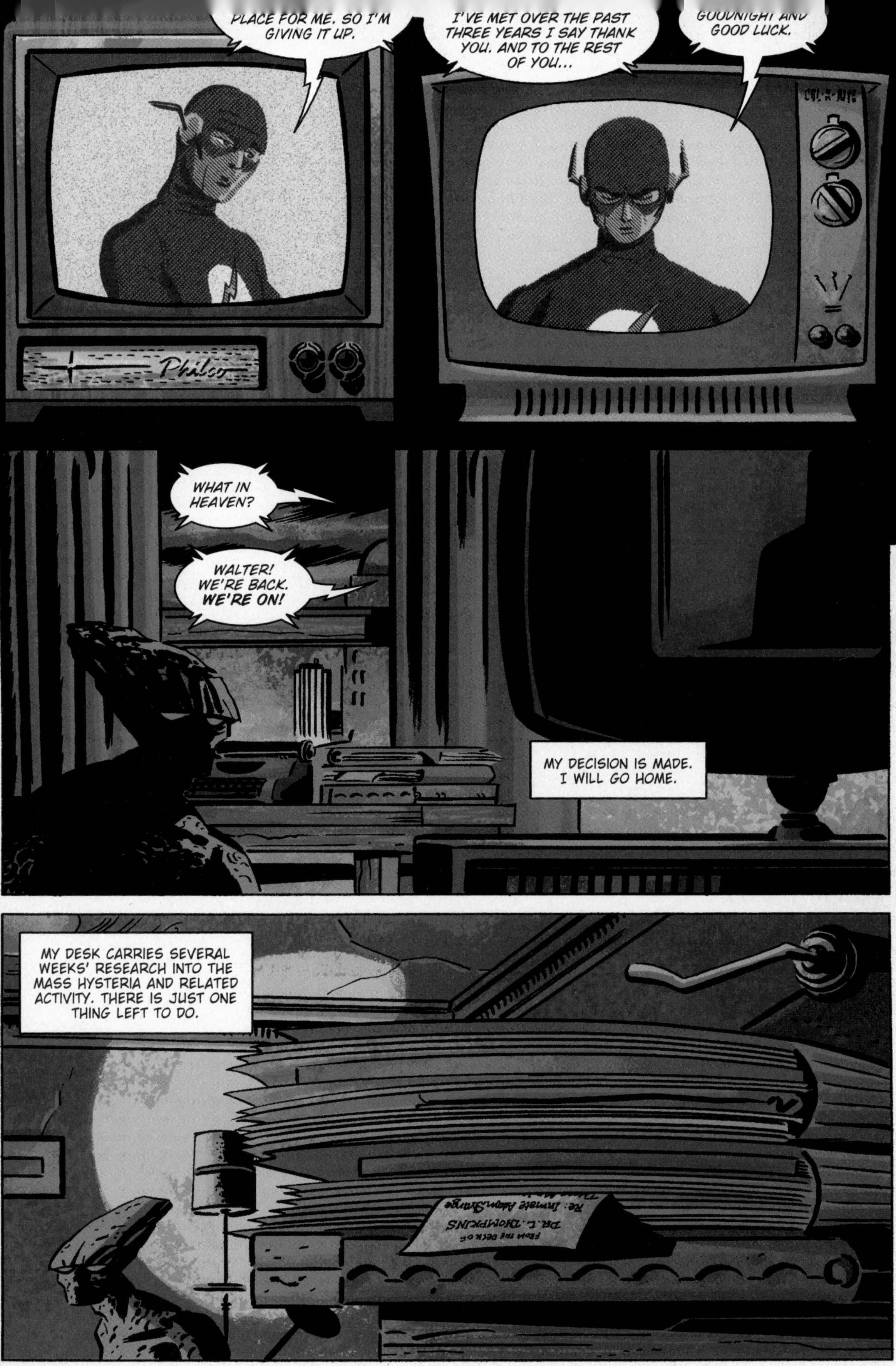
PLACE FOR ME. SO I'M GIVING IT UP.
I'VE MET OVER THE PAST THREE YEARS I SAY THANK YOU. AND TO THE REST OF YOU...
GOOD LUCK.
Philco
WHAT IN HEAVEN?
WALTER! WE'RE BACK. WE'RE ON!
MY DECISION IS MADE. I WILL GO HOME.
MY DESK CARRIES SEVERAL WEEKS' RESEARCH INTO THE MASS HYSTERIA AND RELATED ACTIVITY. THERE IS JUST ONE THING LEFT TO DO.

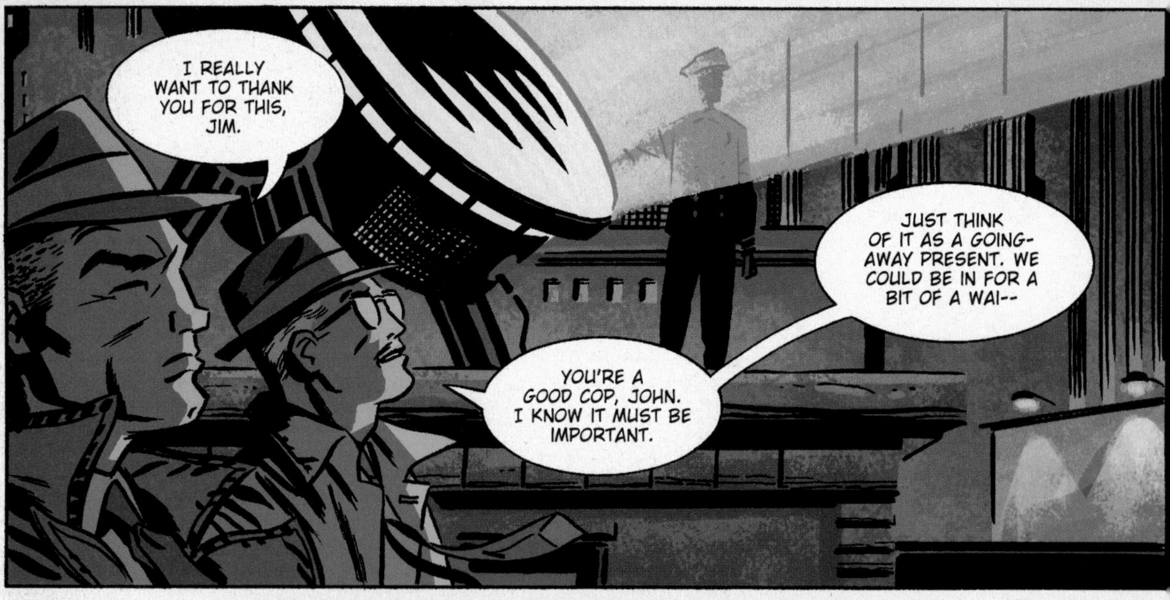
I REALLY WANT TO THANK YOU FOR THIS, JIM.
JUST THINK OF IT AS A GOING-AWAY PRESENT. WE COULD BE IN FOR A BIT OF A WAI--
YOU'RE A GOOD COP, JOHN. I KNOW IT MUST BE IMPORTANT.

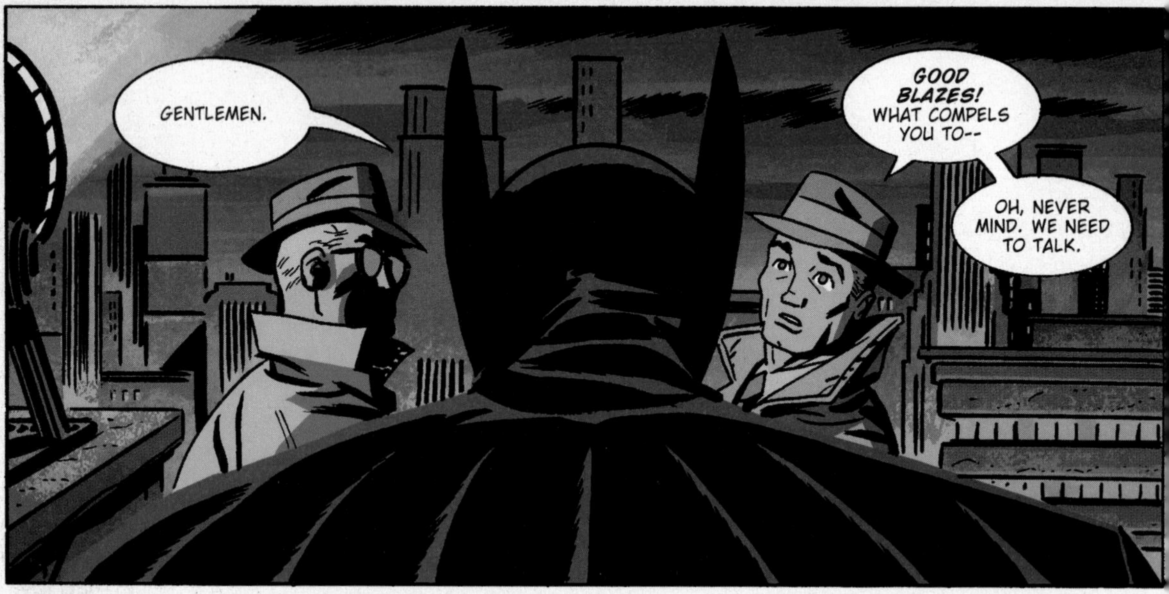
GENTLEMEN.
GOOD BLAZES! WHAT COMPELS YOU TO--
OH, NEVER MIND. WE NEED TO TALK.

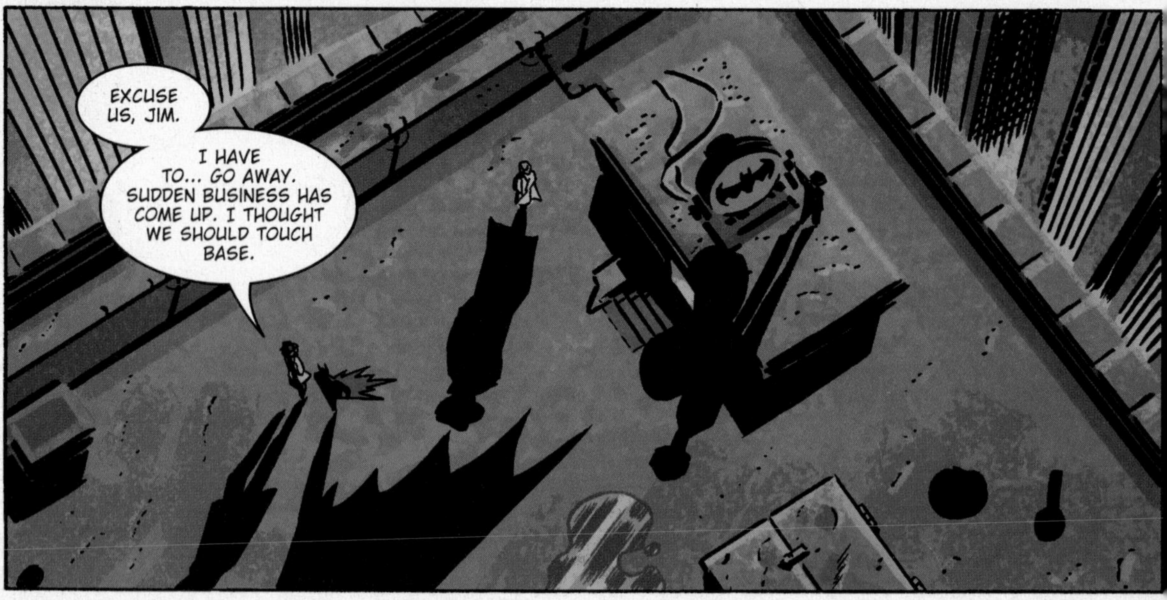
EXCUSE US, JIM.
I HAVE TO... GO AWAY. SUDDEN BUSINESS HAS COME UP. I THOUGHT WE SHOULD TOUCH BASE.

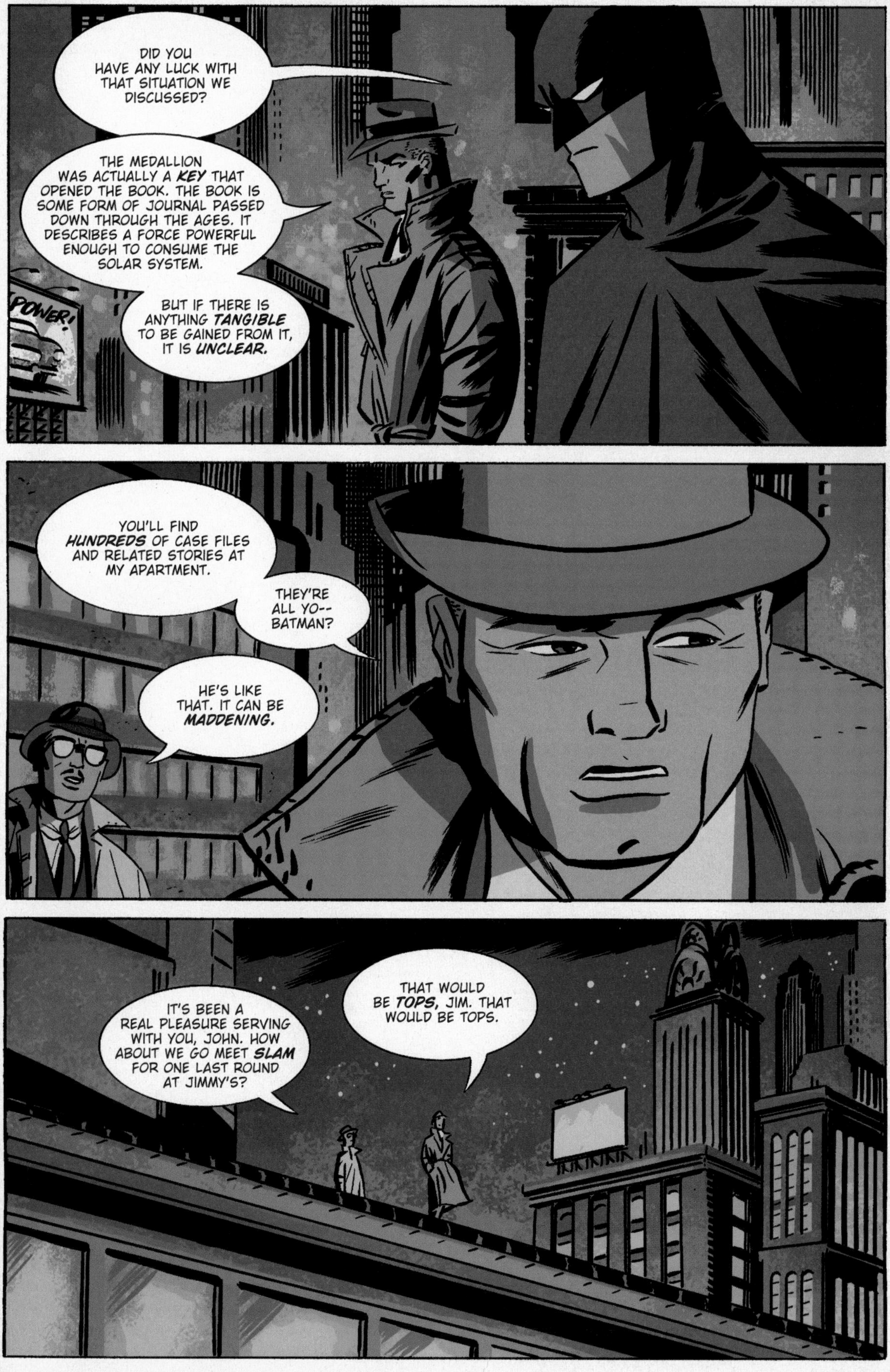
DID YOU HAVE ANY LUCK WITH THAT SITUATION WE DISCUSSED?
THE MEDALLION WAS ACTUALLY A KEY THAT OPENED THE BOOK. THE BOOK IS SOME FORM OF JOURNAL PASSED DOWN THROUGH THE AGES. IT DESCRIBES A FORCE POWERFUL ENOUGH TO CONSUME THE SOLAR SYSTEM.
BUT IF THERE IS ANYTHING TANGIBLE TO BE GAINED FROM IT, IT IS UNCLEAR.
POWER!
YOU'LL FIND HUNDREDS OF CASE FILES AND RELATED STORIES AT MY APARTMENT.
THEY'RE ALL YO-- BATMAN?
HE'S LIKE THAT. IT CAN BE MADDENING.
IT'S BEEN A REAL PLEASURE SERVING WITH YOU, JOHN. HOW ABOUT WE GO MEET SLAM FOR ONE LAST ROUND AT JIMMY'S?
THAT WOULD BE TOPS, JIM. THAT WOULD BE TOPS.

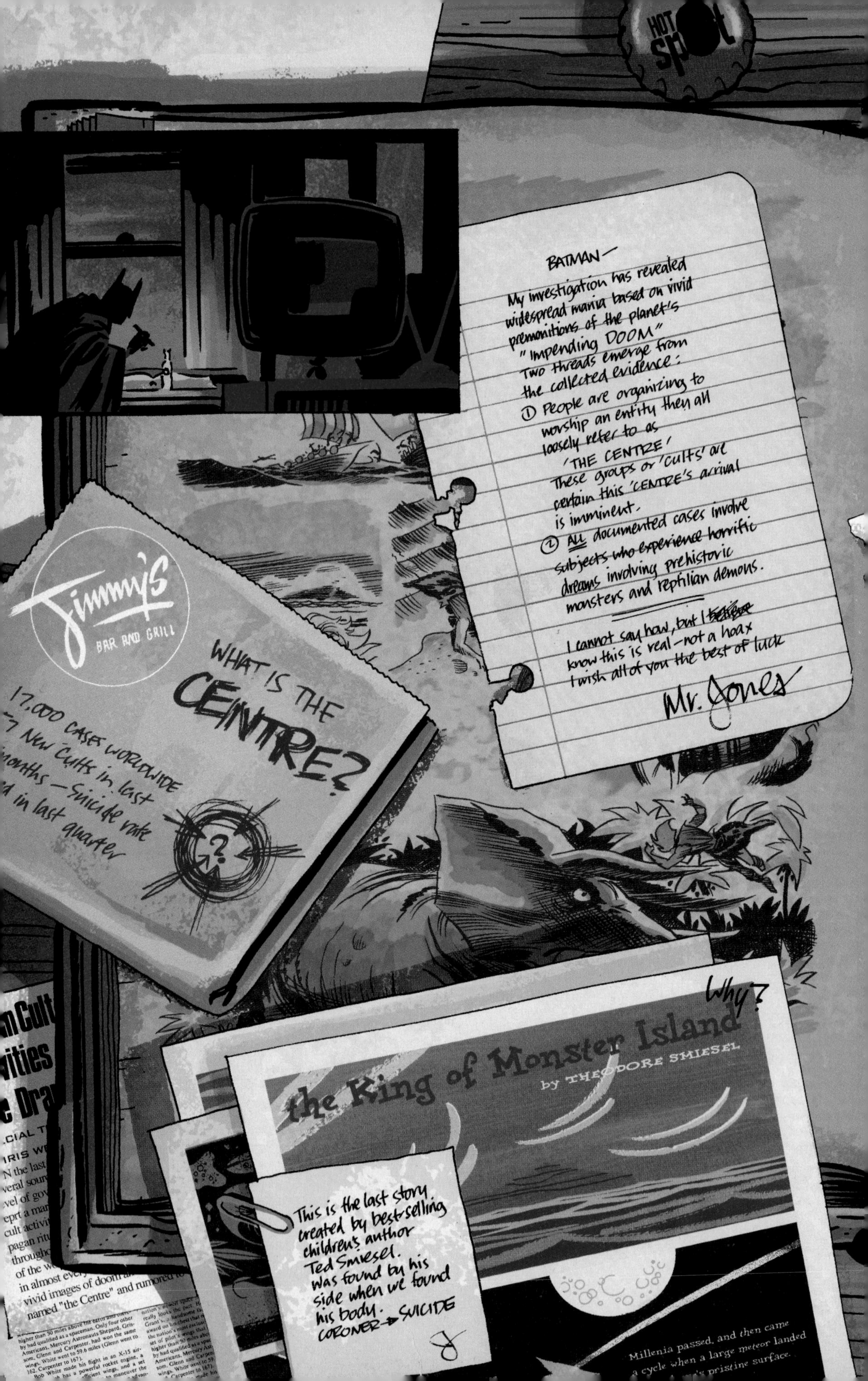
HOT spot
BATMAN—
My investigation has revealed widespread mania based on vivid premonitions of the planet's "Impending DOOM"
Two threads emerge from the collected evidence:
① People are organizing to worship an entity they all loosely refer to as 'THE CENTRE'
These groups or 'cults' are certain this 'CENTRE's arrival is imminent.
② ALL documented cases involve subjects who experience horrific dreams involving prehistoric monsters and reptilian demons.
I cannot say how, but I ~~believe~~ know this is real—not a hoax
I wish all of you the best of luck
Mr. Jones
Jimmy's BAR AND GRILL
WHAT IS THE CENTRE?
17,000 CASES WORLDWIDE
New Cults in last
months—Suicide rate
in last quarter
Why?
the King of Monster Island
by THEODORE SMIESEL
This is the last story created by best-selling children's author Ted Smiesel. Was found by his side when we found his body. CORONER → SUICIDE
Millenia passed, and then came a cycle when a large meteor landed
pristine surface.
vivid images of doom
named "the Centre" and rumored

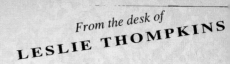

CASE #1494; ADAM STRANGE

(cont)...

Furthermore, it is my opinion that transferring the subject to an undiscl[osed] government facility would be a tremend[ous] step backward in regards to his recovery.

The subject's obsession with an imag[inary] alien world that he "transports" to by way of light beams is both a sensitive and complex psychosis in and of itself.

This case study's value is compoun[ded by] subject's visions of a coming armageddon at the hands of an all-consuming force of some sort. Arkham currently houses 23 such cases, and as such, Mr. Strange seems to be part of a large grou[p] who are experiencing some form o[f] mass hysteria.

(cont)...

OBITUARIES

[CTOR]
[H]UGH EVANS
Renowned Scientist and Patriot

Born—March 9, 1919 Died—June 21, 1958
In what is being referred to as an unfortunate accident resea[rch] [sci]entist Hugh Evans was killed during [ ] in New York City involving [ ] Prehistoric monsters [ ] accident Evans [ ] holid [ ]
un [ ]
E[ ]

Mass Hysteria in Ma[nhattan]
Sunday News January 27th, 1957
A SPECIAL PHOTO-ESSAY BY BORIS SPREMO

Sauron Invas[ion]
New York's finest battle Pr[ ]

pair of co[ ]
plane
tage ov[ ]
flight pa[ ]
Both the[ ]
come und[ ]
Administr[ ]
combining the be[ ]
Immediately af[ ]
pretty wife Doris [ ]
to Washington, D. [ ] California
dent [ ] here they met Presi-
husband's new wings. The[ ] Doris proudly pinned on [ ]
h[ ]
h[ ]
w[ ]

IT'S ME. I'VE GOT SOMETHING HERE I THINK YOU'D BETTER TAKE A LOOK AT. NEXT TUESDAY THEN. USUAL TIME AND PLACE.

HOT SP[OT]

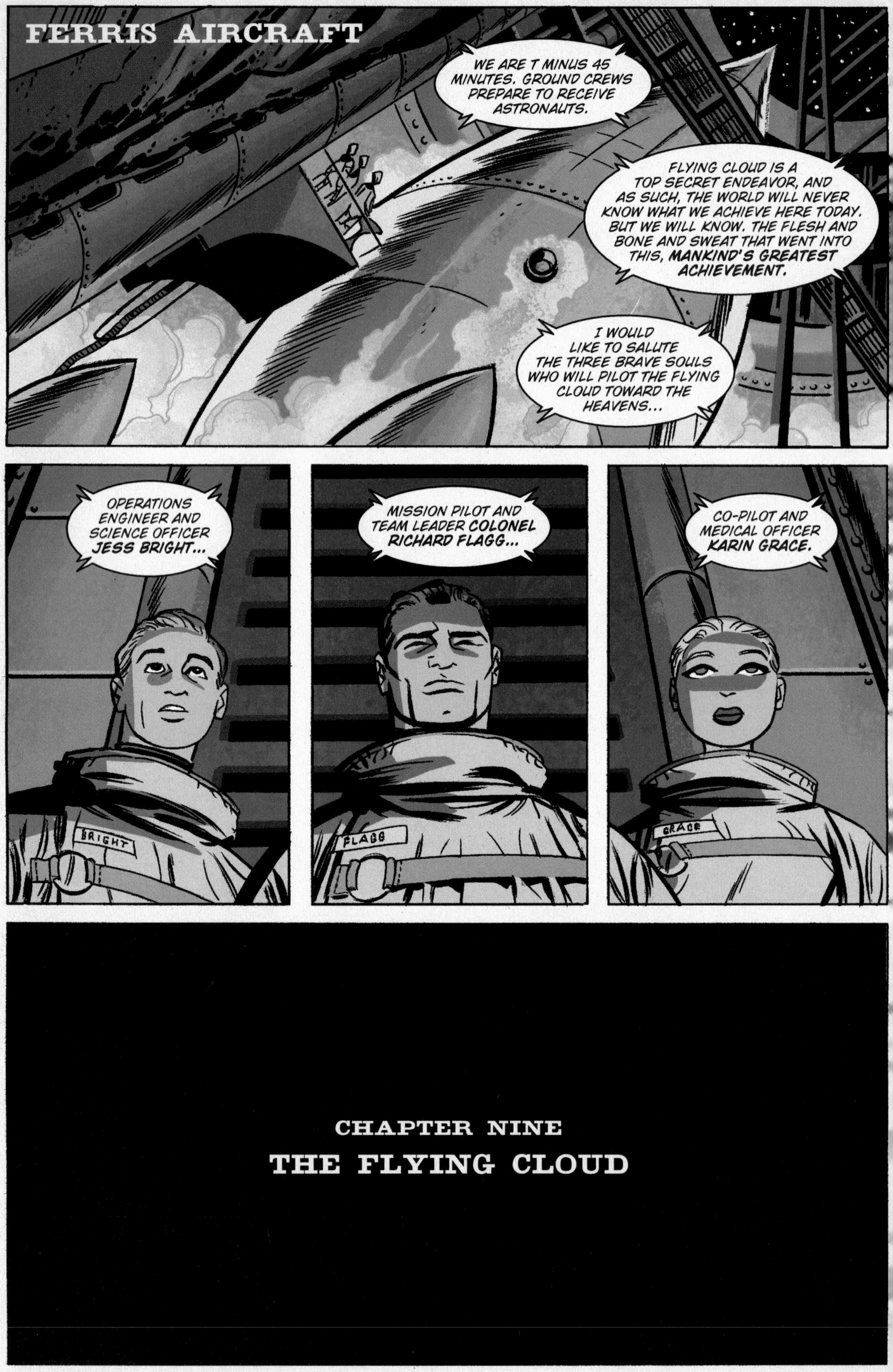
FERRIS AIRCRAFT
WE ARE T MINUS 45 MINUTES. GROUND CREWS PREPARE TO RECEIVE ASTRONAUTS.
FLYING CLOUD IS A TOP SECRET ENDEAVOR, AND AS SUCH, THE WORLD WILL NEVER KNOW WHAT WE ACHIEVE HERE TODAY. BUT WE WILL KNOW. THE FLESH AND BONE AND SWEAT THAT WENT INTO THIS, MANKIND'S GREATEST ACHIEVEMENT.
I WOULD LIKE TO SALUTE THE THREE BRAVE SOULS WHO WILL PILOT THE FLYING CLOUD TOWARD THE HEAVENS...
OPERATIONS ENGINEER AND SCIENCE OFFICER JESS BRIGHT...
BRIGHT
MISSION PILOT AND TEAM LEADER COLONEL RICHARD FLAGG...
FLAGG
CO-PILOT AND MEDICAL OFFICER KARIN GRACE.
GRACE

CHAPTER NINE

THE FLYING CLOUD

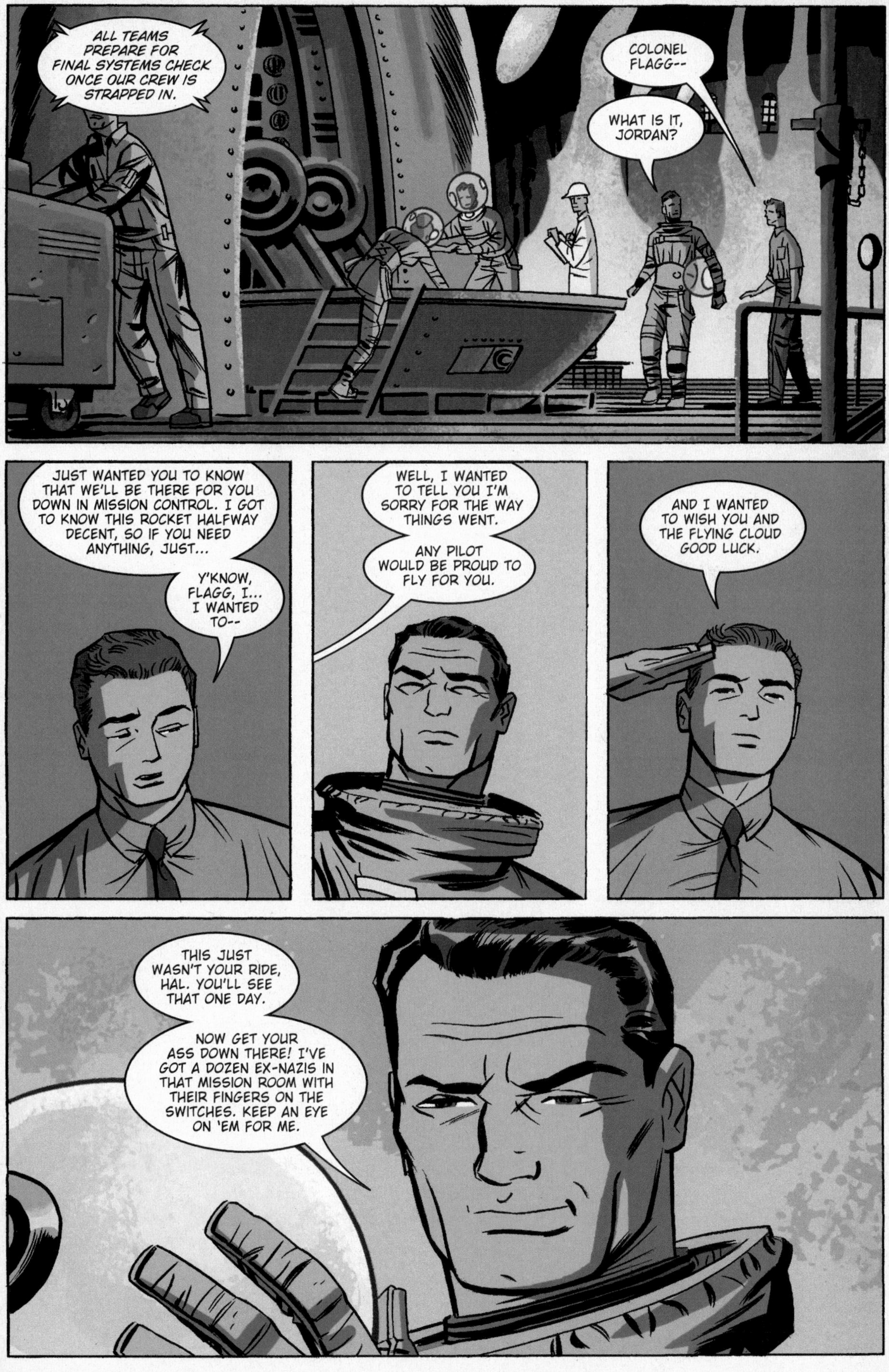
ALL TEAMS PREPARE FOR FINAL SYSTEMS CHECK ONCE OUR CREW IS STRAPPED IN.
COLONEL FLAGG--
WHAT IS IT, JORDAN?
JUST WANTED YOU TO KNOW THAT WE'LL BE THERE FOR YOU DOWN IN MISSION CONTROL. I GOT TO KNOW THIS ROCKET HALFWAY DECENT, SO IF YOU NEED ANYTHING, JUST...
Y'KNOW, FLAGG, I... I WANTED TO--
WELL, I WANTED TO TELL YOU I'M SORRY FOR THE WAY THINGS WENT.
ANY PILOT WOULD BE PROUD TO FLY FOR YOU.
AND I WANTED TO WISH YOU AND THE FLYING CLOUD GOOD LUCK.
THIS JUST WASN'T YOUR RIDE, HAL. YOU'LL SEE THAT ONE DAY.
NOW GET YOUR ASS DOWN THERE! I'VE GOT A DOZEN EX-NAZIS IN THAT MISSION ROOM WITH THEIR FINGERS ON THE SWITCHES. KEEP AN EYE ON 'EM FOR ME.

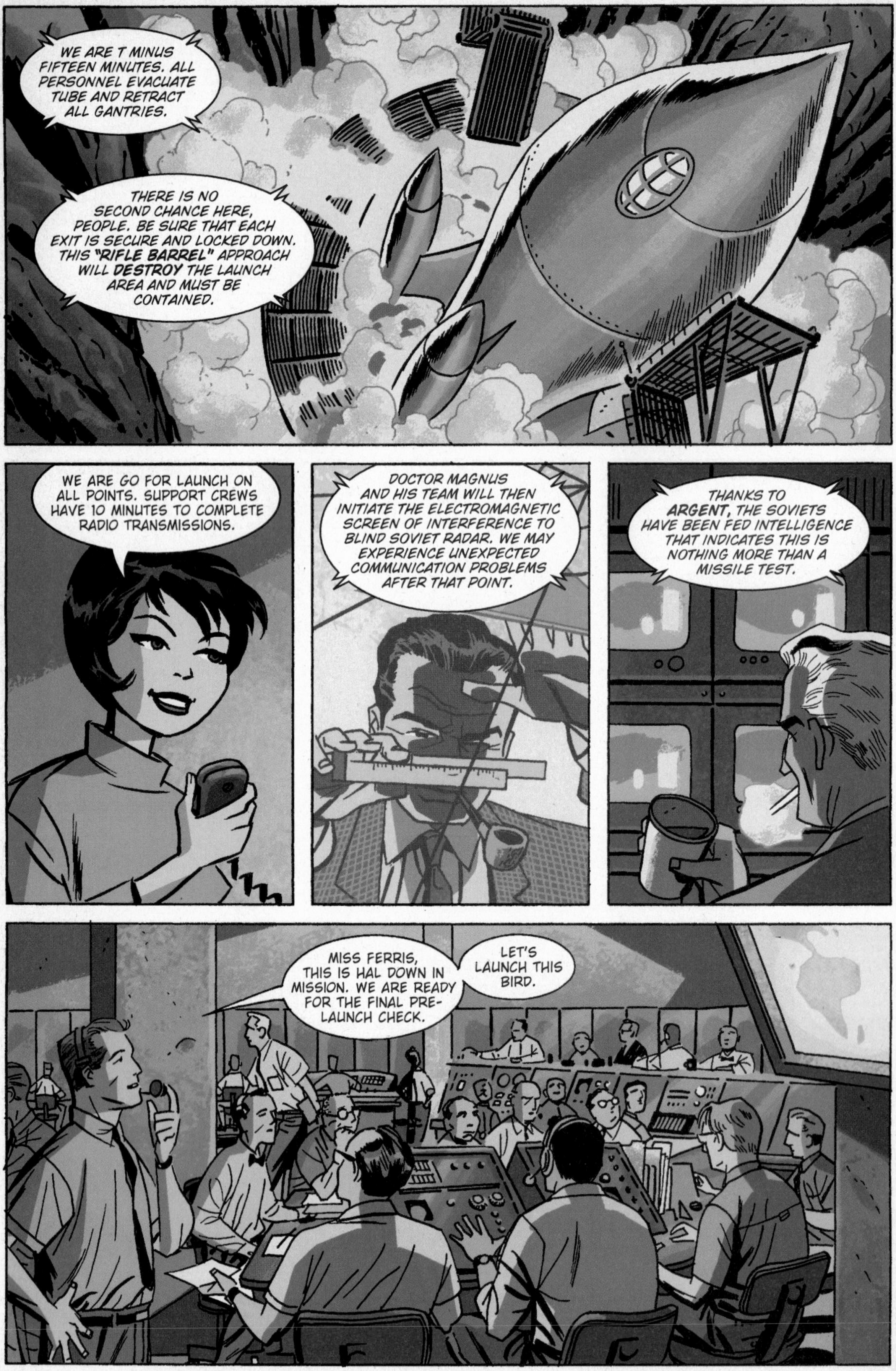
WE ARE T MINUS FIFTEEN MINUTES. ALL PERSONNEL EVACUATE TUBE AND RETRACT ALL GANTRIES.
THERE IS NO SECOND CHANCE HERE, PEOPLE. BE SURE THAT EACH EXIT IS SECURE AND LOCKED DOWN. THIS "RIFLE BARREL" APPROACH WILL DESTROY THE LAUNCH AREA AND MUST BE CONTAINED.
WE ARE GO FOR LAUNCH ON ALL POINTS. SUPPORT CREWS HAVE 10 MINUTES TO COMPLETE RADIO TRANSMISSIONS.
DOCTOR MAGNUS AND HIS TEAM WILL THEN INITIATE THE ELECTROMAGNETIC SCREEN OF INTERFERENCE TO BLIND SOVIET RADAR. WE MAY EXPERIENCE UNEXPECTED COMMUNICATION PROBLEMS AFTER THAT POINT.
THANKS TO ARGENT, THE SOVIETS HAVE BEEN FED INTELLIGENCE THAT INDICATES THIS IS NOTHING MORE THAN A MISSILE TEST.
MISS FERRIS, THIS IS HAL DOWN IN MISSION. WE ARE READY FOR THE FINAL PRE-LAUNCH CHECK.
LET'S LAUNCH THIS BIRD.

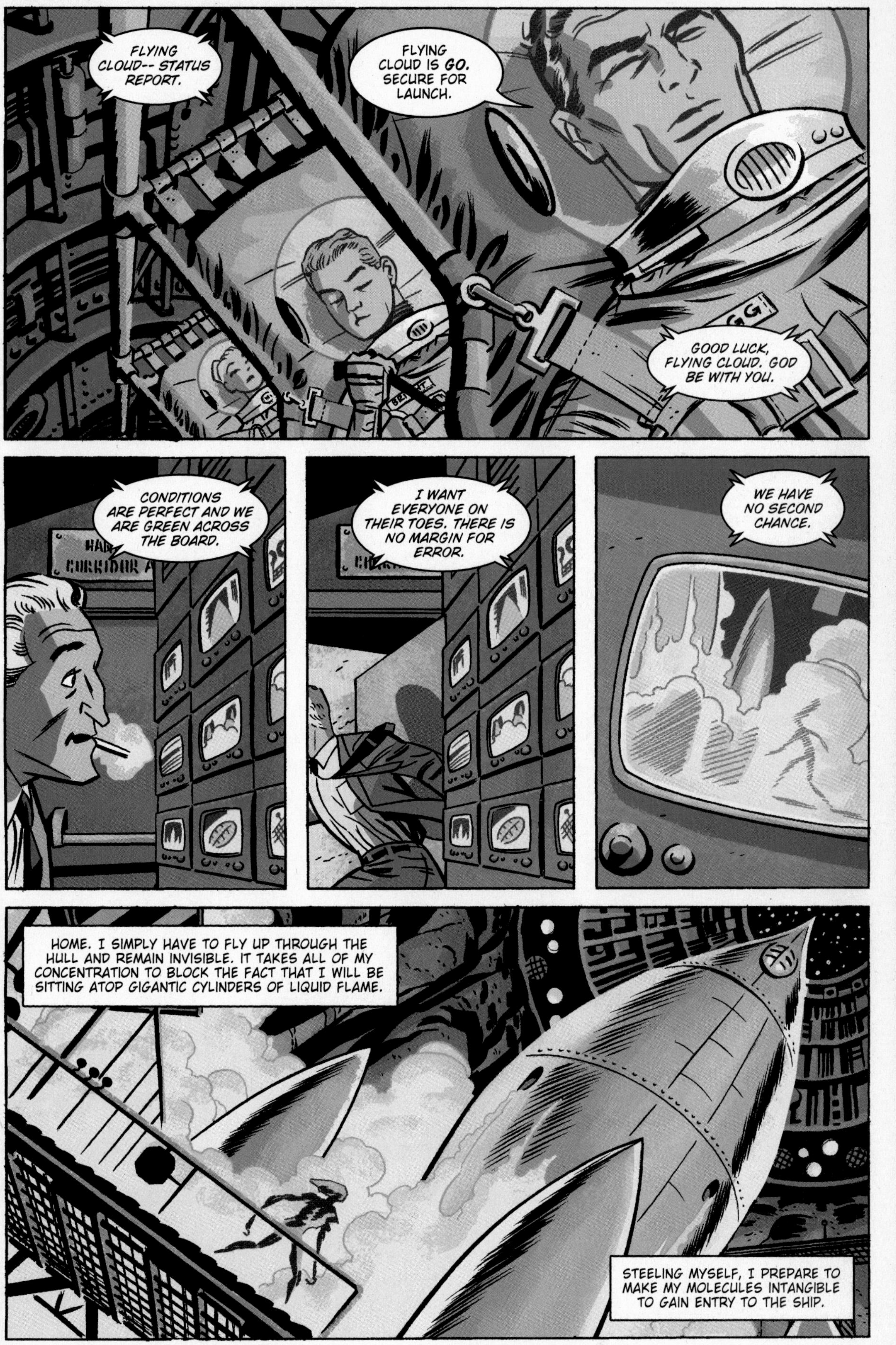
FLYING CLOUD-- STATUS REPORT.
FLYING CLOUD IS GO. SECURE FOR LAUNCH.
GOOD LUCK, FLYING CLOUD. GOD BE WITH YOU.
CONDITIONS ARE PERFECT AND WE ARE GREEN ACROSS THE BOARD.
I WANT EVERYONE ON THEIR TOES. THERE IS NO MARGIN FOR ERROR.
WE HAVE NO SECOND CHANCE.
HOME. I SIMPLY HAVE TO FLY UP THROUGH THE HULL AND REMAIN INVISIBLE. IT TAKES ALL OF MY CONCENTRATION TO BLOCK THE FACT THAT I WILL BE SITTING ATOP GIGANTIC CYLINDERS OF LIQUID FLAME.
STEELING MYSELF, I PREPARE TO MAKE MY MOLECULES INTANGIBLE TO GAIN ENTRY TO THE SHIP.

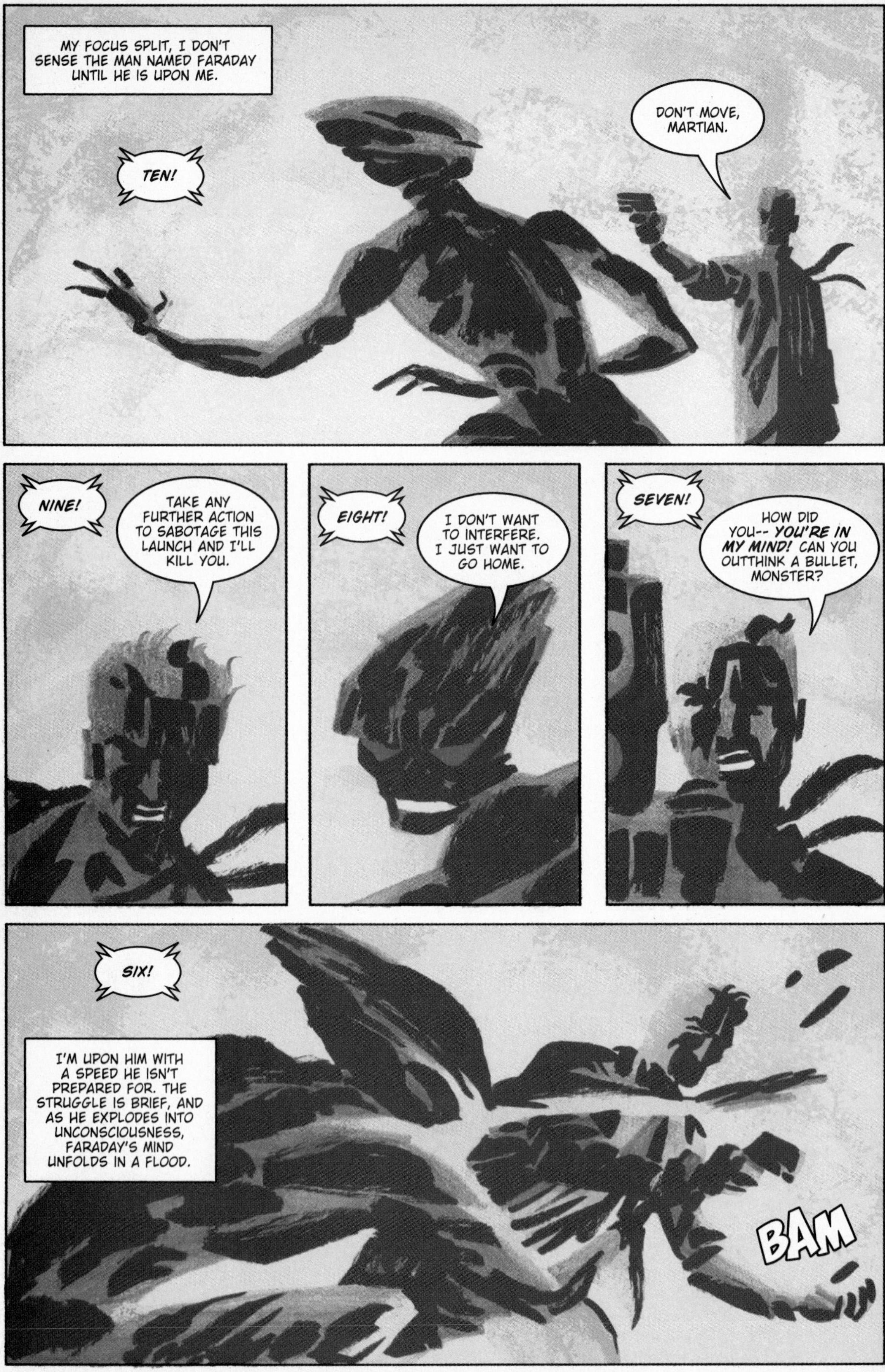

MY FOCUS SPLIT, I DON'T SENSE THE MAN NAMED FARADAY UNTIL HE IS UPON ME.
TEN!
DON'T MOVE, MARTIAN.
NINE!
TAKE ANY FURTHER ACTION TO SABOTAGE THIS LAUNCH AND I'LL KILL YOU.
EIGHT!
I DON'T WANT TO INTERFERE. I JUST WANT TO GO HOME.
SEVEN!
HOW DID YOU-- ***YOU'RE IN MY MIND!*** CAN YOU OUTTHINK A BULLET, MONSTER?
SIX!
I'M UPON HIM WITH A SPEED HE ISN'T PREPARED FOR. THE STRUGGLE IS BRIEF, AND AS HE EXPLODES INTO UNCONSCIOUSNESS, FARADAY'S MIND UNFOLDS IN A FLOOD.
BAM

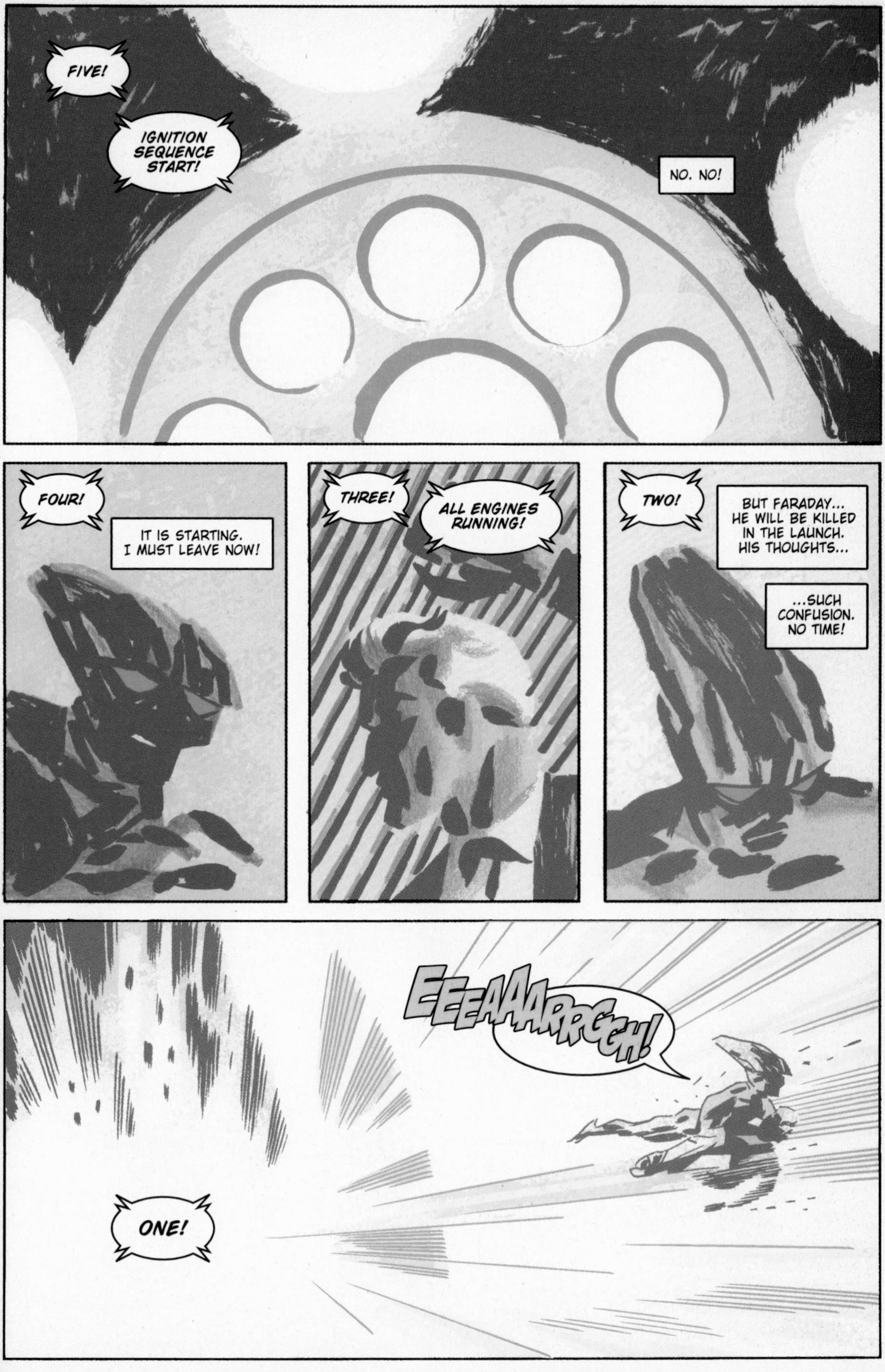
FIVE!
IGNITION SEQUENCE START!
NO. NO!
FOUR!
IT IS STARTING. I MUST LEAVE NOW!
THREE!
ALL ENGINES RUNNING!
TWO!
BUT FARADAY... HE WILL BE KILLED IN THE LAUNCH. HIS THOUGHTS...
...SUCH CONFUSION. NO TIME!
EEEAAARRGGH!
ONE!

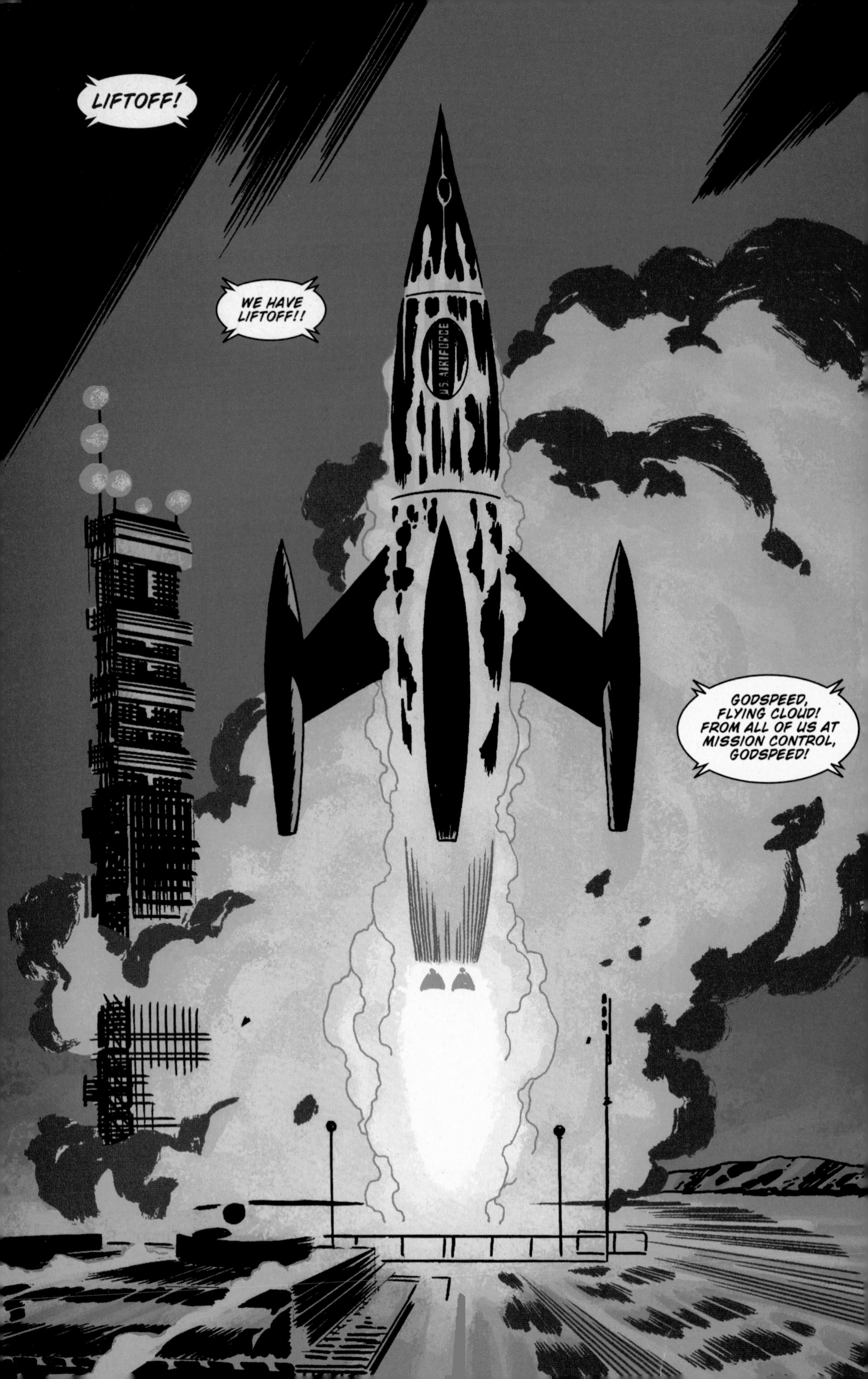
LIFTOFF!
WE HAVE LIFTOFF!!
U.S. AIRFORCE
GODSPEED, FLYING CLOUD! FROM ALL OF US AT MISSION CONTROL, GODSPEED!

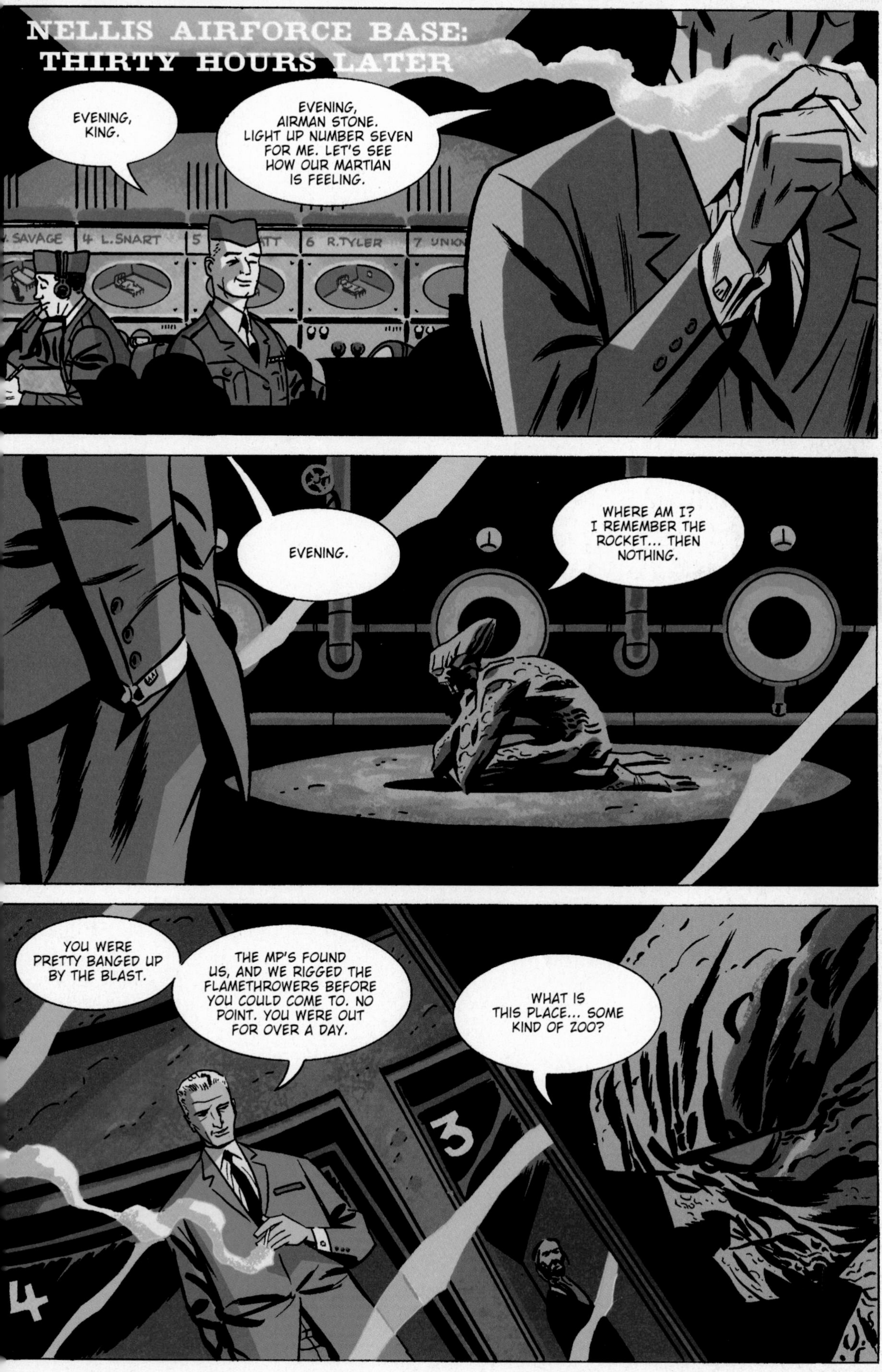
NELLIS AIRFORCE BASE: THIRTY HOURS LATER
EVENING, KING.
EVENING, AIRMAN STONE. LIGHT UP NUMBER SEVEN FOR ME. LET'S SEE HOW OUR MARTIAN IS FEELING.
L.SNART
R.TYLER
EVENING.
WHERE AM I? I REMEMBER THE ROCKET... THEN NOTHING.
YOU WERE PRETTY BANGED UP BY THE BLAST.
THE MP'S FOUND US, AND WE RIGGED THE FLAMETHROWERS BEFORE YOU COULD COME TO. NO POINT. YOU WERE OUT FOR OVER A DAY.
WHAT IS THIS PLACE... SOME KIND OF ZOO?
3
4

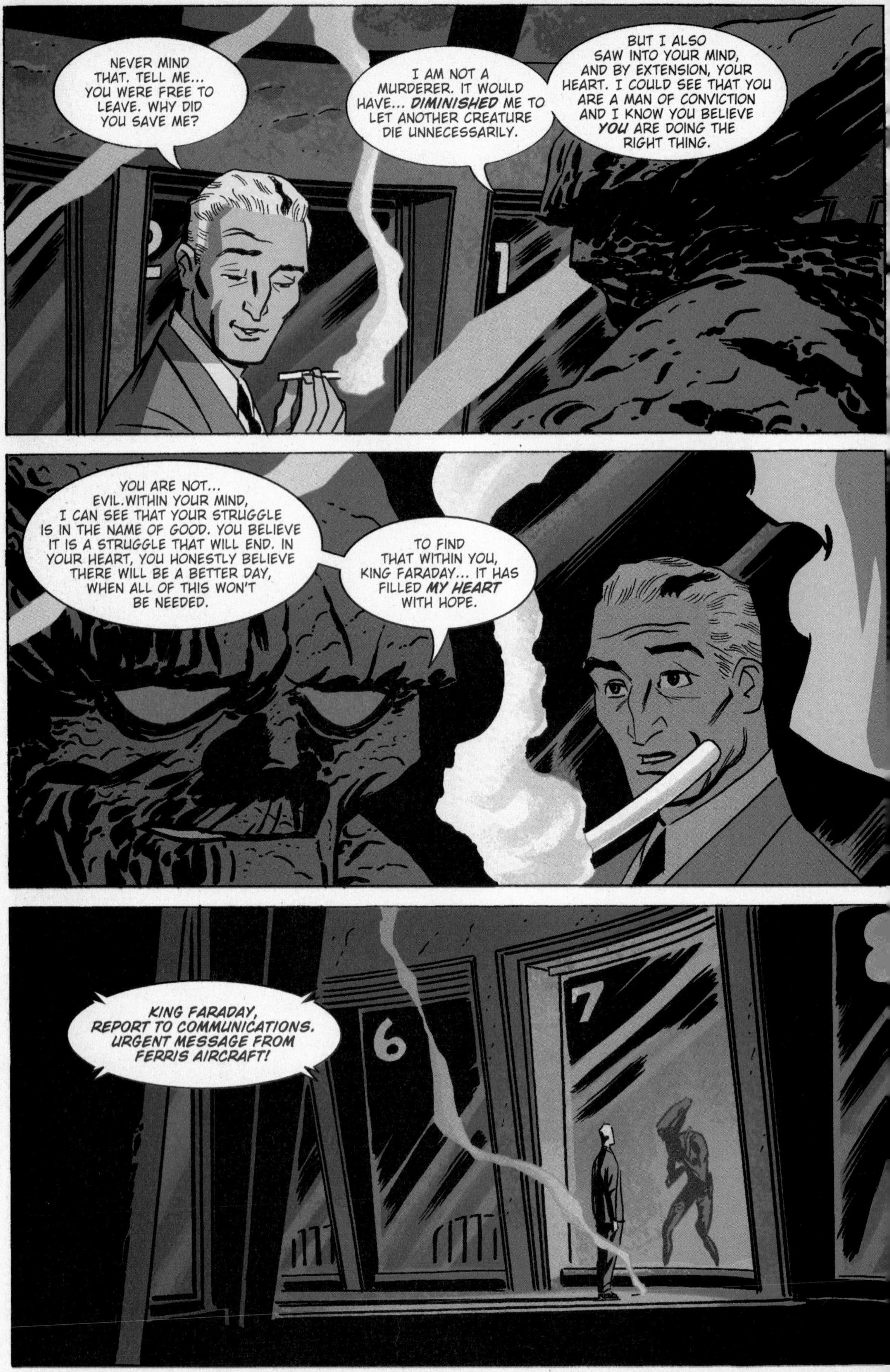
NEVER MIND THAT. TELL ME... YOU WERE FREE TO LEAVE. WHY DID YOU SAVE ME?
I AM NOT A MURDERER. IT WOULD HAVE... DIMINISHED ME TO LET ANOTHER CREATURE DIE UNNECESSARILY.
BUT I ALSO SAW INTO YOUR MIND, AND BY EXTENSION, YOUR HEART. I COULD SEE THAT YOU ARE A MAN OF CONVICTION AND I KNOW YOU BELIEVE YOU ARE DOING THE RIGHT THING.
YOU ARE NOT... EVIL. WITHIN YOUR MIND, I CAN SEE THAT YOUR STRUGGLE IS IN THE NAME OF GOOD. YOU BELIEVE IT IS A STRUGGLE THAT WILL END. IN YOUR HEART, YOU HONESTLY BELIEVE THERE WILL BE A BETTER DAY, WHEN ALL OF THIS WON'T BE NEEDED.
TO FIND THAT WITHIN YOU, KING FARADAY... IT HAS FILLED MY HEART WITH HOPE.
KING FARADAY, REPORT TO COMMUNICATIONS. URGENT MESSAGE FROM FERRIS AIRCRAFT!

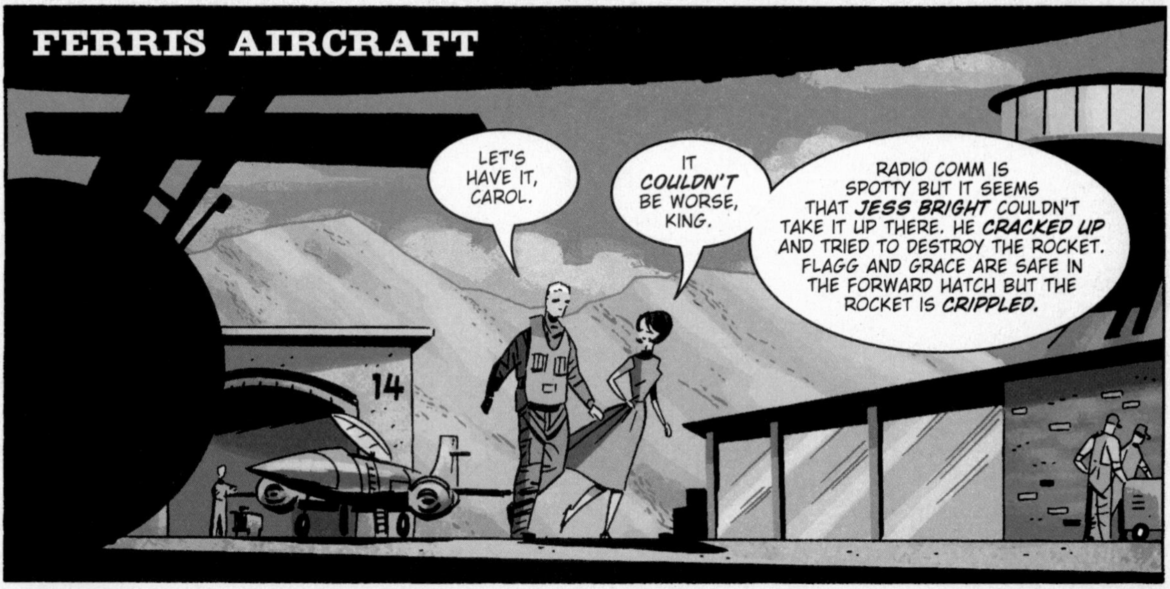
FERRIS AIRCRAFT
LET'S HAVE IT, CAROL.
IT COULDN'T BE WORSE, KING.
RADIO COMM IS SPOTTY BUT IT SEEMS THAT JESS BRIGHT COULDN'T TAKE IT UP THERE. HE CRACKED UP AND TRIED TO DESTROY THE ROCKET. FLAGG AND GRACE ARE SAFE IN THE FORWARD HATCH BUT THE ROCKET IS CRIPPLED.
14

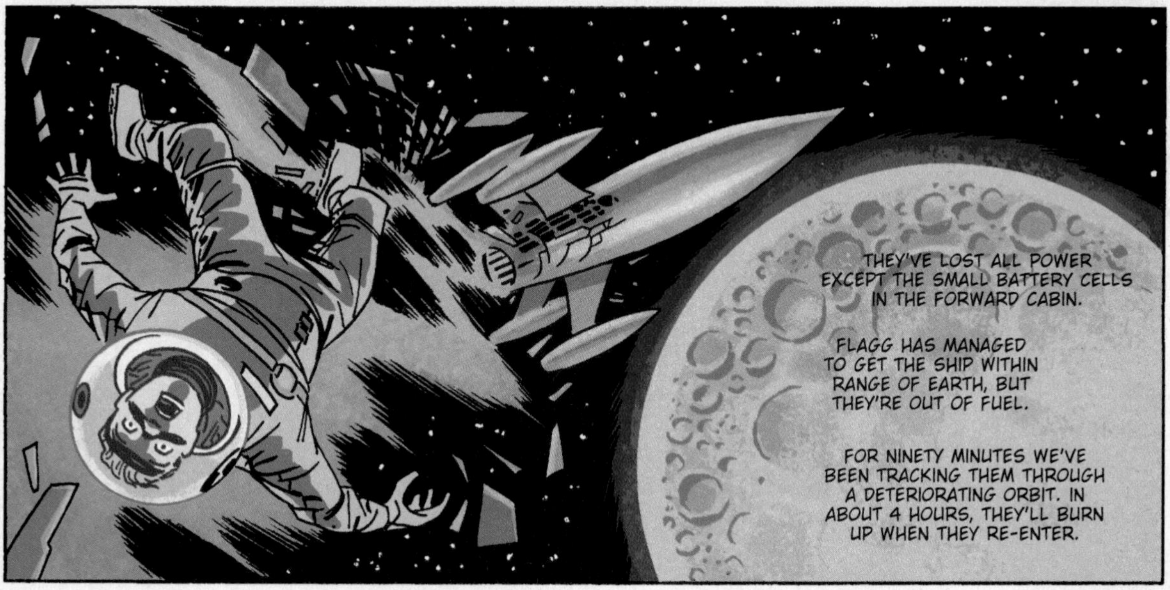
THEY'VE LOST ALL POWER EXCEPT THE SMALL BATTERY CELLS IN THE FORWARD CABIN.
FLAGG HAS MANAGED TO GET THE SHIP WITHIN RANGE OF EARTH, BUT THEY'RE OUT OF FUEL.
FOR NINETY MINUTES WE'VE BEEN TRACKING THEM THROUGH A DETERIORATING ORBIT. IN ABOUT 4 HOURS, THEY'LL BURN UP WHEN THEY RE-ENTER.

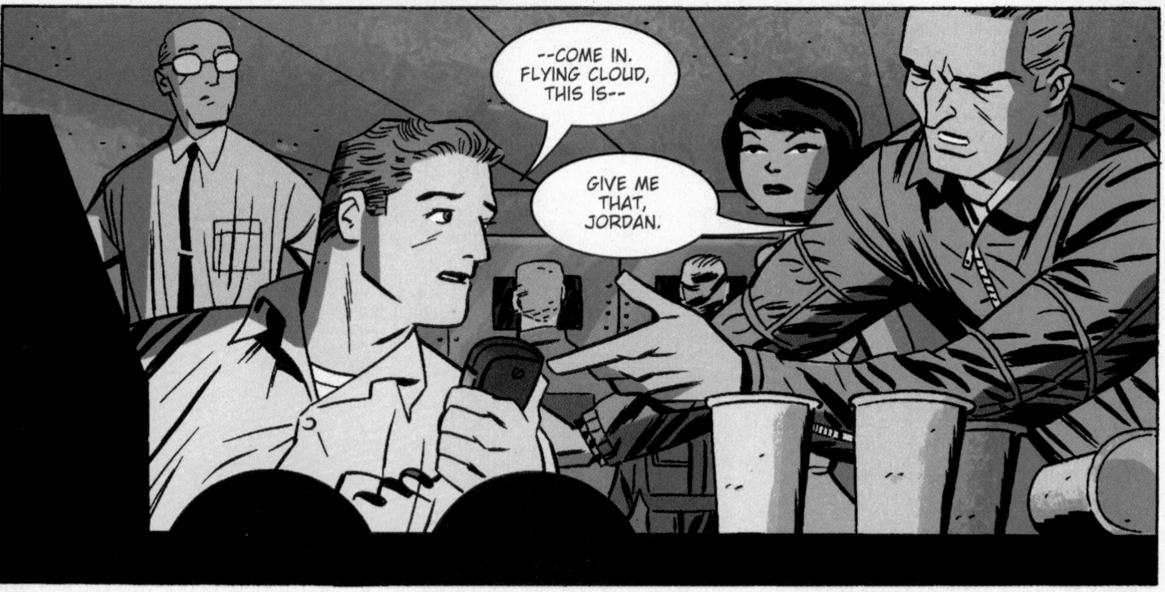
--COME IN. FLYING CLOUD, THIS IS--
GIVE ME THAT, JORDAN.

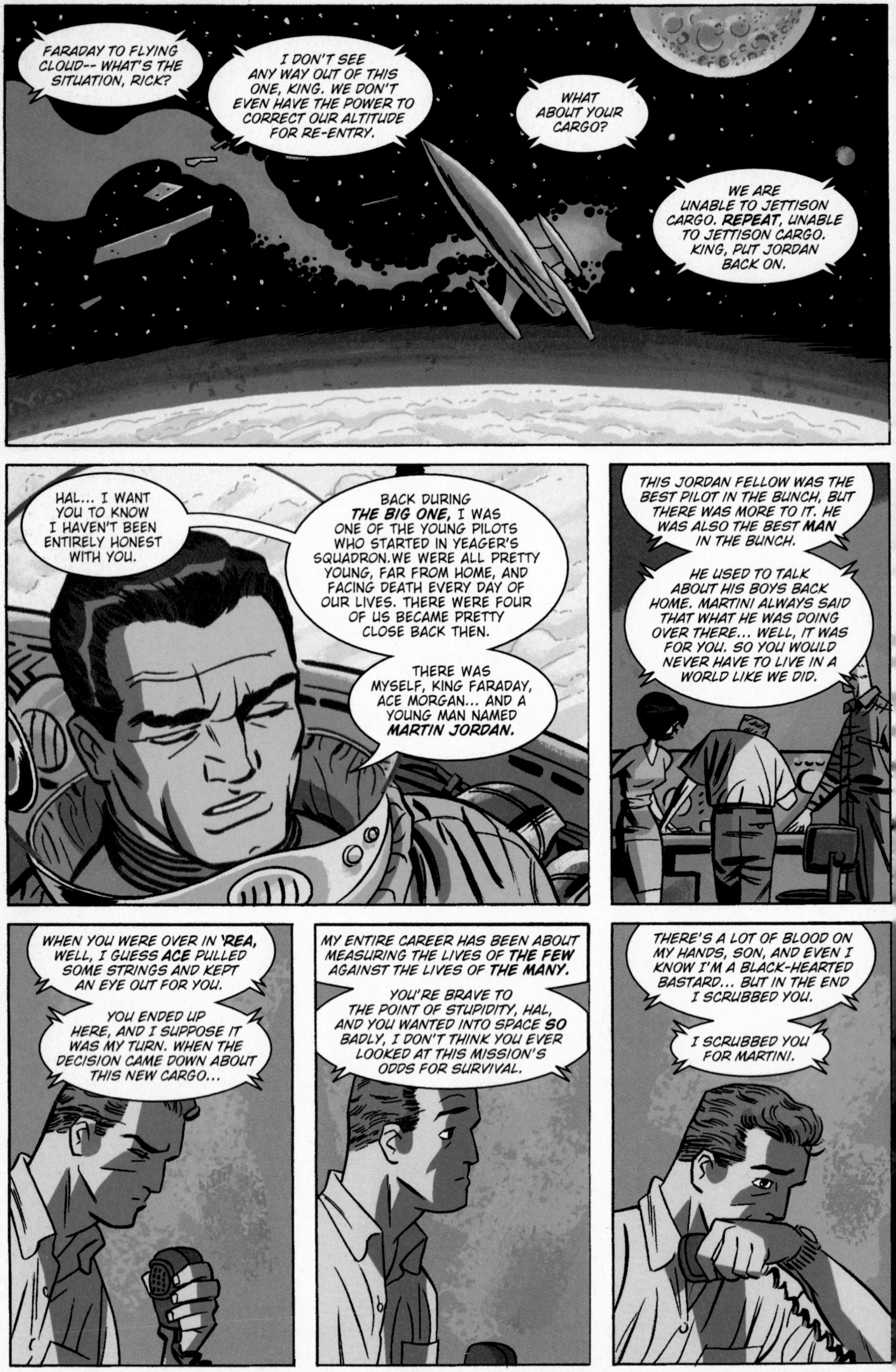
FARADAY TO FLYING CLOUD-- WHAT'S THE SITUATION, RICK?
I DON'T SEE ANY WAY OUT OF THIS ONE, KING. WE DON'T EVEN HAVE THE POWER TO CORRECT OUR ALTITUDE FOR RE-ENTRY.
WHAT ABOUT YOUR CARGO?
WE ARE UNABLE TO JETTISON CARGO. REPEAT, UNABLE TO JETTISON CARGO. KING, PUT JORDAN BACK ON.
HAL... I WANT YOU TO KNOW I HAVEN'T BEEN ENTIRELY HONEST WITH YOU.
BACK DURING THE BIG ONE, I WAS ONE OF THE YOUNG PILOTS WHO STARTED IN YEAGER'S SQUADRON. WE WERE ALL PRETTY YOUNG, FAR FROM HOME, AND FACING DEATH EVERY DAY OF OUR LIVES. THERE WERE FOUR OF US BECAME PRETTY CLOSE BACK THEN.
THERE WAS MYSELF, KING FARADAY, ACE MORGAN... AND A YOUNG MAN NAMED MARTIN JORDAN.
THIS JORDAN FELLOW WAS THE BEST PILOT IN THE BUNCH, BUT THERE WAS MORE TO IT. HE WAS ALSO THE BEST MAN IN THE BUNCH.
HE USED TO TALK ABOUT HIS BOYS BACK HOME. MARTINI ALWAYS SAID THAT WHAT HE WAS DOING OVER THERE... WELL, IT WAS FOR YOU. SO YOU WOULD NEVER HAVE TO LIVE IN A WORLD LIKE WE DID.
WHEN YOU WERE OVER IN 'REA, WELL, I GUESS ACE PULLED SOME STRINGS AND KEPT AN EYE OUT FOR YOU.
YOU ENDED UP HERE, AND I SUPPOSE IT WAS MY TURN. WHEN THE DECISION CAME DOWN ABOUT THIS NEW CARGO...
MY ENTIRE CAREER HAS BEEN ABOUT MEASURING THE LIVES OF THE FEW AGAINST THE LIVES OF THE MANY.
YOU'RE BRAVE TO THE POINT OF STUPIDITY, HAL, AND YOU WANTED INTO SPACE SO BADLY, I DON'T THINK YOU EVER LOOKED AT THIS MISSION'S ODDS FOR SURVIVAL.
THERE'S A LOT OF BLOOD ON MY HANDS, SON, AND EVEN I KNOW I'M A BLACK-HEARTED BASTARD... BUT IN THE END I SCRUBBED YOU.
I SCRUBBED YOU FOR MARTINI.

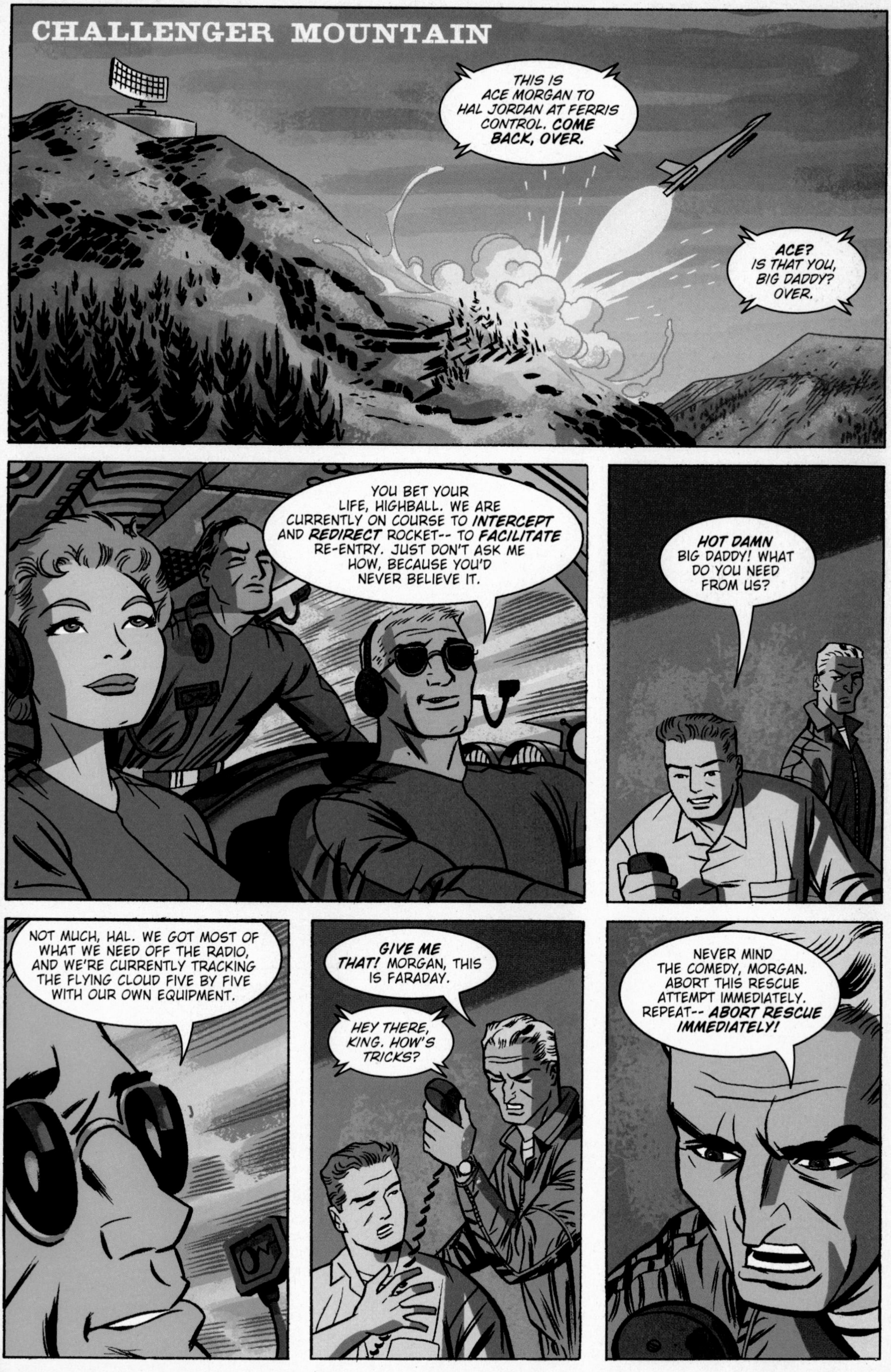
CHALLENGER MOUNTAIN
THIS IS ACE MORGAN TO HAL JORDAN AT FERRIS CONTROL. COME BACK, OVER.
ACE? IS THAT YOU, BIG DADDY? OVER.
YOU BET YOUR LIFE, HIGHBALL. WE ARE CURRENTLY ON COURSE TO INTERCEPT AND REDIRECT ROCKET-- TO FACILITATE RE-ENTRY. JUST DON'T ASK ME HOW, BECAUSE YOU'D NEVER BELIEVE IT.
HOT DAMN BIG DADDY! WHAT DO YOU NEED FROM US?
NOT MUCH, HAL. WE GOT MOST OF WHAT WE NEED OFF THE RADIO, AND WE'RE CURRENTLY TRACKING THE FLYING CLOUD FIVE BY FIVE WITH OUR OWN EQUIPMENT.
GIVE ME THAT! MORGAN, THIS IS FARADAY.
HEY THERE, KING. HOW'S TRICKS?
NEVER MIND THE COMEDY, MORGAN. ABORT THIS RESCUE ATTEMPT IMMEDIATELY. REPEAT-- ABORT RESCUE IMMEDIATELY!

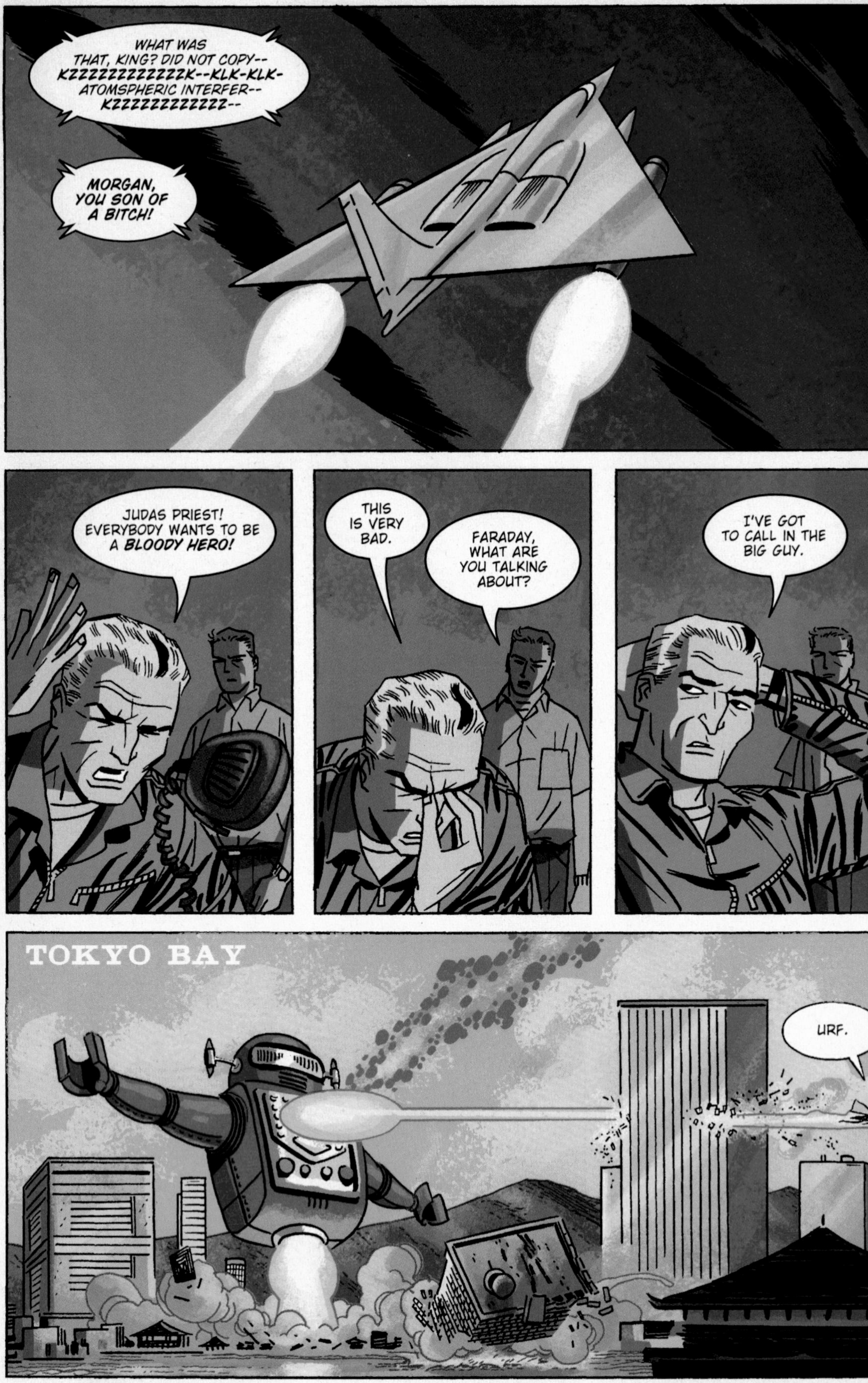
WHAT WAS THAT, KING? DID NOT COPY-- KZZZZZZZZZZZZK--KLK-KLK- ATOMSPHERIC INTERFER-- KZZZZZZZZZZZZ--
MORGAN, YOU SON OF A BITCH!
JUDAS PRIEST! EVERYBODY WANTS TO BE A BLOODY HERO!
THIS IS VERY BAD.
FARADAY, WHAT ARE YOU TALKING ABOUT?
I'VE GOT TO CALL IN THE BIG GUY.
TOKYO BAY
URF.

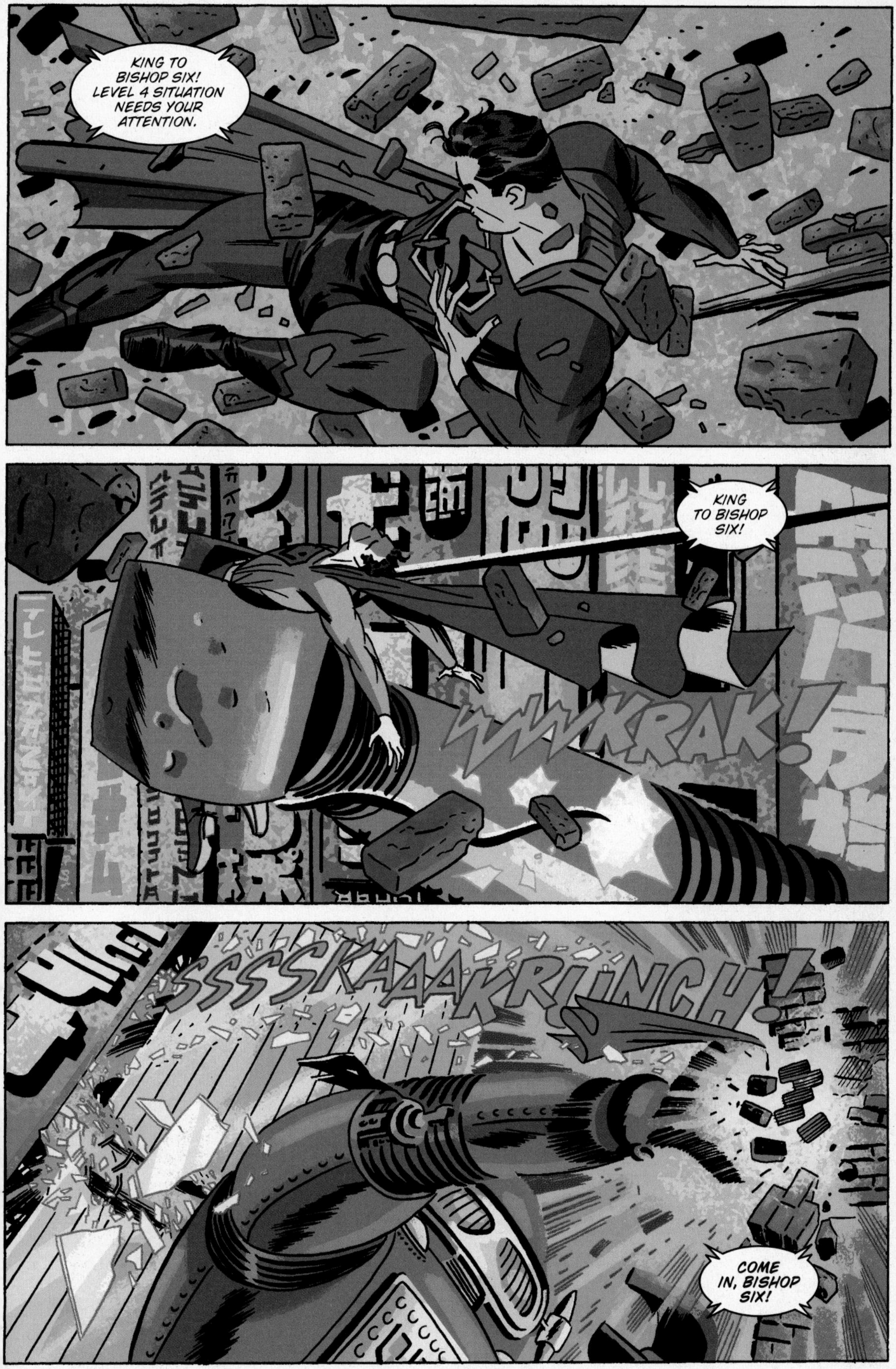
KING TO BISHOP SIX! LEVEL 4 SITUATION NEEDS YOUR ATTENTION.
KING TO BISHOP SIX!
WWKRAK!
SSSSKAAAKRUNCH!
COME IN, BISHOP SIX!

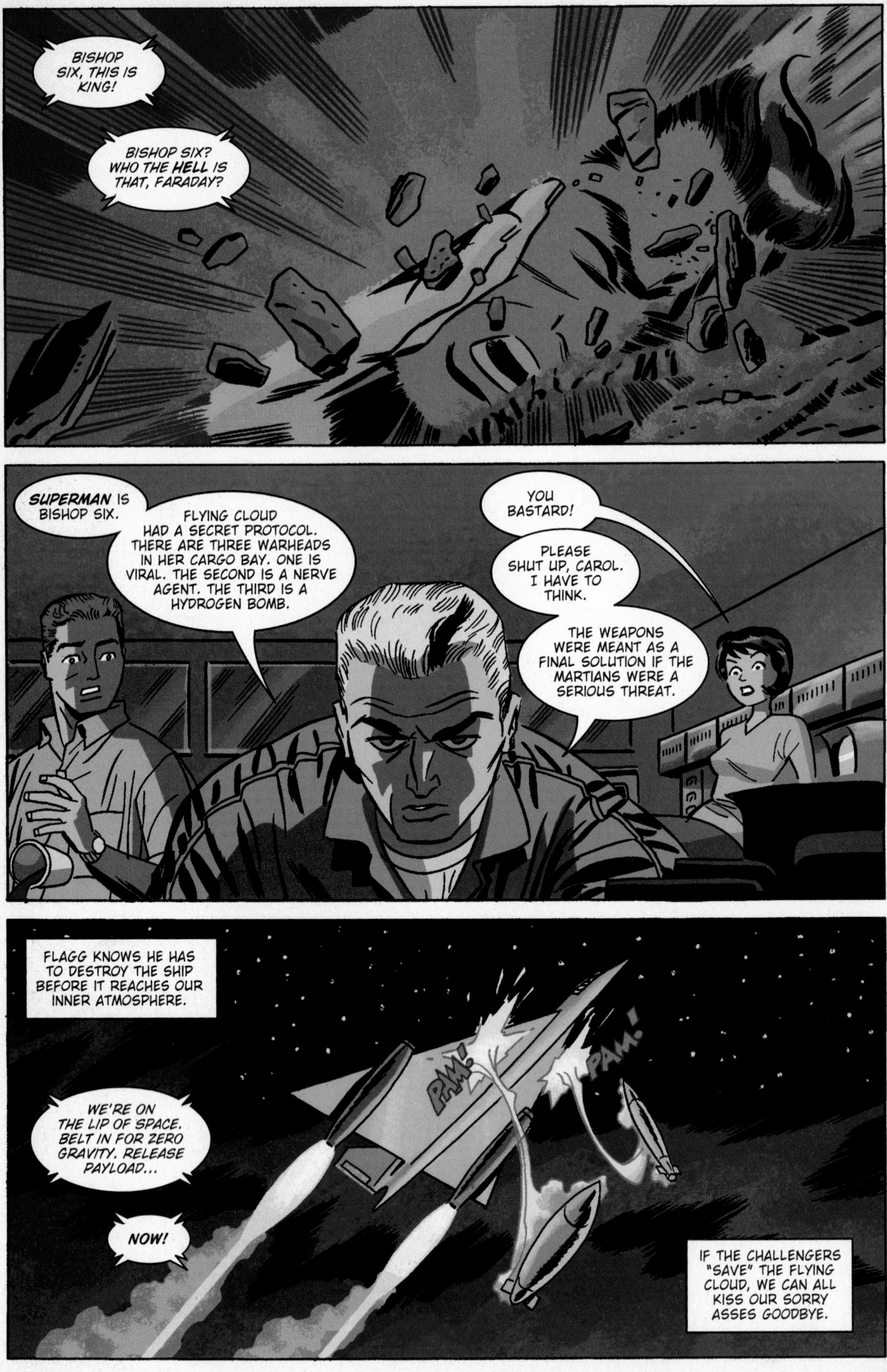

BISHOP SIX, THIS IS KING!
BISHOP SIX? WHO THE **HELL** IS THAT, FARADAY?
SUPERMAN IS BISHOP SIX.
FLYING CLOUD HAD A SECRET PROTOCOL. THERE ARE THREE WARHEADS IN HER CARGO BAY. ONE IS VIRAL. THE SECOND IS A NERVE AGENT. THE THIRD IS A HYDROGEN BOMB.
YOU BASTARD!
PLEASE SHUT UP, CAROL. I HAVE TO THINK.
THE WEAPONS WERE MEANT AS A FINAL SOLUTION IF THE MARTIANS WERE A SERIOUS THREAT.
FLAGG KNOWS HE HAS TO DESTROY THE SHIP BEFORE IT REACHES OUR INNER ATMOSPHERE.
PAM!
PAM!
WE'RE ON THE LIP OF SPACE. BELT IN FOR ZERO GRAVITY. RELEASE PAYLOAD...
NOW!
IF THE CHALLENGERS "SAVE" THE FLYING CLOUD, WE CAN ALL KISS OUR SORRY ASSES GOODBYE.

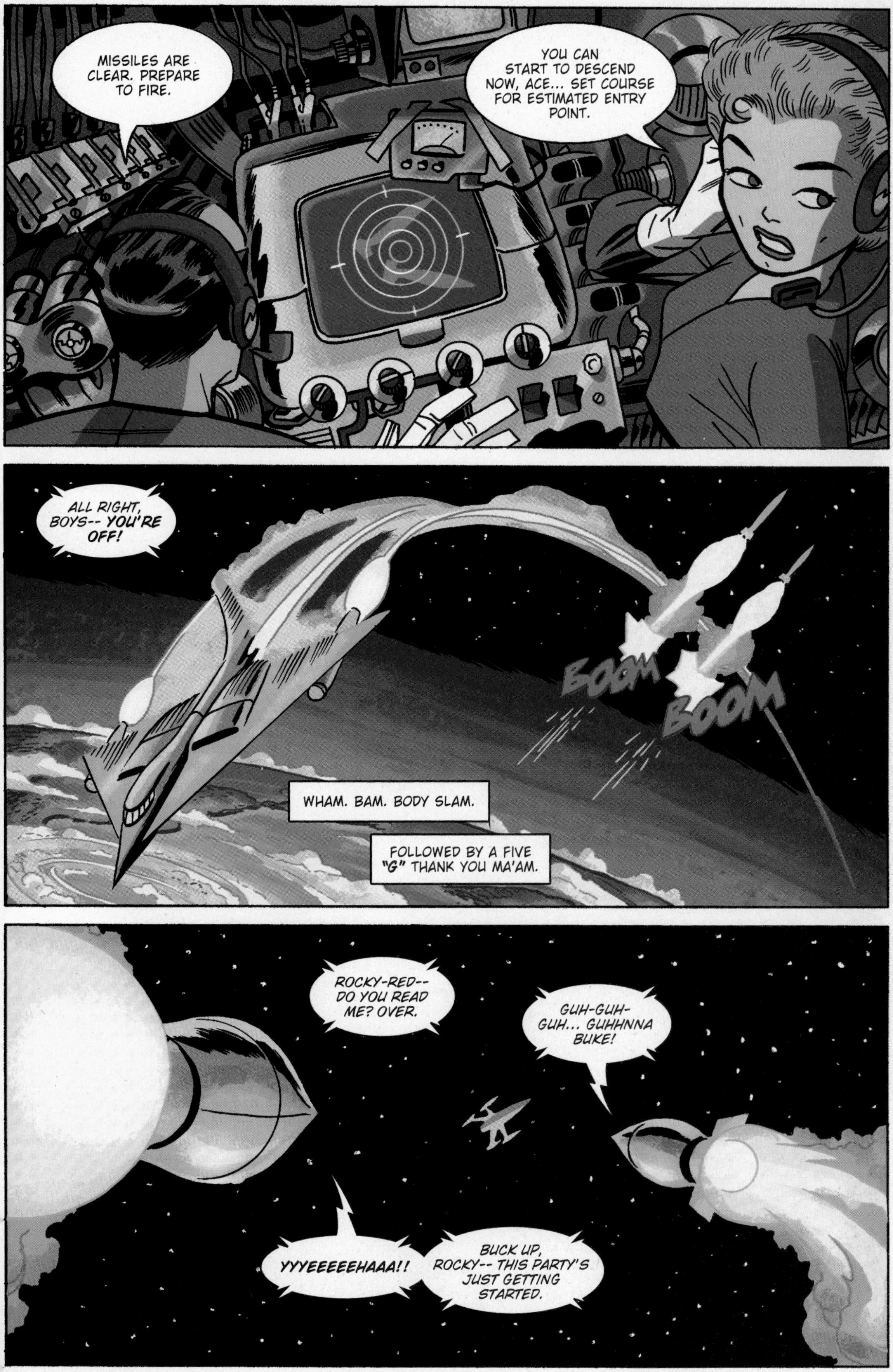

MISSILES ARE CLEAR. PREPARE TO FIRE.
YOU CAN START TO DESCEND NOW, ACE... SET COURSE FOR ESTIMATED ENTRY POINT.
ALL RIGHT, BOYS-- YOU'RE OFF!
BOOM
BOOM
WHAM. BAM. BODY SLAM.
FOLLOWED BY A FIVE "G" THANK YOU MA'AM.
ROCKY-RED-- DO YOU READ ME? OVER.
GUH-GUH-GUH... GUHHNNA BUKE!
YYYEEEEEHAAA!!
BUCK UP, ROCKY-- THIS PARTY'S JUST GETTING STARTED.

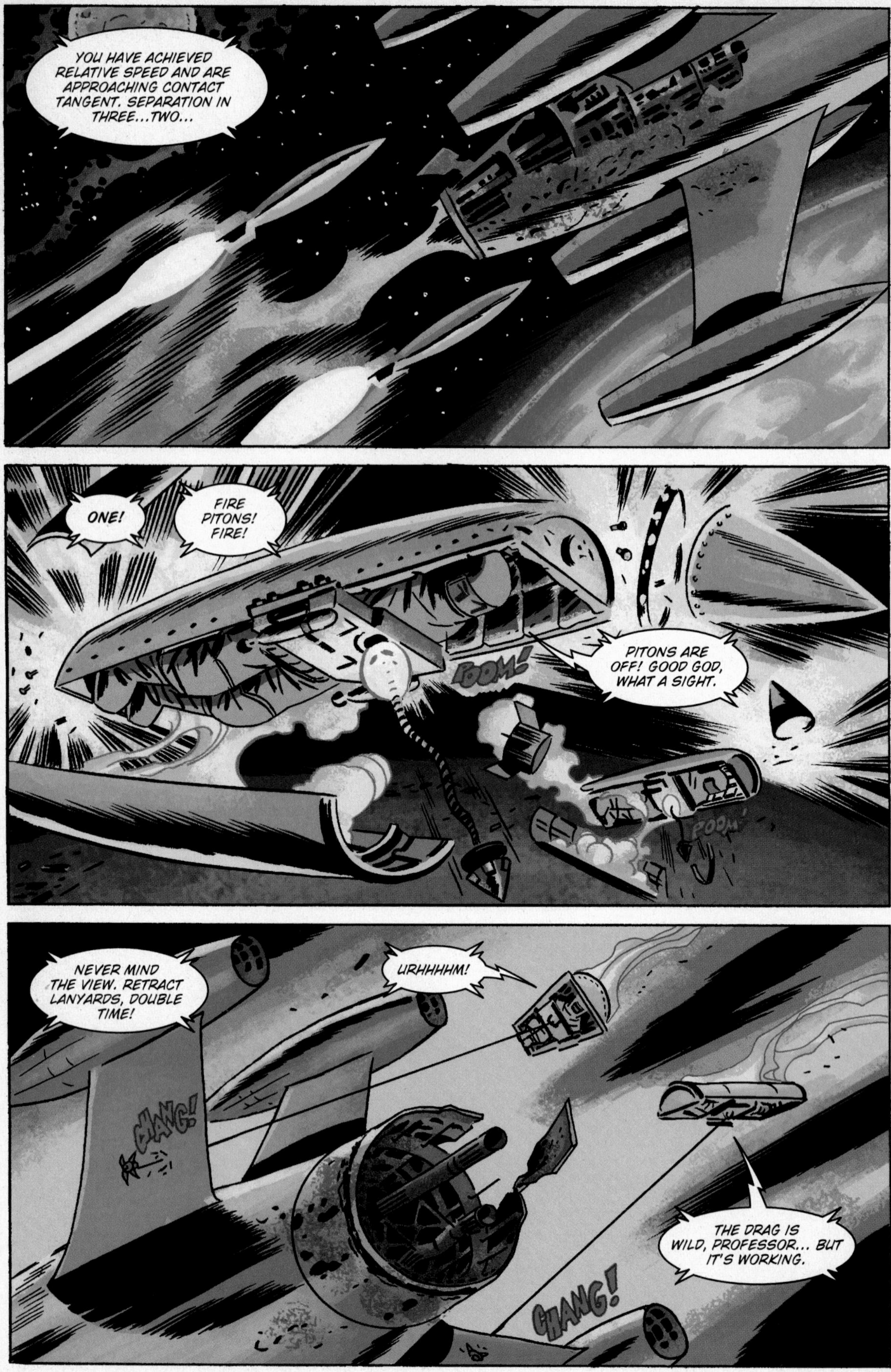
YOU HAVE ACHIEVED RELATIVE SPEED AND ARE APPROACHING CONTACT TANGENT. SEPARATION IN THREE...TWO...
ONE!
FIRE PITONS! FIRE!
POOM!
PITONS ARE OFF! GOOD GOD, WHAT A SIGHT.
POOM!
NEVER MIND THE VIEW. RETRACT LANYARDS, DOUBLE TIME!
URHHHHM!
CHANG!
THE DRAG IS WILD, PROFESSOR... BUT IT'S WORKING.
CHANG!

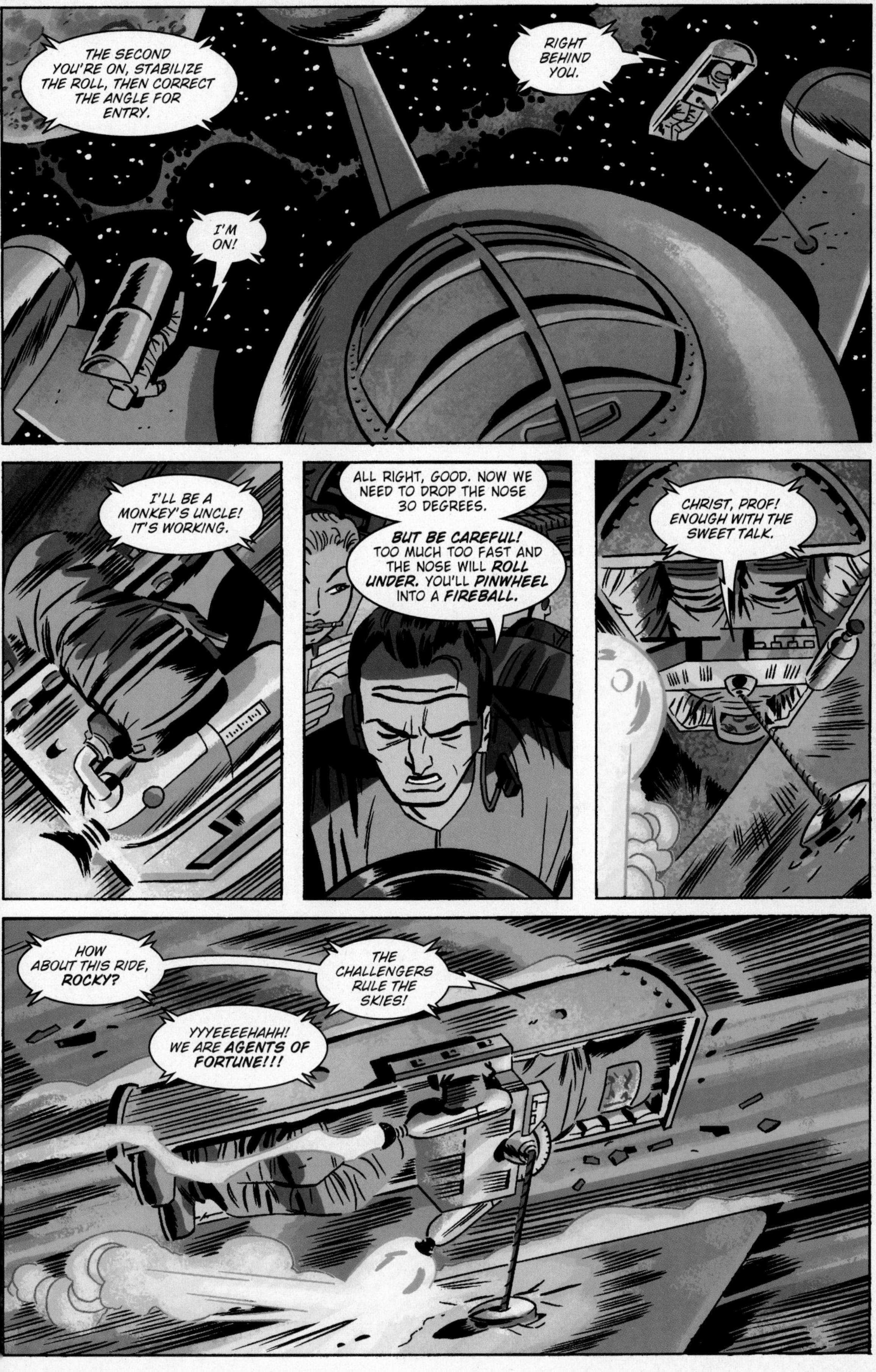
THE SECOND YOU'RE ON, STABILIZE THE ROLL, THEN CORRECT THE ANGLE FOR ENTRY.
RIGHT BEHIND YOU.
I'M ON!
I'LL BE A MONKEY'S UNCLE! IT'S WORKING.
ALL RIGHT, GOOD. NOW WE NEED TO DROP THE NOSE 30 DEGREES.
BUT BE CAREFUL! TOO MUCH TOO FAST AND THE NOSE WILL ROLL UNDER. YOU'LL PINWHEEL INTO A FIREBALL.
CHRIST, PROF! ENOUGH WITH THE SWEET TALK.
HOW ABOUT THIS RIDE, ROCKY?
THE CHALLENGERS RULE THE SKIES!
YYYEEEEHAHH! WE ARE AGENTS OF FORTUNE!!!

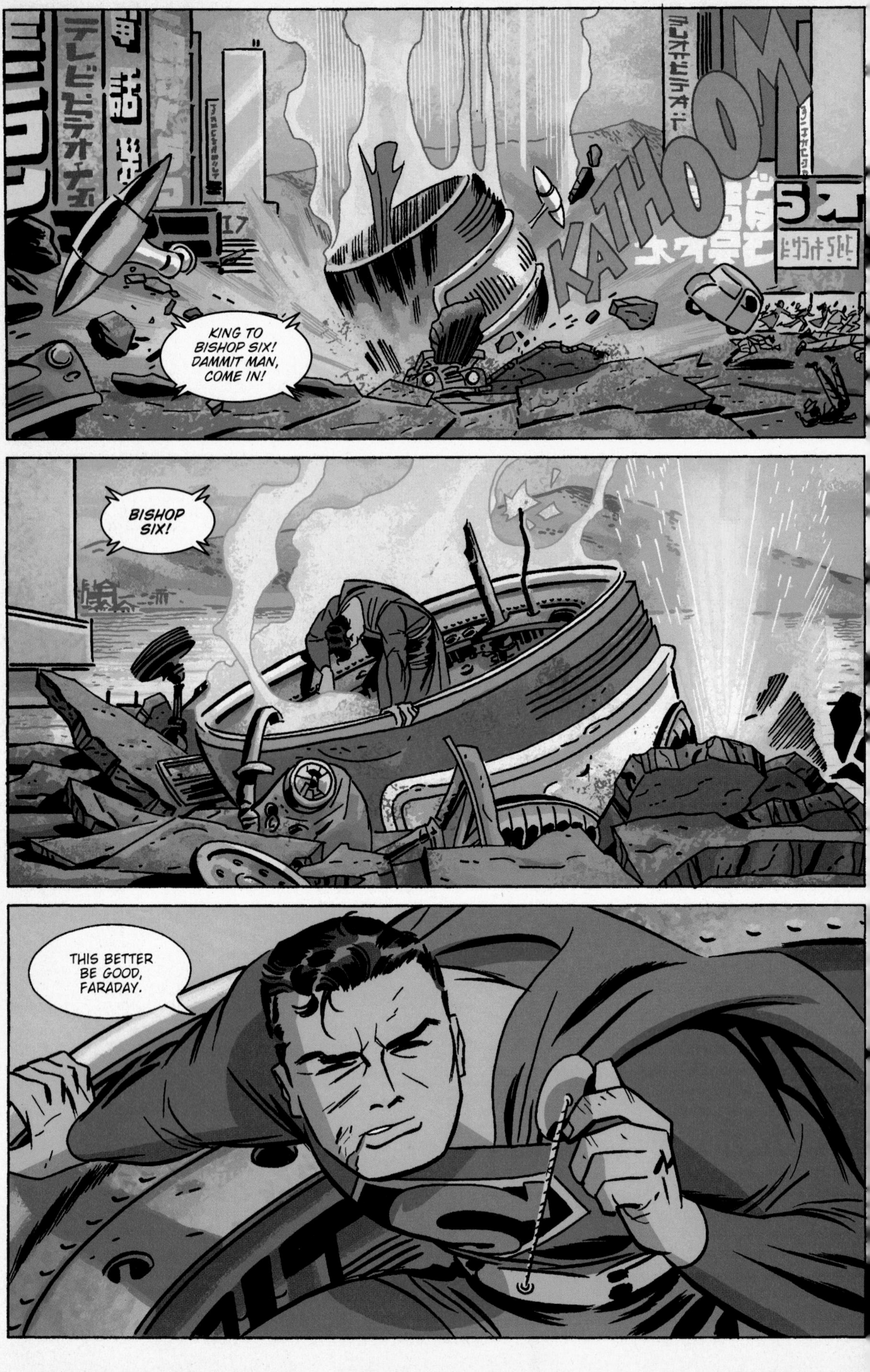
KATHOOM
KING TO BISHOP SIX! DAMMIT MAN, COME IN!
BISHOP SIX!
THIS BETTER BE GOOD, FARADAY.

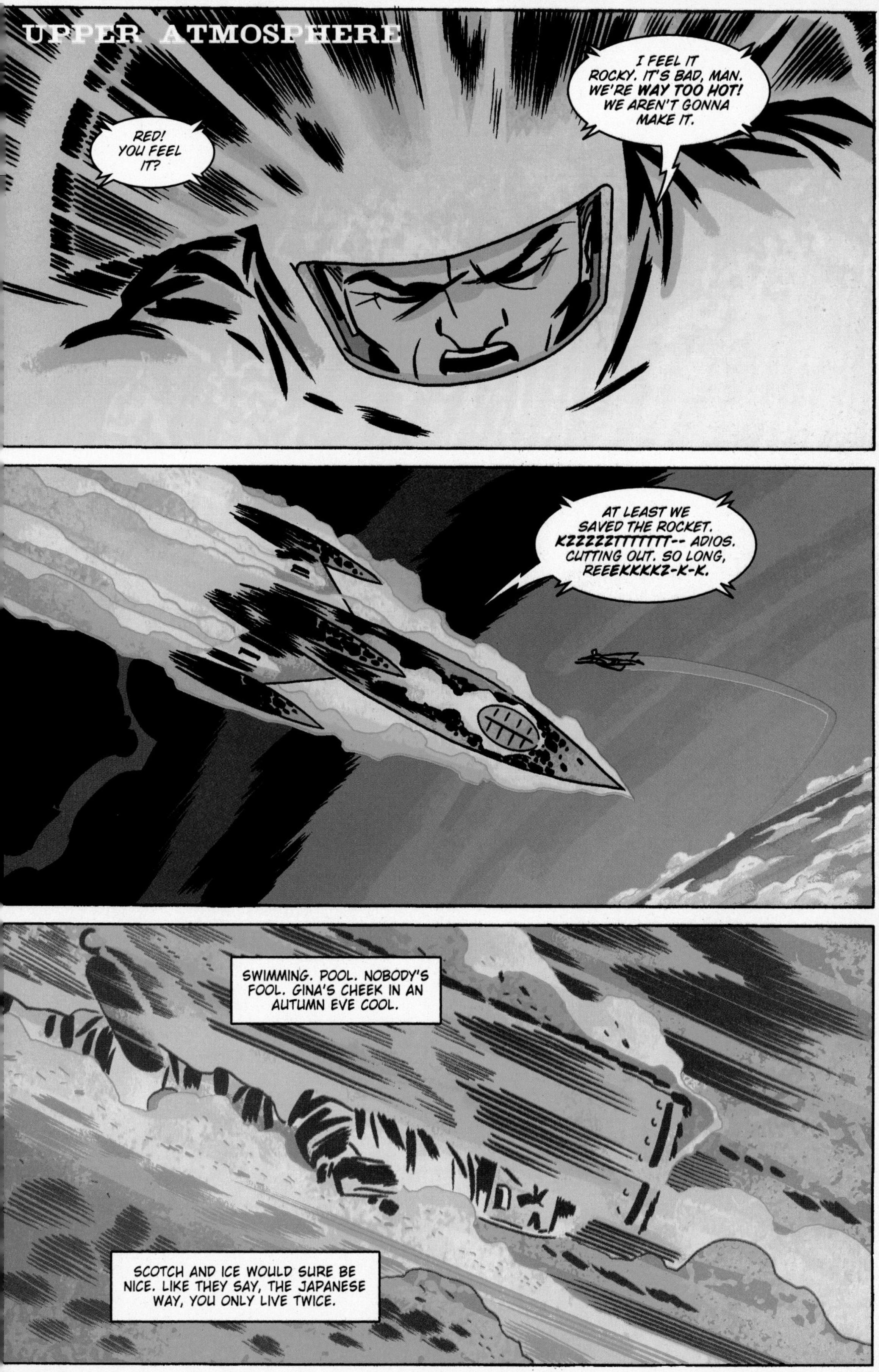
UPPER ATMOSPHERE
RED! YOU FEEL IT?
I FEEL IT ROCKY. IT'S BAD, MAN. WE'RE WAY TOO HOT! WE AREN'T GONNA MAKE IT.
AT LEAST WE SAVED THE ROCKET. KZZZZZTTTTTTT-- ADIOS. CUTTING OUT. SO LONG, REEEKKKKZ-K-K.
SWIMMING. POOL. NOBODY'S FOOL. GINA'S CHEEK IN AN AUTUMN EVE COOL.
SCOTCH AND ICE WOULD SURE BE NICE. LIKE THEY SAY, THE JAPANESE WAY, YOU ONLY LIVE TWICE.

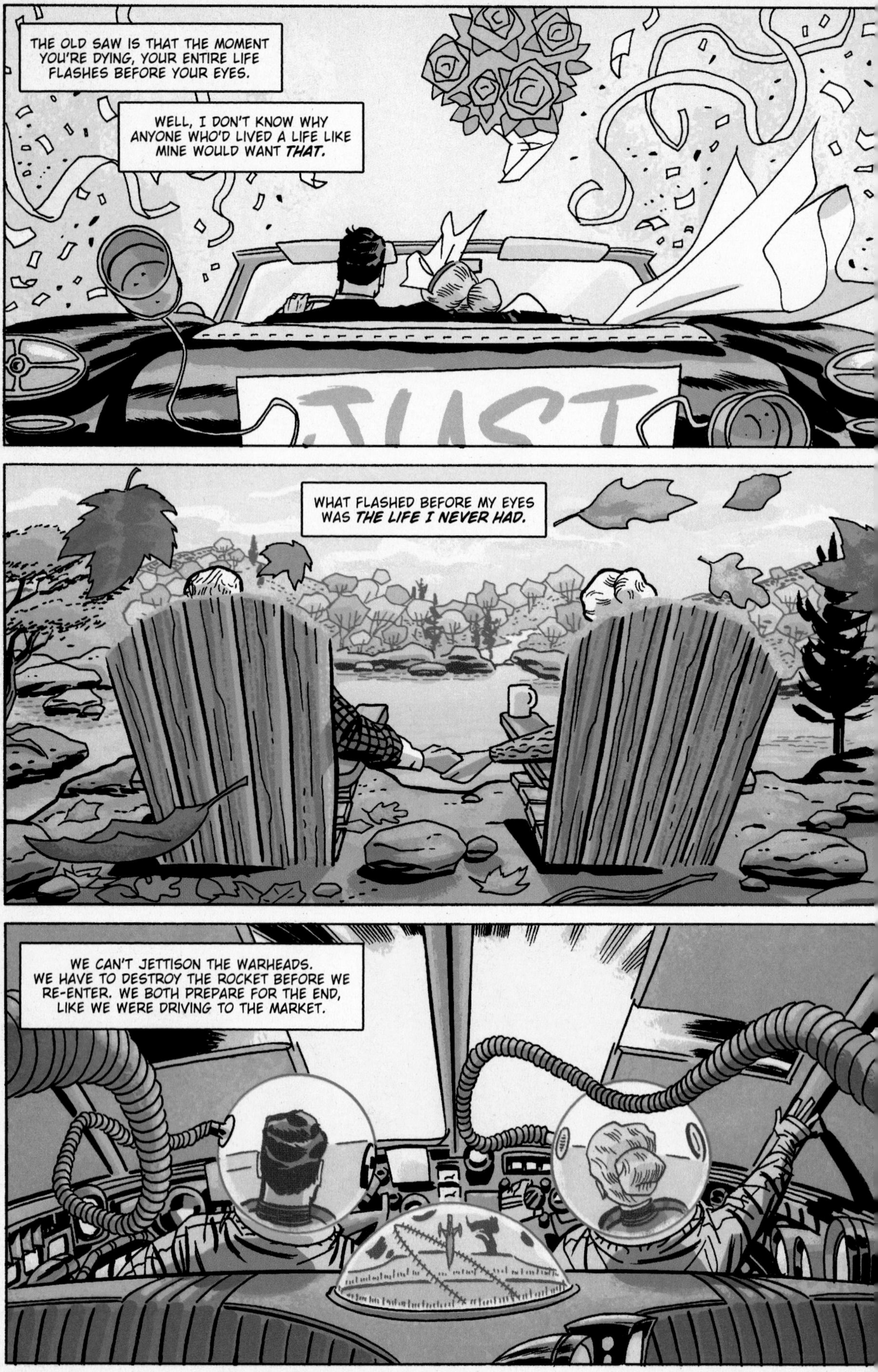
THE OLD SAW IS THAT THE MOMENT YOU'RE DYING, YOUR ENTIRE LIFE FLASHES BEFORE YOUR EYES.
WELL, I DON'T KNOW WHY ANYONE WHO'D LIVED A LIFE LIKE MINE WOULD WANT *THAT.*
JUST
WHAT FLASHED BEFORE MY EYES WAS *THE LIFE I NEVER HAD.*
WE CAN'T JETTISON THE WARHEADS. WE HAVE TO DESTROY THE ROCKET BEFORE WE RE-ENTER. WE BOTH PREPARE FOR THE END, LIKE WE WERE DRIVING TO THE MARKET.

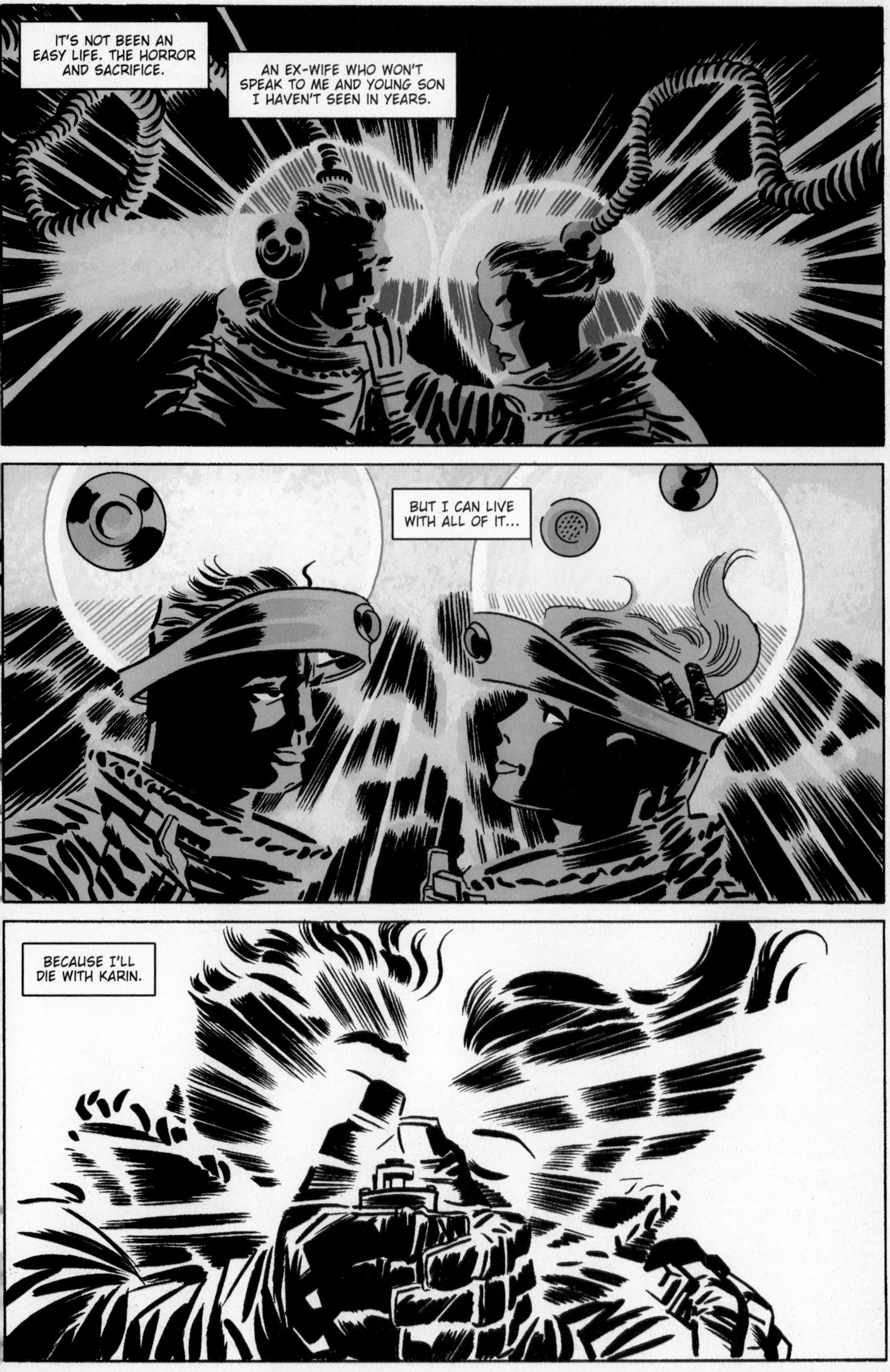
IT'S NOT BEEN AN EASY LIFE. THE HORROR AND SACRIFICE.
AN EX-WIFE WHO WON'T SPEAK TO ME AND YOUNG SON I HAVEN'T SEEN IN YEARS.
BUT I CAN LIVE WITH ALL OF IT...
BECAUSE I'LL DIE WITH KARIN.

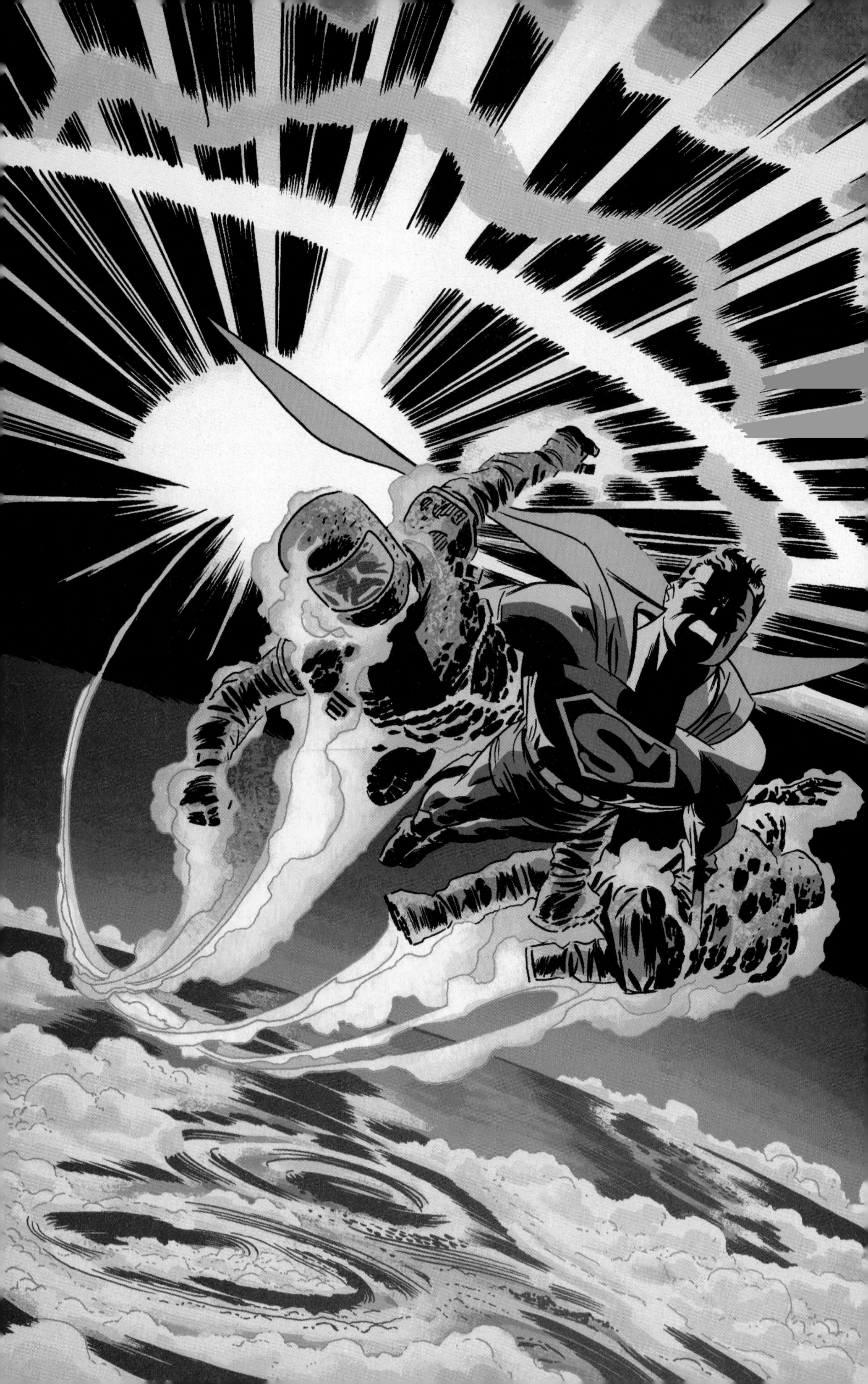

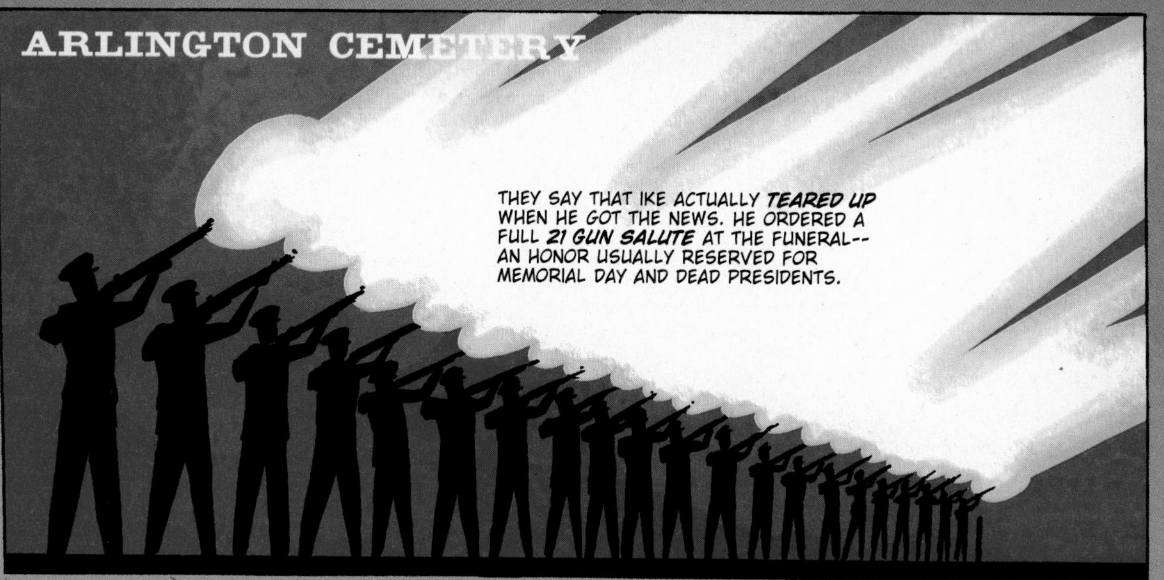
ARLINGTON CEMETERY
THEY SAY THAT IKE ACTUALLY TEARED UP WHEN HE GOT THE NEWS. HE ORDERED A FULL 21 GUN SALUTE AT THE FUNERAL-- AN HONOR USUALLY RESERVED FOR MEMORIAL DAY AND DEAD PRESIDENTS.

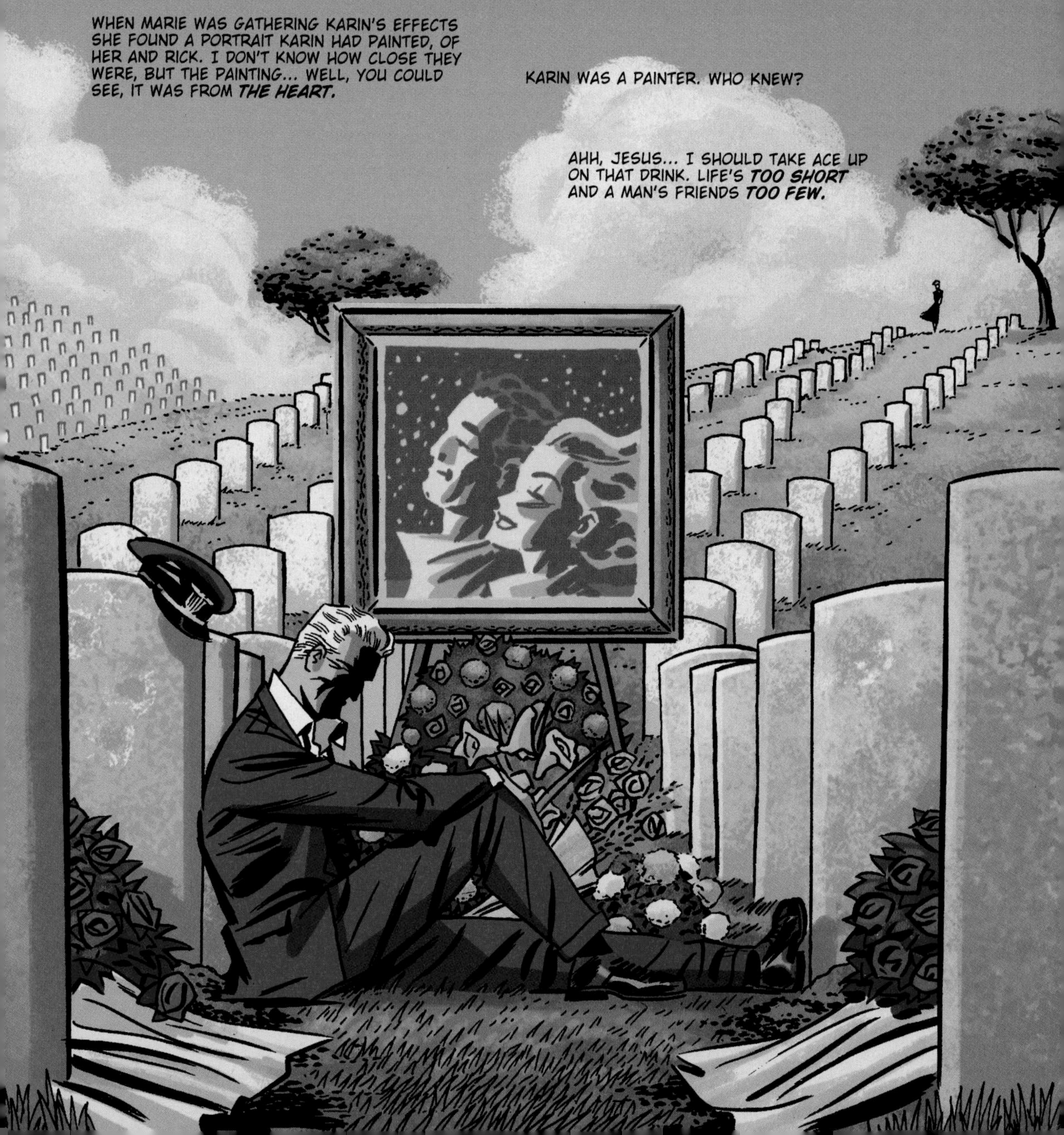
WHEN MARIE WAS GATHERING KARIN'S EFFECTS SHE FOUND A PORTRAIT KARIN HAD PAINTED, OF HER AND RICK. I DON'T KNOW HOW CLOSE THEY WERE, BUT THE PAINTING... WELL, YOU COULD SEE, IT WAS FROM THE HEART.
KARIN WAS A PAINTER. WHO KNEW?
AHH, JESUS... I SHOULD TAKE ACE UP ON THAT DRINK. LIFE'S TOO SHORT AND A MAN'S FRIENDS TOO FEW.

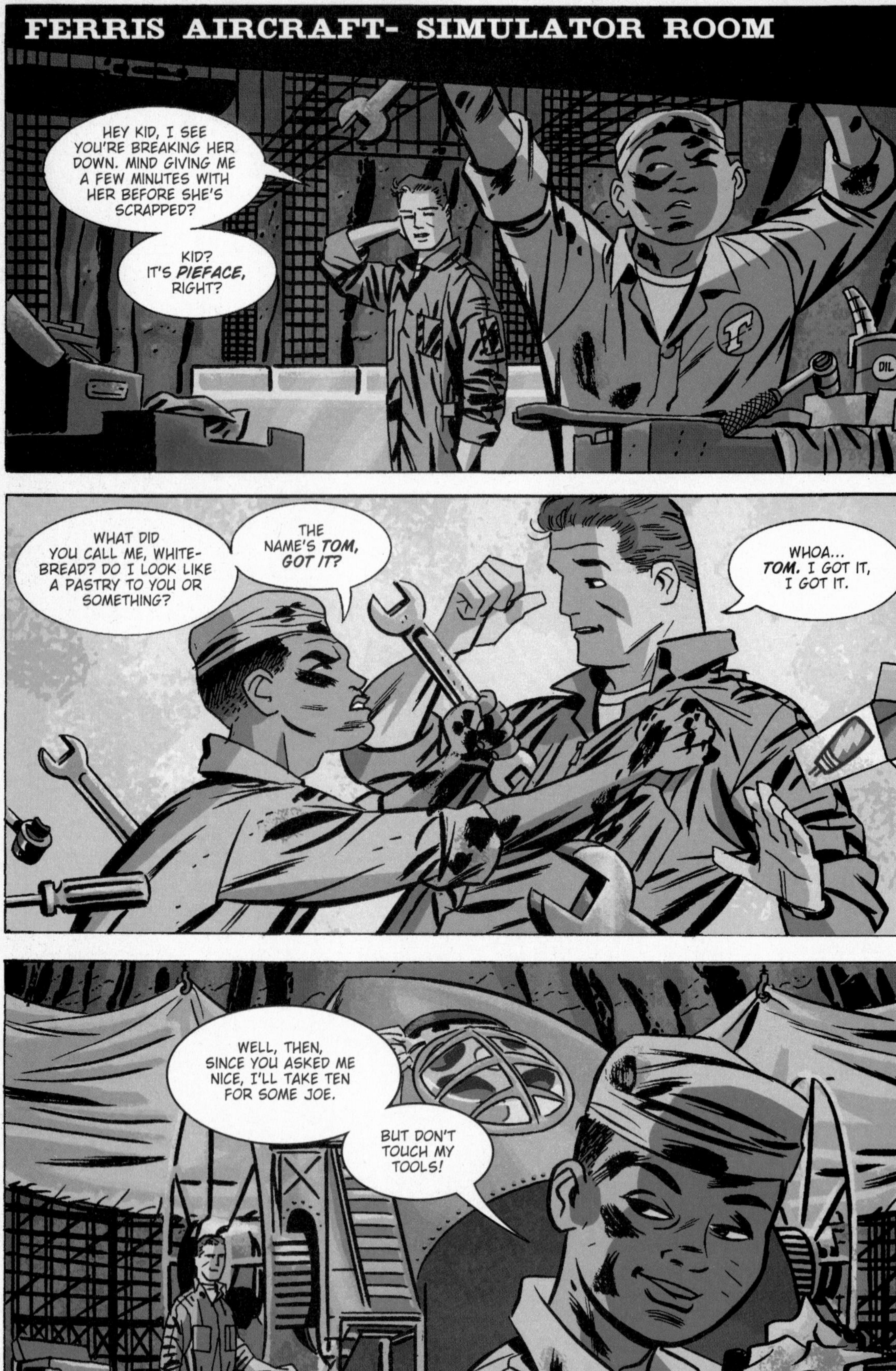
FERRIS AIRCRAFT- SIMULATOR ROOM
HEY KID, I SEE YOU'RE BREAKING HER DOWN. MIND GIVING ME A FEW MINUTES WITH HER BEFORE SHE'S SCRAPPED?
KID? IT'S PIEFACE, RIGHT?
WHAT DID YOU CALL ME, WHITE-BREAD? DO I LOOK LIKE A PASTRY TO YOU OR SOMETHING?
THE NAME'S TOM, GOT IT?
WHOA... TOM. I GOT IT, I GOT IT.
OIL
WELL, THEN, SINCE YOU ASKED ME NICE, I'LL TAKE TEN FOR SOME JOE.
BUT DON'T TOUCH MY TOOLS!

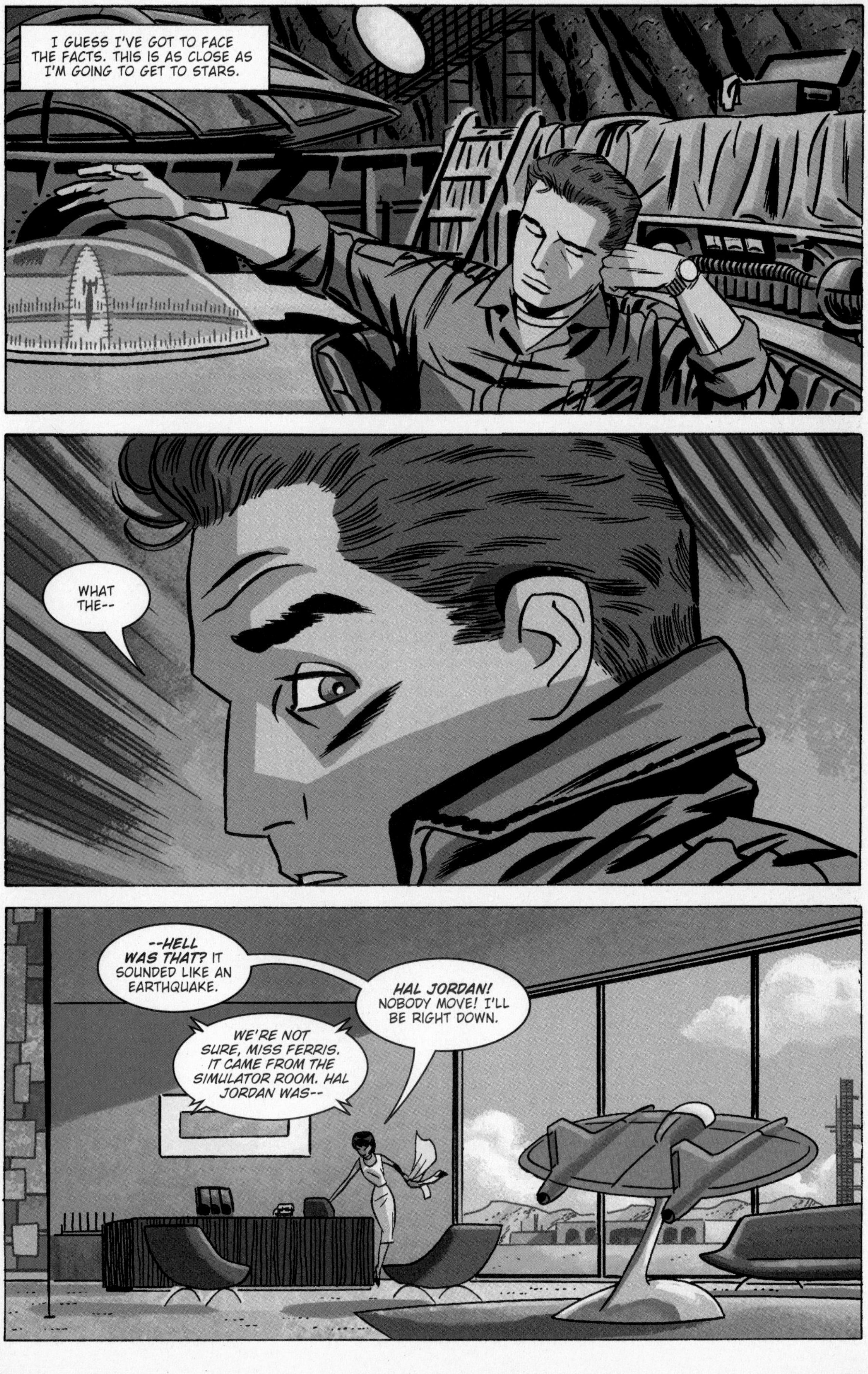
I GUESS I'VE GOT TO FACE THE FACTS. THIS IS AS CLOSE AS I'M GOING TO GET TO STARS.
WHAT THE--
--HELL WAS THAT? IT SOUNDED LIKE AN EARTHQUAKE.
WE'RE NOT SURE, MISS FERRIS. IT CAME FROM THE SIMULATOR ROOM. HAL JORDAN WAS--
HAL JORDAN! NOBODY MOVE! I'LL BE RIGHT DOWN.

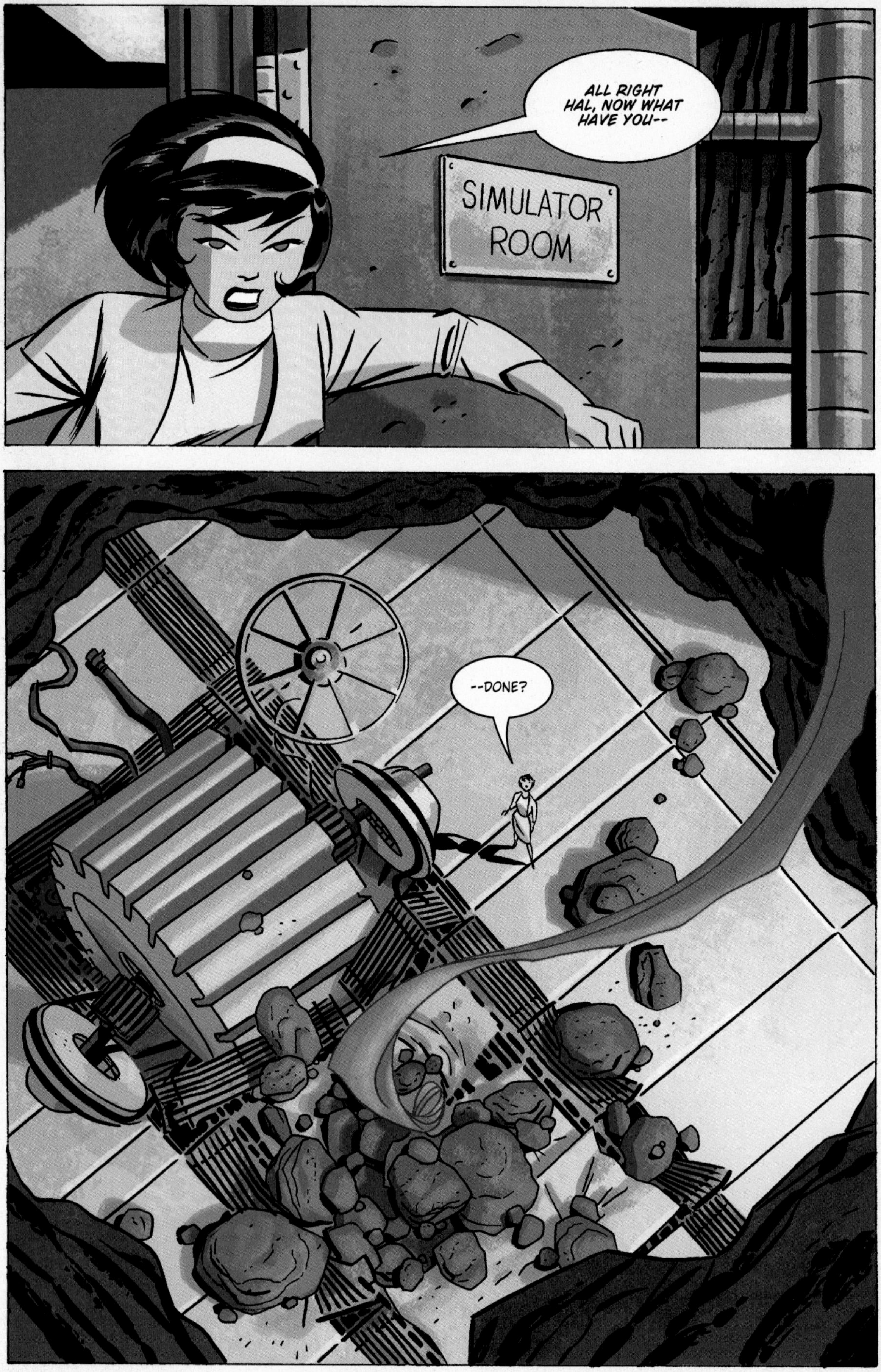
ALL RIGHT HAL, NOW WHAT HAVE YOU--
SIMULATOR ROOM
--DONE?

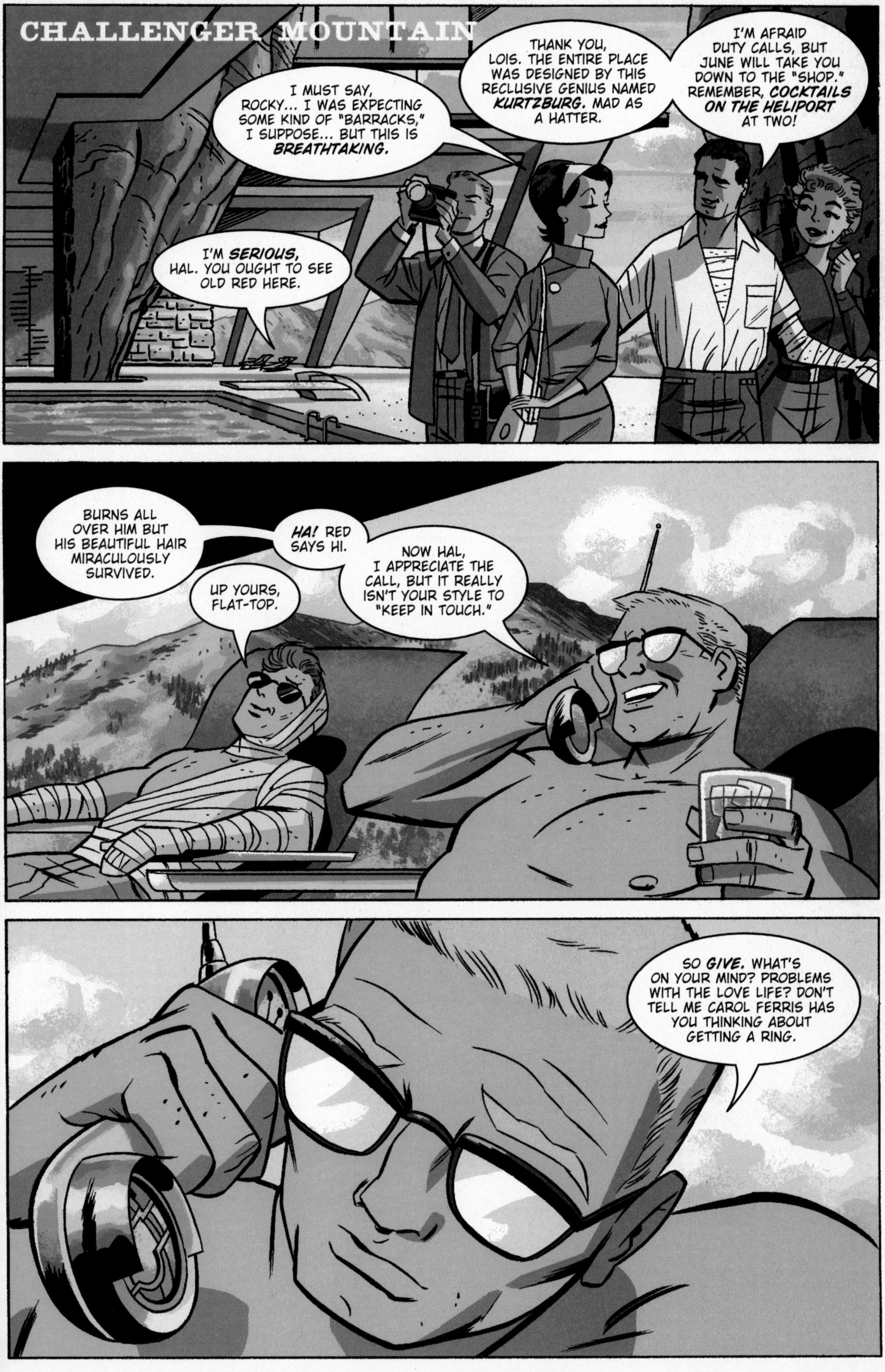
CHALLENGER MOUNTAIN
I MUST SAY, ROCKY... I WAS EXPECTING SOME KIND OF "BARRACKS," I SUPPOSE... BUT THIS IS BREATHTAKING.
THANK YOU, LOIS. THE ENTIRE PLACE WAS DESIGNED BY THIS RECLUSIVE GENIUS NAMED KURTZBURG. MAD AS A HATTER.
I'M AFRAID DUTY CALLS, BUT JUNE WILL TAKE YOU DOWN TO THE "SHOP." REMEMBER, COCKTAILS ON THE HELIPORT AT TWO!
I'M SERIOUS, HAL. YOU OUGHT TO SEE OLD RED HERE.
BURNS ALL OVER HIM BUT HIS BEAUTIFUL HAIR MIRACULOUSLY SURVIVED.
UP YOURS, FLAT-TOP.
HA! RED SAYS HI.
NOW HAL, I APPRECIATE THE CALL, BUT IT REALLY ISN'T YOUR STYLE TO "KEEP IN TOUCH."
SO GIVE. WHAT'S ON YOUR MIND? PROBLEMS WITH THE LOVE LIFE? DON'T TELL ME CAROL FERRIS HAS YOU THINKING ABOUT GETTING A RING.

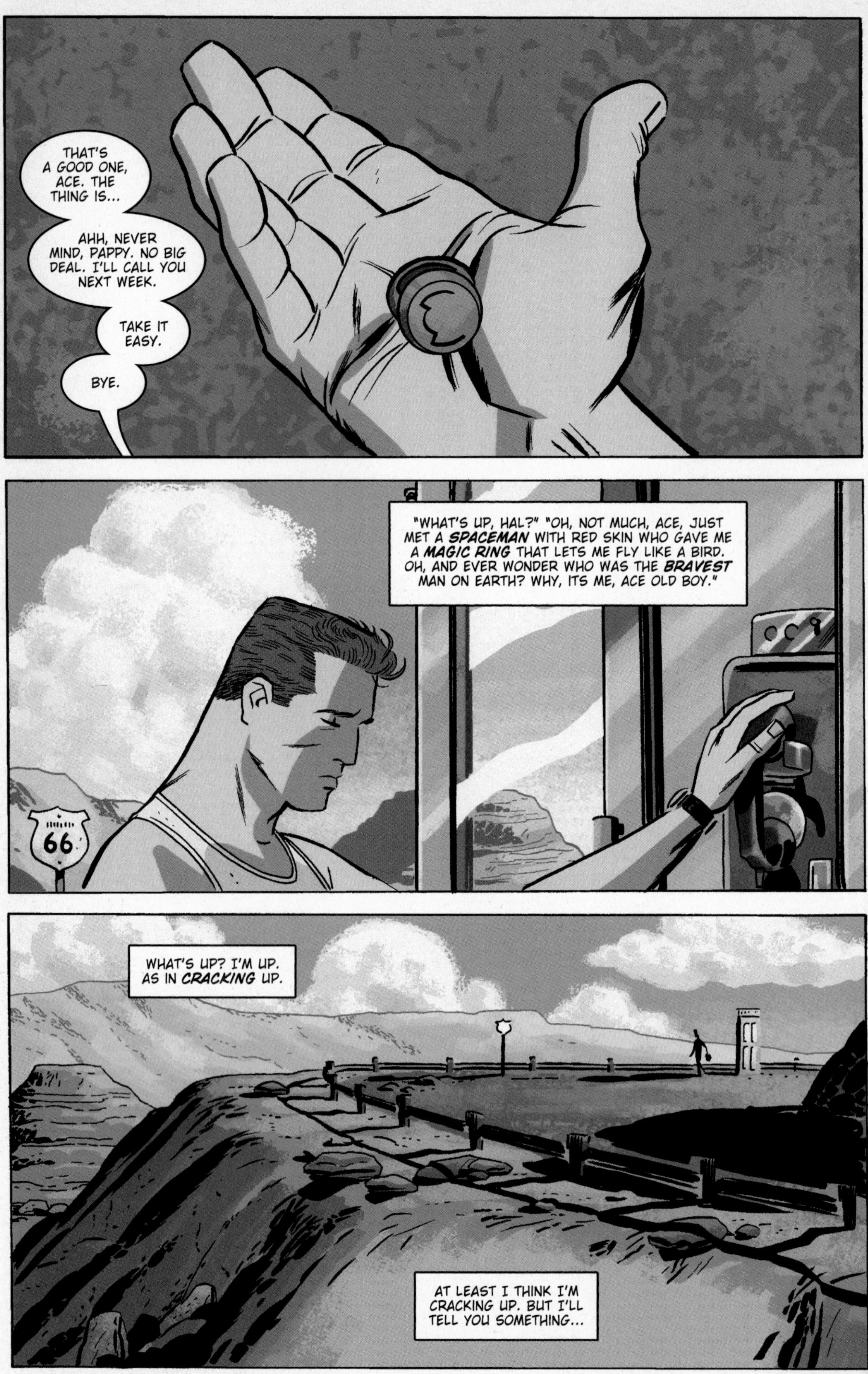
THAT'S A GOOD ONE, ACE. THE THING IS...
AHH, NEVER MIND, PAPPY. NO BIG DEAL. I'LL CALL YOU NEXT WEEK.
TAKE IT EASY.
BYE.
"WHAT'S UP, HAL?" "OH, NOT MUCH, ACE, JUST MET A SPACEMAN WITH RED SKIN WHO GAVE ME A MAGIC RING THAT LETS ME FLY LIKE A BIRD. OH, AND EVER WONDER WHO WAS THE BRAVEST MAN ON EARTH? WHY, ITS ME, ACE OLD BOY."
66
WHAT'S UP? I'M UP. AS IN CRACKING UP.
AT LEAST I THINK I'M CRACKING UP. BUT I'LL TELL YOU SOMETHING...

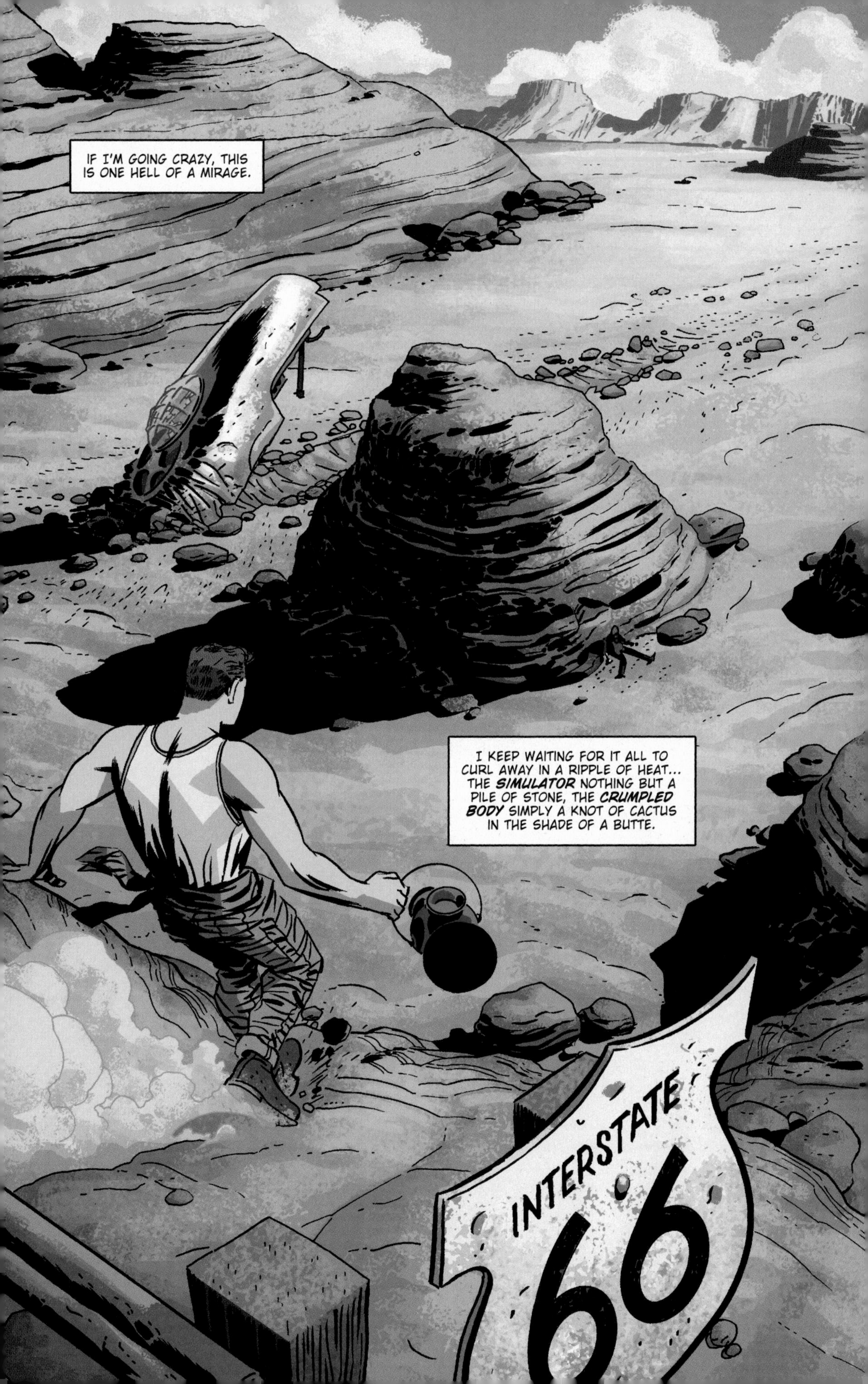
IF I'M GOING CRAZY, THIS IS ONE HELL OF A MIRAGE.
I KEEP WAITING FOR IT ALL TO CURL AWAY IN A RIPPLE OF HEAT... THE **SIMULATOR** NOTHING BUT A PILE OF STONE, THE **CRUMPLED BODY** SIMPLY A KNOT OF CACTUS IN THE SHADE OF A BUTTE.
INTERSTATE 66

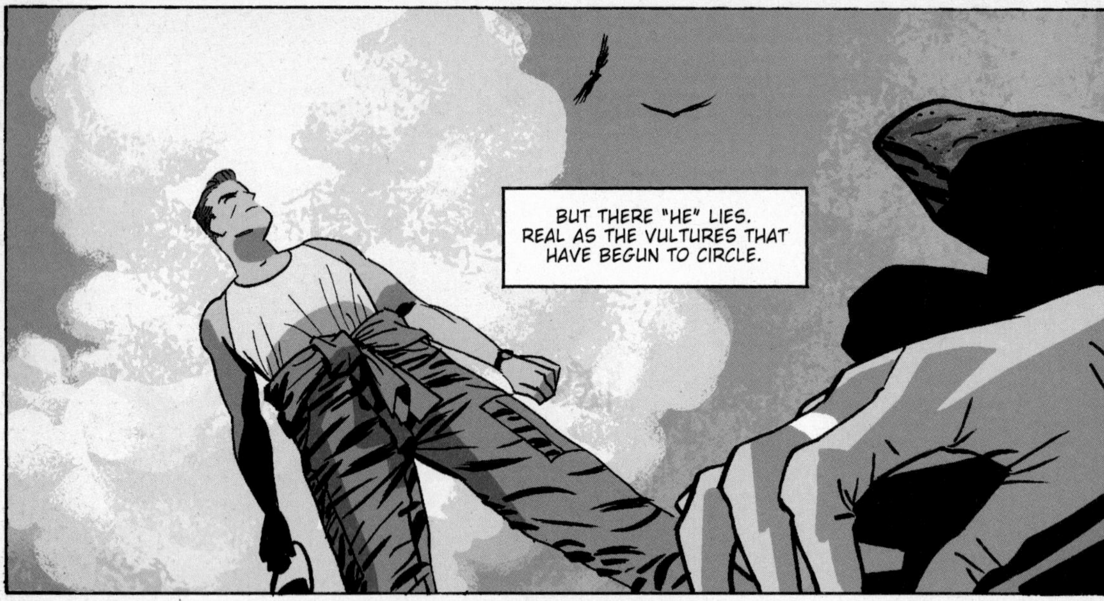
BUT THERE "HE" LIES. REAL AS THE VULTURES THAT HAVE BEGUN TO CIRCLE.

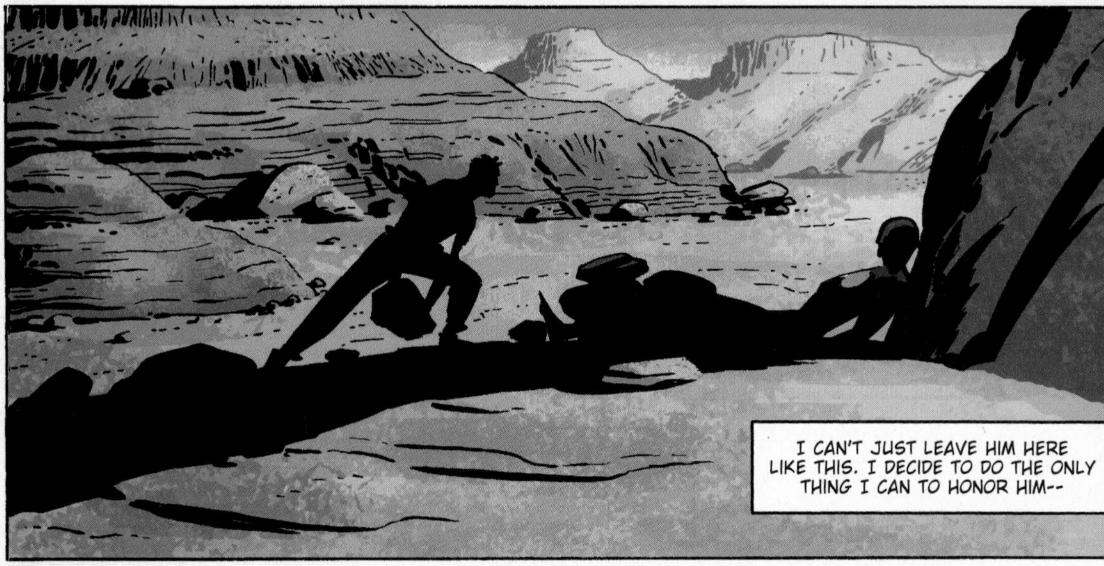
I CAN'T JUST LEAVE HIM HERE LIKE THIS. I DECIDE TO DO THE ONLY THING I CAN TO HONOR HIM--

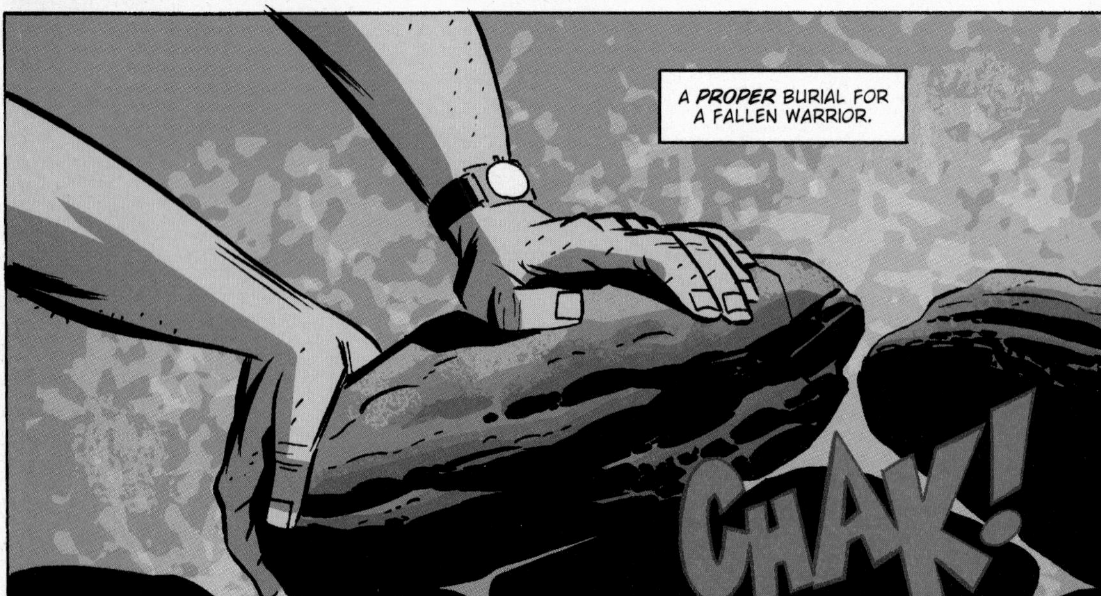
A ***PROPER*** BURIAL FOR A FALLEN WARRIOR.
CHAK!

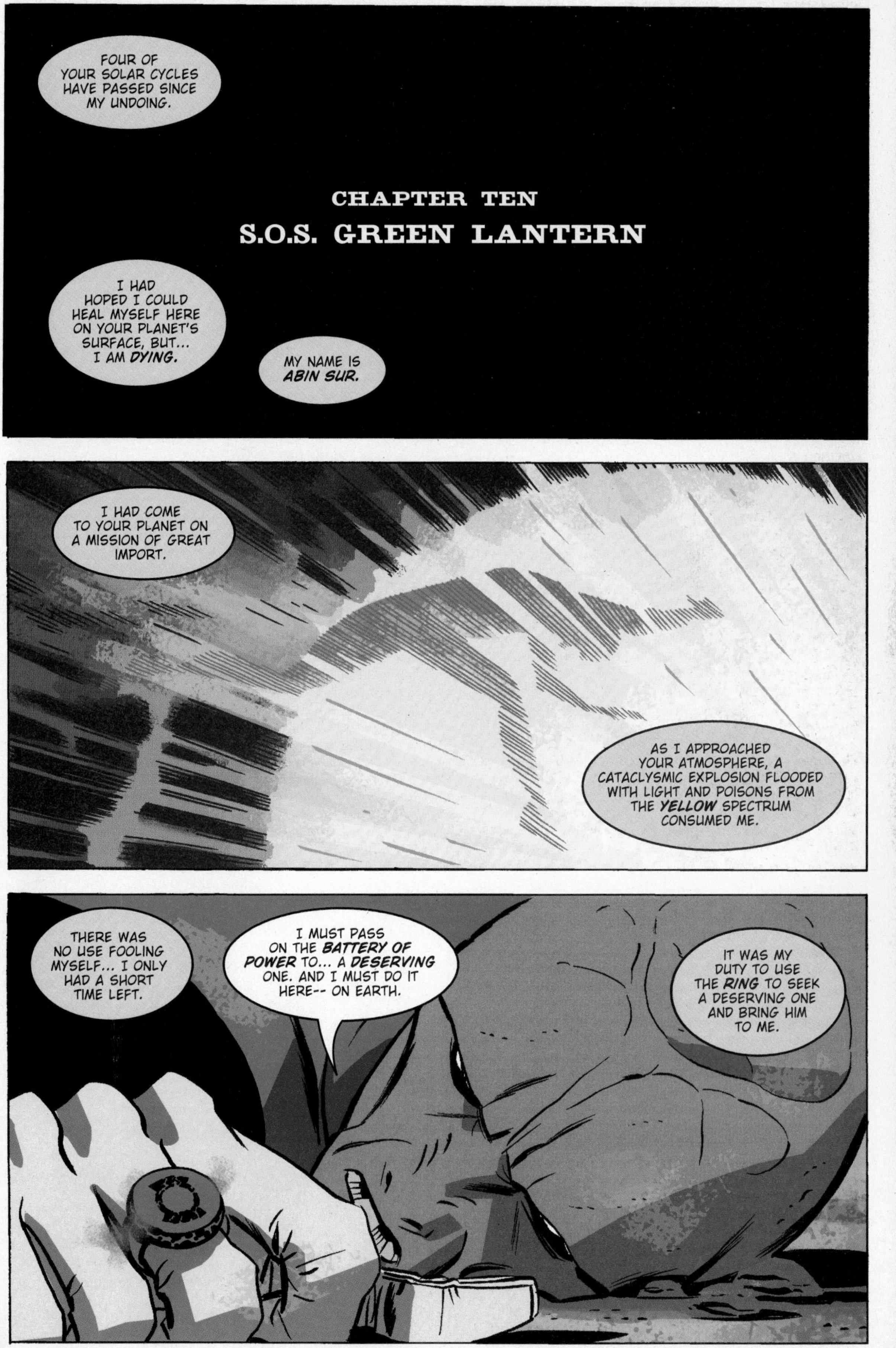
FOUR OF YOUR SOLAR CYCLES HAVE PASSED SINCE MY UNDOING.
CHAPTER TEN
S.O.S. GREEN LANTERN
I HAD HOPED I COULD HEAL MYSELF HERE ON YOUR PLANET'S SURFACE, BUT... I AM *DYING.*
MY NAME IS *ABIN SUR.*
I HAD COME TO YOUR PLANET ON A MISSION OF GREAT IMPORT.
AS I APPROACHED YOUR ATMOSPHERE, A CATACLYSMIC EXPLOSION FLOODED WITH LIGHT AND POISONS FROM THE *YELLOW* SPECTRUM CONSUMED ME.
THERE WAS NO USE FOOLING MYSELF... I ONLY HAD A SHORT TIME LEFT.
I MUST PASS ON THE *BATTERY OF POWER* TO... A *DESERVING* ONE. AND I MUST DO IT HERE-- ON EARTH.
IT WAS MY DUTY TO USE THE *RING* TO SEEK A DESERVING ONE AND BRING HIM TO ME.

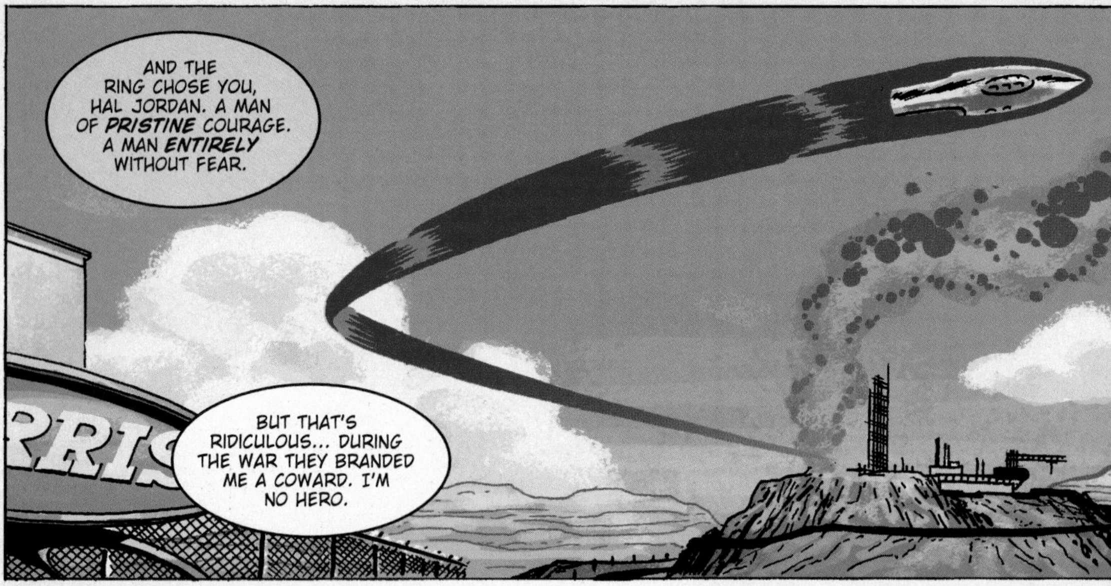
AND THE RING CHOSE YOU, HAL JORDAN. A MAN OF **PRISTINE** COURAGE. A MAN **ENTIRELY** WITHOUT FEAR.
BUT THAT'S RIDICULOUS... DURING THE WAR THEY BRANDED ME A COWARD. I'M NO HERO.

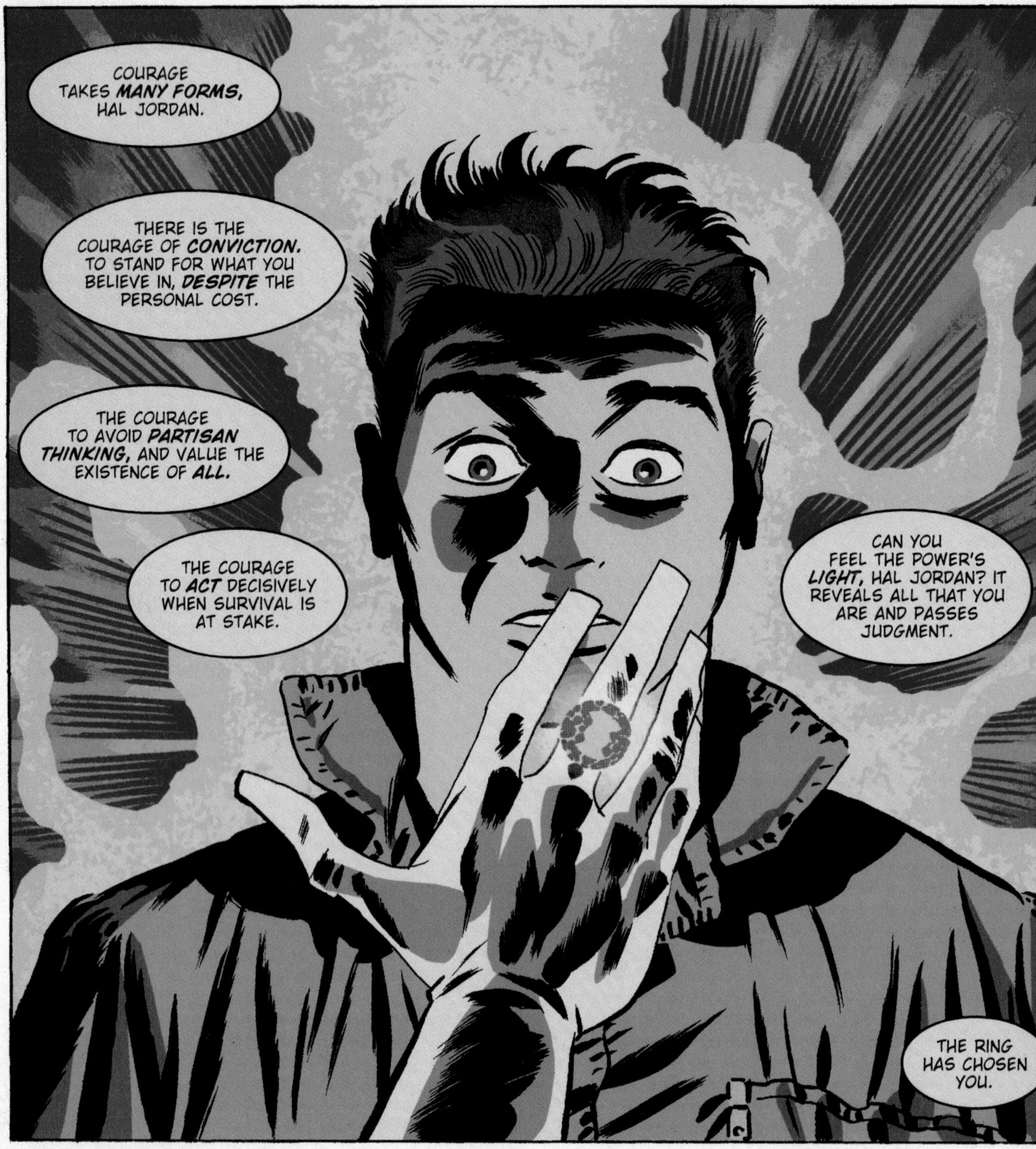
COURAGE TAKES **MANY FORMS,** HAL JORDAN.
THERE IS THE COURAGE OF **CONVICTION.** TO STAND FOR WHAT YOU BELIEVE IN, **DESPITE** THE PERSONAL COST.
THE COURAGE TO AVOID **PARTISAN THINKING,** AND VALUE THE EXISTENCE OF **ALL.**
THE COURAGE TO **ACT** DECISIVELY WHEN SURVIVAL IS AT STAKE.
CAN YOU FEEL THE POWER'S **LIGHT,** HAL JORDAN? IT REVEALS ALL THAT YOU ARE AND PASSES JUDGMENT.
THE RING HAS CHOSEN YOU.

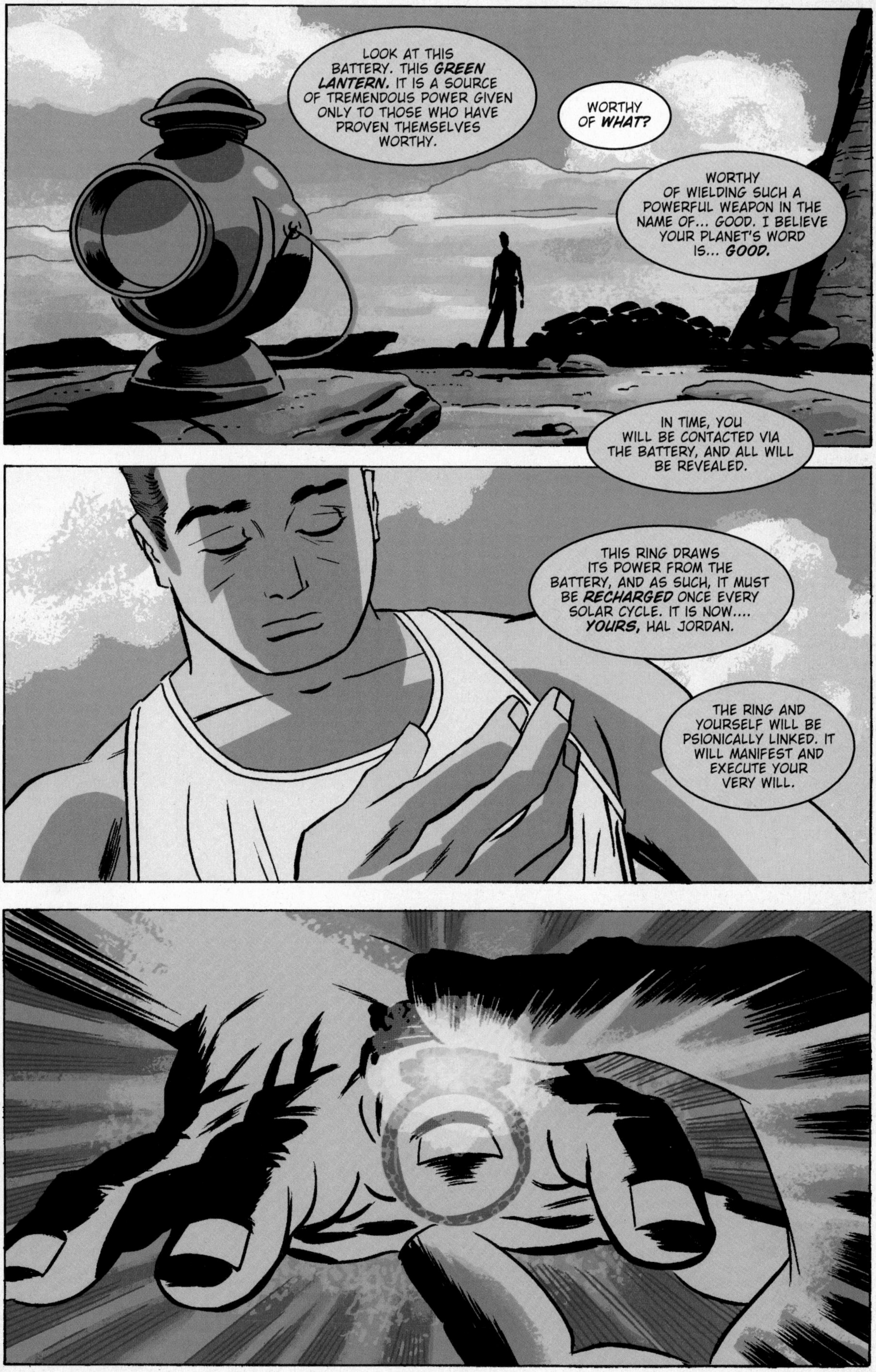
LOOK AT THIS BATTERY. THIS GREEN LANTERN. IT IS A SOURCE OF TREMENDOUS POWER GIVEN ONLY TO THOSE WHO HAVE PROVEN THEMSELVES WORTHY.
WORTHY OF WHAT?
WORTHY OF WIELDING SUCH A POWERFUL WEAPON IN THE NAME OF... GOOD. I BELIEVE YOUR PLANET'S WORD IS... GOOD.
IN TIME, YOU WILL BE CONTACTED VIA THE BATTERY, AND ALL WILL BE REVEALED.
THIS RING DRAWS ITS POWER FROM THE BATTERY, AND AS SUCH, IT MUST BE RECHARGED ONCE EVERY SOLAR CYCLE. IT IS NOW.... YOURS, HAL JORDAN.
THE RING AND YOURSELF WILL BE PSIONICALLY LINKED. IT WILL MANIFEST AND EXECUTE YOUR VERY WILL.

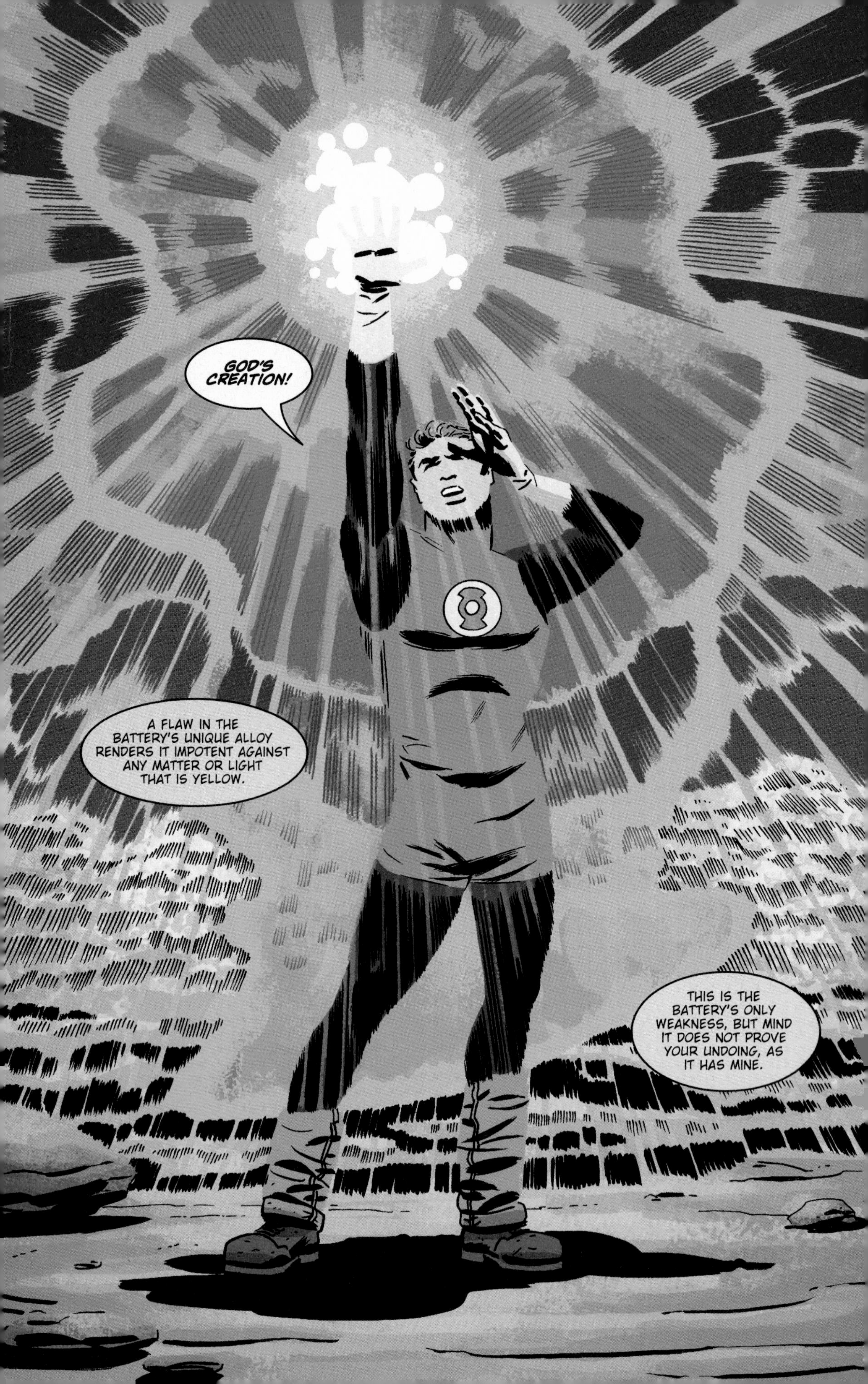
GOD'S CREATION!
A FLAW IN THE BATTERY'S UNIQUE ALLOY RENDERS IT IMPOTENT AGAINST ANY MATTER OR LIGHT THAT IS YELLOW.
THIS IS THE BATTERY'S ONLY WEAKNESS, BUT MIND IT DOES NOT PROVE YOUR UNDOING, AS IT HAS MINE.

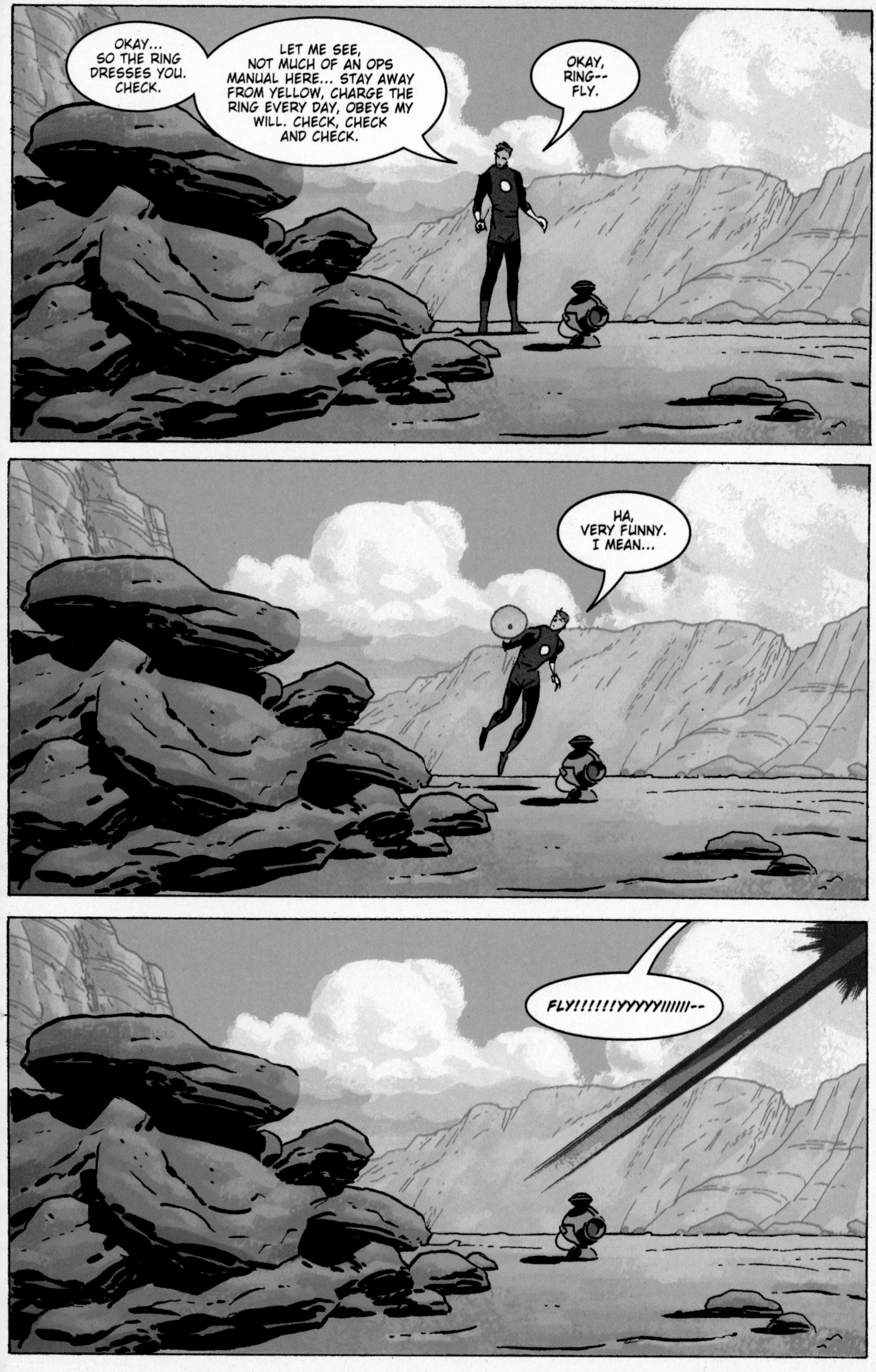
OKAY... SO THE RING DRESSES YOU. CHECK.
LET ME SEE, NOT MUCH OF AN OPS MANUAL HERE... STAY AWAY FROM YELLOW, CHARGE THE RING EVERY DAY, OBEYS MY WILL. CHECK, CHECK AND CHECK.
OKAY, RING-- FLY.
HA, VERY FUNNY. I MEAN...
FLY!!!!!!YYYYYIIIIII--

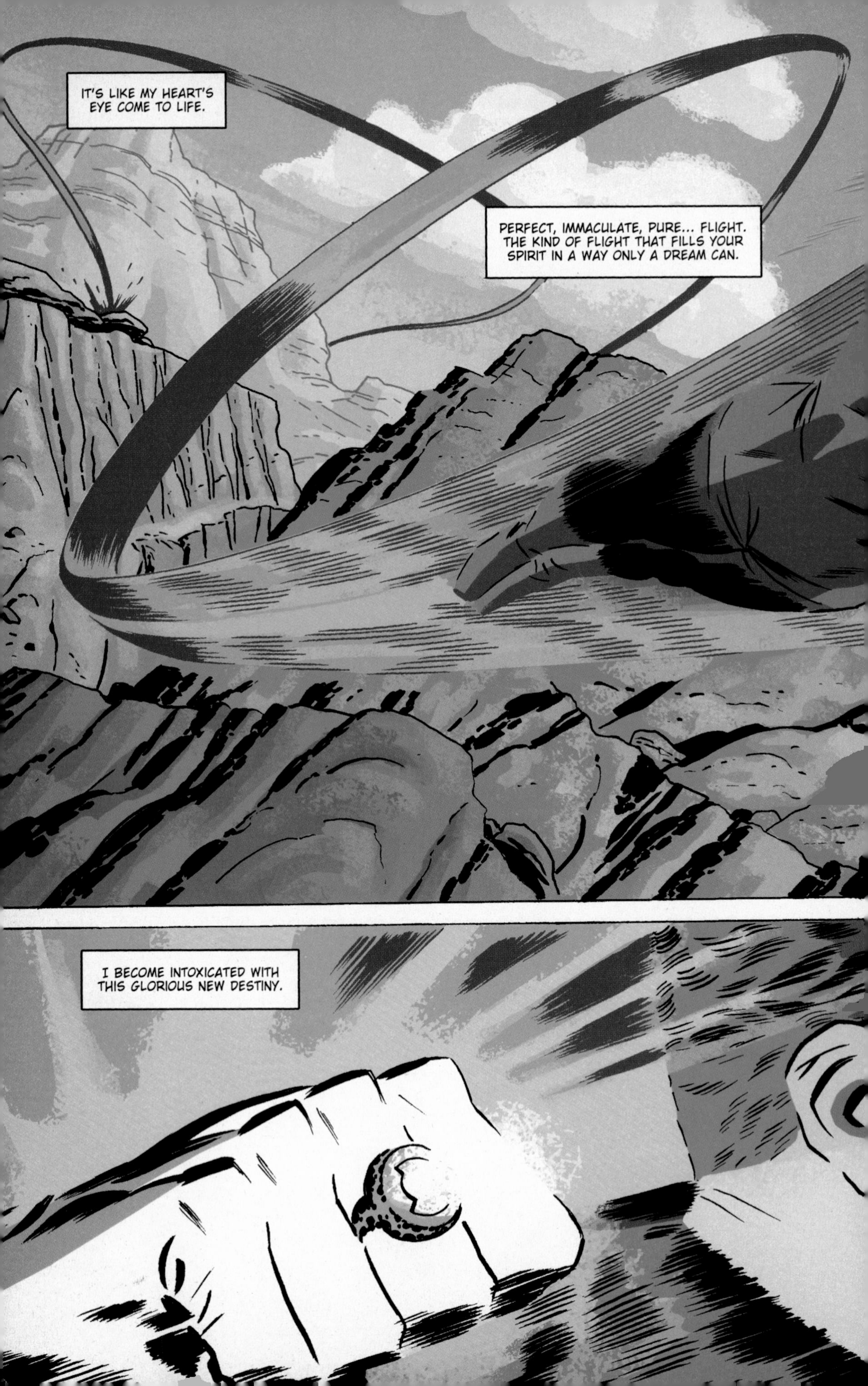
IT'S LIKE MY HEART'S EYE COME TO LIFE.
PERFECT, IMMACULATE, PURE... FLIGHT. THE KIND OF FLIGHT THAT FILLS YOUR SPIRIT IN A WAY ONLY A DREAM CAN.
I BECOME INTOXICATED WITH THIS GLORIOUS NEW DESTINY.

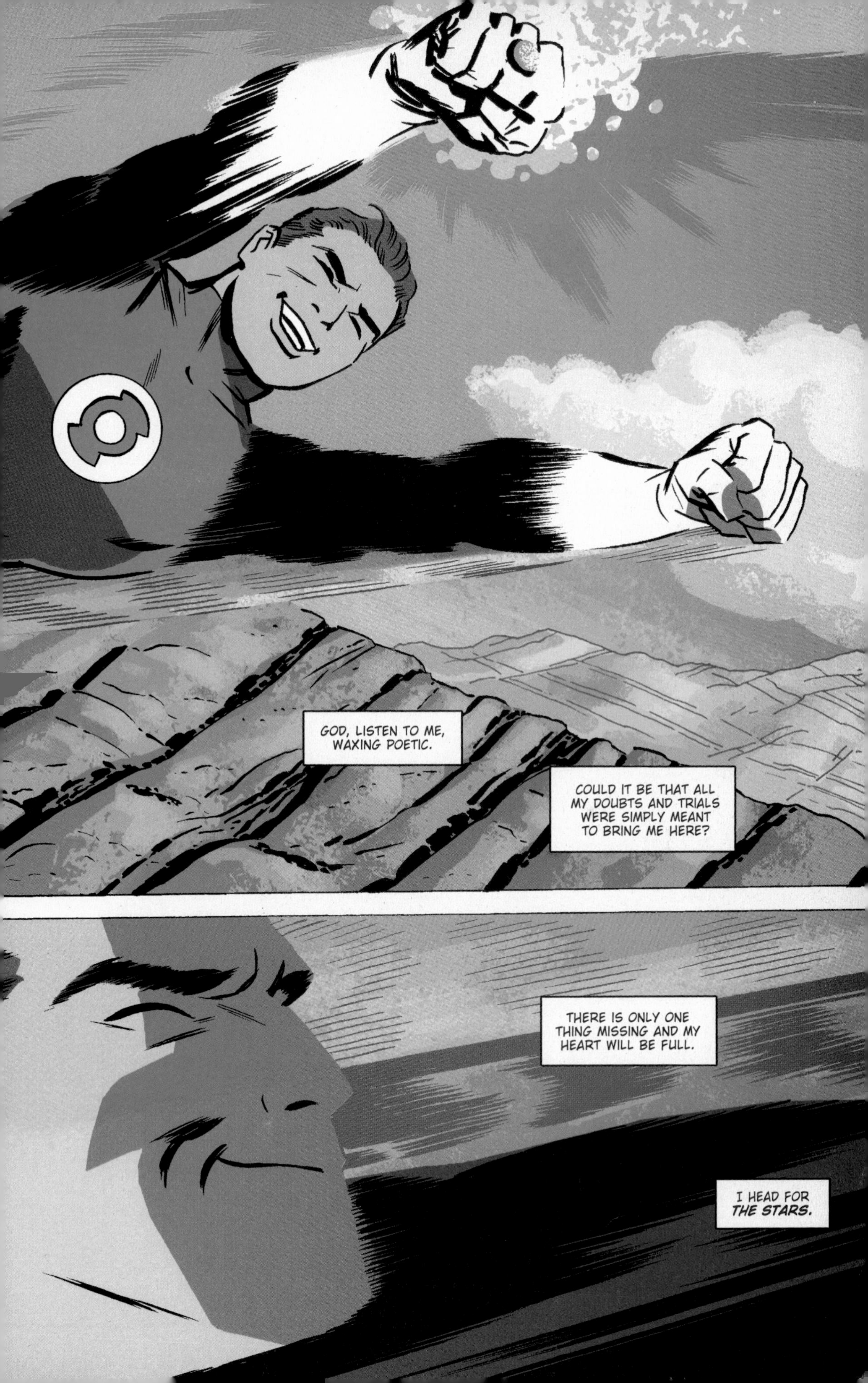
GOD, LISTEN TO ME, WAXING POETIC.
COULD IT BE THAT ALL MY DOUBTS AND TRIALS WERE SIMPLY MEANT TO BRING ME HERE?
THERE IS ONLY ONE THING MISSING AND MY HEART WILL BE FULL.
I HEAD FOR *THE STARS.*

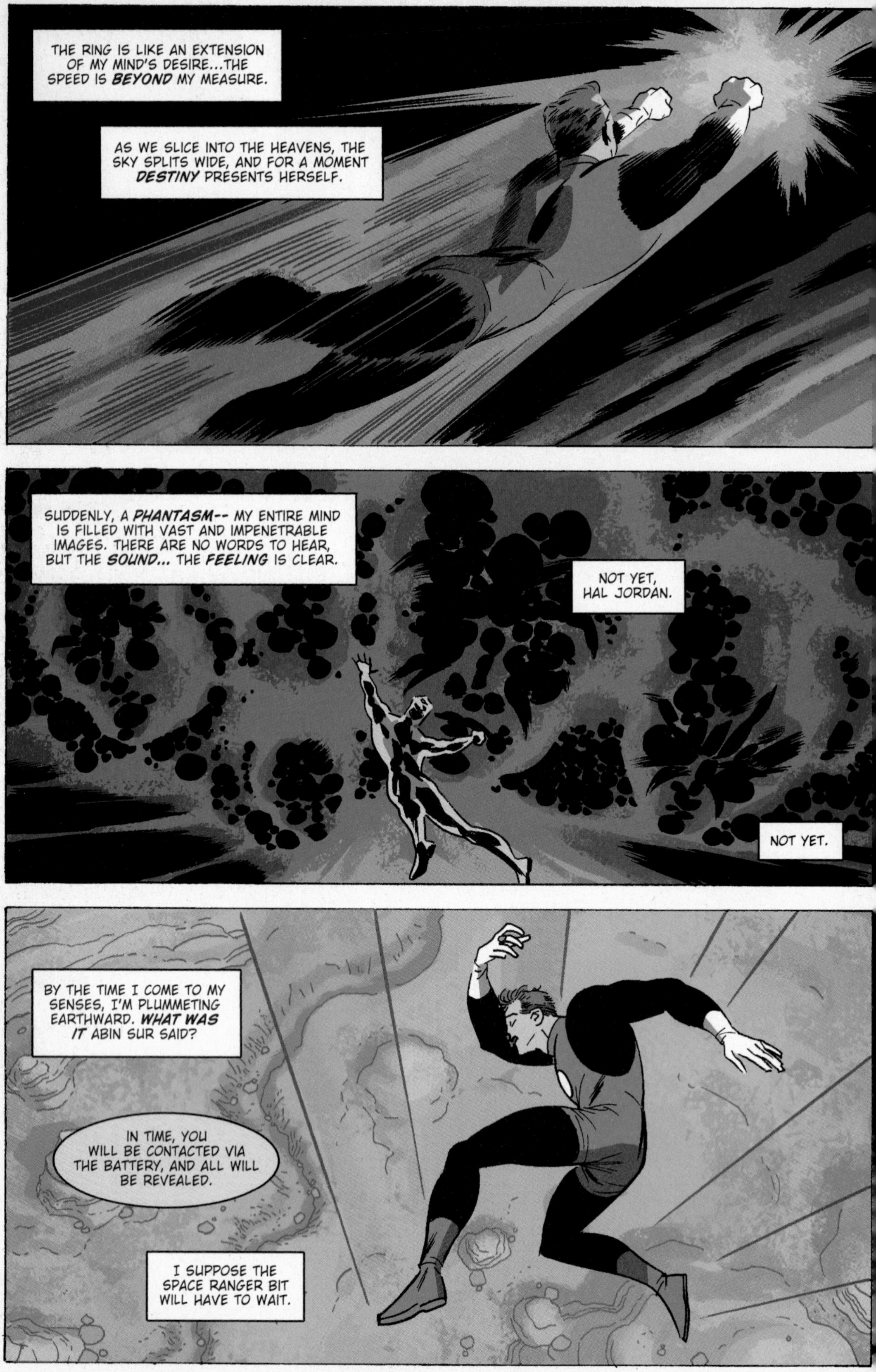

THE RING IS LIKE AN EXTENSION OF MY MIND'S DESIRE...THE SPEED IS BEYOND MY MEASURE.
AS WE SLICE INTO THE HEAVENS, THE SKY SPLITS WIDE, AND FOR A MOMENT DESTINY PRESENTS HERSELF.
SUDDENLY, A PHANTASM-- MY ENTIRE MIND IS FILLED WITH VAST AND IMPENETRABLE IMAGES. THERE ARE NO WORDS TO HEAR, BUT THE SOUND... THE FEELING IS CLEAR.
NOT YET, HAL JORDAN.
NOT YET.
BY THE TIME I COME TO MY SENSES, I'M PLUMMETING EARTHWARD. WHAT WAS IT ABIN SUR SAID?
IN TIME, YOU WILL BE CONTACTED VIA THE BATTERY, AND ALL WILL BE REVEALED.
I SUPPOSE THE SPACE RANGER BIT WILL HAVE TO WAIT.

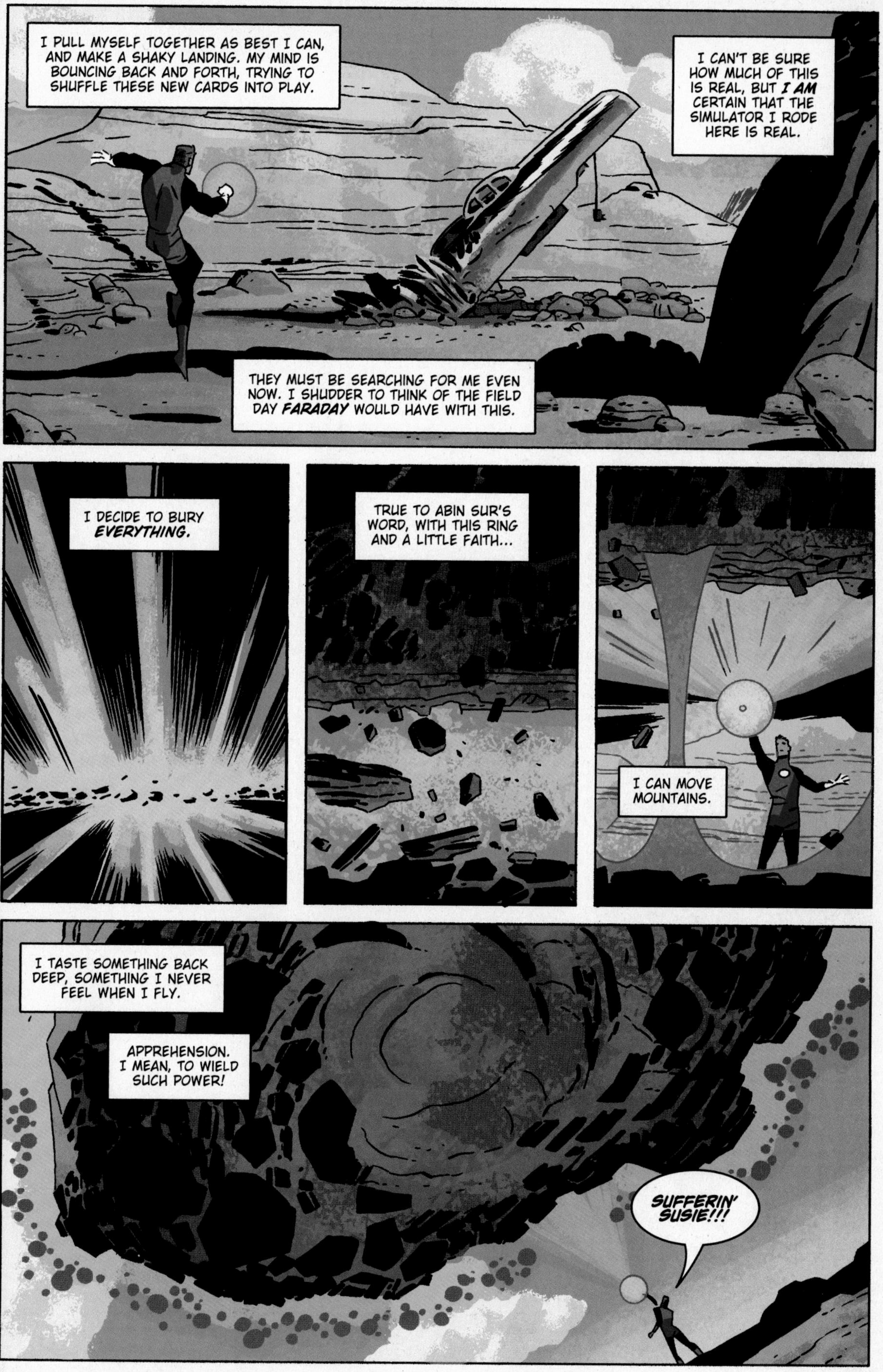
I PULL MYSELF TOGETHER AS BEST I CAN, AND MAKE A SHAKY LANDING. MY MIND IS BOUNCING BACK AND FORTH, TRYING TO SHUFFLE THESE NEW CARDS INTO PLAY.
I CAN'T BE SURE HOW MUCH OF THIS IS REAL, BUT *I AM* CERTAIN THAT THE SIMULATOR I RODE HERE IS REAL.
THEY MUST BE SEARCHING FOR ME EVEN NOW. I SHUDDER TO THINK OF THE FIELD DAY *FARADAY* WOULD HAVE WITH THIS.
I DECIDE TO BURY *EVERYTHING.*
TRUE TO ABIN SUR'S WORD, WITH THIS RING AND A LITTLE FAITH...
I CAN MOVE MOUNTAINS.
I TASTE SOMETHING BACK DEEP, SOMETHING I NEVER FEEL WHEN I FLY.
APPREHENSION. I MEAN, TO WIELD SUCH POWER!
SUFFERIN' SUSIE!!!

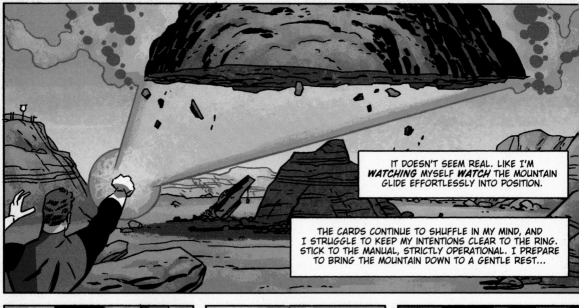

IT DOESN'T SEEM REAL. LIKE I'M *WATCHING* MYSELF *WATCH* THE MOUNTAIN GLIDE EFFORTLESSLY INTO POSITION.

THE CARDS CONTINUE TO SHUFFLE IN MY MIND, AND I STRUGGLE TO KEEP MY INTENTIONS CLEAR TO THE RING. STICK TO THE MANUAL, STRICTLY OPERATIONAL. I PREPARE TO BRING THE MOUNTAIN DOWN TO A GENTLE REST...

...BUT EVEN THE SIMPLEST OPERATIONS CAN *SNAFU.*

TSSSS

WHOA!

REFLEXES TAKE OVER, AND THOUGH IT ONLY TAKES A DISTRACTED SECOND...

NAP!

WELL, LIKE THEY SAY, GRAVITY IS A HARSH MISTRESS.

KRRAKAKABOOOM

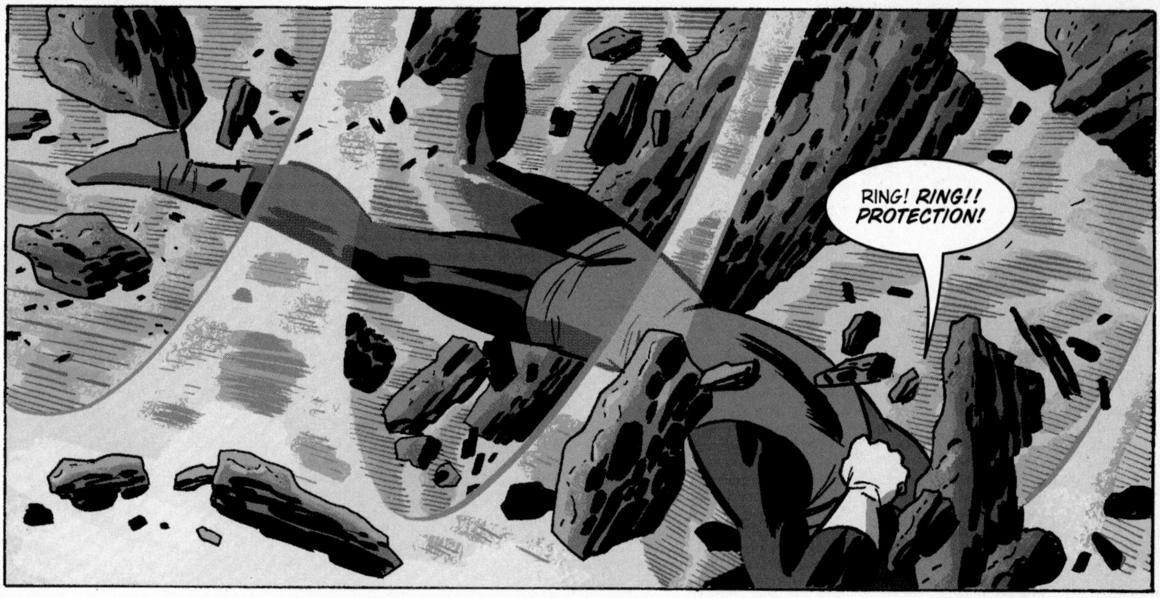
RING! RING!! PROTECTION!

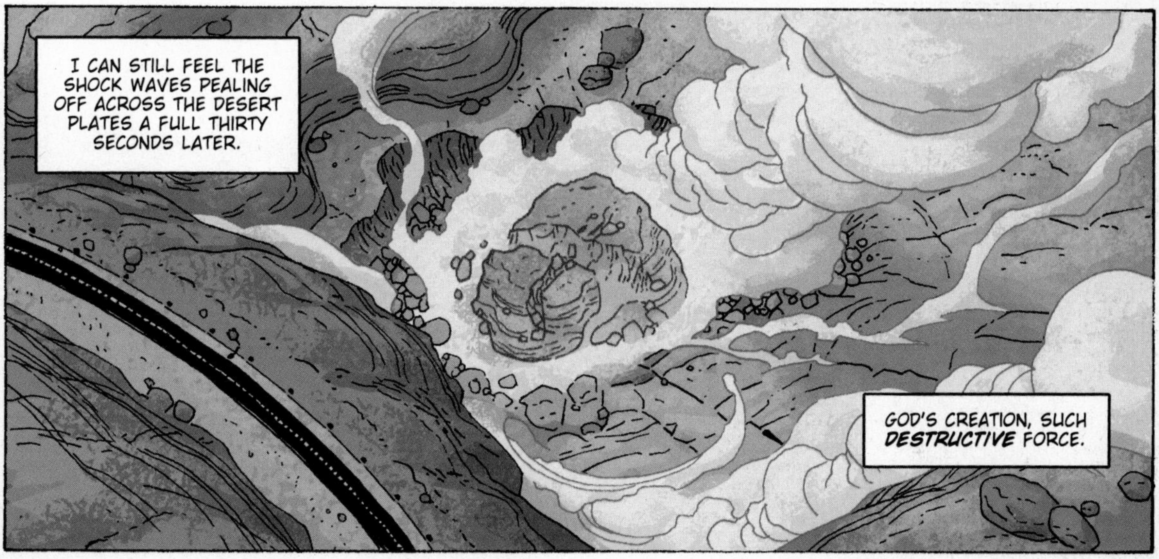
I CAN STILL FEEL THE SHOCK WAVES PEALING OFF ACROSS THE DESERT PLATES A FULL THIRTY SECONDS LATER.
GOD'S CREATION, SUCH DESTRUCTIVE FORCE.

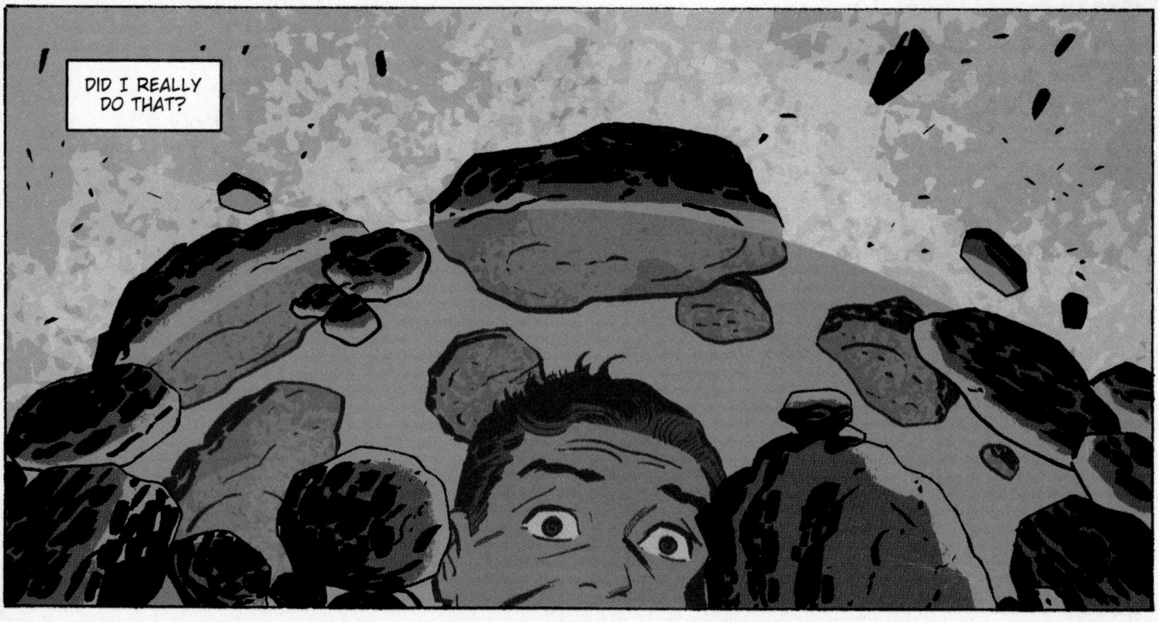
DID I REALLY DO THAT?

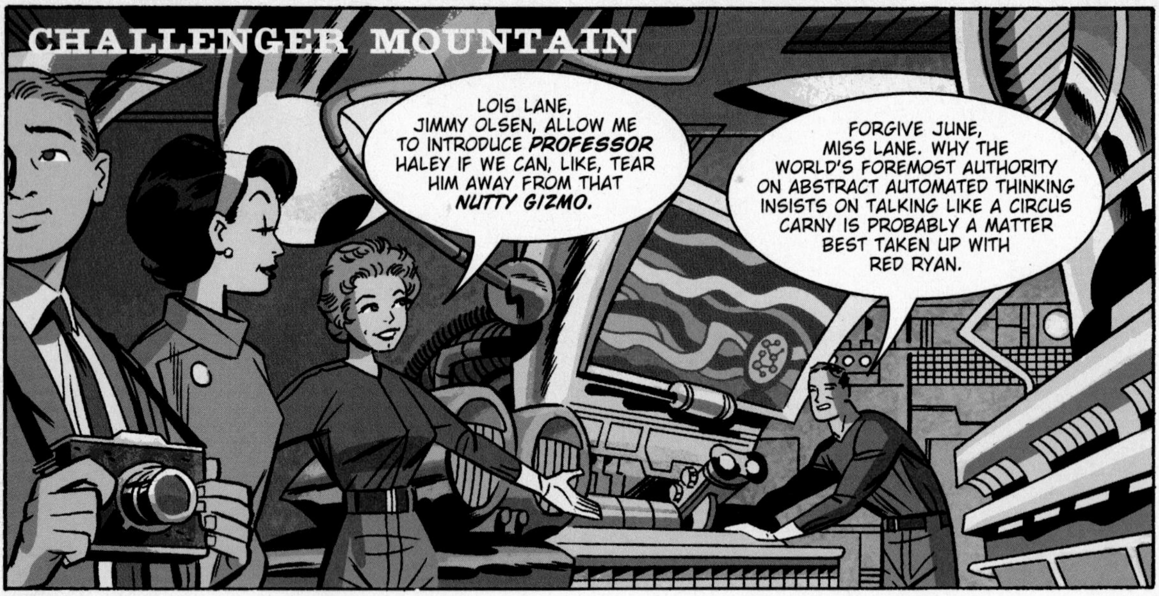
CHALLENGER MOUNTAIN
LOIS LANE, JIMMY OLSEN, ALLOW ME TO INTRODUCE PROFESSOR HALEY IF WE CAN, LIKE, TEAR HIM AWAY FROM THAT NUTTY GIZMO.
FORGIVE JUNE, MISS LANE. WHY THE WORLD'S FOREMOST AUTHORITY ON ABSTRACT AUTOMATED THINKING INSISTS ON TALKING LIKE A CIRCUS CARNY IS PROBABLY A MATTER BEST TAKEN UP WITH RED RYAN.

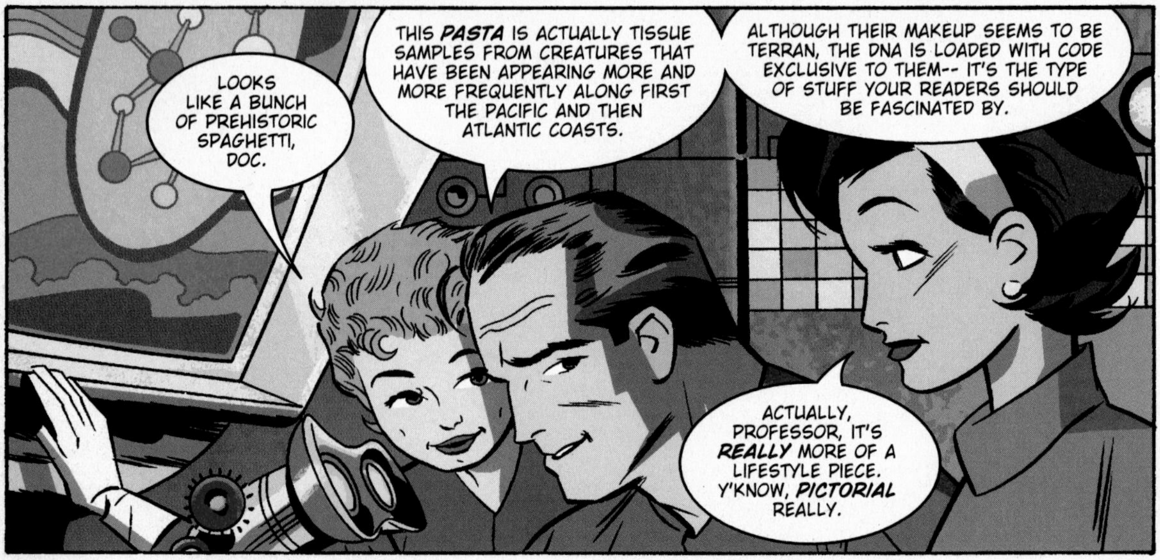
LOOKS LIKE A BUNCH OF PREHISTORIC SPAGHETTI, DOC.
THIS PASTA IS ACTUALLY TISSUE SAMPLES FROM CREATURES THAT HAVE BEEN APPEARING MORE AND MORE FREQUENTLY ALONG FIRST THE PACIFIC AND THEN ATLANTIC COASTS.
ALTHOUGH THEIR MAKEUP SEEMS TO BE TERRAN, THE DNA IS LOADED WITH CODE EXCLUSIVE TO THEM-- IT'S THE TYPE OF STUFF YOUR READERS SHOULD BE FASCINATED BY.
ACTUALLY, PROFESSOR, IT'S REALLY MORE OF A LIFESTYLE PIECE. Y'KNOW, PICTORIAL REALLY.

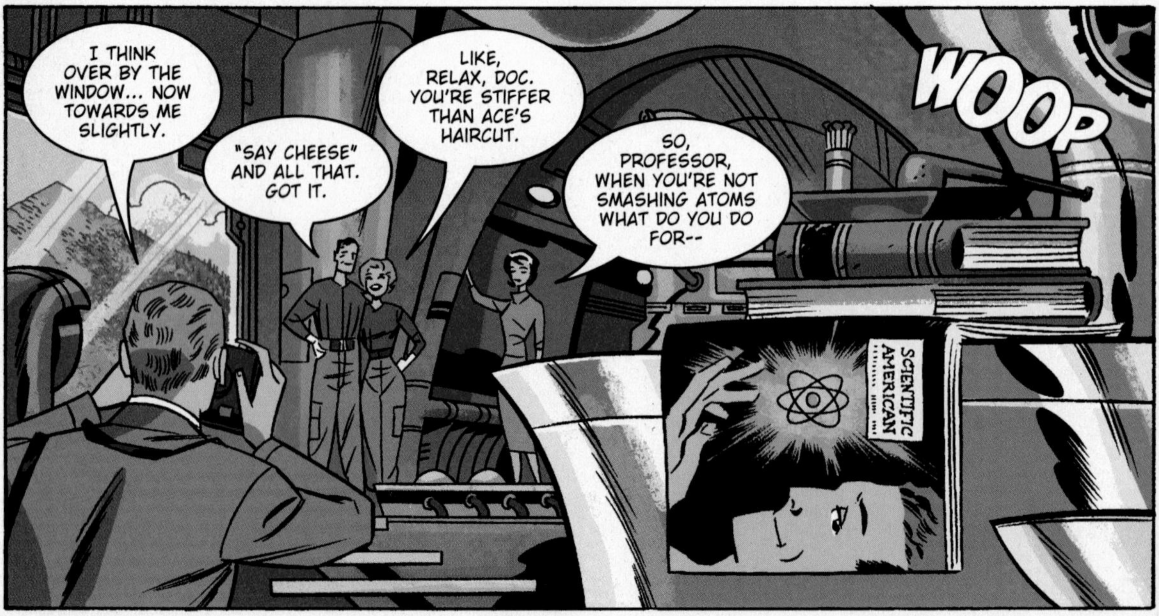
I THINK OVER BY THE WINDOW... NOW TOWARDS ME SLIGHTLY.
"SAY CHEESE" AND ALL THAT. GOT IT.
LIKE, RELAX, DOC. YOU'RE STIFFER THAN ACE'S HAIRCUT.
SO, PROFESSOR, WHEN YOU'RE NOT SMASHING ATOMS WHAT DO YOU DO FOR--
WOOP
SCIENTIFIC AMERICAN

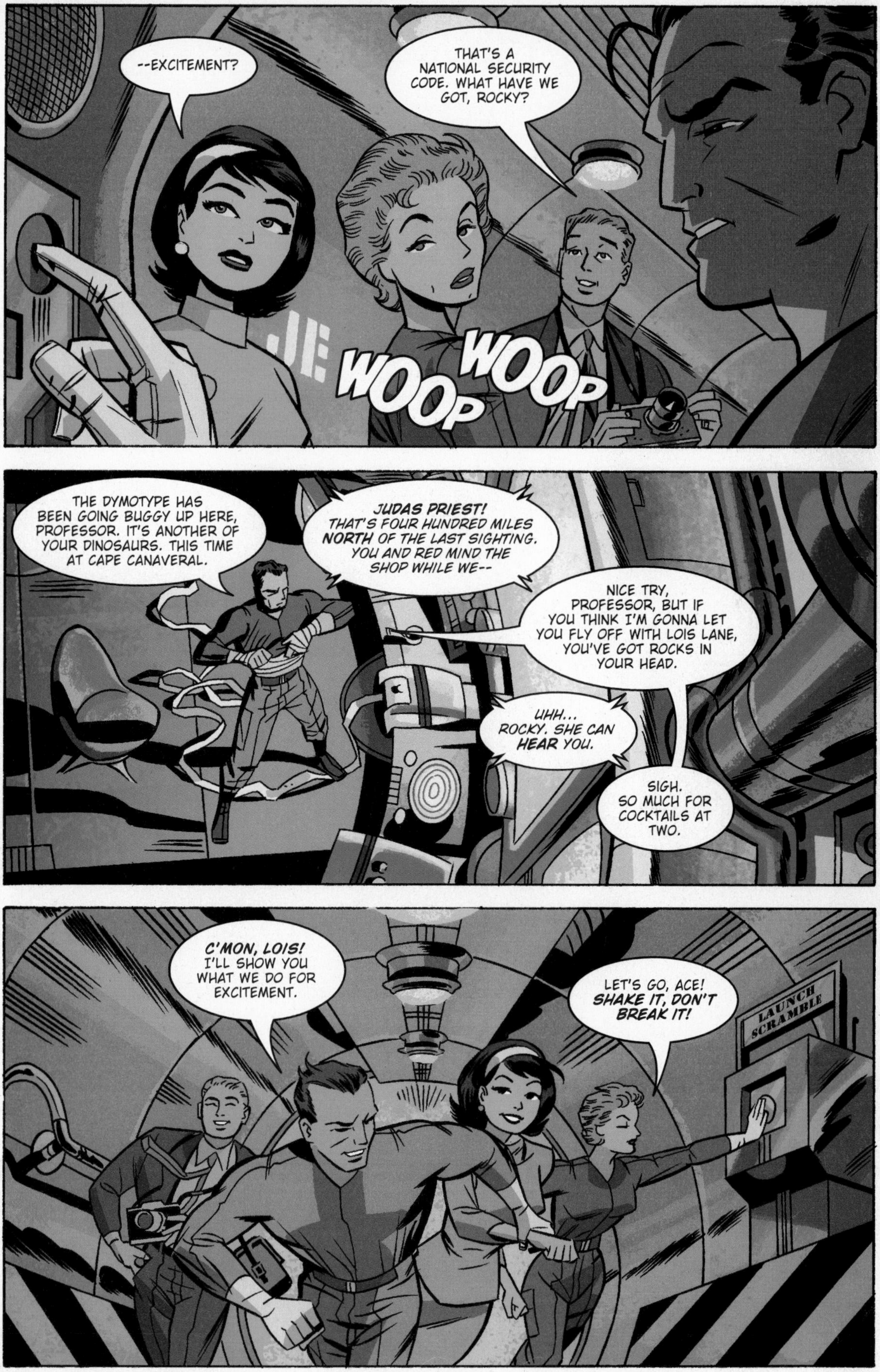
--EXCITEMENT?
THAT'S A NATIONAL SECURITY CODE. WHAT HAVE WE GOT, ROCKY?
WOOP WOOP
THE DYMOTYPE HAS BEEN GOING BUGGY UP HERE, PROFESSOR. IT'S ANOTHER OF YOUR DINOSAURS. THIS TIME AT CAPE CANAVERAL.
JUDAS PRIEST! THAT'S FOUR HUNDRED MILES NORTH OF THE LAST SIGHTING. YOU AND RED MIND THE SHOP WHILE WE--
NICE TRY, PROFESSOR, BUT IF YOU THINK I'M GONNA LET YOU FLY OFF WITH LOIS LANE, YOU'VE GOT ROCKS IN YOUR HEAD.
UHH... ROCKY. SHE CAN HEAR YOU.
SIGH. SO MUCH FOR COCKTAILS AT TWO.
C'MON, LOIS! I'LL SHOW YOU WHAT WE DO FOR EXCITEMENT.
LET'S GO, ACE! SHAKE IT, DON'T BREAK IT!
LAUNCH SCRAMBLE

CHAPTER ELEVEN

TOWARDS THE CENTRE

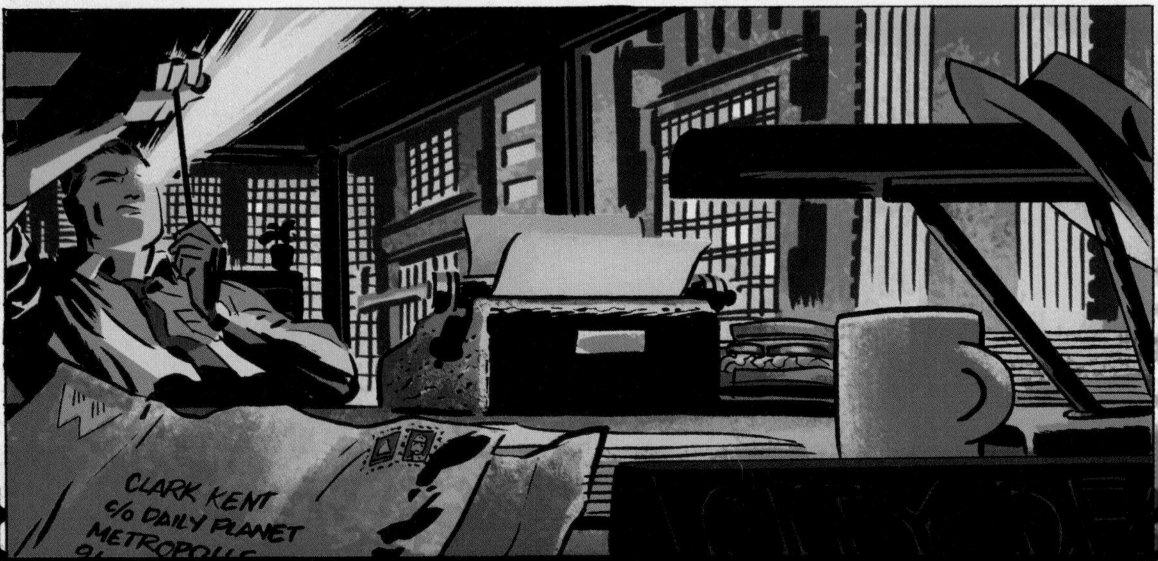
CLARK KENT
c/o DAILY PLANET

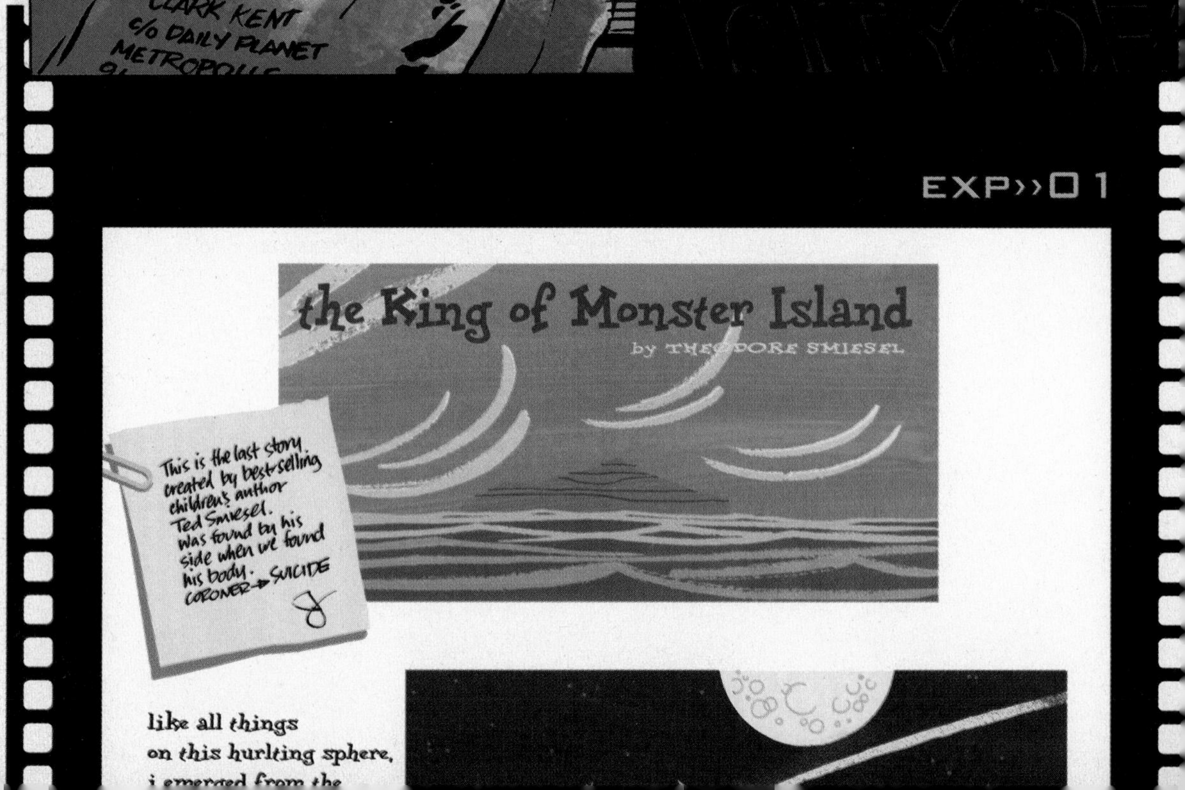
EXP››01
the King of Monster Island
by THEODORE SMIESEL
This is the last story created by best-selling children's author Ted Smiesel. Was found by his side when we found his body. CORONER→SUICIDE
like all things
on this hurlting sphere,

created
children's author
Ted Smiesel.
Was found by his
side when we found
his body.
CORONER → SUICIDE
J

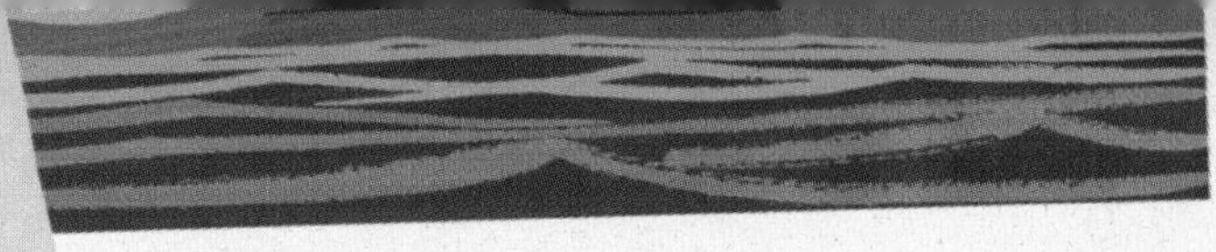

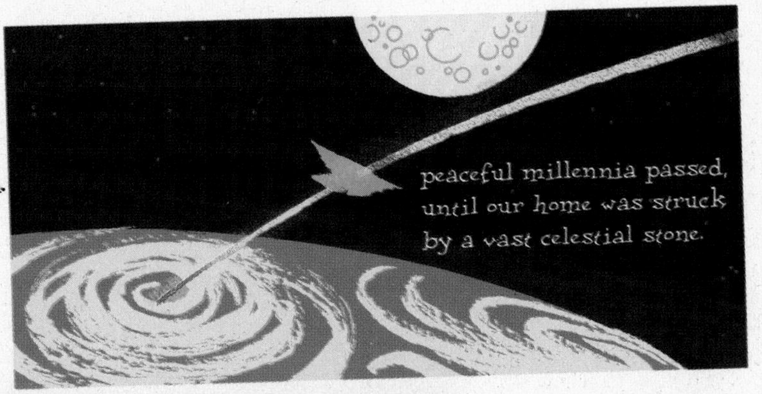
peaceful millennia passed,
until our home was struck
by a vast celestial stone.

like all things
on this hurlting sphere,
i emerged from the
molten centre of creation.
but mine has been a
unique path.
isolated, i developed
attributes beyond those
of lesser things.

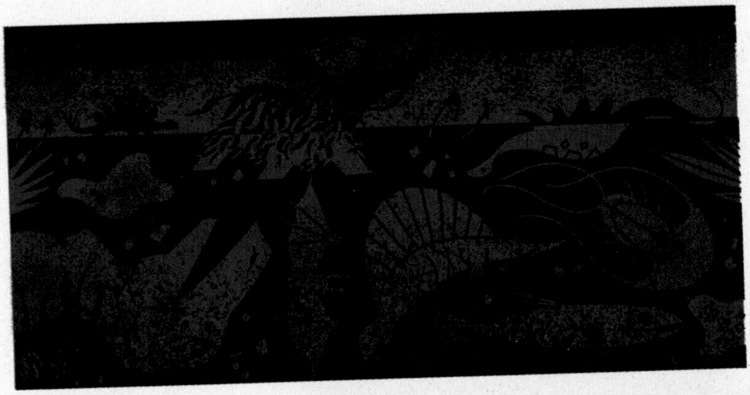

the force of contact
plunged our idyllic
sphere into a chaotic
garden of death.
light was life, and
black chunks of death
had filled the skies.

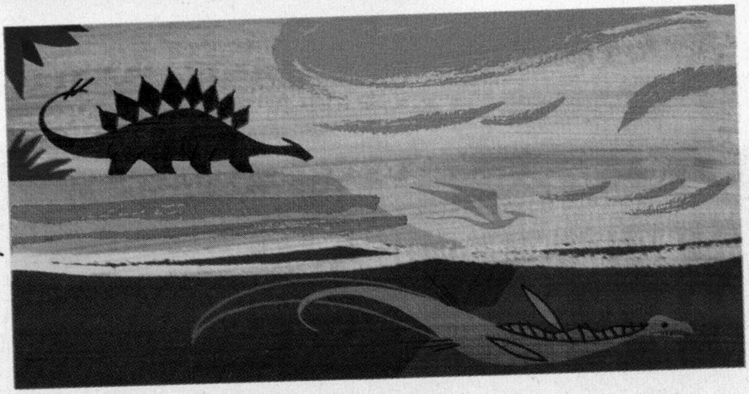

with great haste, i set
to the task of preparing
an environment in
which i could sustain
the lesser things.
with flora and flesh,
i would find sustenance.
at the centre of
the great ocean i would
ensure that life
would survive.

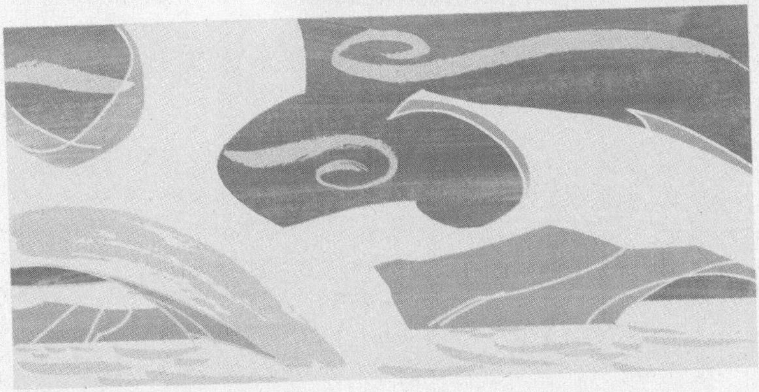

then came an era
of pristine beauty
and blessed quiet.
our sphere lay dead
under a glistening pearl
coat, but life prevailed
through my will.
i lived and fed on
the lesser things,
growing from the centre.

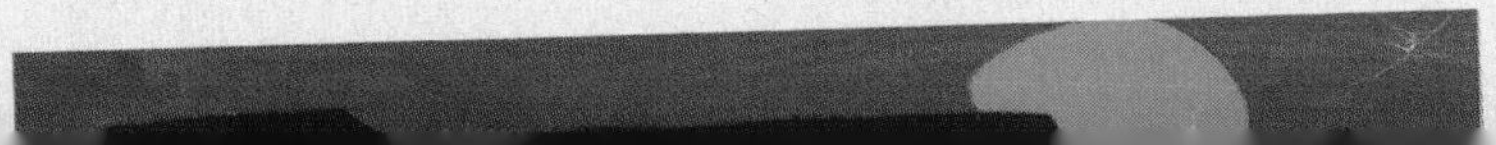

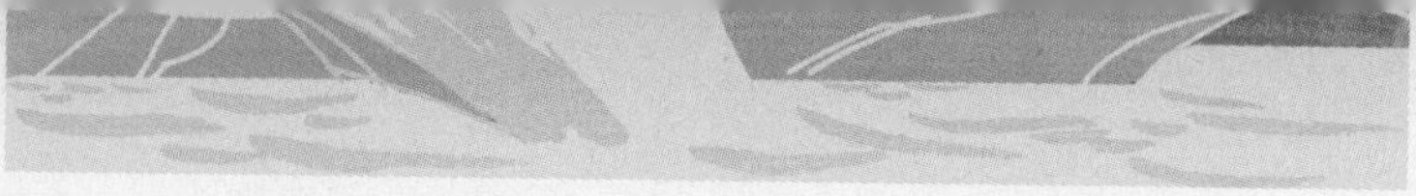

the lesser things,
growing from the centre.

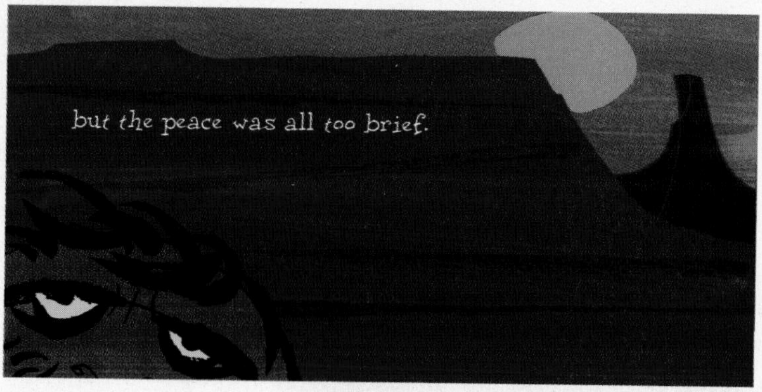
but the peace was all too brief.

soon the heavens opened, and the sphere began to nurture and sustain curious new kinds of life. all were lesser things, but there was one creature that stood above the rest.

unlike my things, the blood ran hot through this one's impatient heart. its fragile shell belied a vicious nature, and its clever mind was quick to find new ways to control the sphere.

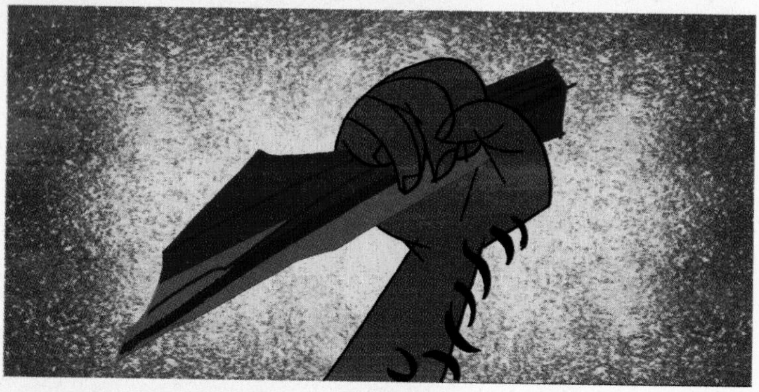

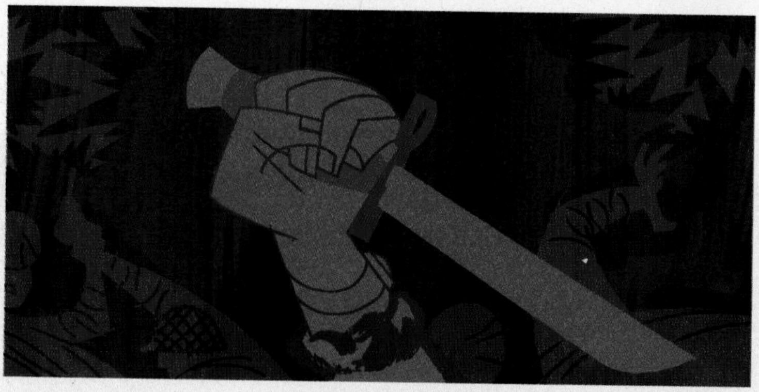

in what seemed a heartbeat, these things had proliferated in both numbers, and destructive means. another heartbeat, and they had brought their conflicts to my haven.

by the time they had harnessed the most destructive forces on our sphere, i concluded it was time to leave my azure home. long have i dreamt of traveling the spheres beyond mine, claiming them for the centre's glory.

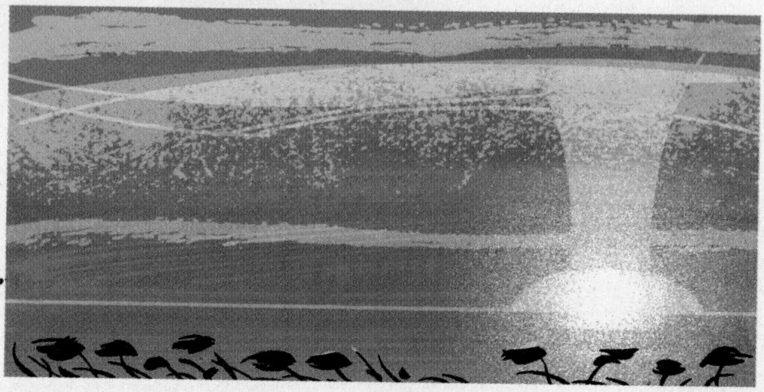

i sent forth an airborne

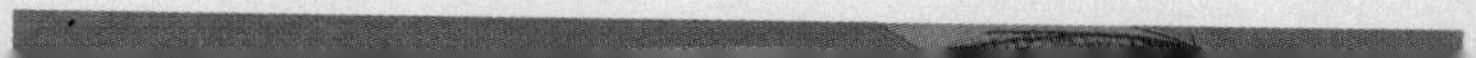

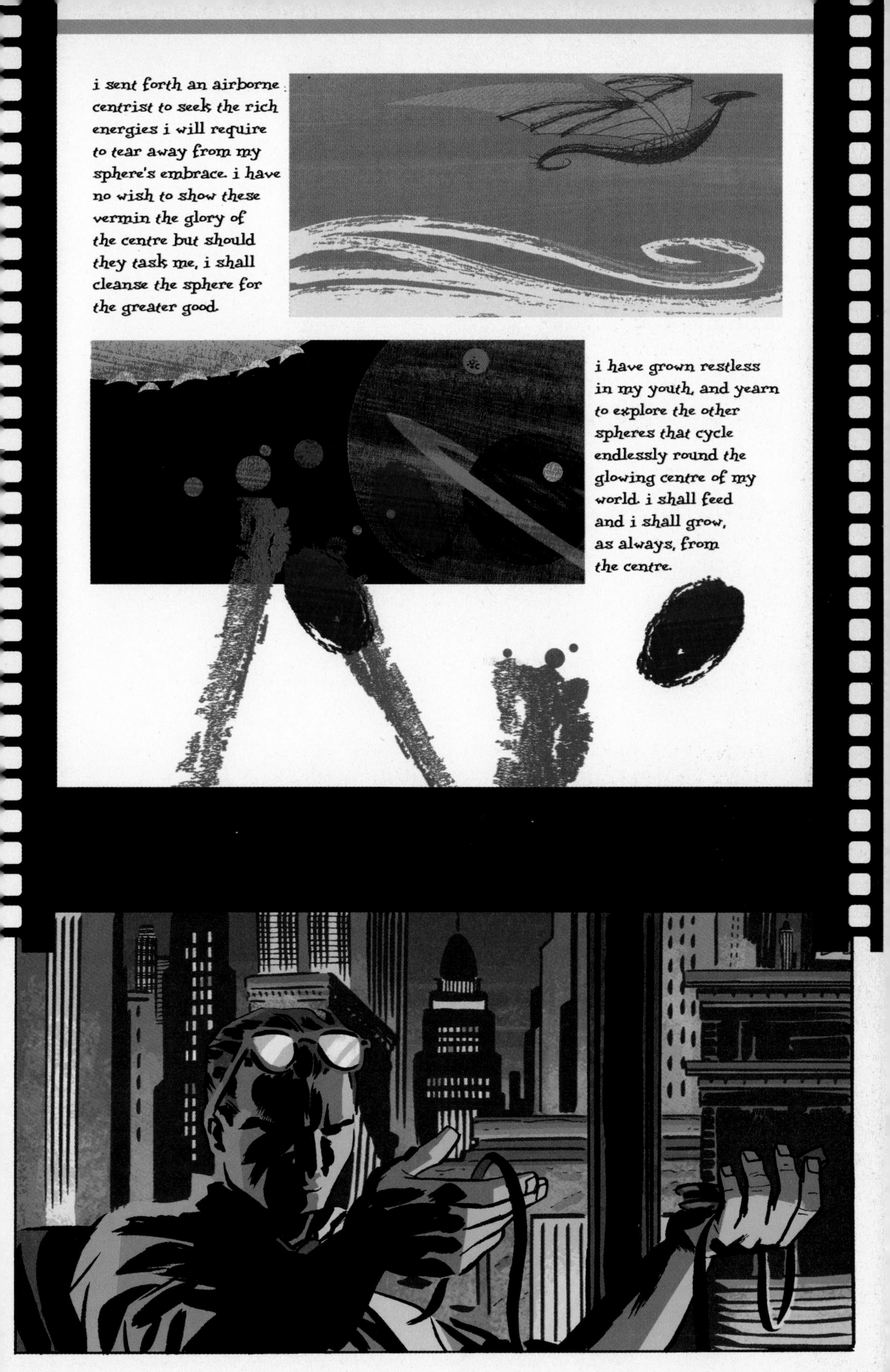
i sent forth an airborne centrist to seek the rich energies i will require to tear away from my sphere's embrace. i have no wish to show these vermin the glory of the centre but should they task me, i shall cleanse the sphere for the greater good.
i have grown restless in my youth, and yearn to explore the other spheres that cycle endlessly round the glowing centre of my world. i shall feed and i shall grow, as always, from the centre.

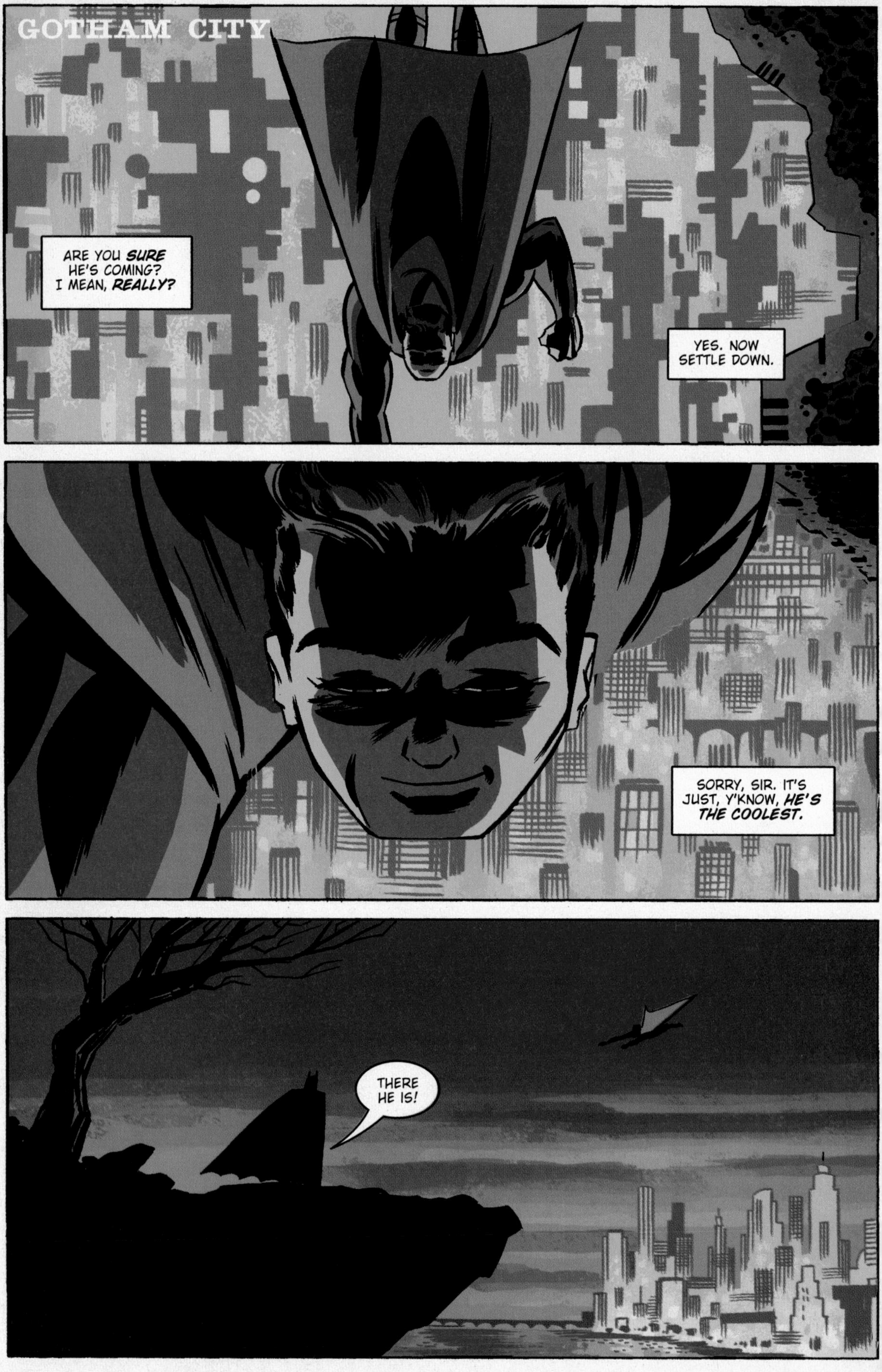
GOTHAM CITY
ARE YOU SURE HE'S COMING? I MEAN, REALLY?
YES. NOW SETTLE DOWN.
SORRY, SIR. IT'S JUST, Y'KNOW, HE'S THE COOLEST.
THERE HE IS!

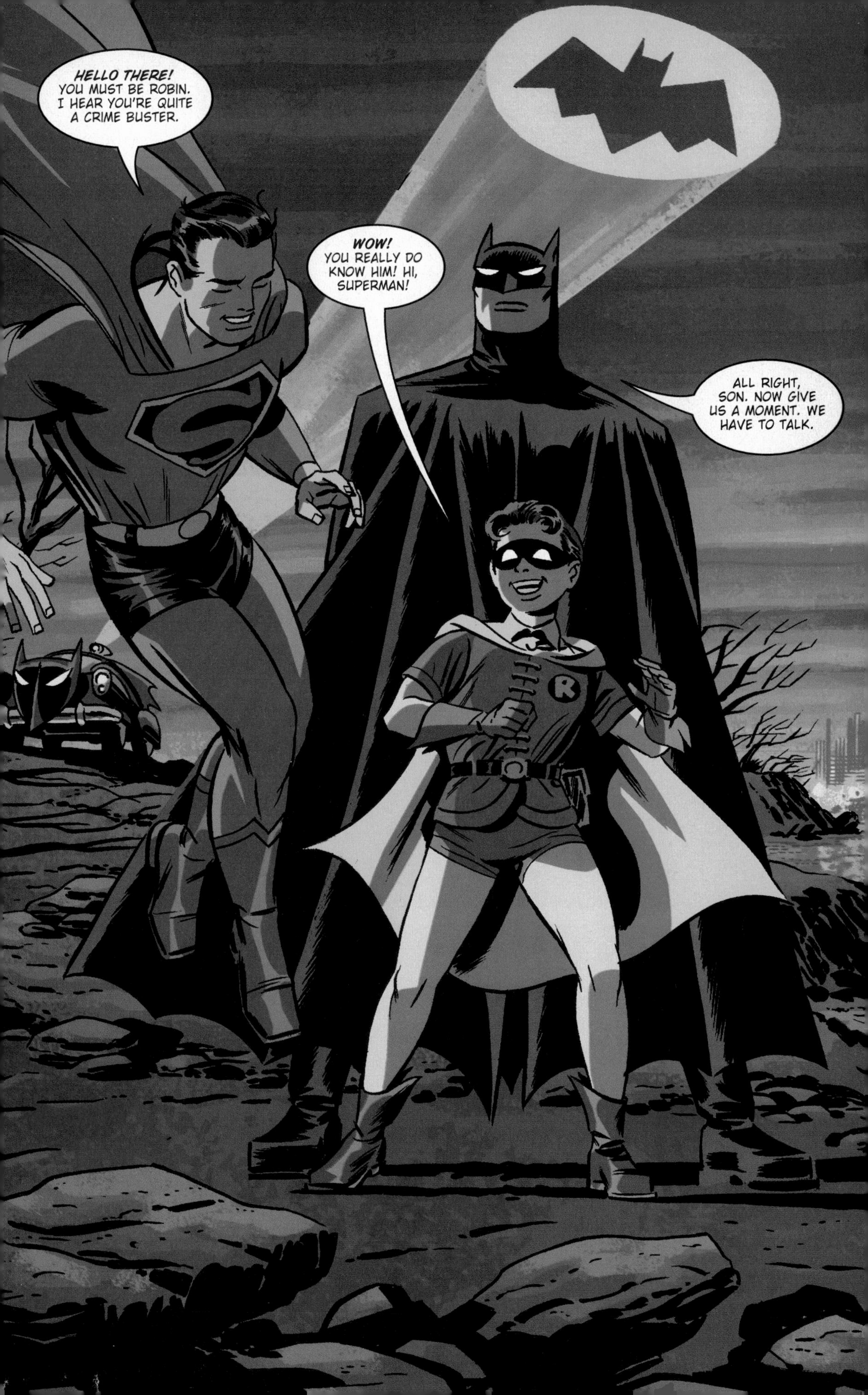
HELLO THERE! YOU MUST BE ROBIN. I HEAR YOU'RE QUITE A CRIME BUSTER.
WOW! YOU REALLY DO KNOW HIM! HI, SUPERMAN!
ALL RIGHT, SON. NOW GIVE US A MOMENT. WE HAVE TO TALK.

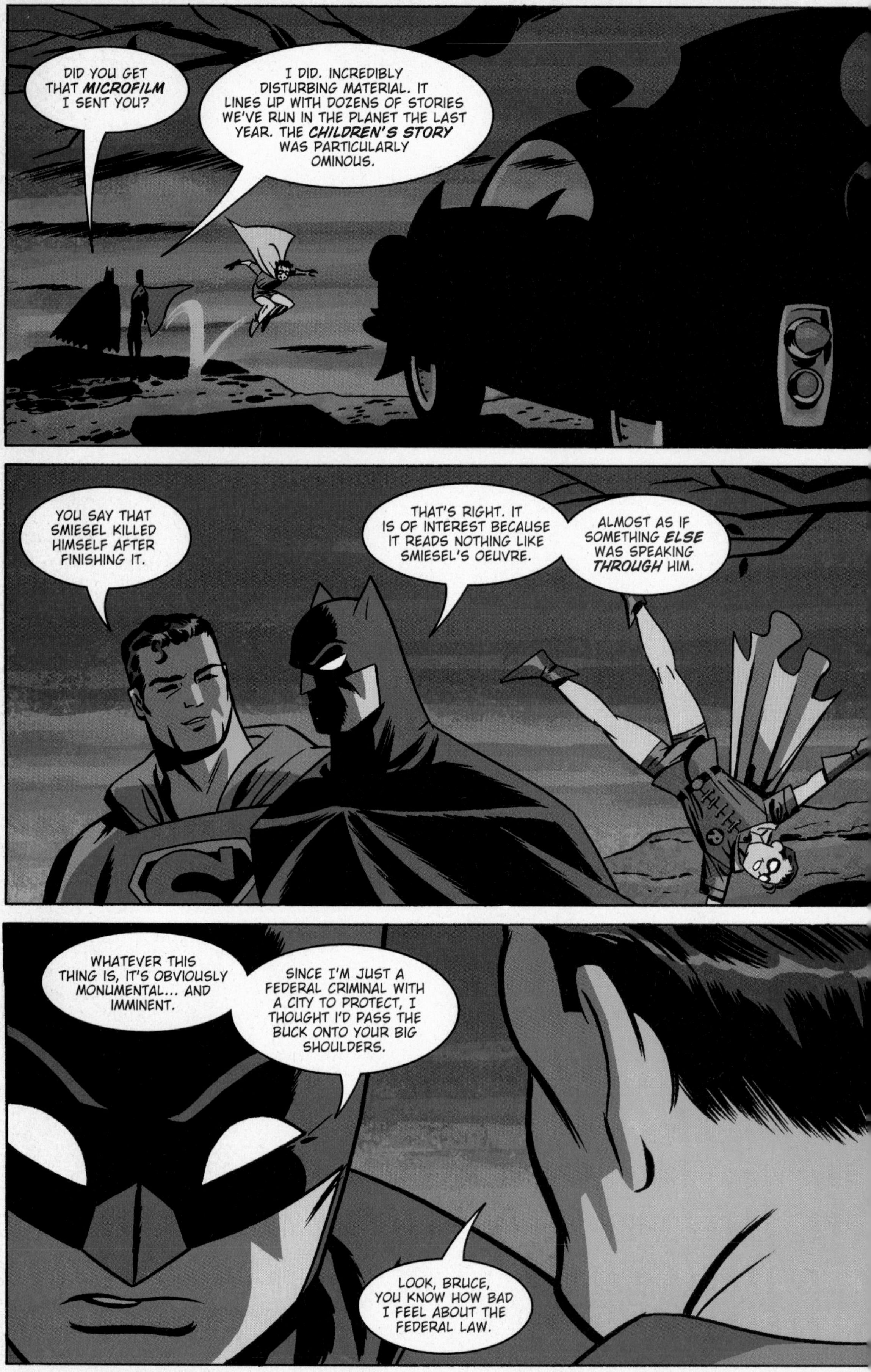
DID YOU GET THAT MICROFILM I SENT YOU?
I DID. INCREDIBLY DISTURBING MATERIAL. IT LINES UP WITH DOZENS OF STORIES WE'VE RUN IN THE PLANET THE LAST YEAR. THE CHILDREN'S STORY WAS PARTICULARLY OMINOUS.
YOU SAY THAT SMIESEL KILLED HIMSELF AFTER FINISHING IT.
THAT'S RIGHT. IT IS OF INTEREST BECAUSE IT READS NOTHING LIKE SMIESEL'S OEUVRE.
ALMOST AS IF SOMETHING ELSE WAS SPEAKING THROUGH HIM.
WHATEVER THIS THING IS, IT'S OBVIOUSLY MONUMENTAL... AND IMMINENT.
SINCE I'M JUST A FEDERAL CRIMINAL WITH A CITY TO PROTECT, I THOUGHT I'D PASS THE BUCK ONTO YOUR BIG SHOULDERS.
LOOK, BRUCE, YOU KNOW HOW BAD I FEEL ABOUT THE FEDERAL LAW.

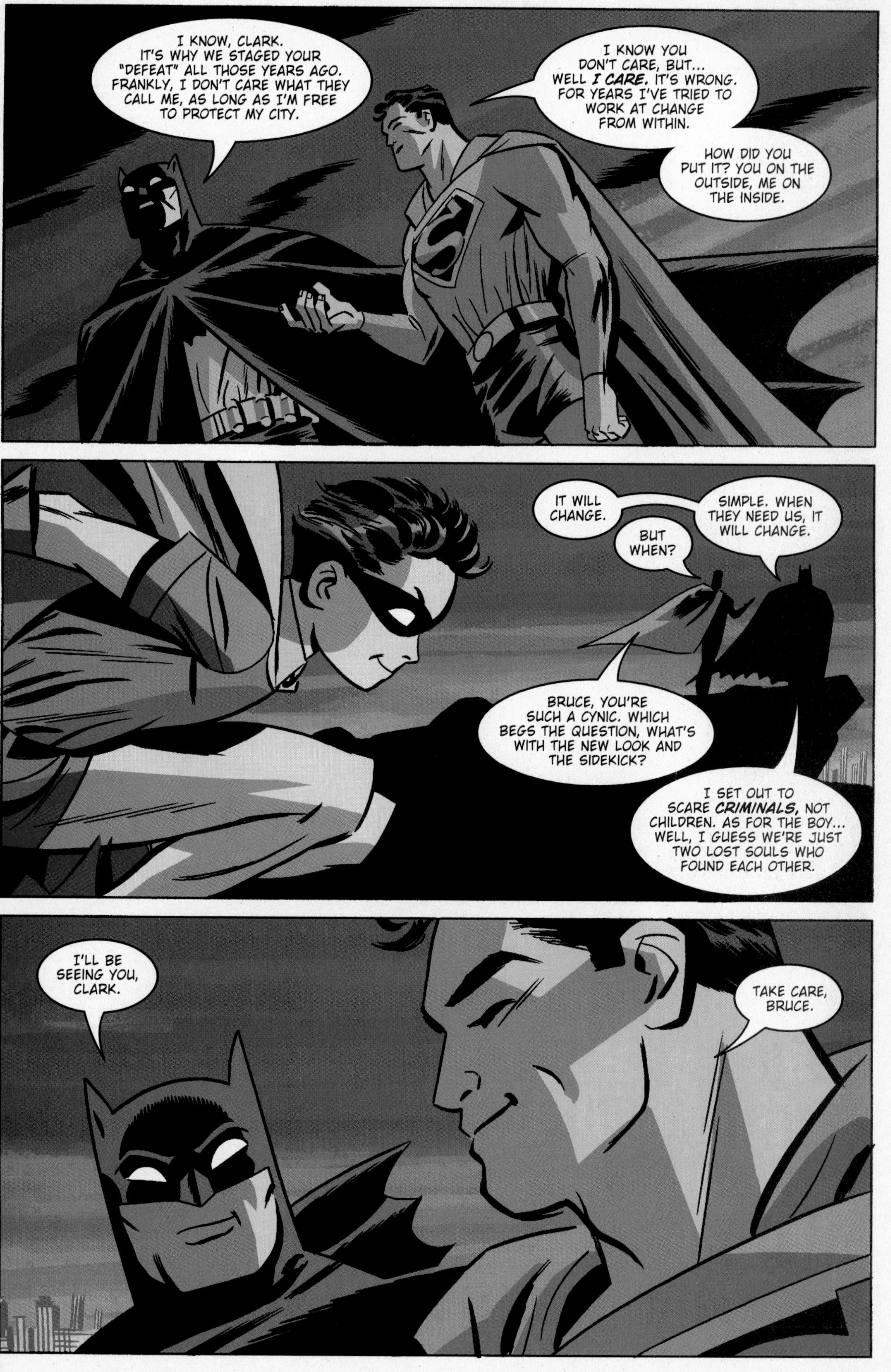

I KNOW, CLARK. IT'S WHY WE STAGED YOUR "DEFEAT" ALL THOSE YEARS AGO. FRANKLY, I DON'T CARE WHAT THEY CALL ME, AS LONG AS I'M FREE TO PROTECT MY CITY.
I KNOW YOU DON'T CARE, BUT... WELL *I CARE.* IT'S WRONG. FOR YEARS I'VE TRIED TO WORK AT CHANGE FROM WITHIN.
HOW DID YOU PUT IT? YOU ON THE OUTSIDE, ME ON THE INSIDE.
IT WILL CHANGE.
BUT WHEN?
SIMPLE. WHEN THEY NEED US, IT WILL CHANGE.
BRUCE, YOU'RE SUCH A CYNIC. WHICH BEGS THE QUESTION, WHAT'S WITH THE NEW LOOK AND THE SIDEKICK?
I SET OUT TO SCARE *CRIMINALS,* NOT CHILDREN. AS FOR THE BOY... WELL, I GUESS WE'RE JUST TWO LOST SOULS WHO FOUND EACH OTHER.
I'LL BE SEEING YOU, CLARK.
TAKE CARE, BRUCE.

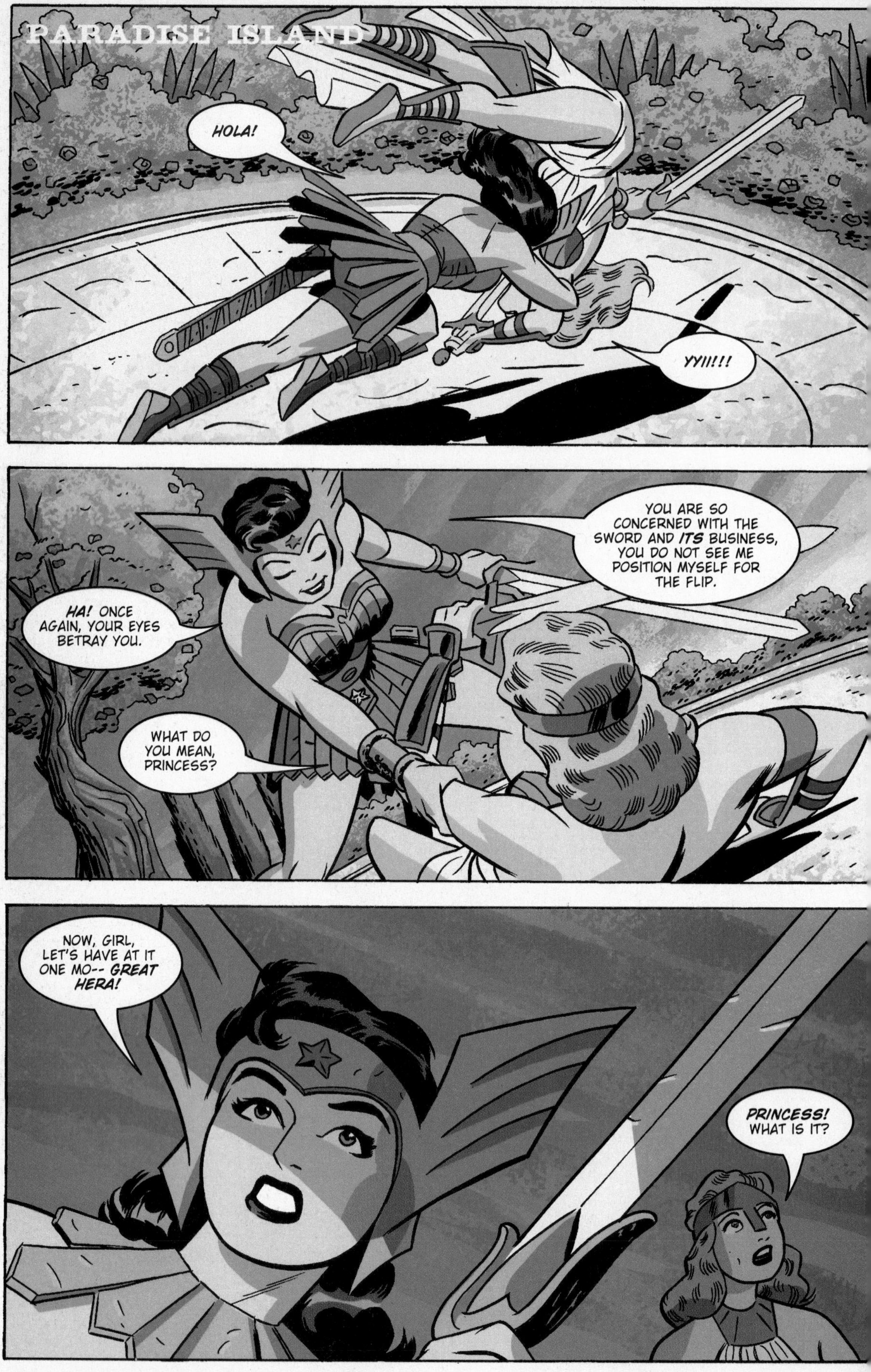
PARADISE ISLAND
HOLA!
YYII!!!
HA! ONCE AGAIN, YOUR EYES BETRAY YOU.
YOU ARE SO CONCERNED WITH THE SWORD AND ITS BUSINESS, YOU DO NOT SEE ME POSITION MYSELF FOR THE FLIP.
WHAT DO YOU MEAN, PRINCESS?
NOW, GIRL, LET'S HAVE AT IT ONE MO-- GREAT HERA!
PRINCESS! WHAT IS IT?

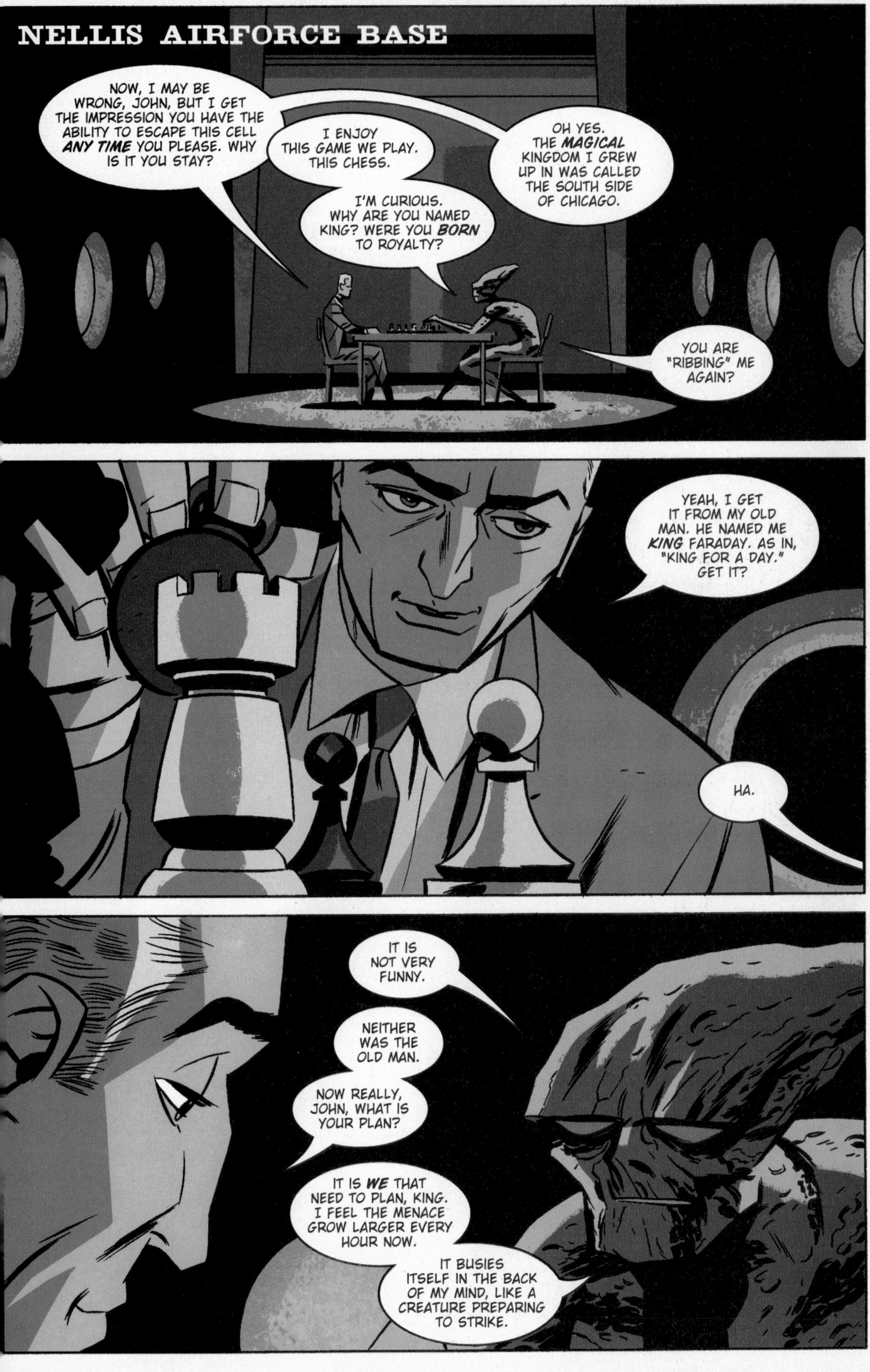
NELLIS AIRFORCE BASE
NOW, I MAY BE WRONG, JOHN, BUT I GET THE IMPRESSION YOU HAVE THE ABILITY TO ESCAPE THIS CELL ANY TIME YOU PLEASE. WHY IS IT YOU STAY?
I ENJOY THIS GAME WE PLAY. THIS CHESS.
I'M CURIOUS. WHY ARE YOU NAMED KING? WERE YOU BORN TO ROYALTY?
OH YES. THE MAGICAL KINGDOM I GREW UP IN WAS CALLED THE SOUTH SIDE OF CHICAGO.
YOU ARE "RIBBING" ME AGAIN?
YEAH, I GET IT FROM MY OLD MAN. HE NAMED ME KING FARADAY. AS IN, "KING FOR A DAY." GET IT?
HA.
IT IS NOT VERY FUNNY.
NEITHER WAS THE OLD MAN.
NOW REALLY, JOHN, WHAT IS YOUR PLAN?
IT IS WE THAT NEED TO PLAN, KING. I FEEL THE MENACE GROW LARGER EVERY HOUR NOW.
IT BUSIES ITSELF IN THE BACK OF MY MIND, LIKE A CREATURE PREPARING TO STRIKE.

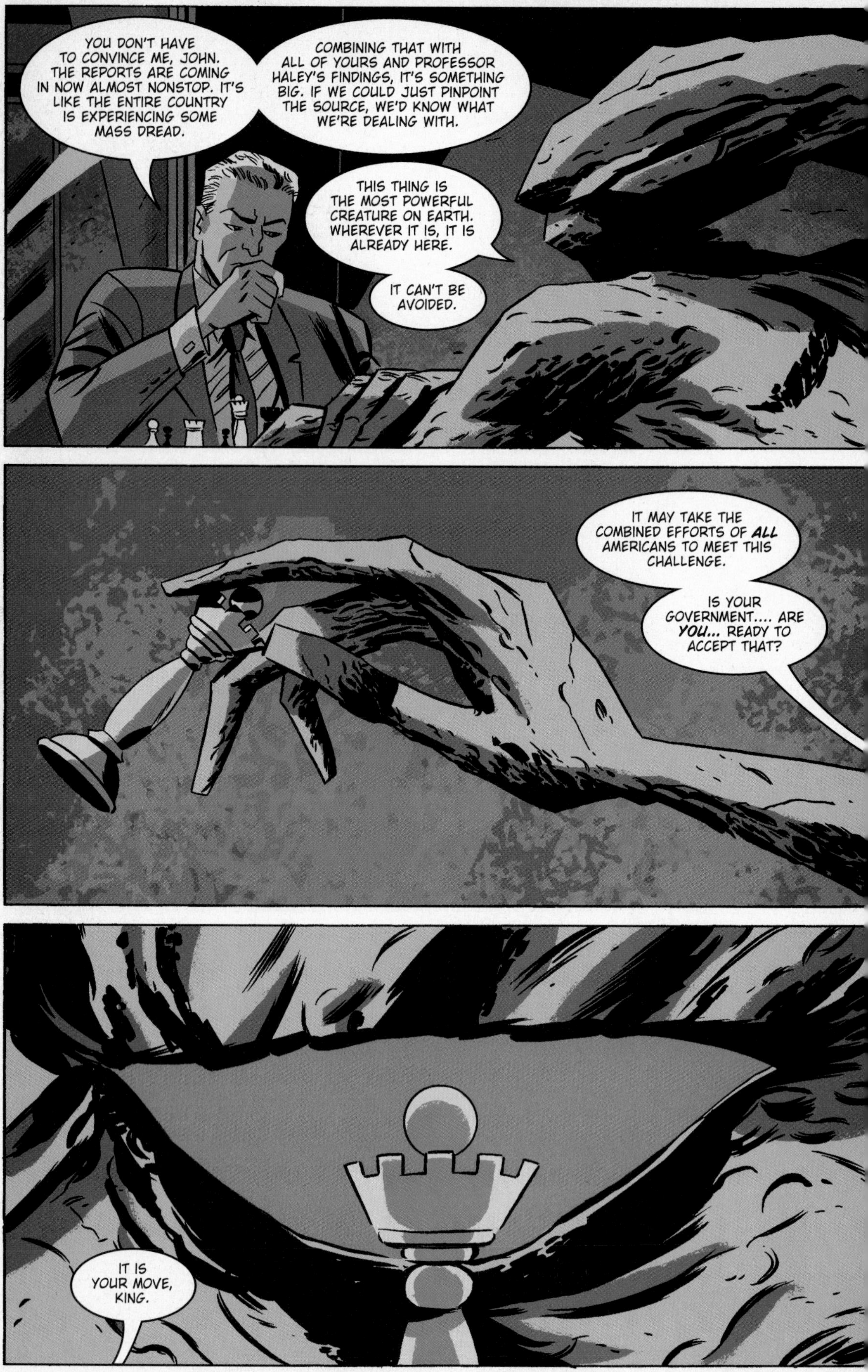
YOU DON'T HAVE TO CONVINCE ME, JOHN. THE REPORTS ARE COMING IN NOW ALMOST NONSTOP. IT'S LIKE THE ENTIRE COUNTRY IS EXPERIENCING SOME MASS DREAD.
COMBINING THAT WITH ALL OF YOURS AND PROFESSOR HALEY'S FINDINGS, IT'S SOMETHING BIG. IF WE COULD JUST PINPOINT THE SOURCE, WE'D KNOW WHAT WE'RE DEALING WITH.
THIS THING IS THE MOST POWERFUL CREATURE ON EARTH. WHEREVER IT IS, IT IS ALREADY HERE.
IT CAN'T BE AVOIDED.
IT MAY TAKE THE COMBINED EFFORTS OF ALL AMERICANS TO MEET THIS CHALLENGE.
IS YOUR GOVERNMENT.... ARE YOU... READY TO ACCEPT THAT?
IT IS YOUR MOVE, KING.

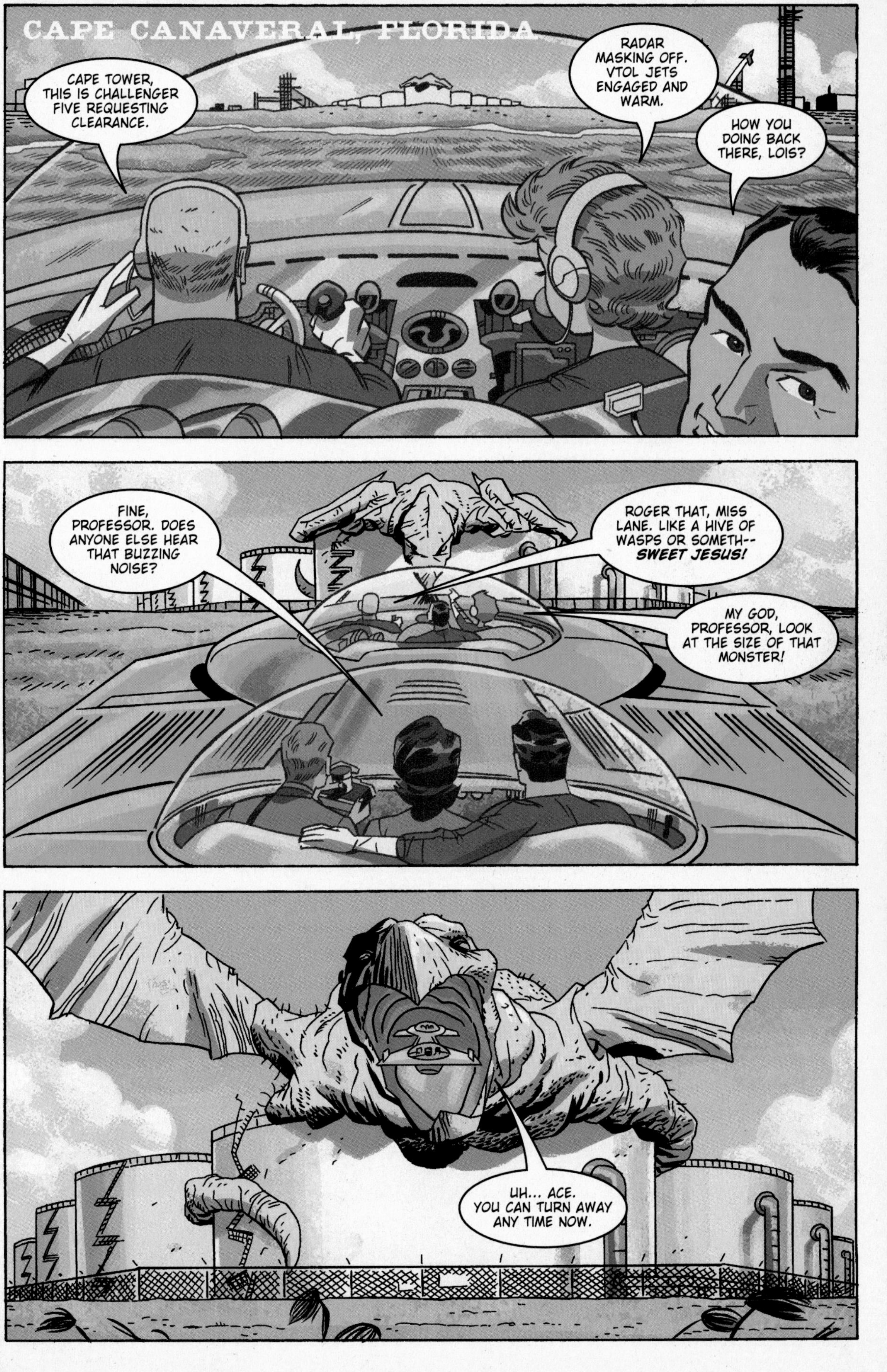
CAPE CANAVERAL, FLORIDA
CAPE TOWER, THIS IS CHALLENGER FIVE REQUESTING CLEARANCE.
RADAR MASKING OFF. VTOL JETS ENGAGED AND WARM.
HOW YOU DOING BACK THERE, LOIS?
FINE, PROFESSOR. DOES ANYONE ELSE HEAR THAT BUZZING NOISE?
ROGER THAT, MISS LANE. LIKE A HIVE OF WASPS OR SOMETH-- *SWEET JESUS!*
MY GOD, PROFESSOR, LOOK AT THE SIZE OF THAT MONSTER!
UH... ACE. YOU CAN TURN AWAY ANY TIME NOW.

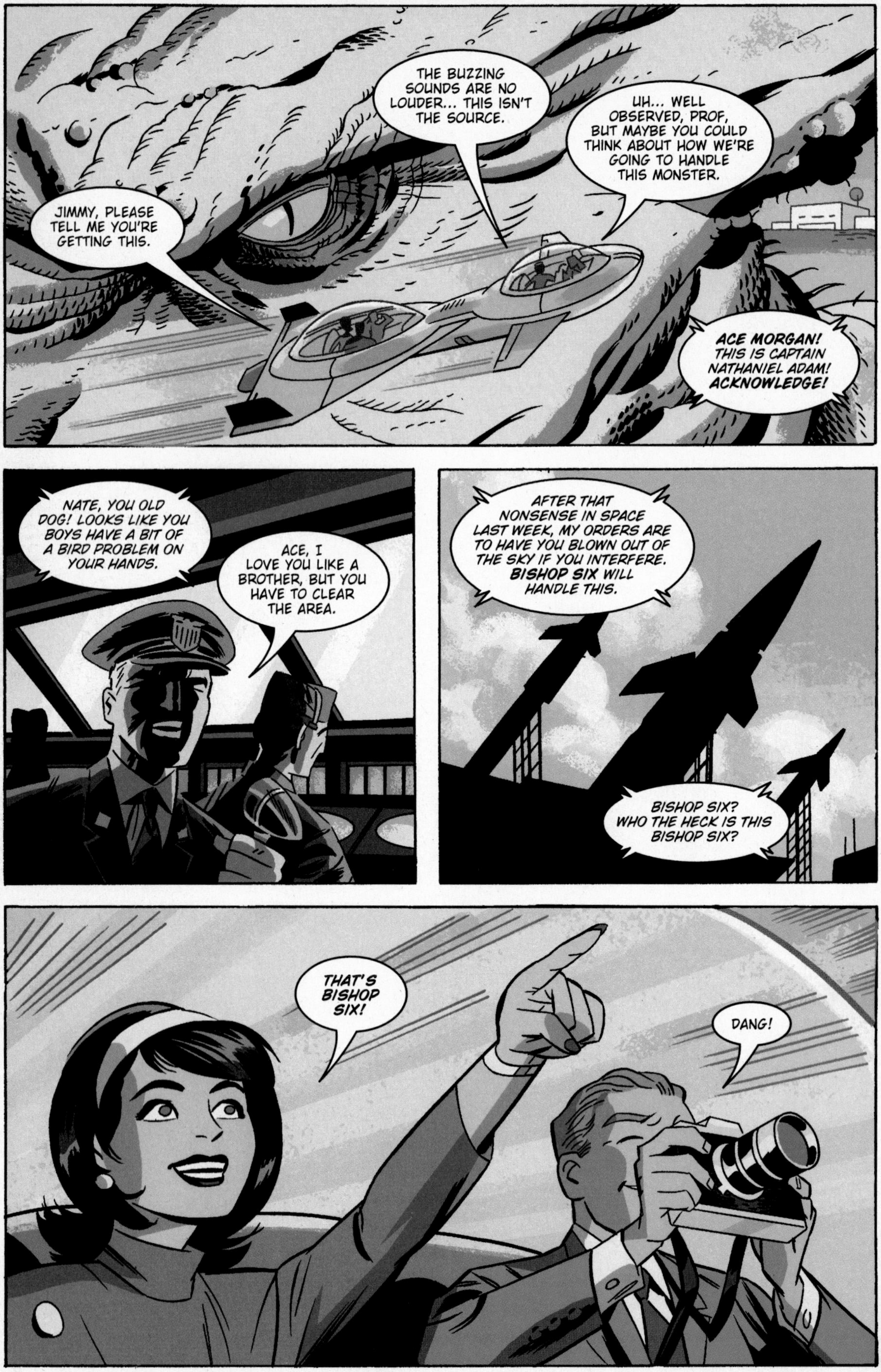
THE BUZZING SOUNDS ARE NO LOUDER... THIS ISN'T THE SOURCE.
UH... WELL OBSERVED, PROF, BUT MAYBE YOU COULD THINK ABOUT HOW WE'RE GOING TO HANDLE THIS MONSTER.
JIMMY, PLEASE TELL ME YOU'RE GETTING THIS.
ACE MORGAN! THIS IS CAPTAIN NATHANIEL ADAM! ACKNOWLEDGE!
NATE, YOU OLD DOG! LOOKS LIKE YOU BOYS HAVE A BIT OF A BIRD PROBLEM ON YOUR HANDS.
ACE, I LOVE YOU LIKE A BROTHER, BUT YOU HAVE TO CLEAR THE AREA.
AFTER THAT NONSENSE IN SPACE LAST WEEK, MY ORDERS ARE TO HAVE YOU BLOWN OUT OF THE SKY IF YOU INTERFERE. BISHOP SIX WILL HANDLE THIS.
BISHOP SIX? WHO THE HECK IS THIS BISHOP SIX?
THAT'S BISHOP SIX!
DANG!

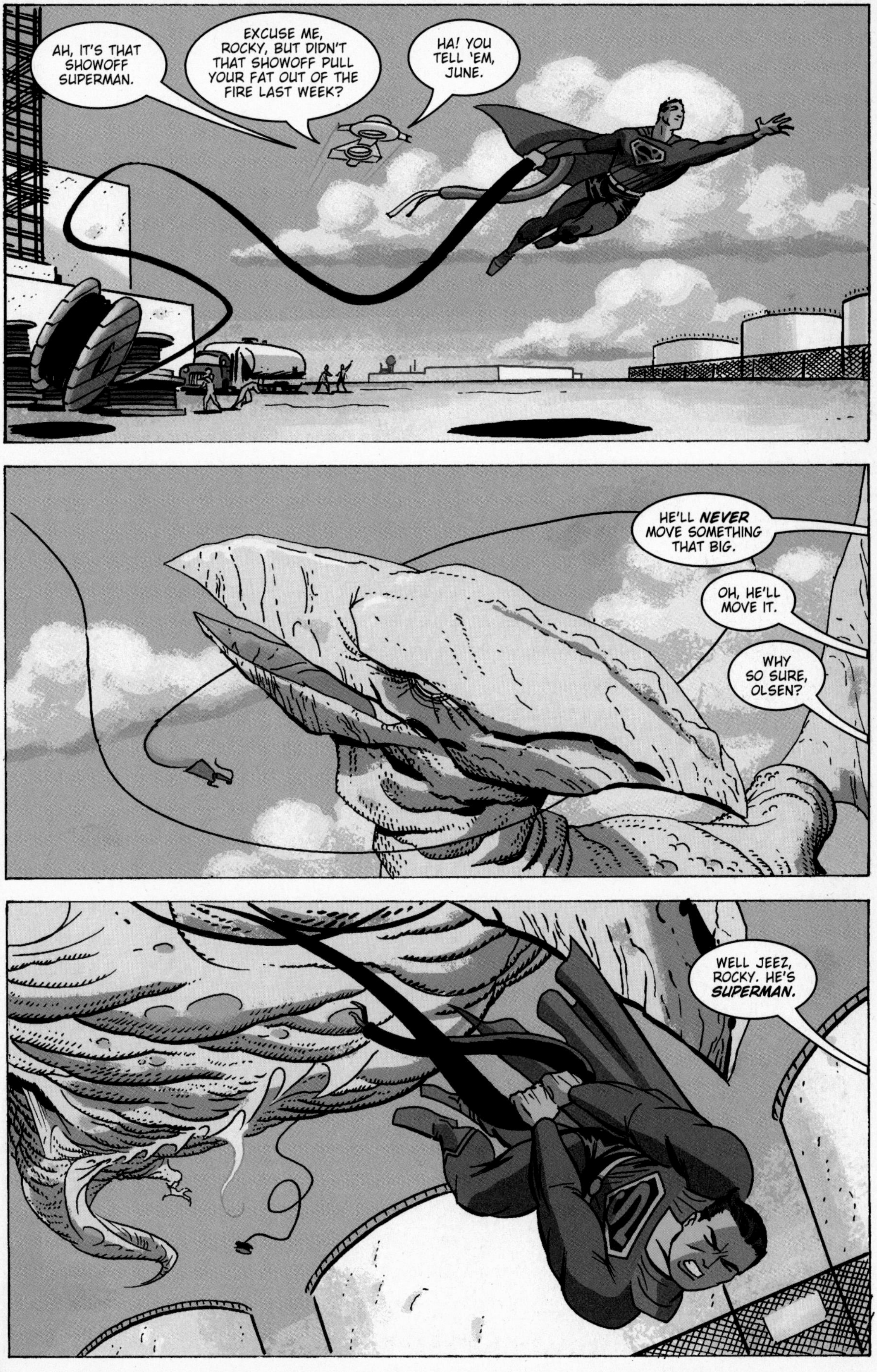
AH, IT'S THAT SHOWOFF SUPERMAN.
EXCUSE ME, ROCKY, BUT DIDN'T THAT SHOWOFF PULL YOUR FAT OUT OF THE FIRE LAST WEEK?
HA! YOU TELL 'EM, JUNE.
HE'LL *NEVER* MOVE SOMETHING THAT BIG.
OH, HE'LL MOVE IT.
WHY SO SURE, OLSEN?
WELL JEEZ, ROCKY. HE'S *SUPERMAN.*

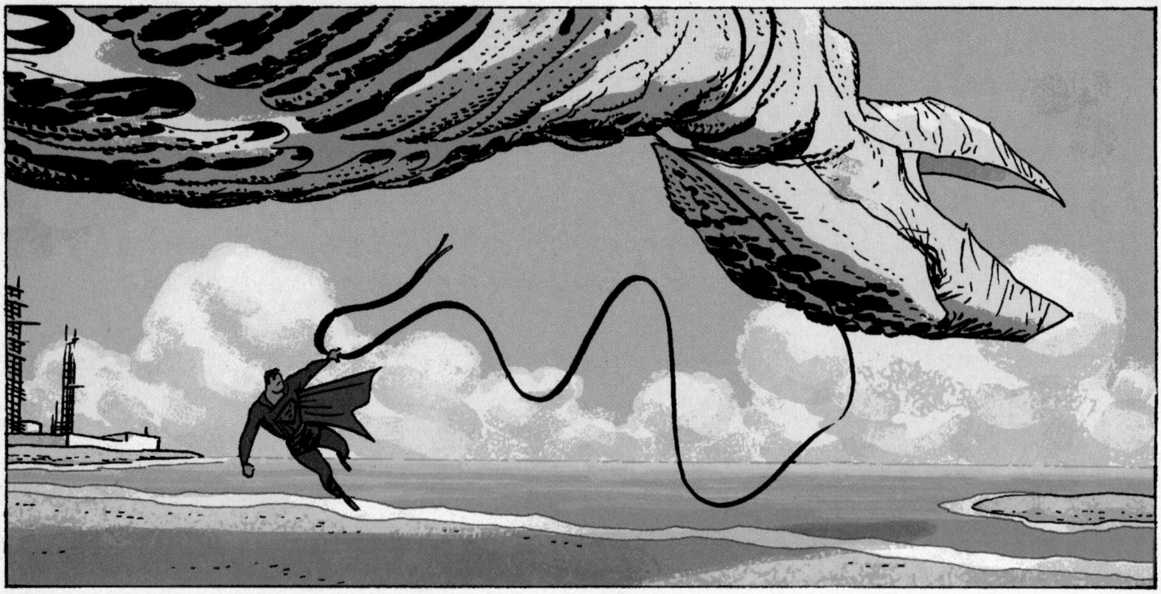

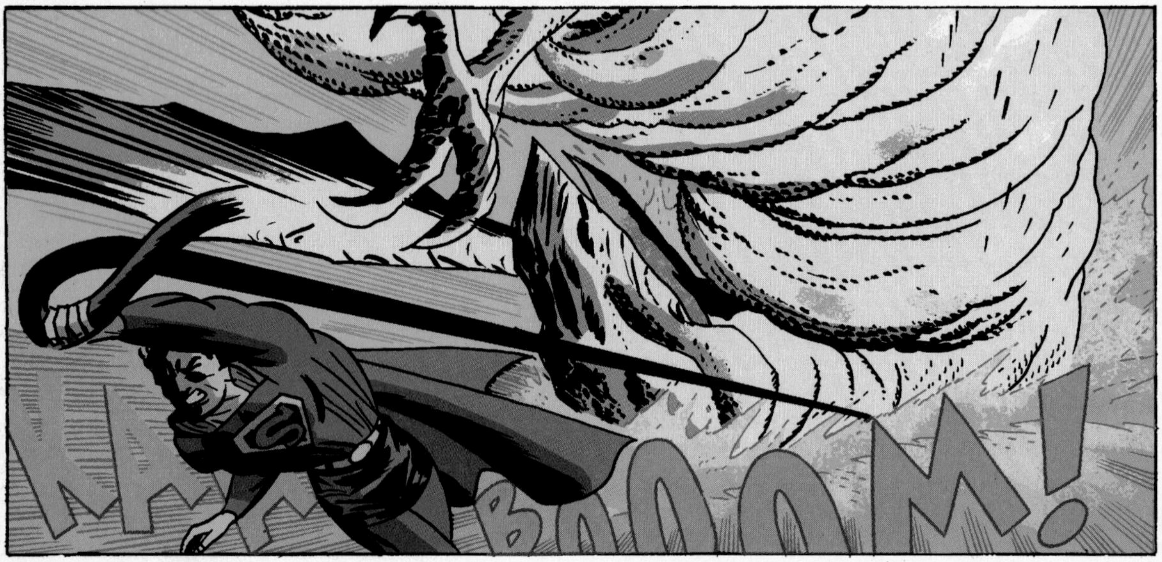
BOOOM!

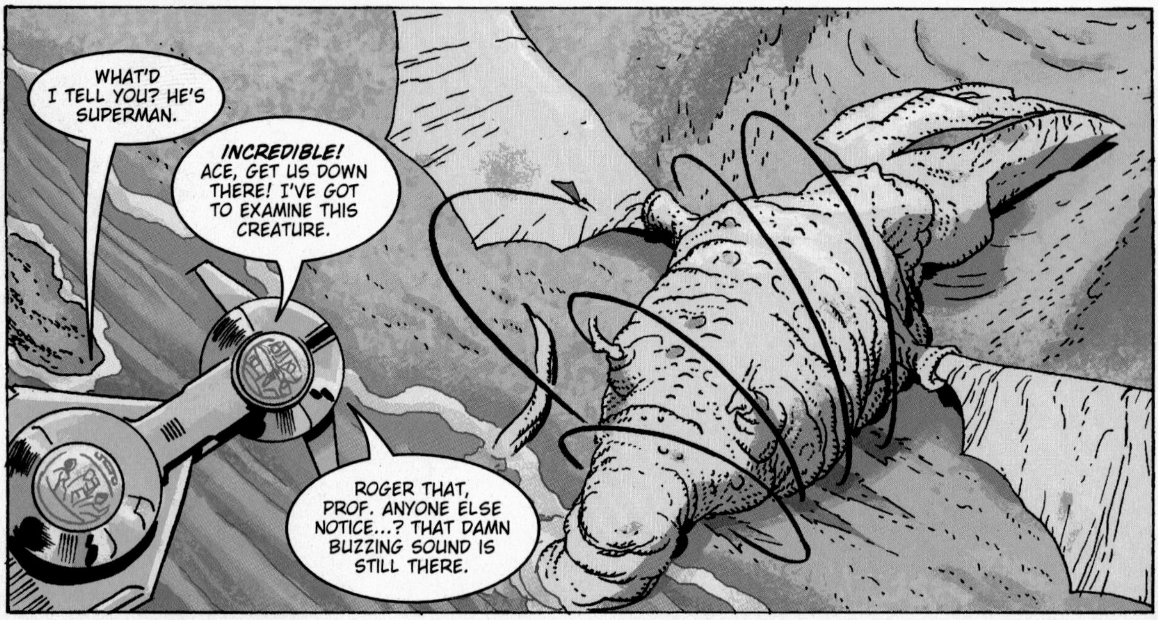
WHAT'D I TELL YOU? HE'S SUPERMAN.
INCREDIBLE! ACE, GET US DOWN THERE! I'VE GOT TO EXAMINE THIS CREATURE.
ROGER THAT, PROF. ANYONE ELSE NOTICE...? THAT DAMN BUZZING SOUND IS STILL THERE.

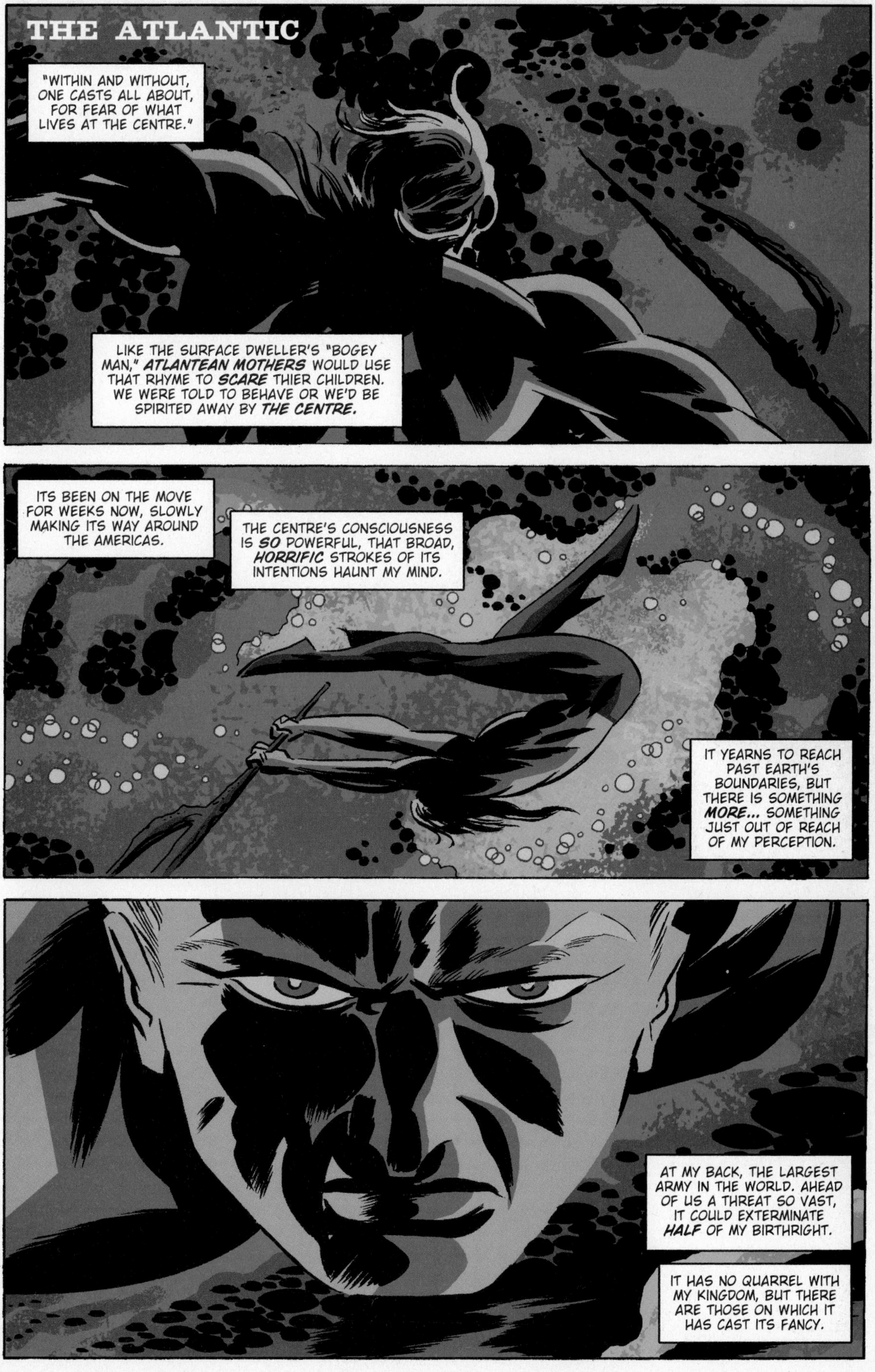
THE ATLANTIC
"WITHIN AND WITHOUT, ONE CASTS ALL ABOUT, FOR FEAR OF WHAT LIVES AT THE CENTRE."
LIKE THE SURFACE DWELLER'S "BOGEY MAN," ATLANTEAN MOTHERS WOULD USE THAT RHYME TO SCARE THIER CHILDREN. WE WERE TOLD TO BEHAVE OR WE'D BE SPIRITED AWAY BY THE CENTRE.
ITS BEEN ON THE MOVE FOR WEEKS NOW, SLOWLY MAKING ITS WAY AROUND THE AMERICAS.
THE CENTRE'S CONSCIOUSNESS IS SO POWERFUL, THAT BROAD, HORRIFIC STROKES OF ITS INTENTIONS HAUNT MY MIND.
IT YEARNS TO REACH PAST EARTH'S BOUNDARIES, BUT THERE IS SOMETHING MORE... SOMETHING JUST OUT OF REACH OF MY PERCEPTION.
AT MY BACK, THE LARGEST ARMY IN THE WORLD. AHEAD OF US A THREAT SO VAST, IT COULD EXTERMINATE HALF OF MY BIRTHRIGHT.
IT HAS NO QUARREL WITH MY KINGDOM, BUT THERE ARE THOSE ON WHICH IT HAS CAST ITS FANCY.

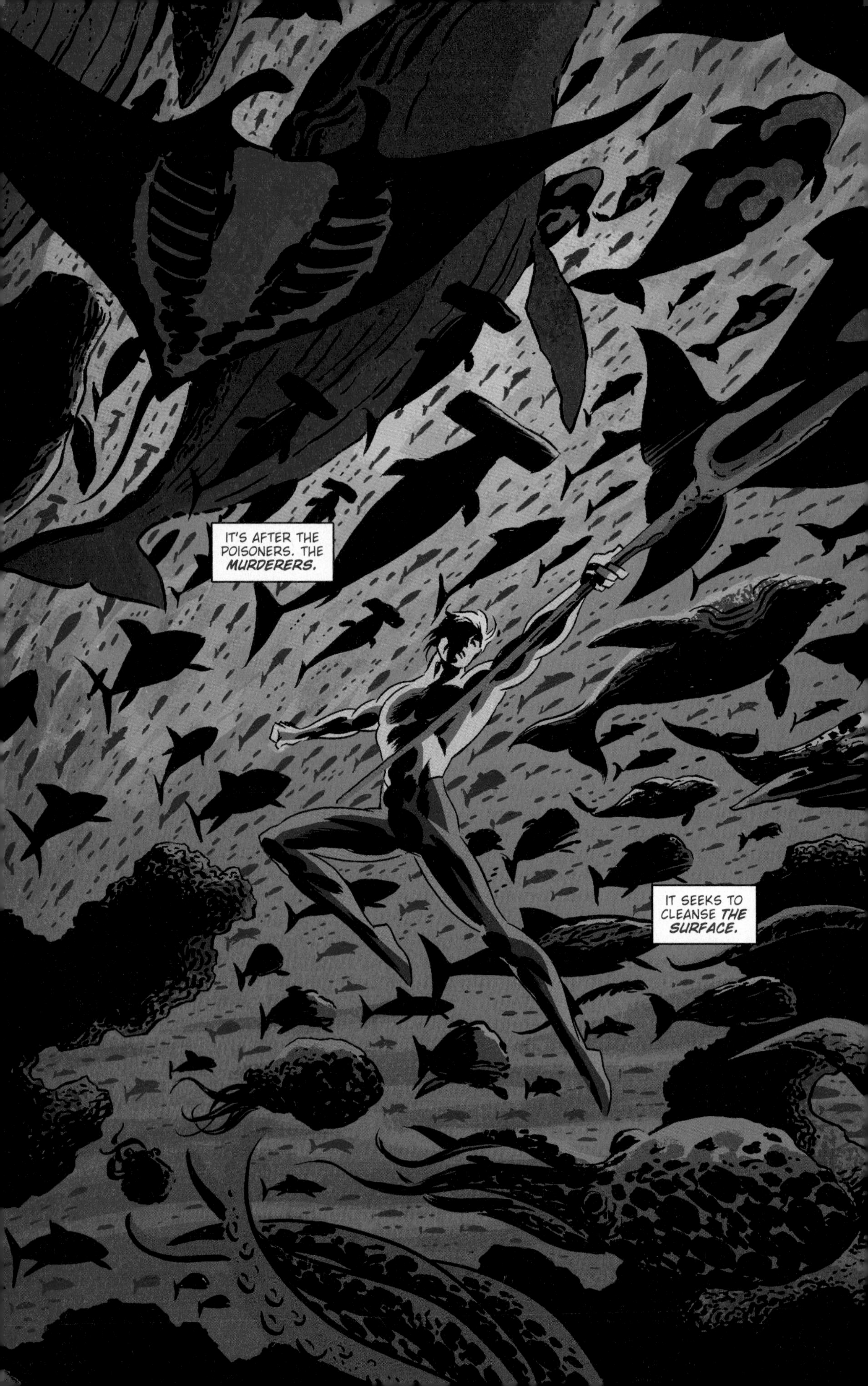
IT'S AFTER THE POISONERS. THE *MURDERERS.*
IT SEEKS TO CLEANSE *THE SURFACE.*

CHAPTER TWELVE
THE WAR THAT TIME FORGOT

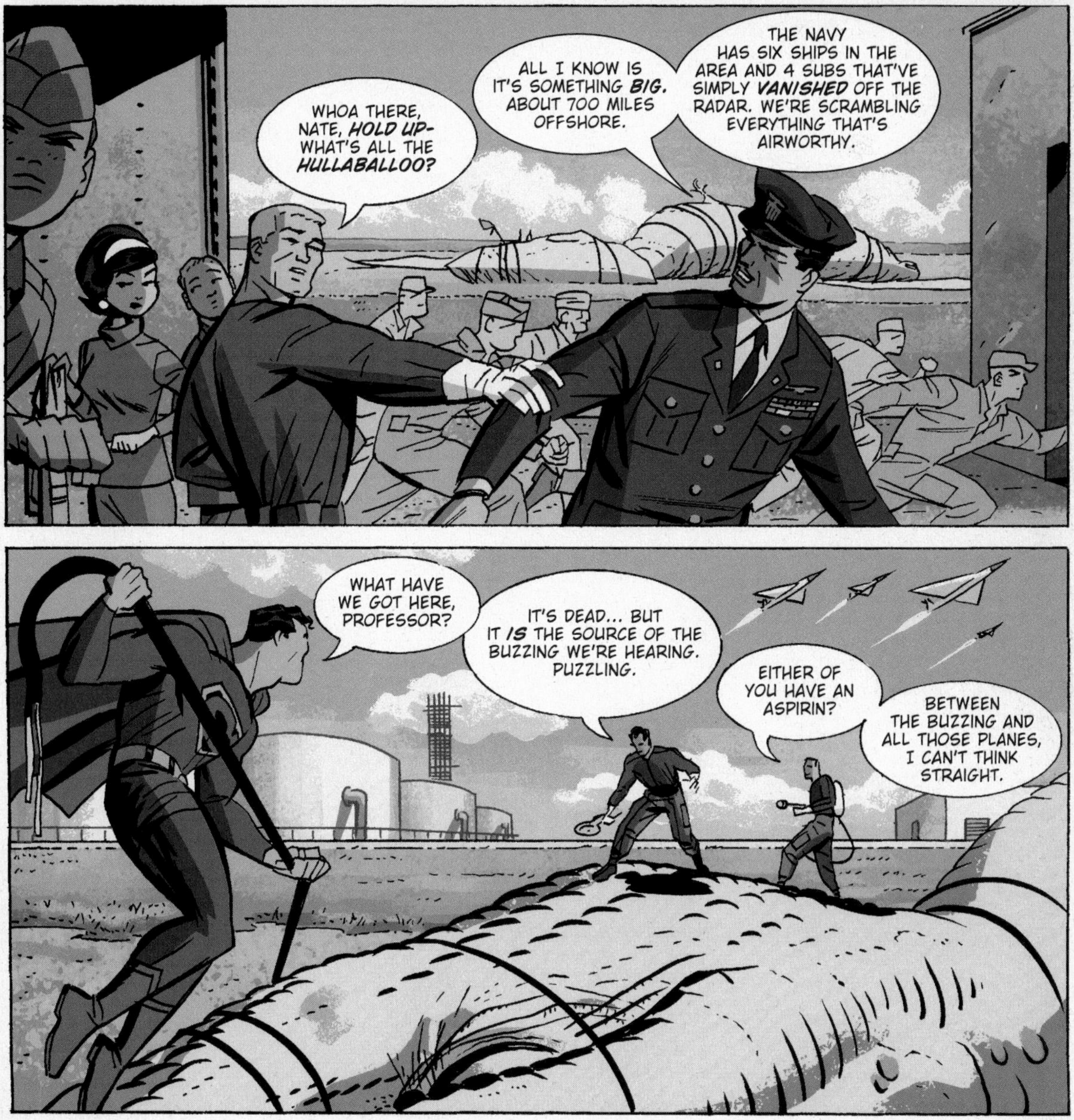

WHOA THERE, NATE, *HOLD UP*- WHAT'S ALL THE *HULLABALLOO?*
ALL I KNOW IS IT'S SOMETHING *BIG.* ABOUT 700 MILES OFFSHORE.
THE NAVY HAS SIX SHIPS IN THE AREA AND 4 SUBS THAT'VE SIMPLY *VANISHED* OFF THE RADAR. WE'RE SCRAMBLING EVERYTHING THAT'S AIRWORTHY.
WHAT HAVE WE GOT HERE, PROFESSOR?
IT'S DEAD... BUT IT *IS* THE SOURCE OF THE BUZZING WE'RE HEARING. PUZZLING.
EITHER OF YOU HAVE AN ASPIRIN?
BETWEEN THE BUZZING AND ALL THOSE PLANES, I CAN'T THINK STRAIGHT.

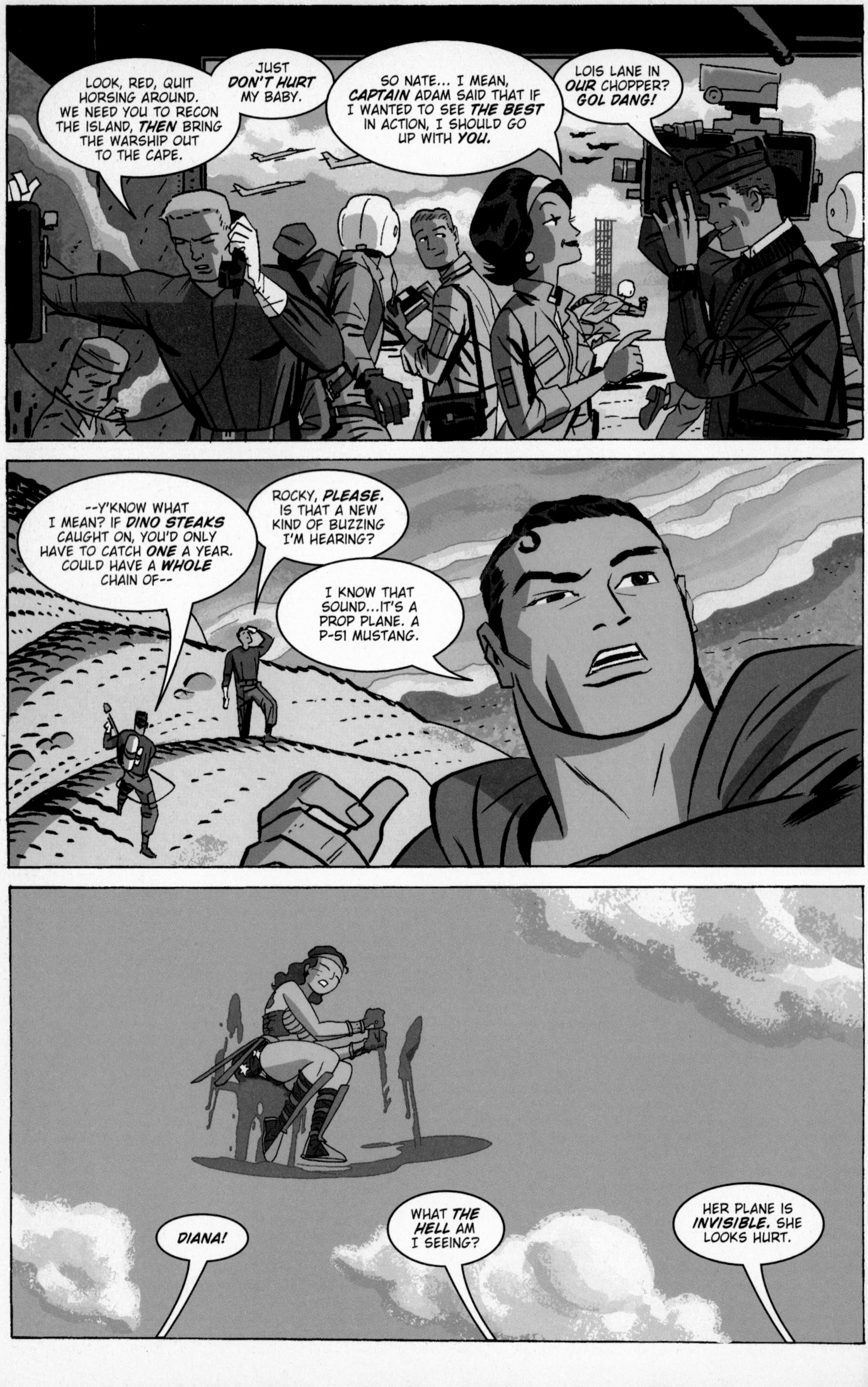
LOOK, RED, QUIT HORSING AROUND. WE NEED YOU TO RECON THE ISLAND, THEN BRING THE WARSHIP OUT TO THE CAPE.
JUST DON'T HURT MY BABY.
SO NATE... I MEAN, CAPTAIN ADAM SAID THAT IF I WANTED TO SEE THE BEST IN ACTION, I SHOULD GO UP WITH YOU.
LOIS LANE IN OUR CHOPPER? GOL DANG!
--Y'KNOW WHAT I MEAN? IF DINO STEAKS CAUGHT ON, YOU'D ONLY HAVE TO CATCH ONE A YEAR. COULD HAVE A WHOLE CHAIN OF--
ROCKY, PLEASE. IS THAT A NEW KIND OF BUZZING I'M HEARING?
I KNOW THAT SOUND...IT'S A PROP PLANE. A P-51 MUSTANG.
DIANA!
WHAT THE HELL AM I SEEING?
HER PLANE IS INVISIBLE. SHE LOOKS HURT.

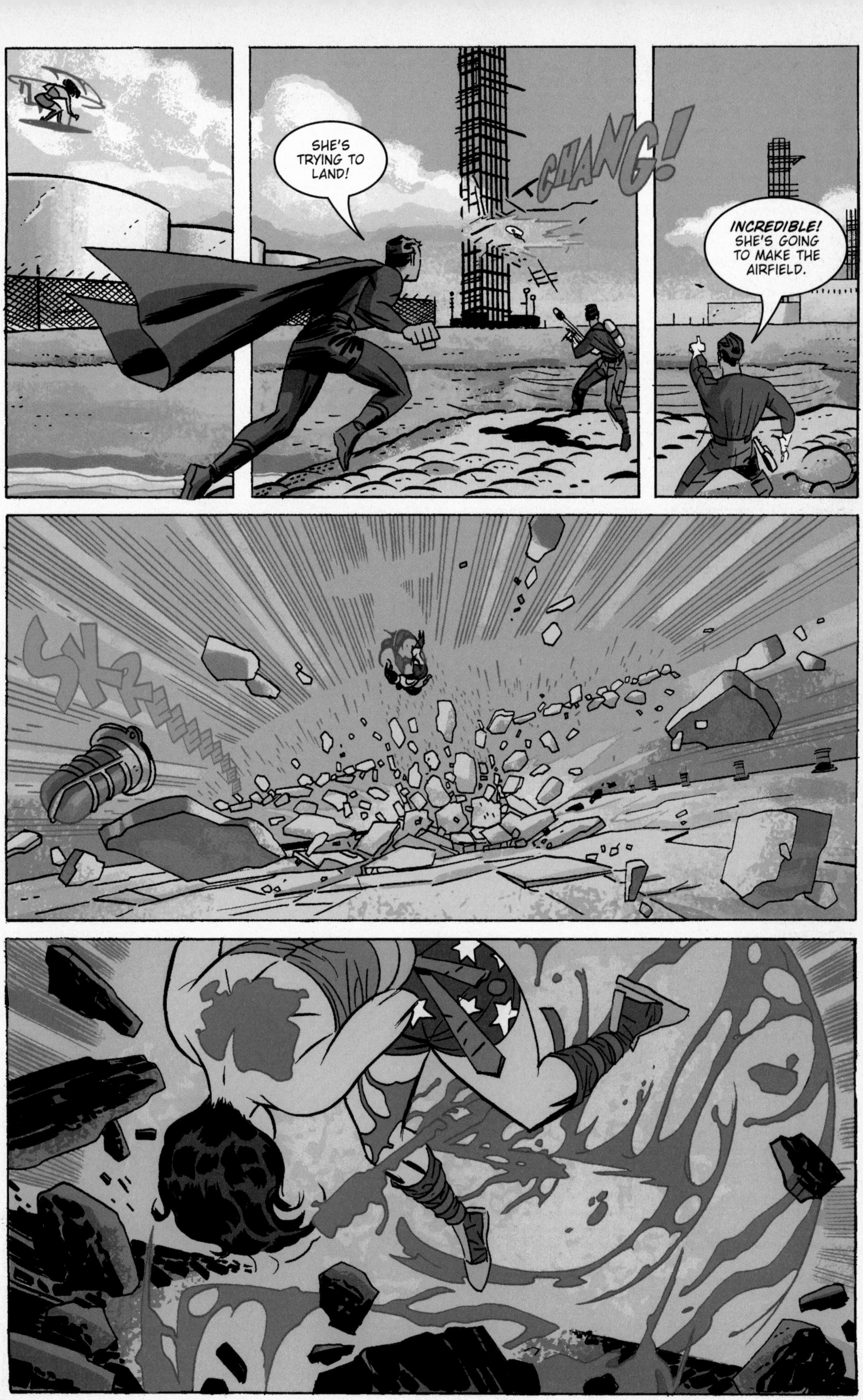
SHE'S TRYING TO LAND!
CHANG!
INCREDIBLE! SHE'S GOING TO MAKE THE AIRFIELD.
SKREEEEEEE

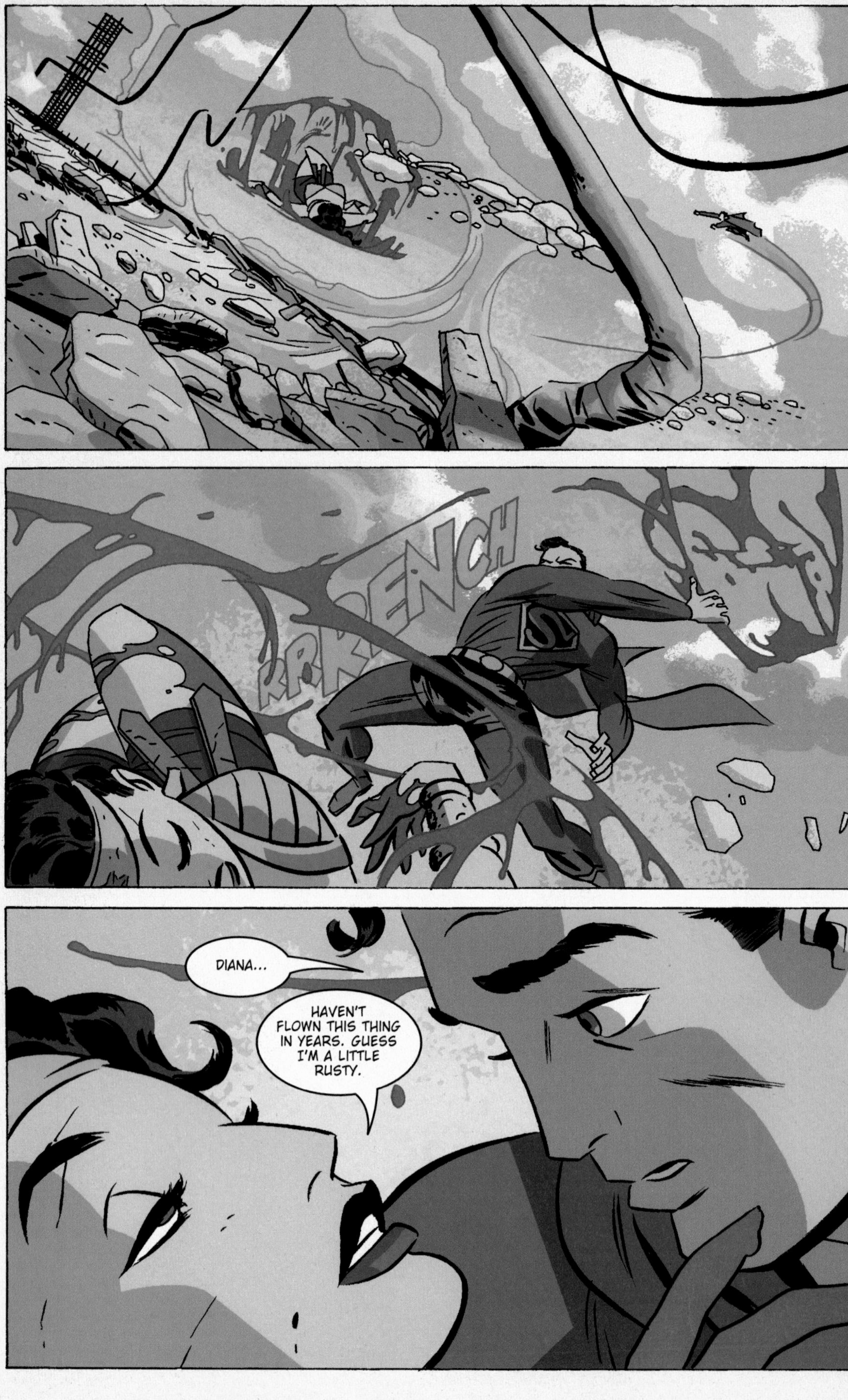

KRRRENCH
DIANA...
HAVEN'T FLOWN THIS THING IN YEARS. GUESS I'M A LITTLE RUSTY.

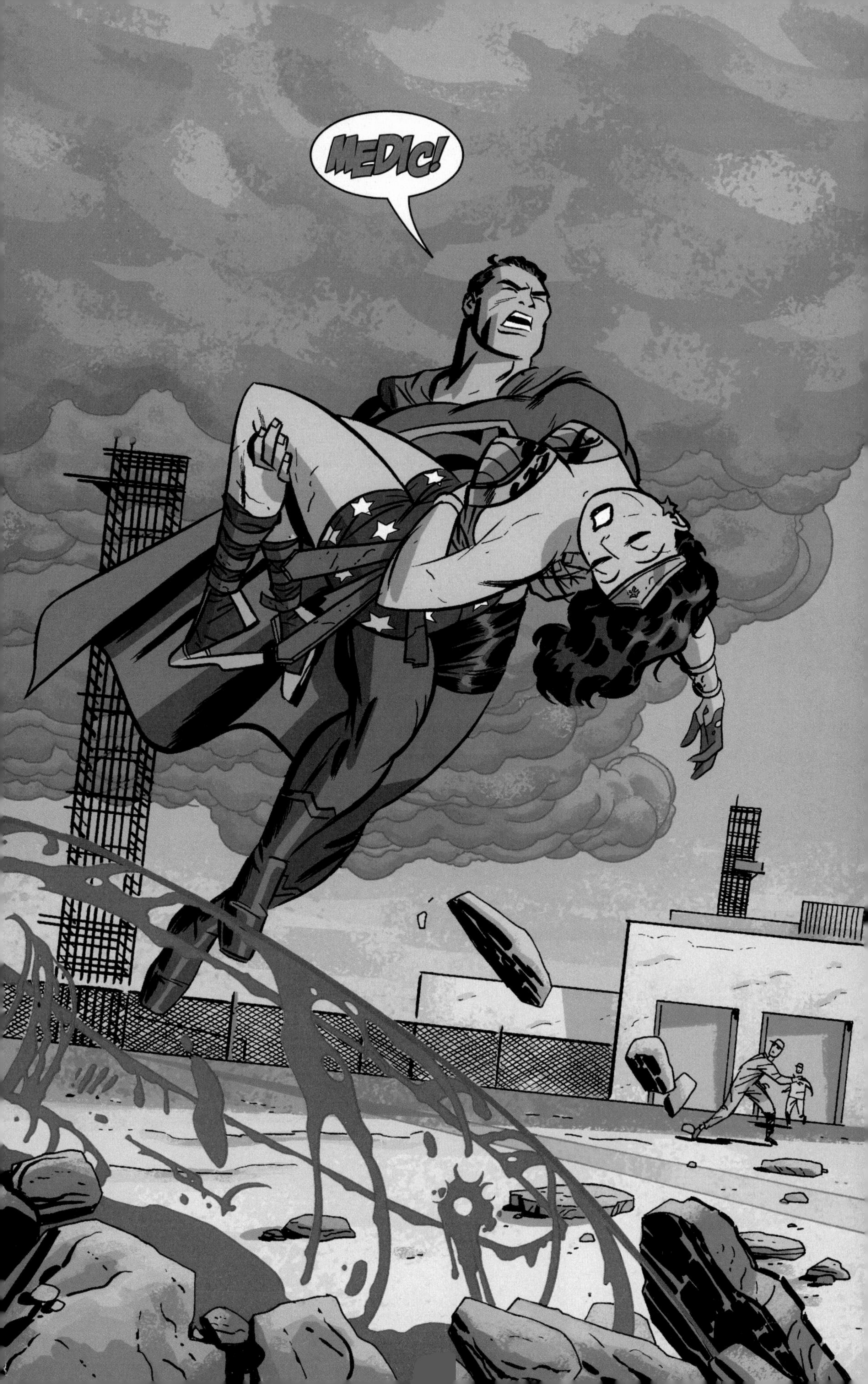
MEDIC!

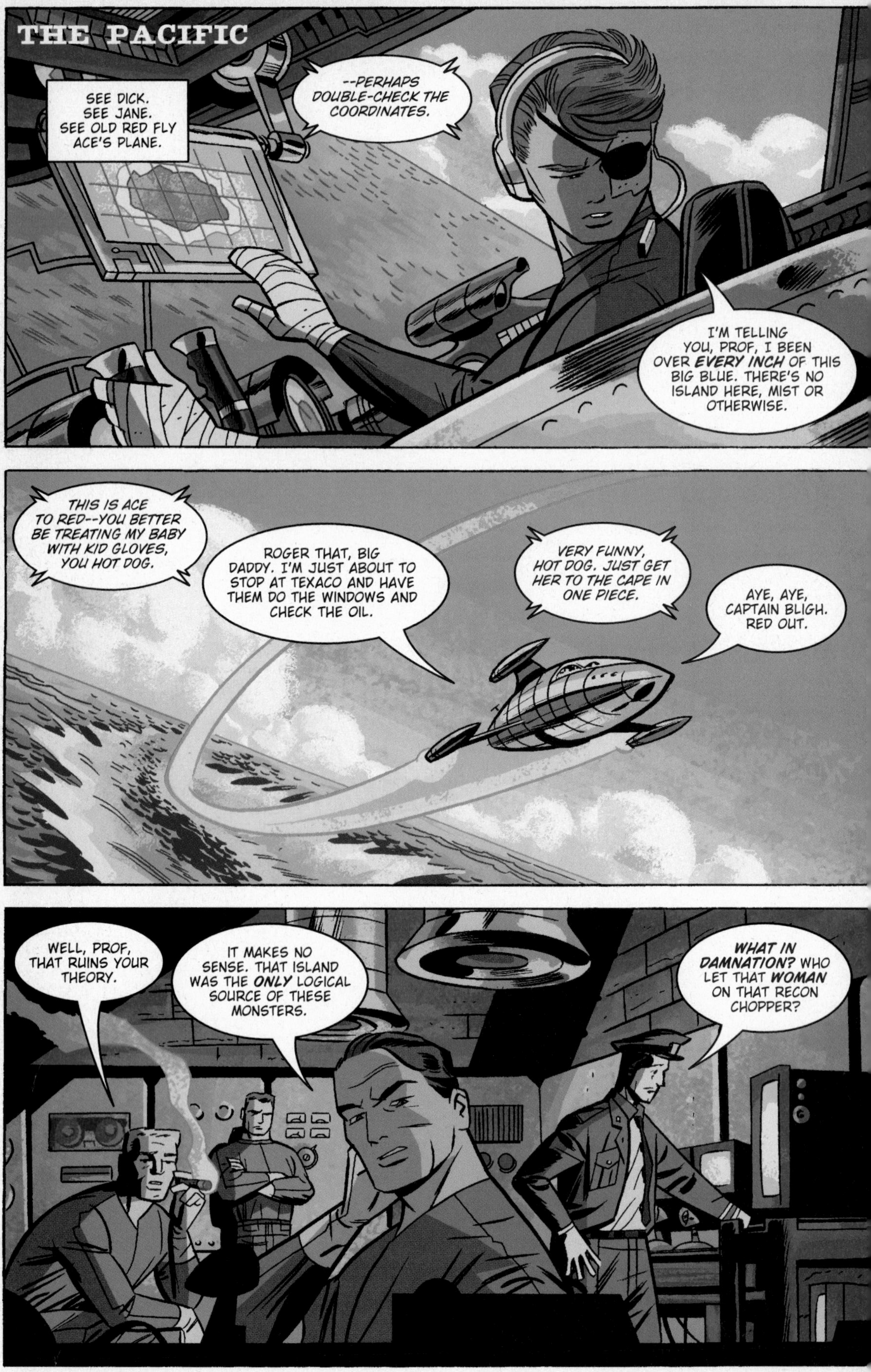
THE PACIFIC
SEE DICK. SEE JANE. SEE OLD RED FLY ACE'S PLANE.
--PERHAPS DOUBLE-CHECK THE COORDINATES.
I'M TELLING YOU, PROF, I BEEN OVER EVERY INCH OF THIS BIG BLUE. THERE'S NO ISLAND HERE, MIST OR OTHERWISE.
THIS IS ACE TO RED--YOU BETTER BE TREATING MY BABY WITH KID GLOVES, YOU HOT DOG.
ROGER THAT, BIG DADDY. I'M JUST ABOUT TO STOP AT TEXACO AND HAVE THEM DO THE WINDOWS AND CHECK THE OIL.
VERY FUNNY, HOT DOG. JUST GET HER TO THE CAPE IN ONE PIECE.
AYE, AYE, CAPTAIN BLIGH. RED OUT.
WELL, PROF, THAT RUINS YOUR THEORY.
IT MAKES NO SENSE. THAT ISLAND WAS THE ONLY LOGICAL SOURCE OF THESE MONSTERS.
WHAT IN DAMNATION? WHO LET THAT WOMAN ON THAT RECON CHOPPER?

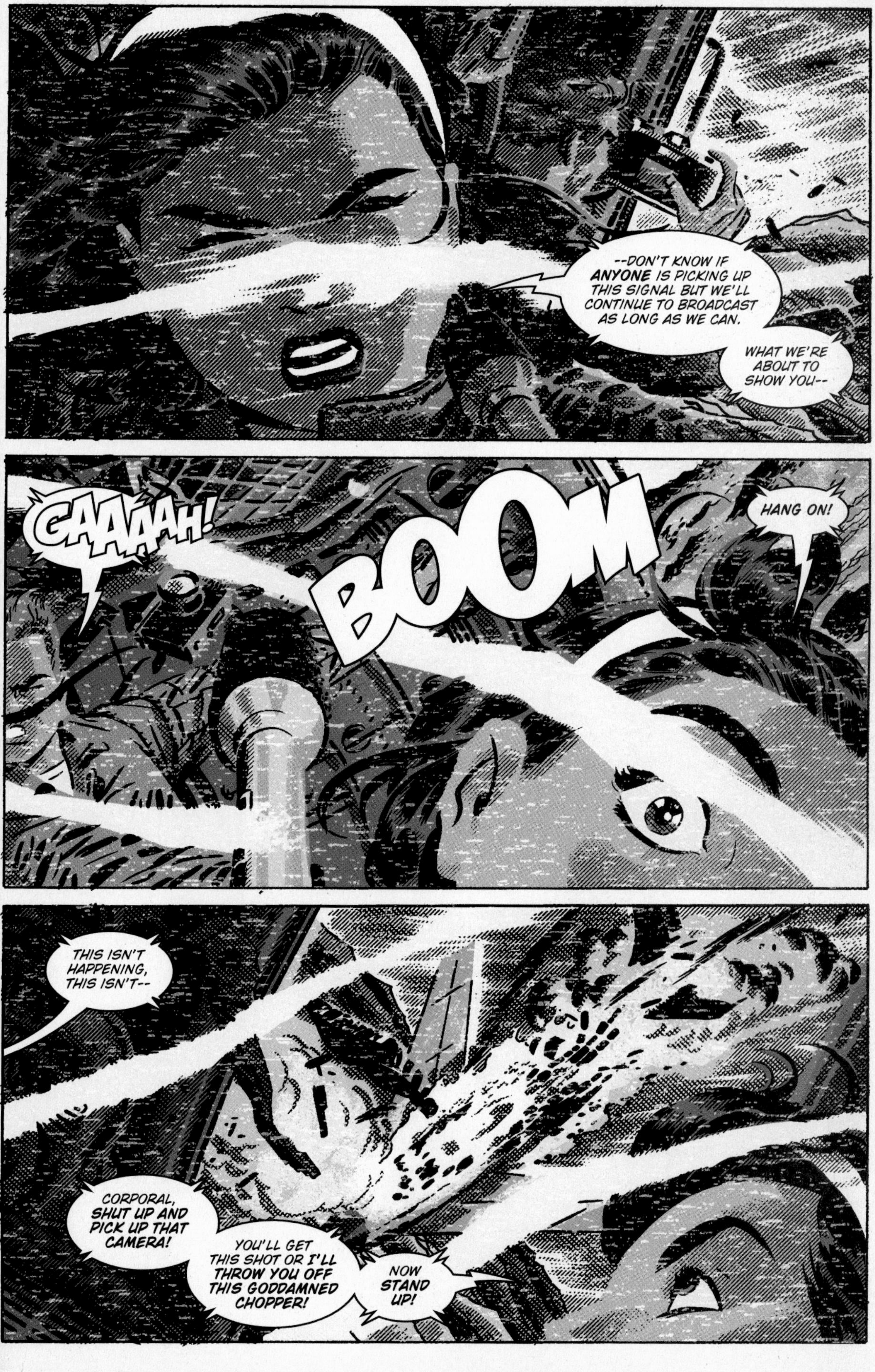
--DON'T KNOW IF ANYONE IS PICKING UP THIS SIGNAL BUT WE'LL CONTINUE TO BROADCAST AS LONG AS WE CAN.
WHAT WE'RE ABOUT TO SHOW YOU--
GAAAAH!
BOOM
HANG ON!
THIS ISN'T HAPPENING, THIS ISN'T--
CORPORAL, SHUT UP AND PICK UP THAT CAMERA!
YOU'LL GET THIS SHOT OR I'LL THROW YOU OFF THIS GODDAMNED CHOPPER!
NOW STAND UP!

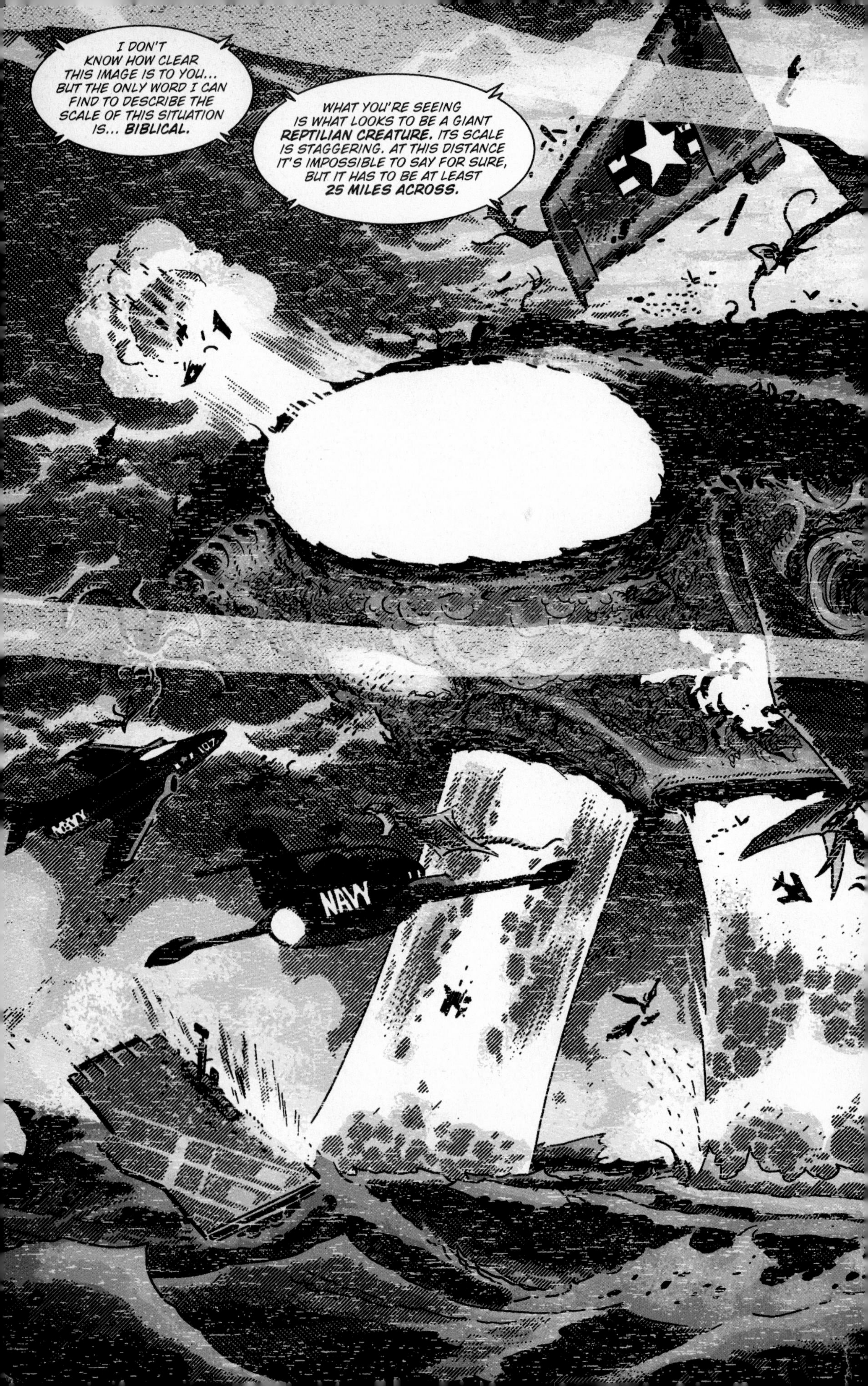
I DON'T KNOW HOW CLEAR THIS IMAGE IS TO YOU... BUT THE ONLY WORD I CAN FIND TO DESCRIBE THE SCALE OF THIS SITUATION IS... BIBLICAL.
WHAT YOU'RE SEEING IS WHAT LOOKS TO BE A GIANT REPTILIAN CREATURE. ITS SCALE IS STAGGERING. AT THIS DISTANCE IT'S IMPOSSIBLE TO SAY FOR SURE, BUT IT HAS TO BE AT LEAST 25 MILES ACROSS.
107
NAVY
NAVY

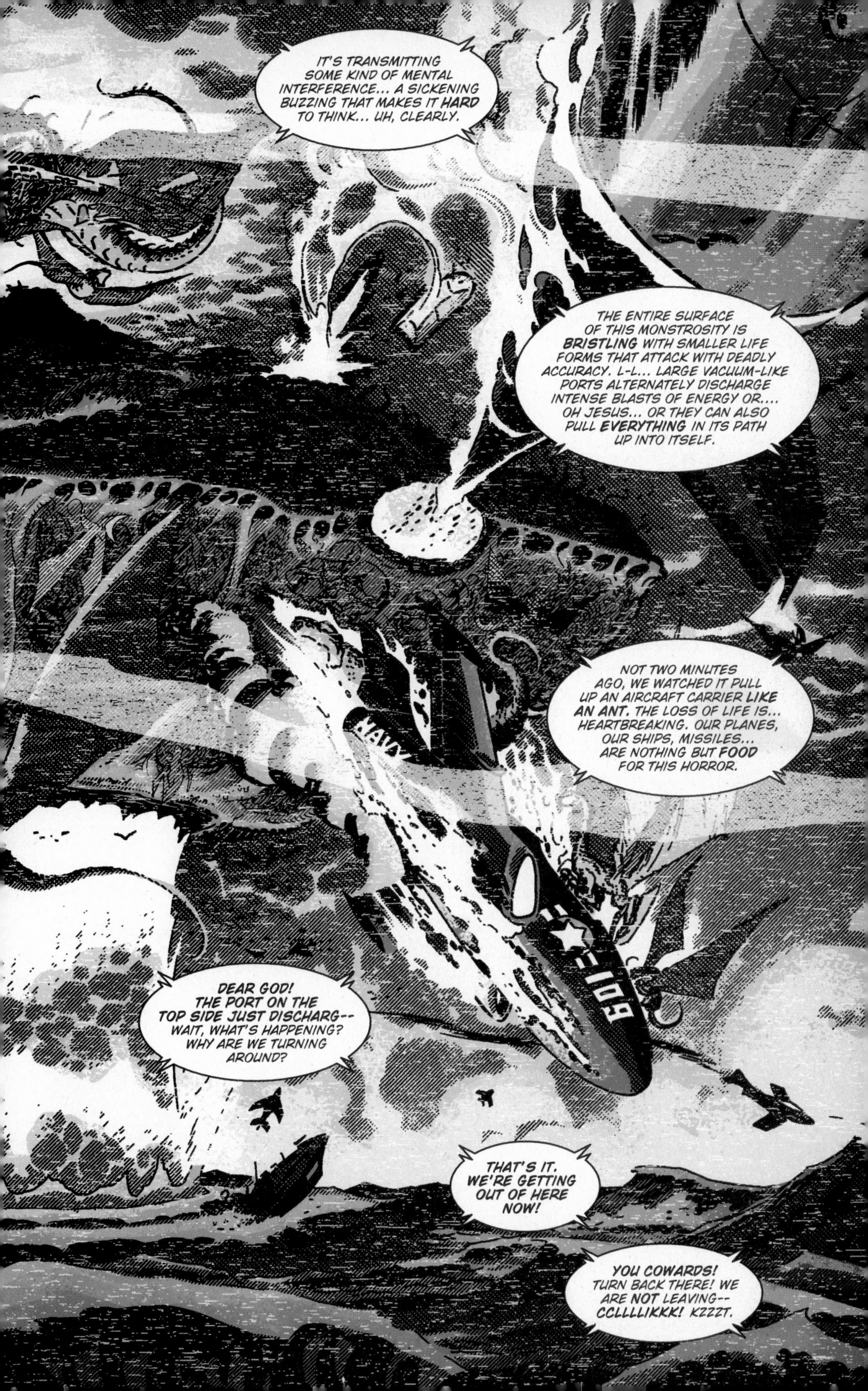
IT'S TRANSMITTING SOME KIND OF MENTAL INTERFERENCE... A SICKENING BUZZING THAT MAKES IT HARD TO THINK... UH, CLEARLY.
THE ENTIRE SURFACE OF THIS MONSTROSITY IS BRISTLING WITH SMALLER LIFE FORMS THAT ATTACK WITH DEADLY ACCURACY. L-L... LARGE VACUUM-LIKE PORTS ALTERNATELY DISCHARGE INTENSE BLASTS OF ENERGY OR.... OH JESUS... OR THEY CAN ALSO PULL EVERYTHING IN ITS PATH UP INTO ITSELF.
NOT TWO MINUTES AGO, WE WATCHED IT PULL UP AN AIRCRAFT CARRIER LIKE AN ANT. THE LOSS OF LIFE IS... HEARTBREAKING. OUR PLANES, OUR SHIPS, MISSILES... ARE NOTHING BUT FOOD FOR THIS HORROR.
NAVY
DEAR GOD! THE PORT ON THE TOP SIDE JUST DISCHARG-- WAIT, WHAT'S HAPPENING? WHY ARE WE TURNING AROUND?
THAT'S IT. WE'RE GETTING OUT OF HERE NOW!
YOU COWARDS! TURN BACK THERE! WE ARE NOT LEAVING-- CCLLLLIKKK! KZZZT.

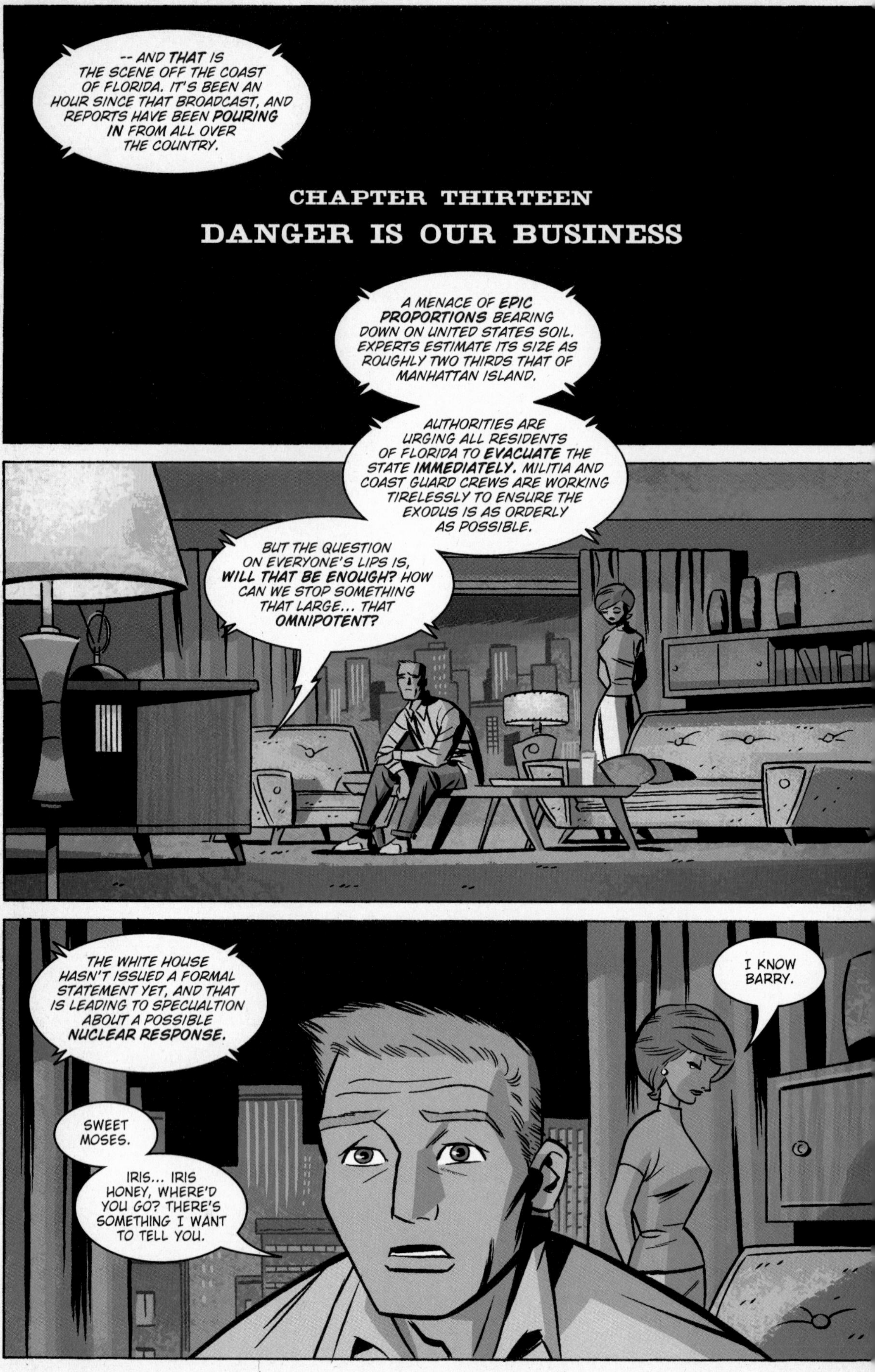
-- AND THAT IS THE SCENE OFF THE COAST OF FLORIDA. IT'S BEEN AN HOUR SINCE THAT BROADCAST, AND REPORTS HAVE BEEN POURING IN FROM ALL OVER THE COUNTRY.
CHAPTER THIRTEEN
DANGER IS OUR BUSINESS
A MENACE OF EPIC PROPORTIONS BEARING DOWN ON UNITED STATES SOIL. EXPERTS ESTIMATE ITS SIZE AS ROUGHLY TWO THIRDS THAT OF MANHATTAN ISLAND.
AUTHORITIES ARE URGING ALL RESIDENTS OF FLORIDA TO EVACUATE THE STATE IMMEDIATELY. MILITIA AND COAST GUARD CREWS ARE WORKING TIRELESSLY TO ENSURE THE EXODUS IS AS ORDERLY AS POSSIBLE.
BUT THE QUESTION ON EVERYONE'S LIPS IS, WILL THAT BE ENOUGH? HOW CAN WE STOP SOMETHING THAT LARGE... THAT OMNIPOTENT?
THE WHITE HOUSE HASN'T ISSUED A FORMAL STATEMENT YET, AND THAT IS LEADING TO SPECUALTION ABOUT A POSSIBLE NUCLEAR RESPONSE.
SWEET MOSES.
IRIS... IRIS HONEY, WHERE'D YOU GO? THERE'S SOMETHING I WANT TO TELL YOU.
I KNOW BARRY.

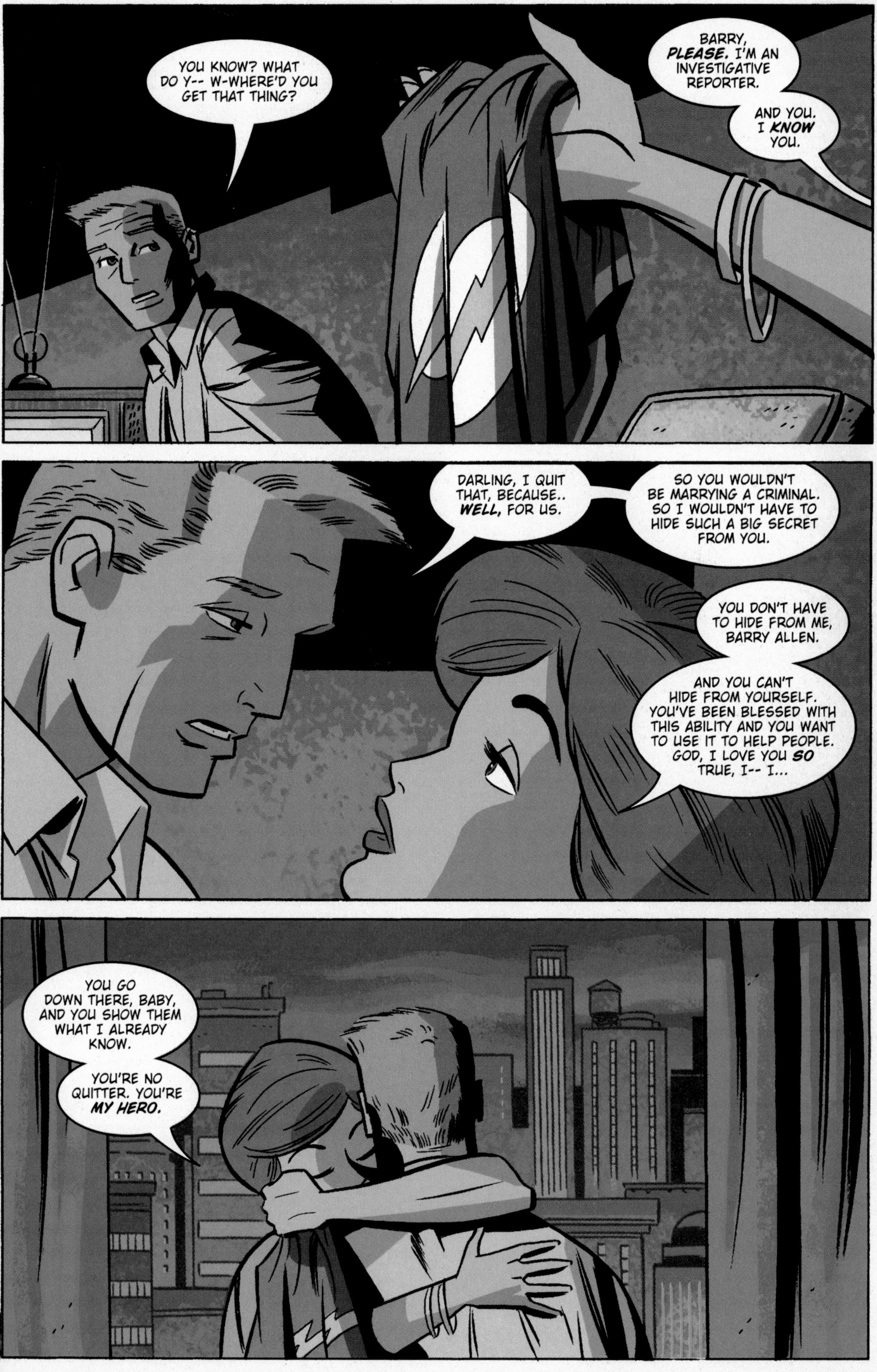
YOU KNOW? WHAT DO Y-- W-WHERE'D YOU GET THAT THING?
BARRY, **PLEASE.** I'M AN INVESTIGATIVE REPORTER.
AND YOU. I **KNOW** YOU.
DARLING, I QUIT THAT, BECAUSE.. **WELL,** FOR US.
SO YOU WOULDN'T BE MARRYING A CRIMINAL. SO I WOULDN'T HAVE TO HIDE SUCH A BIG SECRET FROM YOU.
YOU DON'T HAVE TO HIDE FROM ME, BARRY ALLEN.
AND YOU CAN'T HIDE FROM YOURSELF. YOU'VE BEEN BLESSED WITH THIS ABILITY AND YOU WANT TO USE IT TO HELP PEOPLE. GOD, I LOVE YOU **SO** TRUE, I-- I...
YOU GO DOWN THERE, BABY, AND YOU SHOW THEM WHAT I ALREADY KNOW.
YOU'RE NO QUITTER. YOU'RE **MY HERO.**

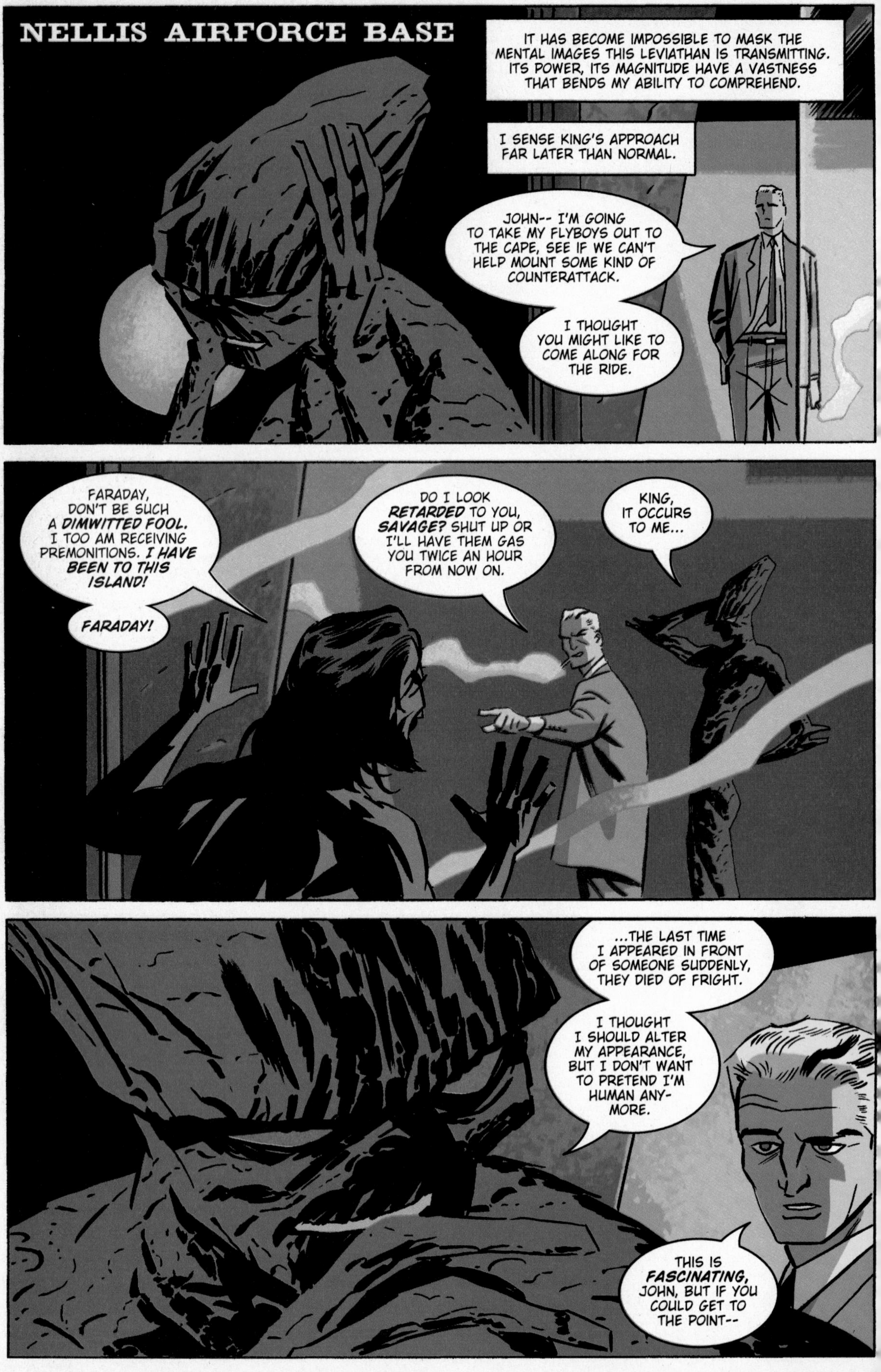
NELLIS AIRFORCE BASE
IT HAS BECOME IMPOSSIBLE TO MASK THE MENTAL IMAGES THIS LEVIATHAN IS TRANSMITTING. ITS POWER, ITS MAGNITUDE HAVE A VASTNESS THAT BENDS MY ABILITY TO COMPREHEND.
I SENSE KING'S APPROACH FAR LATER THAN NORMAL.
JOHN-- I'M GOING TO TAKE MY FLYBOYS OUT TO THE CAPE, SEE IF WE CAN'T HELP MOUNT SOME KIND OF COUNTERATTACK.
I THOUGHT YOU MIGHT LIKE TO COME ALONG FOR THE RIDE.
FARADAY, DON'T BE SUCH A ***DIMWITTED FOOL.*** I TOO AM RECEIVING PREMONITIONS. ***I HAVE BEEN TO THIS ISLAND!***
FARADAY!
DO I LOOK ***RETARDED*** TO YOU, ***SAVAGE?*** SHUT UP OR I'LL HAVE THEM GAS YOU TWICE AN HOUR FROM NOW ON.
KING, IT OCCURS TO ME...
...THE LAST TIME I APPEARED IN FRONT OF SOMEONE SUDDENLY, THEY DIED OF FRIGHT.
I THOUGHT I SHOULD ALTER MY APPEARANCE, BUT I DON'T WANT TO PRETEND I'M HUMAN ANYMORE.
THIS IS ***FASCINATING,*** JOHN, BUT IF YOU COULD GET TO THE POINT--

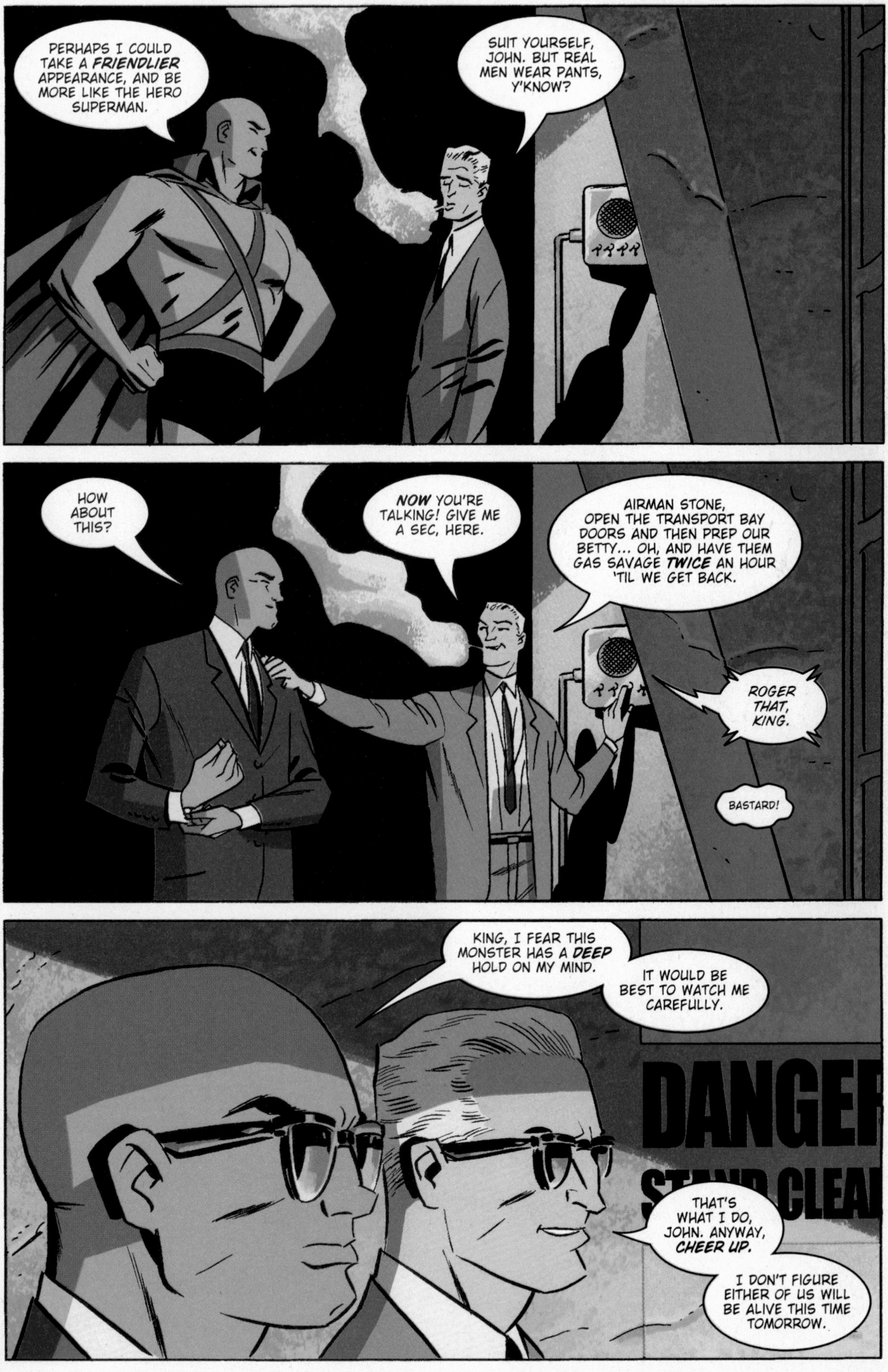
PERHAPS I COULD TAKE A **FRIENDLIER** APPEARANCE, AND BE MORE LIKE THE HERO SUPERMAN.
SUIT YOURSELF, JOHN. BUT REAL MEN WEAR PANTS, Y'KNOW?
HOW ABOUT THIS?
NOW YOU'RE TALKING! GIVE ME A SEC, HERE.
AIRMAN STONE, OPEN THE TRANSPORT BAY DOORS AND THEN PREP OUR BETTY... OH, AND HAVE THEM GAS SAVAGE **TWICE** AN HOUR 'TIL WE GET BACK.
ROGER THAT, KING.
BASTARD!
KING, I FEAR THIS MONSTER HAS A **DEEP** HOLD ON MY MIND.
IT WOULD BE BEST TO WATCH ME CAREFULLY.
DANGER
THAT'S WHAT I DO, JOHN. ANYWAY, **CHEER UP.**
I DON'T FIGURE EITHER OF US WILL BE ALIVE THIS TIME TOMORROW.

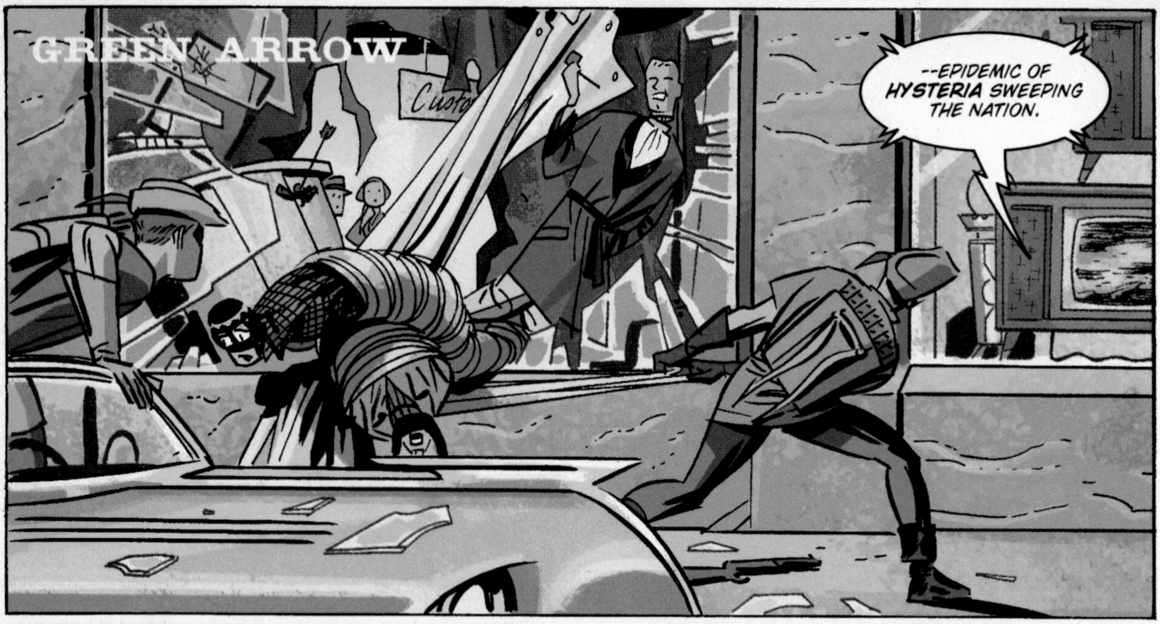
GREEN ARROW
--EPIDEMIC OF HYSTERIA SWEEPING THE NATION.

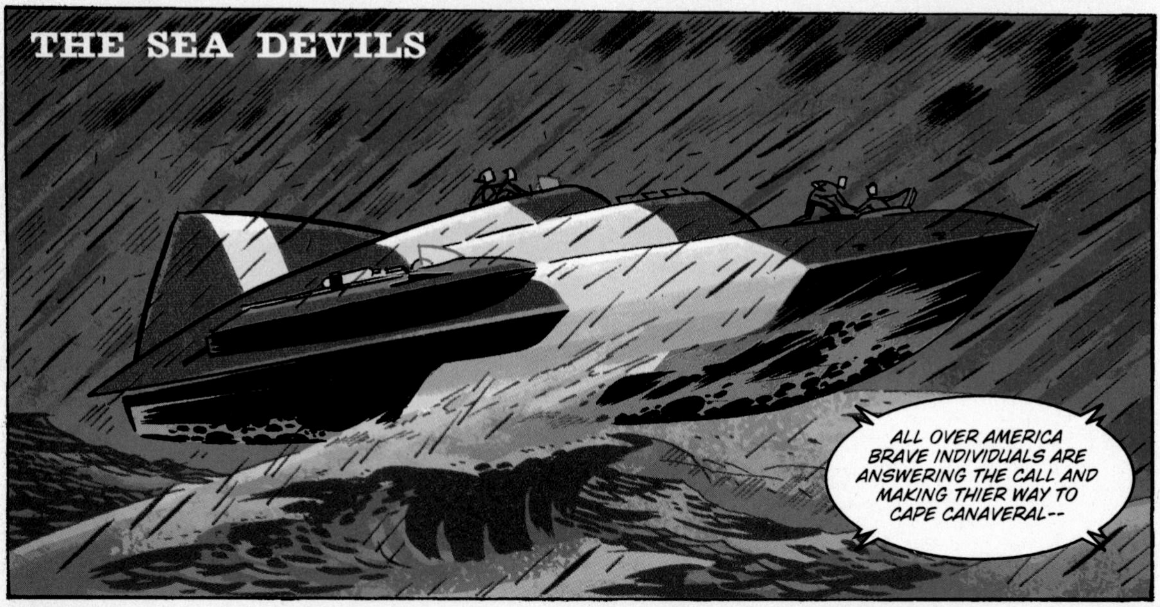
THE SEA DEVILS
ALL OVER AMERICA BRAVE INDIVIDUALS ARE ANSWERING THE CALL AND MAKING THIER WAY TO CAPE CANAVERAL--

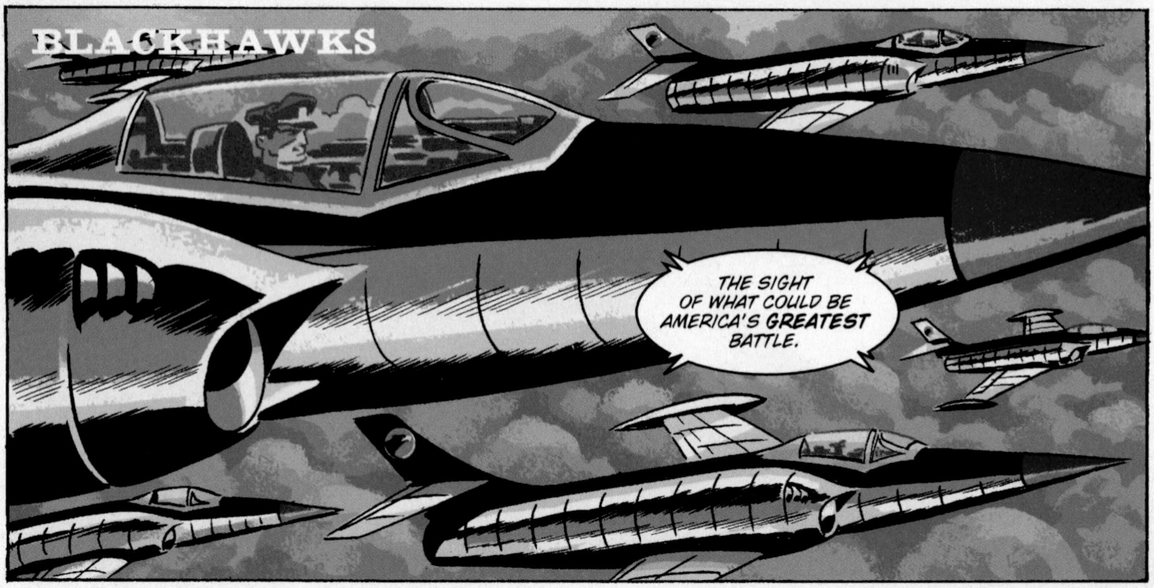
BLACKHAWKS
THE SIGHT OF WHAT COULD BE AMERICA'S GREATEST BATTLE.

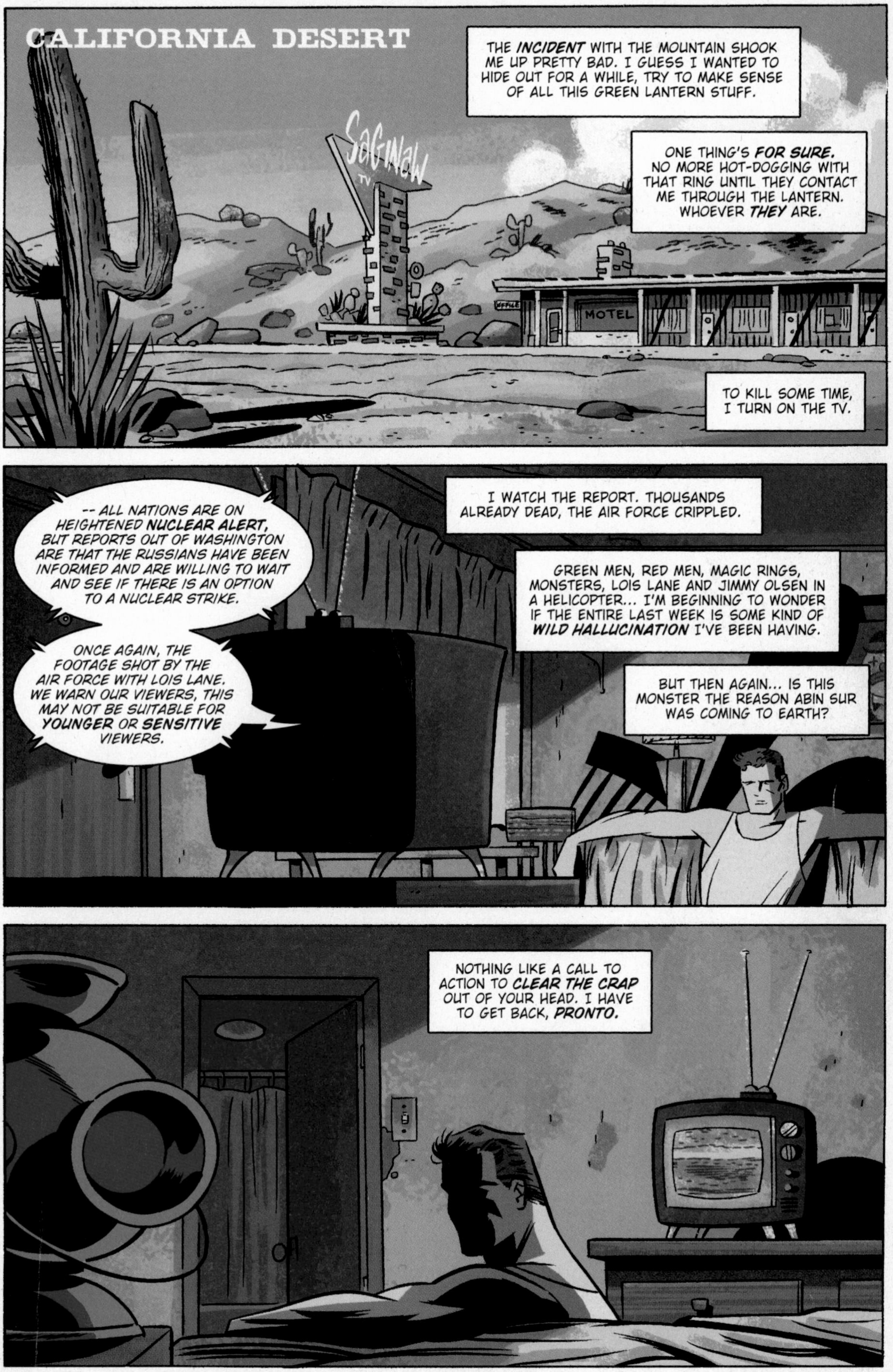

CALIFORNIA DESERT
THE INCIDENT WITH THE MOUNTAIN SHOOK ME UP PRETTY BAD. I GUESS I WANTED TO HIDE OUT FOR A WHILE, TRY TO MAKE SENSE OF ALL THIS GREEN LANTERN STUFF.
ONE THING'S FOR SURE. NO MORE HOT-DOGGING WITH THAT RING UNTIL THEY CONTACT ME THROUGH THE LANTERN. WHOEVER THEY ARE.
SAGINAW
TV
MOTEL
TO KILL SOME TIME, I TURN ON THE TV.
-- ALL NATIONS ARE ON HEIGHTENED NUCLEAR ALERT, BUT REPORTS OUT OF WASHINGTON ARE THAT THE RUSSIANS HAVE BEEN INFORMED AND ARE WILLING TO WAIT AND SEE IF THERE IS AN OPTION TO A NUCLEAR STRIKE.
ONCE AGAIN, THE FOOTAGE SHOT BY THE AIR FORCE WITH LOIS LANE. WE WARN OUR VIEWERS, THIS MAY NOT BE SUITABLE FOR YOUNGER OR SENSITIVE VIEWERS.
I WATCH THE REPORT. THOUSANDS ALREADY DEAD, THE AIR FORCE CRIPPLED.
GREEN MEN, RED MEN, MAGIC RINGS, MONSTERS, LOIS LANE AND JIMMY OLSEN IN A HELICOPTER... I'M BEGINNING TO WONDER IF THE ENTIRE LAST WEEK IS SOME KIND OF WILD HALLUCINATION I'VE BEEN HAVING.
BUT THEN AGAIN... IS THIS MONSTER THE REASON ABIN SUR WAS COMING TO EARTH?
NOTHING LIKE A CALL TO ACTION TO CLEAR THE CRAP OUT OF YOUR HEAD. I HAVE TO GET BACK, PRONTO.

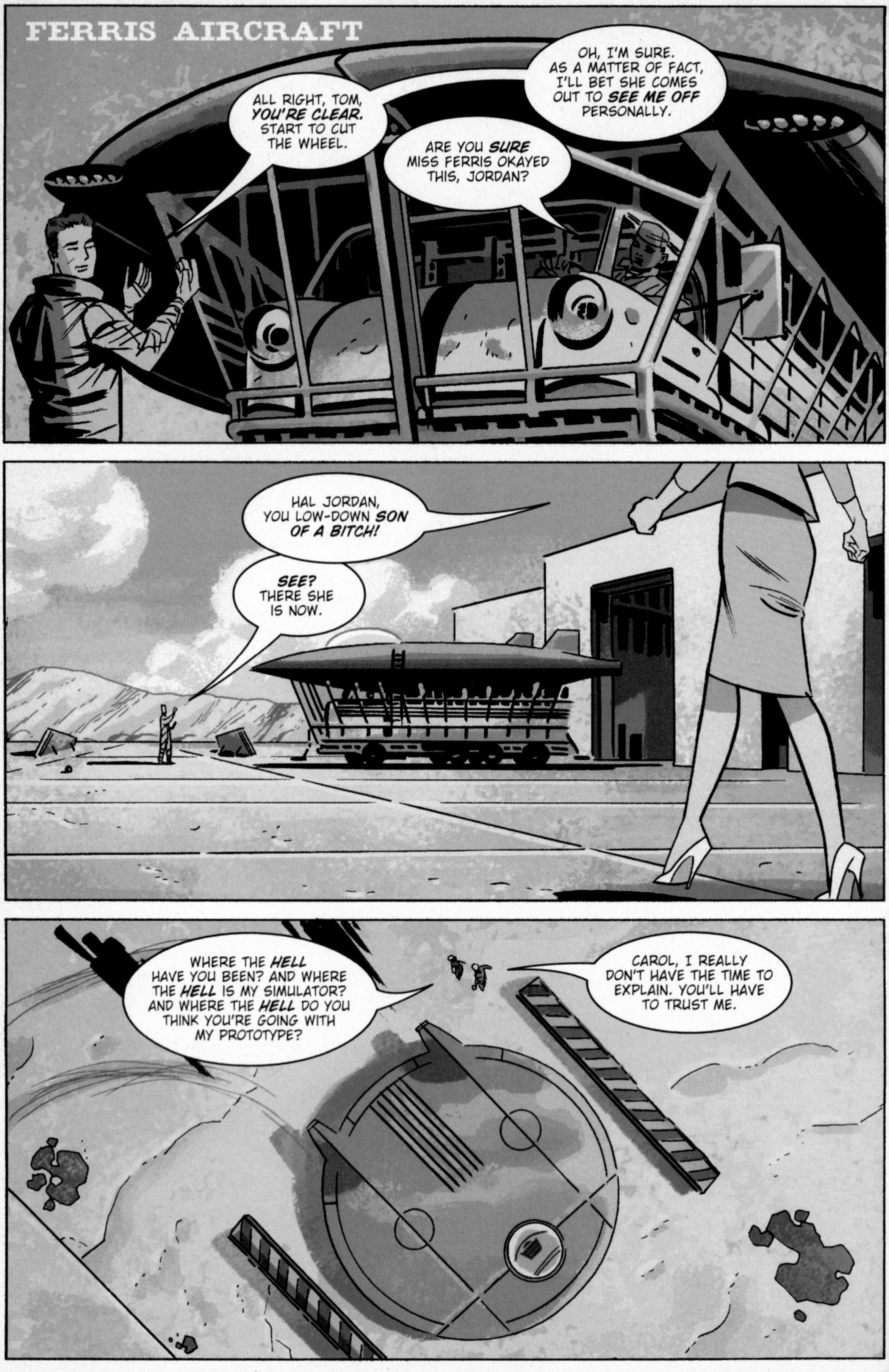
FERRIS AIRCRAFT
ALL RIGHT, TOM, YOU'RE CLEAR. START TO CUT THE WHEEL.
ARE YOU SURE MISS FERRIS OKAYED THIS, JORDAN?
OH, I'M SURE. AS A MATTER OF FACT, I'LL BET SHE COMES OUT TO SEE ME OFF PERSONALLY.
HAL JORDAN, YOU LOW-DOWN SON OF A BITCH!
SEE? THERE SHE IS NOW.
WHERE THE HELL HAVE YOU BEEN? AND WHERE THE HELL IS MY SIMULATOR? AND WHERE THE HELL DO YOU THINK YOU'RE GOING WITH MY PROTOTYPE?
CAROL, I REALLY DON'T HAVE THE TIME TO EXPLAIN. YOU'LL HAVE TO TRUST ME.

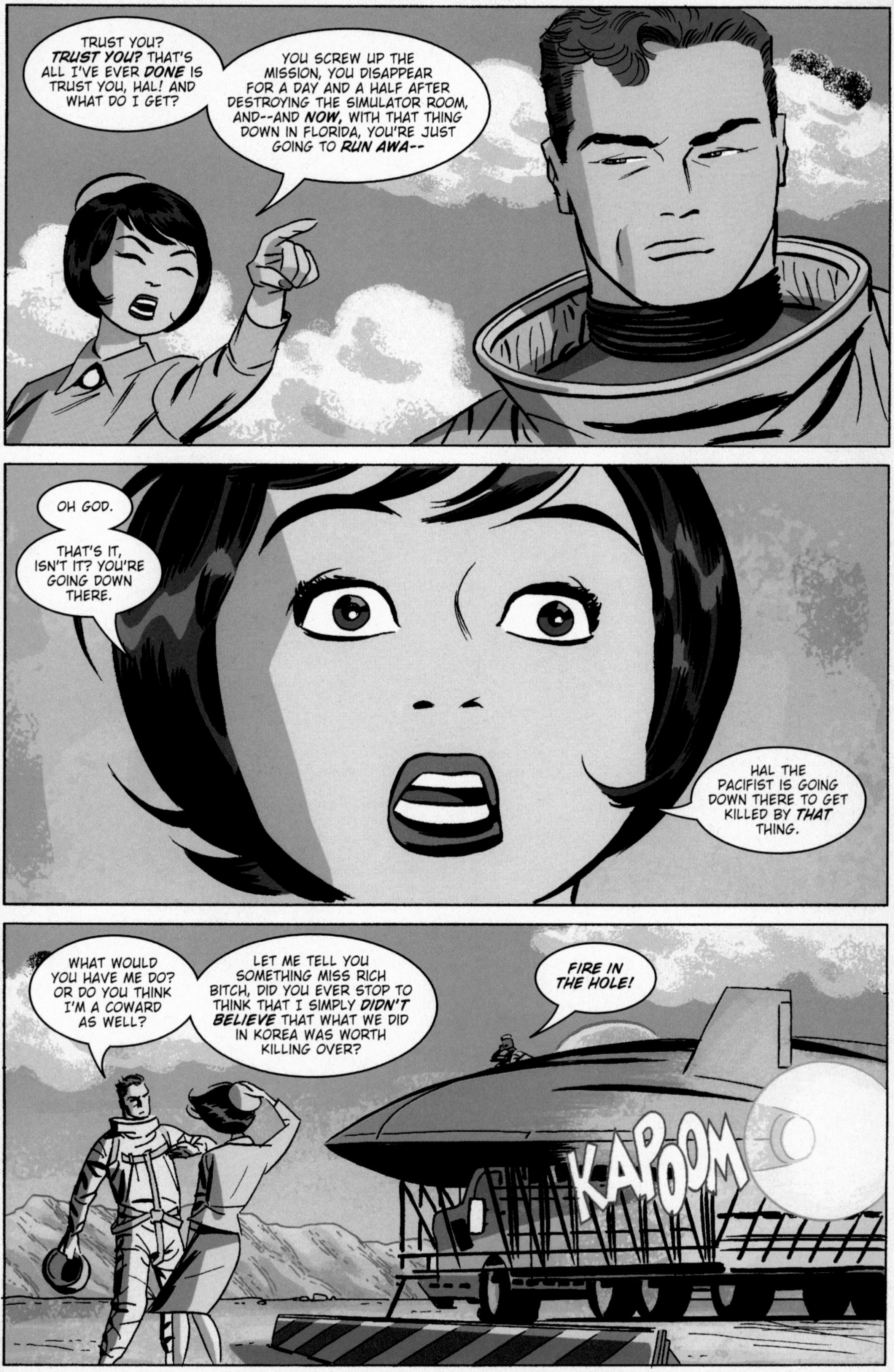
TRUST YOU? **TRUST YOU?** THAT'S ALL I'VE EVER **DONE** IS TRUST YOU, HAL! AND WHAT DO I GET?
YOU SCREW UP THE MISSION, YOU DISAPPEAR FOR A DAY AND A HALF AFTER DESTROYING THE SIMULATOR ROOM, AND--AND **NOW,** WITH THAT THING DOWN IN FLORIDA, YOU'RE JUST GOING TO **RUN AWA--**
OH GOD.
THAT'S IT, ISN'T IT? YOU'RE GOING DOWN THERE.
HAL THE PACIFIST IS GOING DOWN THERE TO GET KILLED BY **THAT** THING.
WHAT WOULD YOU HAVE ME DO? OR DO YOU THINK I'M A COWARD AS WELL?
LET ME TELL YOU SOMETHING MISS RICH BITCH, DID YOU EVER STOP TO THINK THAT I SIMPLY **DIDN'T BELIEVE** THAT WHAT WE DID IN KOREA WAS WORTH KILLING OVER?
FIRE IN THE HOLE!
KAPOOM

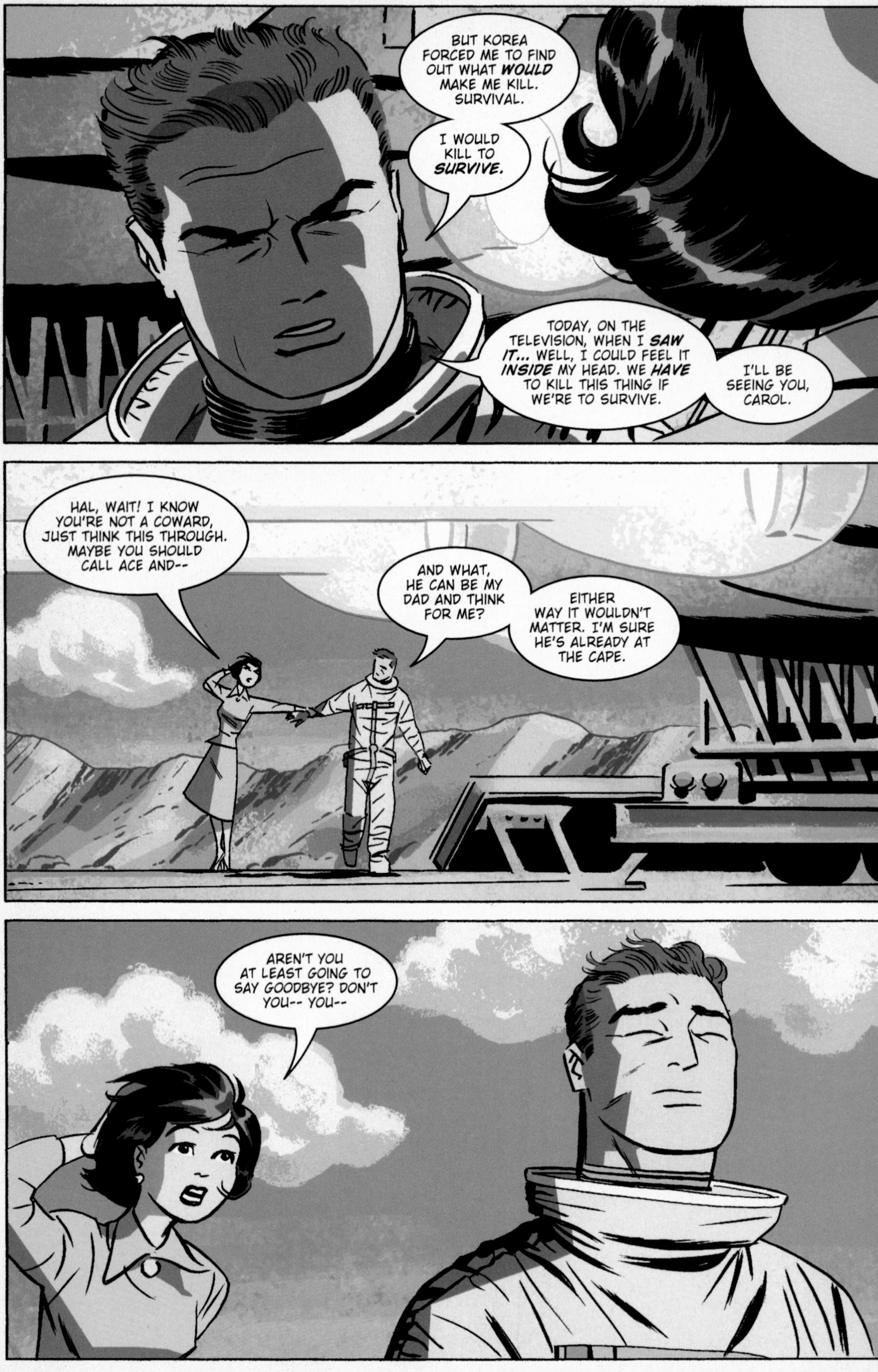
BUT KOREA FORCED ME TO FIND OUT WHAT **WOULD** MAKE ME KILL. SURVIVAL.
I WOULD KILL TO ***SURVIVE.***
TODAY, ON THE TELEVISION, WHEN I ***SAW IT...*** WELL, I COULD FEEL IT ***INSIDE*** MY HEAD. WE ***HAVE*** TO KILL THIS THING IF WE'RE TO SURVIVE.
I'LL BE SEEING YOU, CAROL.
HAL, WAIT! I KNOW YOU'RE NOT A COWARD, JUST THINK THIS THROUGH. MAYBE YOU SHOULD CALL ACE AND--
AND WHAT, HE CAN BE MY DAD AND THINK FOR ME?
EITHER WAY IT WOULDN'T MATTER. I'M SURE HE'S ALREADY AT THE CAPE.
AREN'T YOU AT LEAST GOING TO SAY GOODBYE? DON'T YOU-- YOU--

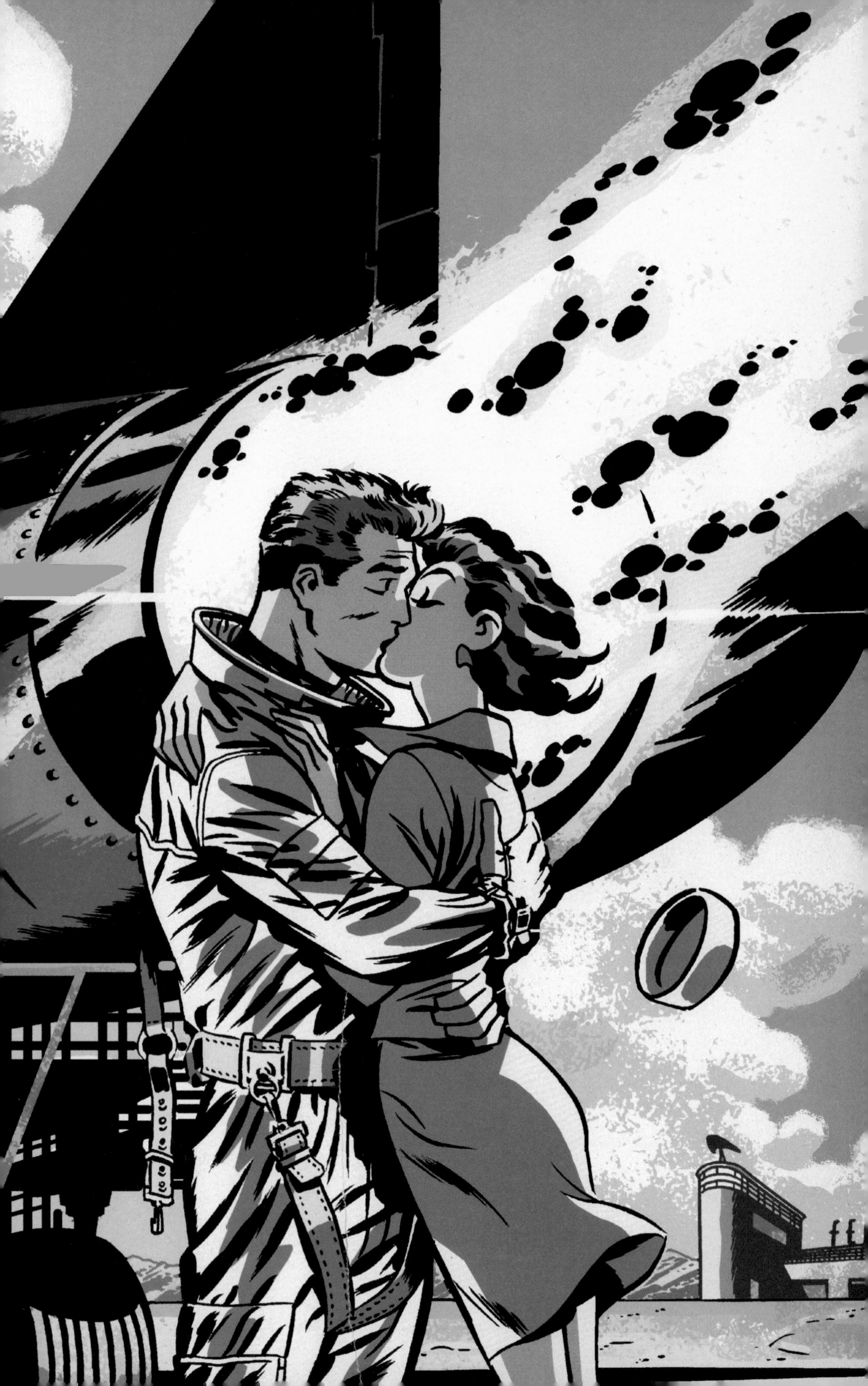

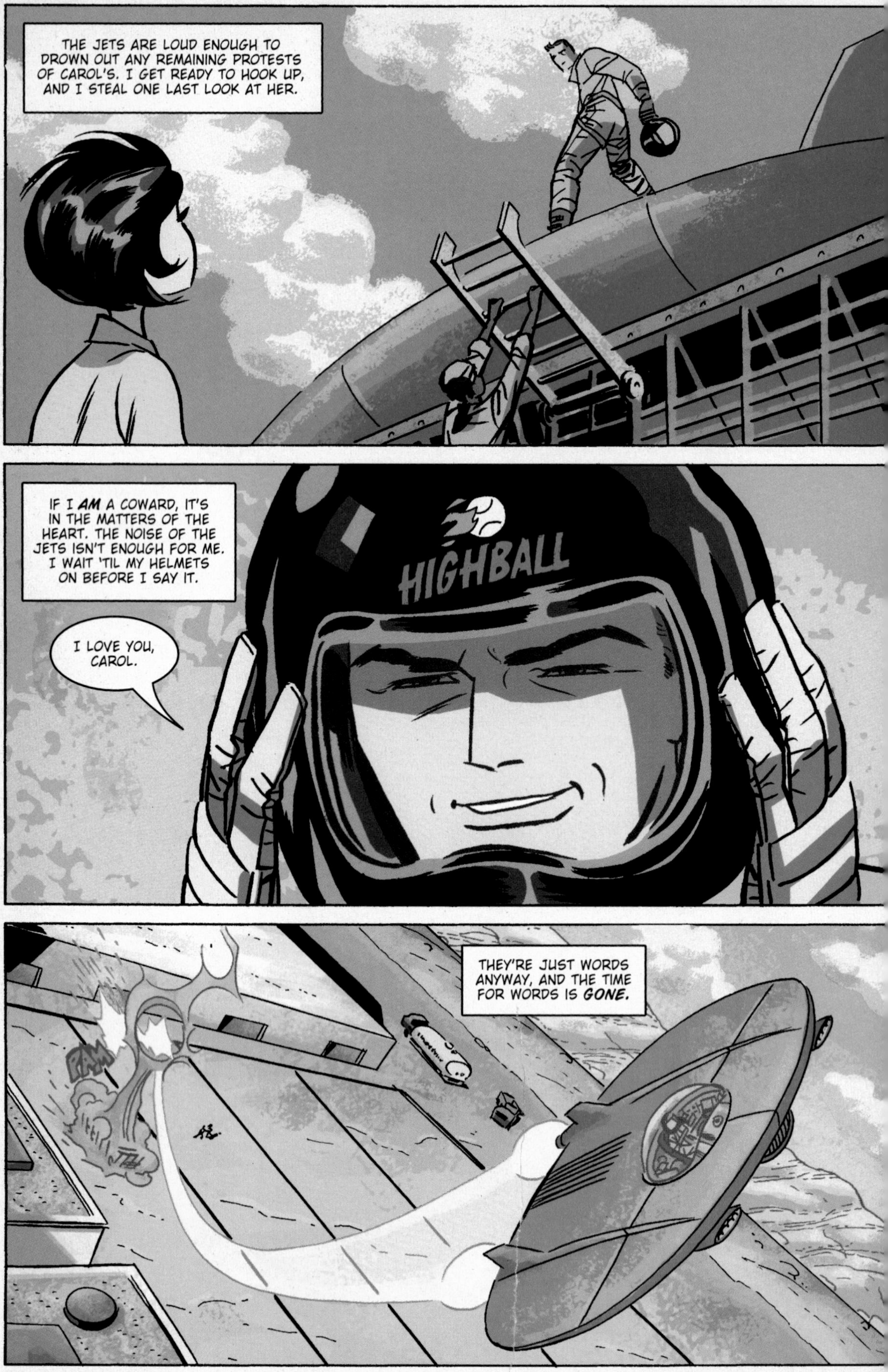
THE JETS ARE LOUD ENOUGH TO DROWN OUT ANY REMAINING PROTESTS OF CAROL'S. I GET READY TO HOOK UP, AND I STEAL ONE LAST LOOK AT HER.
IF I *AM* A COWARD, IT'S IN THE MATTERS OF THE HEART. THE NOISE OF THE JETS ISN'T ENOUGH FOR ME. I WAIT 'TIL MY HELMETS ON BEFORE I SAY IT.
HIGHBALL
I LOVE YOU, CAROL.
THEY'RE JUST WORDS ANYWAY, AND THE TIME FOR WORDS IS *GONE.*

CHAPTER FOURTEEN
THE BOY SCOUT'S LAST

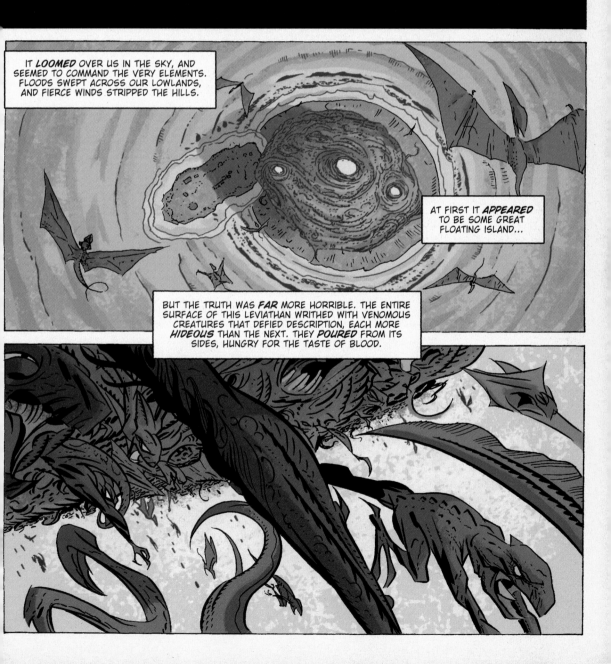

IT *LOOMED* OVER US IN THE SKY, AND SEEMED TO COMMAND THE VERY ELEMENTS. FLOODS SWEPT ACROSS OUR LOWLANDS, AND FIERCE WINDS STRIPPED THE HILLS.

AT FIRST IT *APPEARED* TO BE SOME GREAT FLOATING ISLAND...

BUT THE TRUTH WAS *FAR* MORE HORRIBLE. THE ENTIRE SURFACE OF THIS LEVIATHAN WRITHED WITH VENOMOUS CREATURES THAT DEFIED DESCRIPTION, EACH MORE *HIDEOUS* THAN THE NEXT. THEY *POURED* FROM ITS SIDES, HUNGRY FOR THE TASTE OF BLOOD.

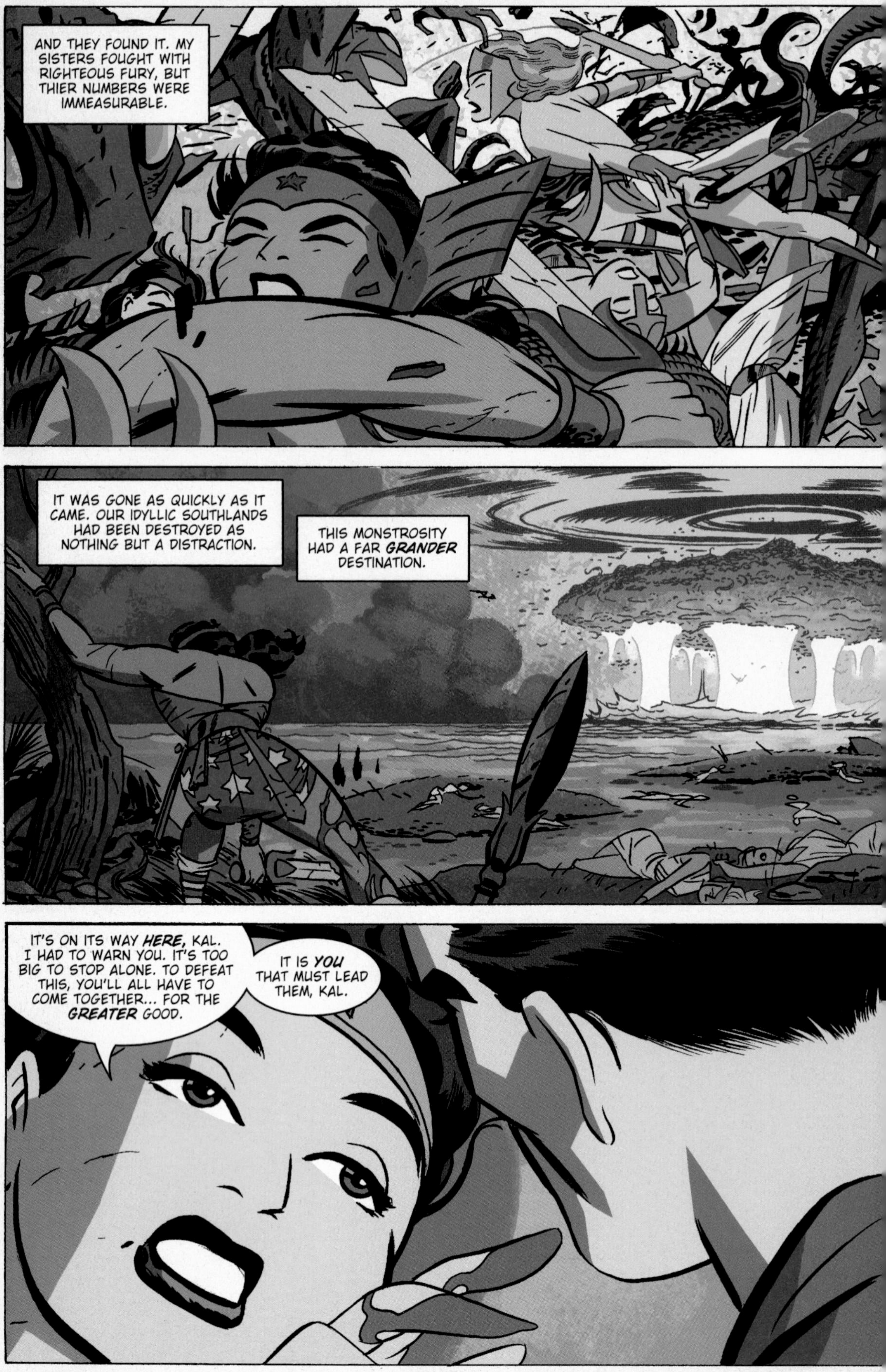
AND THEY FOUND IT. MY SISTERS FOUGHT WITH RIGHTEOUS FURY, BUT THIER NUMBERS WERE IMMEASURABLE.
IT WAS GONE AS QUICKLY AS IT CAME. OUR IDYLLIC SOUTHLANDS HAD BEEN DESTROYED AS NOTHING BUT A DISTRACTION.
THIS MONSTROSITY HAD A FAR GRANDER DESTINATION.
IT'S ON ITS WAY HERE, KAL. I HAD TO WARN YOU. IT'S TOO BIG TO STOP ALONE. TO DEFEAT THIS, YOU'LL ALL HAVE TO COME TOGETHER... FOR THE GREATER GOOD.
IT IS YOU THAT MUST LEAD THEM, KAL.

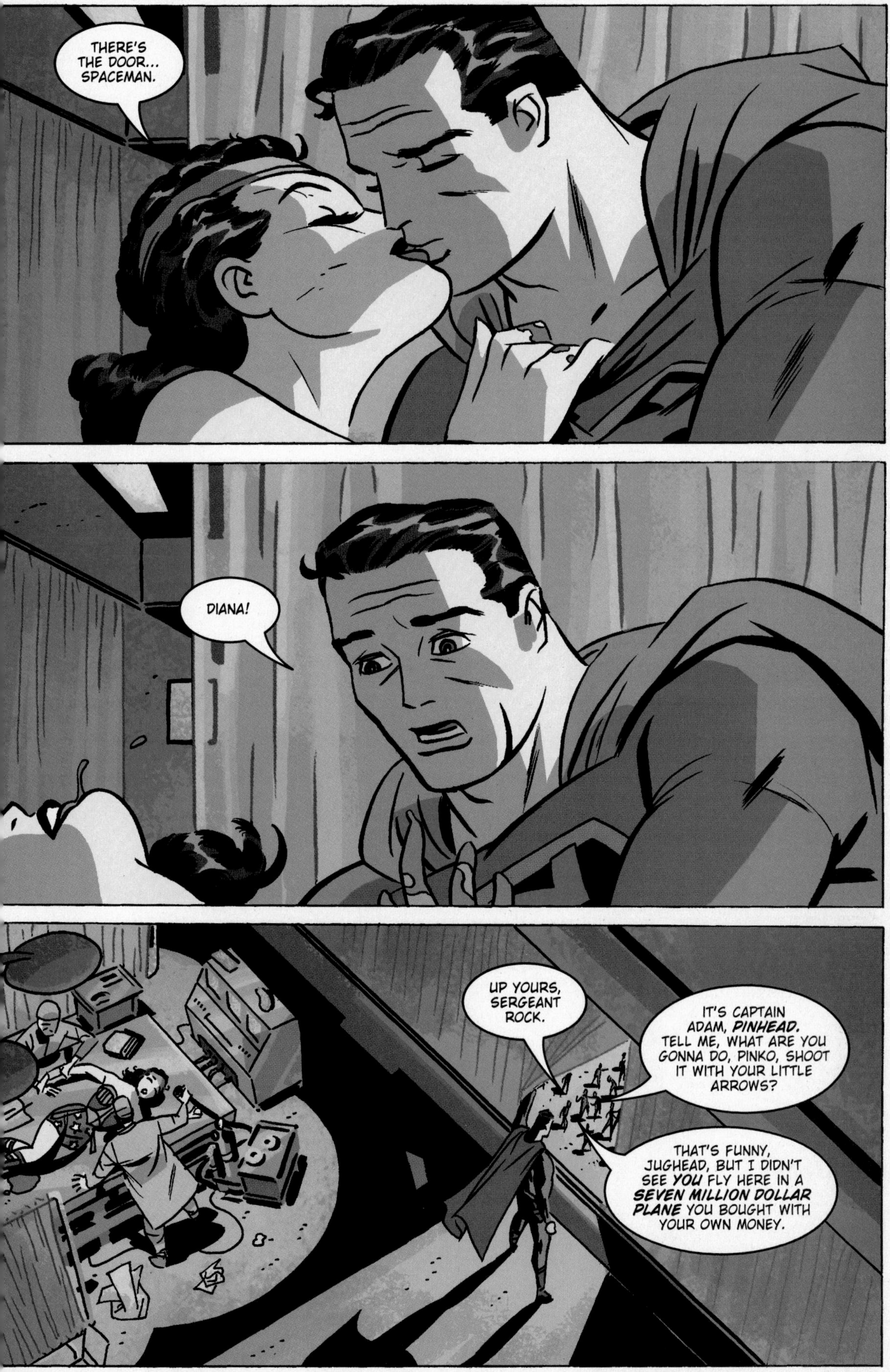
THERE'S THE DOOR... SPACEMAN.
DIANA!
UP YOURS, SERGEANT ROCK.
IT'S CAPTAIN ADAM, PINHEAD. TELL ME, WHAT ARE YOU GONNA DO, PINKO, SHOOT IT WITH YOUR LITTLE ARROWS?
THAT'S FUNNY, JUGHEAD, BUT I DIDN'T SEE YOU FLY HERE IN A SEVEN MILLION DOLLAR PLANE YOU BOUGHT WITH YOUR OWN MONEY.

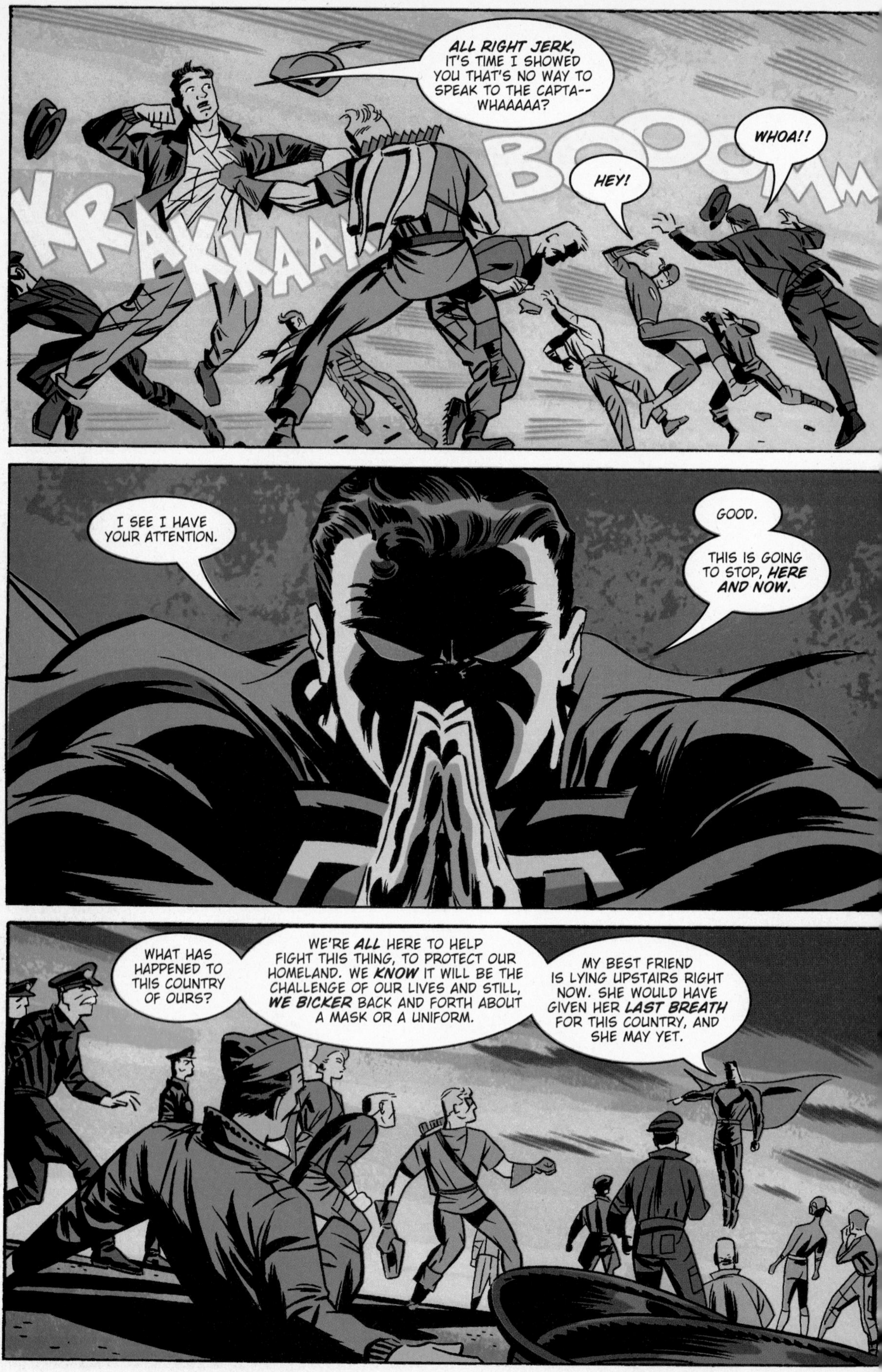
ALL RIGHT JERK, IT'S TIME I SHOWED YOU THAT'S NO WAY TO SPEAK TO THE CAPTA-- WHAAAAA?
KRAKKAAA
BOOOOMM
HEY!
WHOA!!
I SEE I HAVE YOUR ATTENTION.
GOOD.
THIS IS GOING TO STOP, HERE AND NOW.
WHAT HAS HAPPENED TO THIS COUNTRY OF OURS?
WE'RE ALL HERE TO HELP FIGHT THIS THING, TO PROTECT OUR HOMELAND. WE KNOW IT WILL BE THE CHALLENGE OF OUR LIVES AND STILL, WE BICKER BACK AND FORTH ABOUT A MASK OR A UNIFORM.
MY BEST FRIEND IS LYING UPSTAIRS RIGHT NOW. SHE WOULD HAVE GIVEN HER LAST BREATH FOR THIS COUNTRY, AND SHE MAY YET.

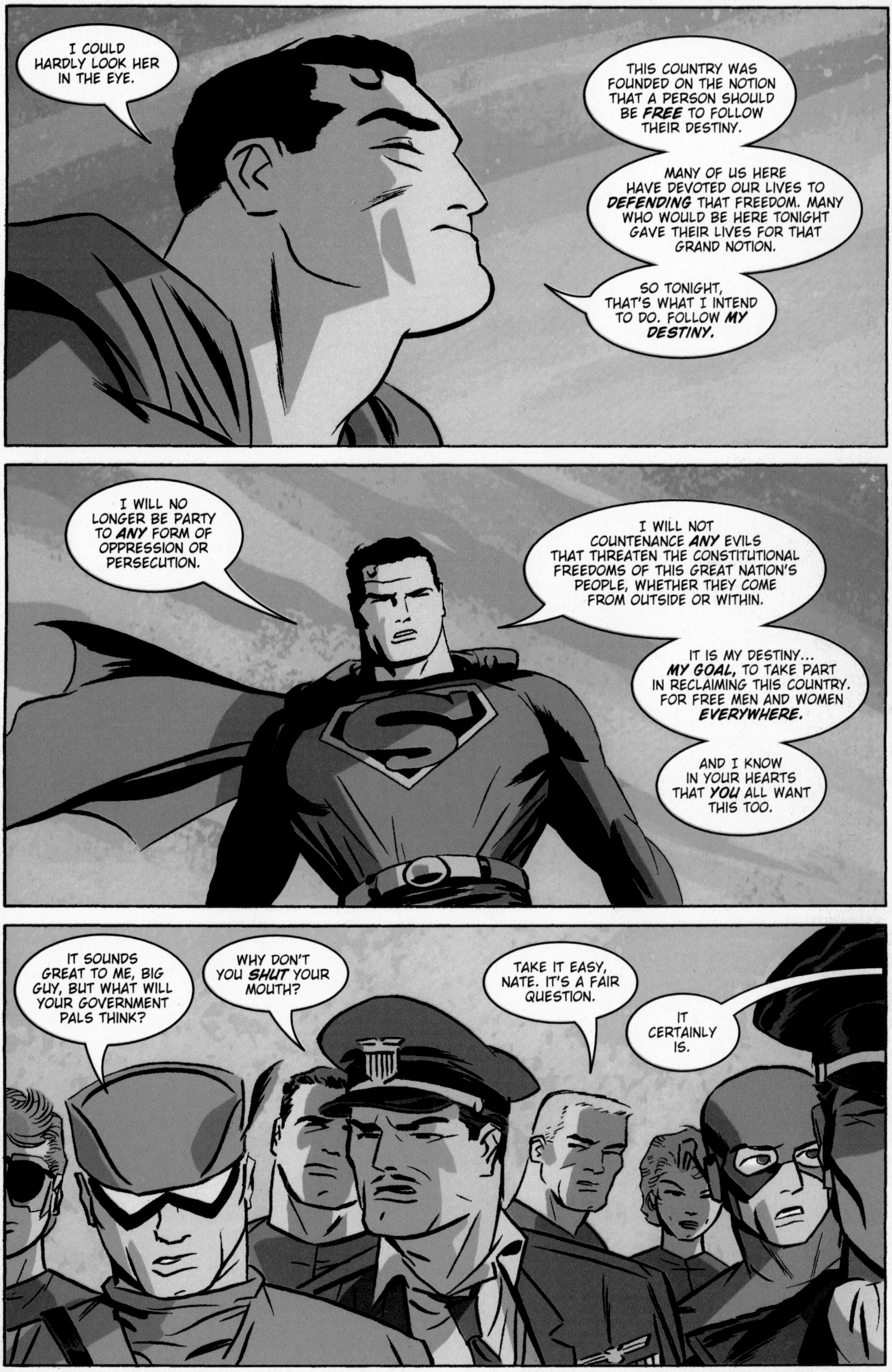
I COULD HARDLY LOOK HER IN THE EYE.
THIS COUNTRY WAS FOUNDED ON THE NOTION THAT A PERSON SHOULD BE FREE TO FOLLOW THEIR DESTINY.
MANY OF US HERE HAVE DEVOTED OUR LIVES TO DEFENDING THAT FREEDOM. MANY WHO WOULD BE HERE TONIGHT GAVE THEIR LIVES FOR THAT GRAND NOTION.
SO TONIGHT, THAT'S WHAT I INTEND TO DO. FOLLOW MY DESTINY.
I WILL NO LONGER BE PARTY TO ANY FORM OF OPPRESSION OR PERSECUTION.
I WILL NOT COUNTENANCE ANY EVILS THAT THREATEN THE CONSTITUTIONAL FREEDOMS OF THIS GREAT NATION'S PEOPLE, WHETHER THEY COME FROM OUTSIDE OR WITHIN.
IT IS MY DESTINY... MY GOAL, TO TAKE PART IN RECLAIMING THIS COUNTRY. FOR FREE MEN AND WOMEN EVERYWHERE.
AND I KNOW IN YOUR HEARTS THAT YOU ALL WANT THIS TOO.
IT SOUNDS GREAT TO ME, BIG GUY, BUT WHAT WILL YOUR GOVERNMENT PALS THINK?
WHY DON'T YOU SHUT YOUR MOUTH?
TAKE IT EASY, NATE. IT'S A FAIR QUESTION.
IT CERTAINLY IS.

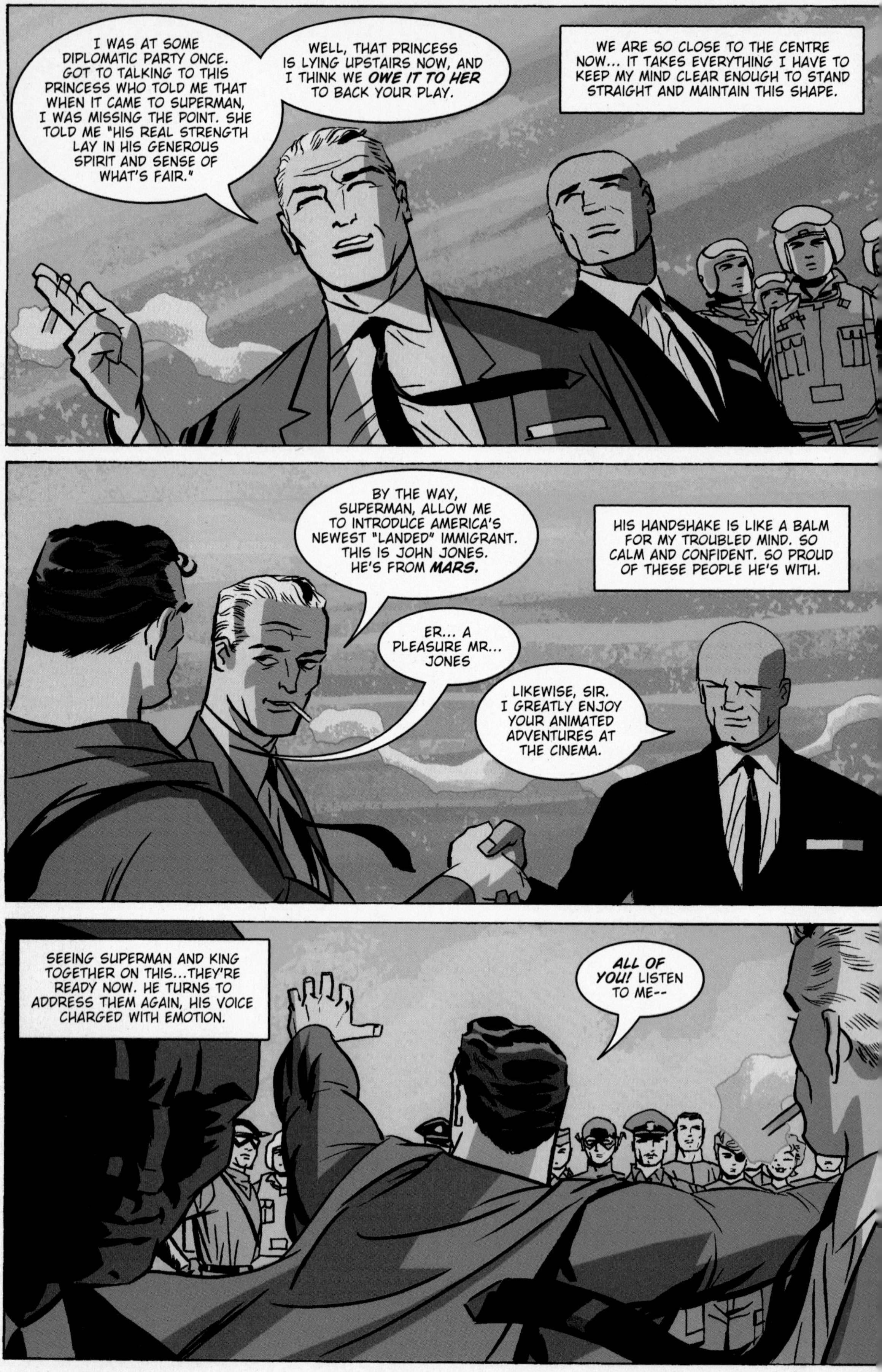
I WAS AT SOME DIPLOMATIC PARTY ONCE. GOT TO TALKING TO THIS PRINCESS WHO TOLD ME THAT WHEN IT CAME TO SUPERMAN, I WAS MISSING THE POINT. SHE TOLD ME "HIS REAL STRENGTH LAY IN HIS GENEROUS SPIRIT AND SENSE OF WHAT'S FAIR."
WELL, THAT PRINCESS IS LYING UPSTAIRS NOW, AND I THINK WE *OWE IT TO HER* TO BACK YOUR PLAY.
WE ARE SO CLOSE TO THE CENTRE NOW... IT TAKES EVERYTHING I HAVE TO KEEP MY MIND CLEAR ENOUGH TO STAND STRAIGHT AND MAINTAIN THIS SHAPE.
BY THE WAY, SUPERMAN, ALLOW ME TO INTRODUCE AMERICA'S NEWEST "LANDED" IMMIGRANT. THIS IS JOHN JONES. HE'S FROM *MARS.*
HIS HANDSHAKE IS LIKE A BALM FOR MY TROUBLED MIND. SO CALM AND CONFIDENT. SO PROUD OF THESE PEOPLE HE'S WITH.
ER... A PLEASURE MR... JONES
LIKEWISE, SIR. I GREATLY ENJOY YOUR ANIMATED ADVENTURES AT THE CINEMA.
SEEING SUPERMAN AND KING TOGETHER ON THIS...THEY'RE READY NOW. HE TURNS TO ADDRESS THEM AGAIN, HIS VOICE CHARGED WITH EMOTION.
ALL OF YOU! LISTEN TO ME--

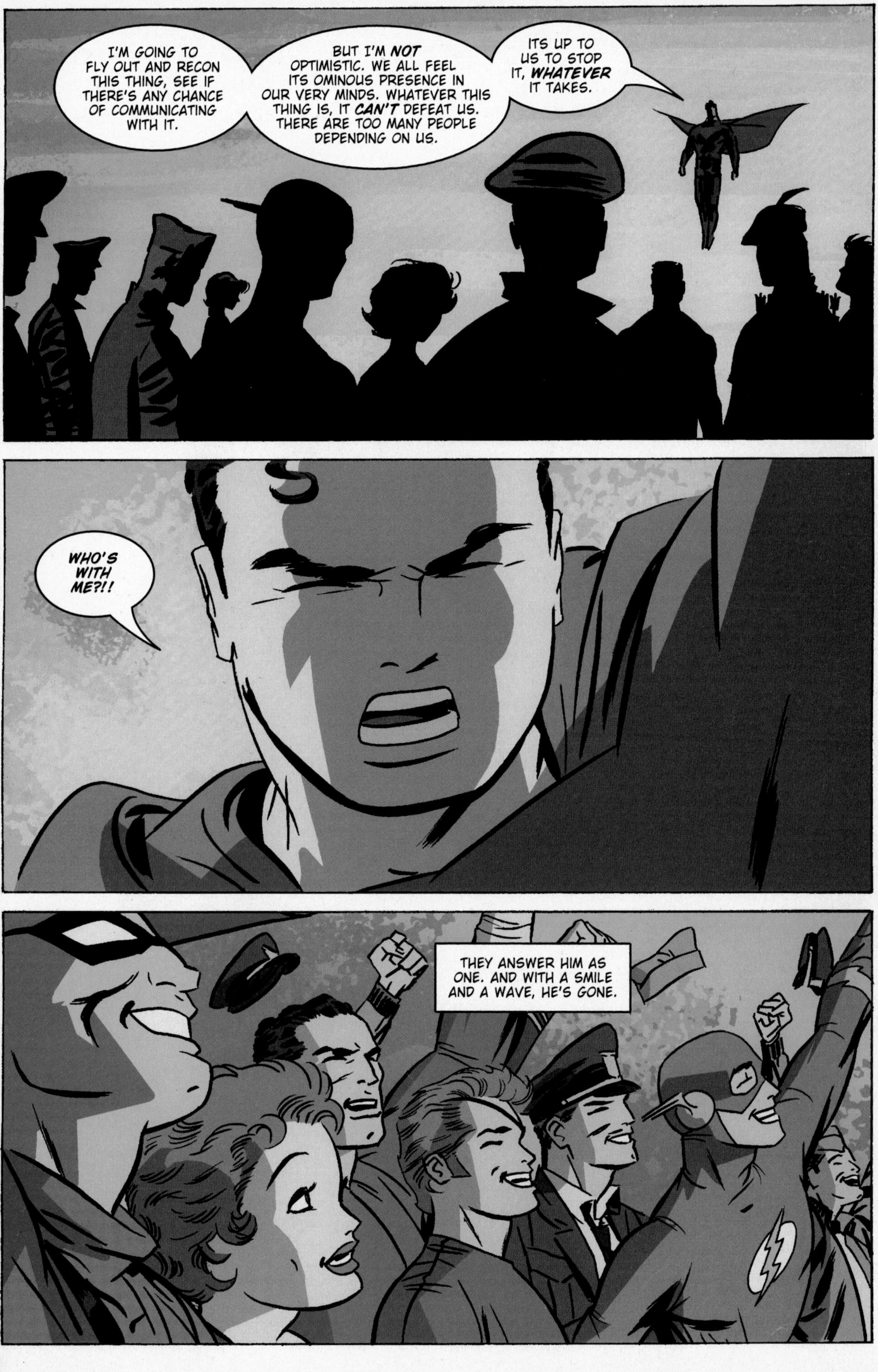
I'M GOING TO FLY OUT AND RECON THIS THING, SEE IF THERE'S ANY CHANCE OF COMMUNICATING WITH IT.
BUT I'M NOT OPTIMISTIC. WE ALL FEEL ITS OMINOUS PRESENCE IN OUR VERY MINDS. WHATEVER THIS THING IS, IT CAN'T DEFEAT US. THERE ARE TOO MANY PEOPLE DEPENDING ON US.
ITS UP TO US TO STOP IT, WHATEVER IT TAKES.
WHO'S WITH ME?!!
THEY ANSWER HIM AS ONE. AND WITH A SMILE AND A WAVE, HE'S GONE.

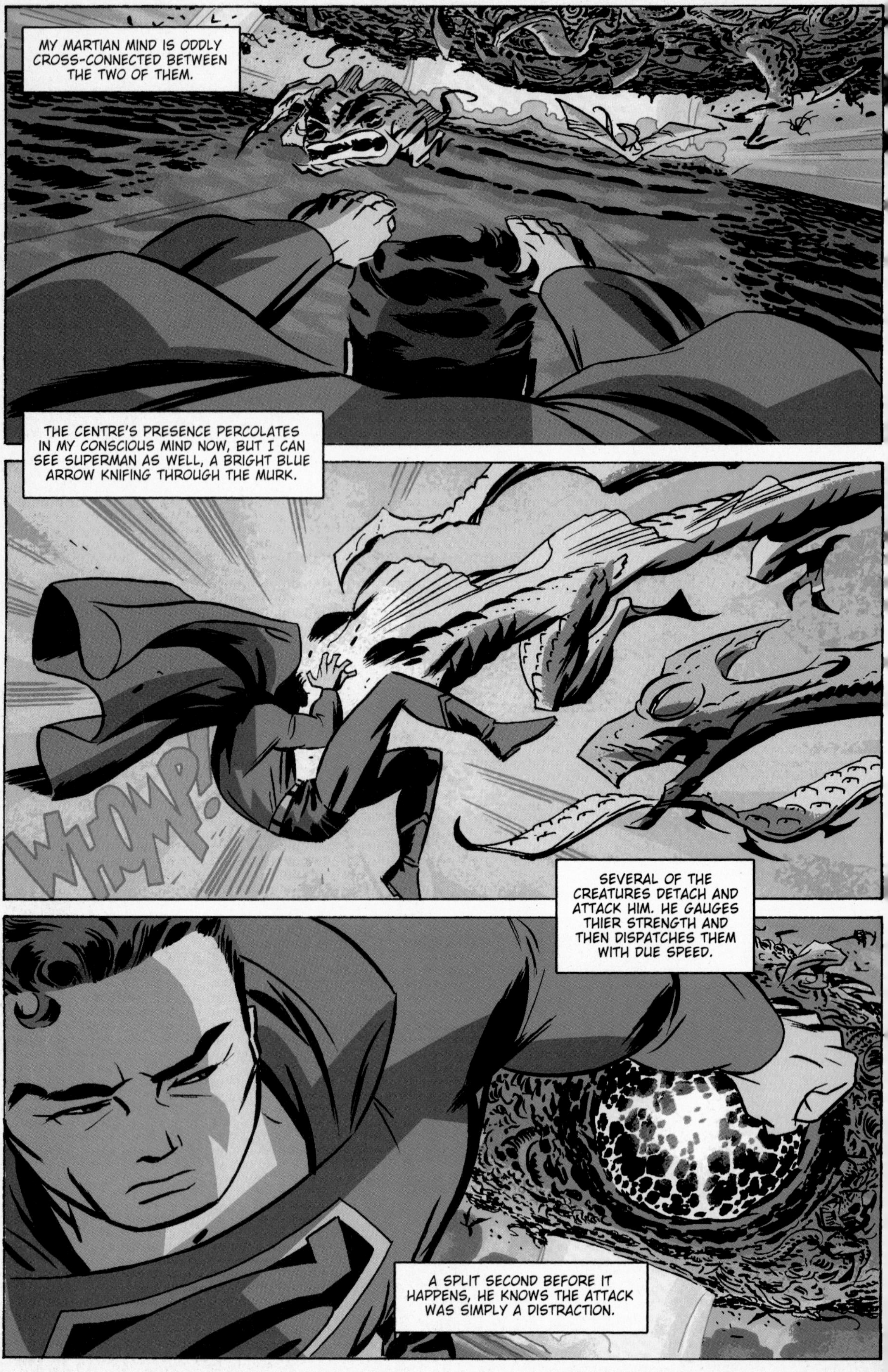
MY MARTIAN MIND IS ODDLY CROSS-CONNECTED BETWEEN THE TWO OF THEM.
THE CENTRE'S PRESENCE PERCOLATES IN MY CONSCIOUS MIND NOW, BUT I CAN SEE SUPERMAN AS WELL, A BRIGHT BLUE ARROW KNIFING THROUGH THE MURK.
WHOMP!
SEVERAL OF THE CREATURES DETACH AND ATTACK HIM. HE GAUGES THIER STRENGTH AND THEN DISPATCHES THEM WITH DUE SPEED.
A SPLIT SECOND BEFORE IT HAPPENS, HE KNOWS THE ATTACK WAS SIMPLY A DISTRACTION.

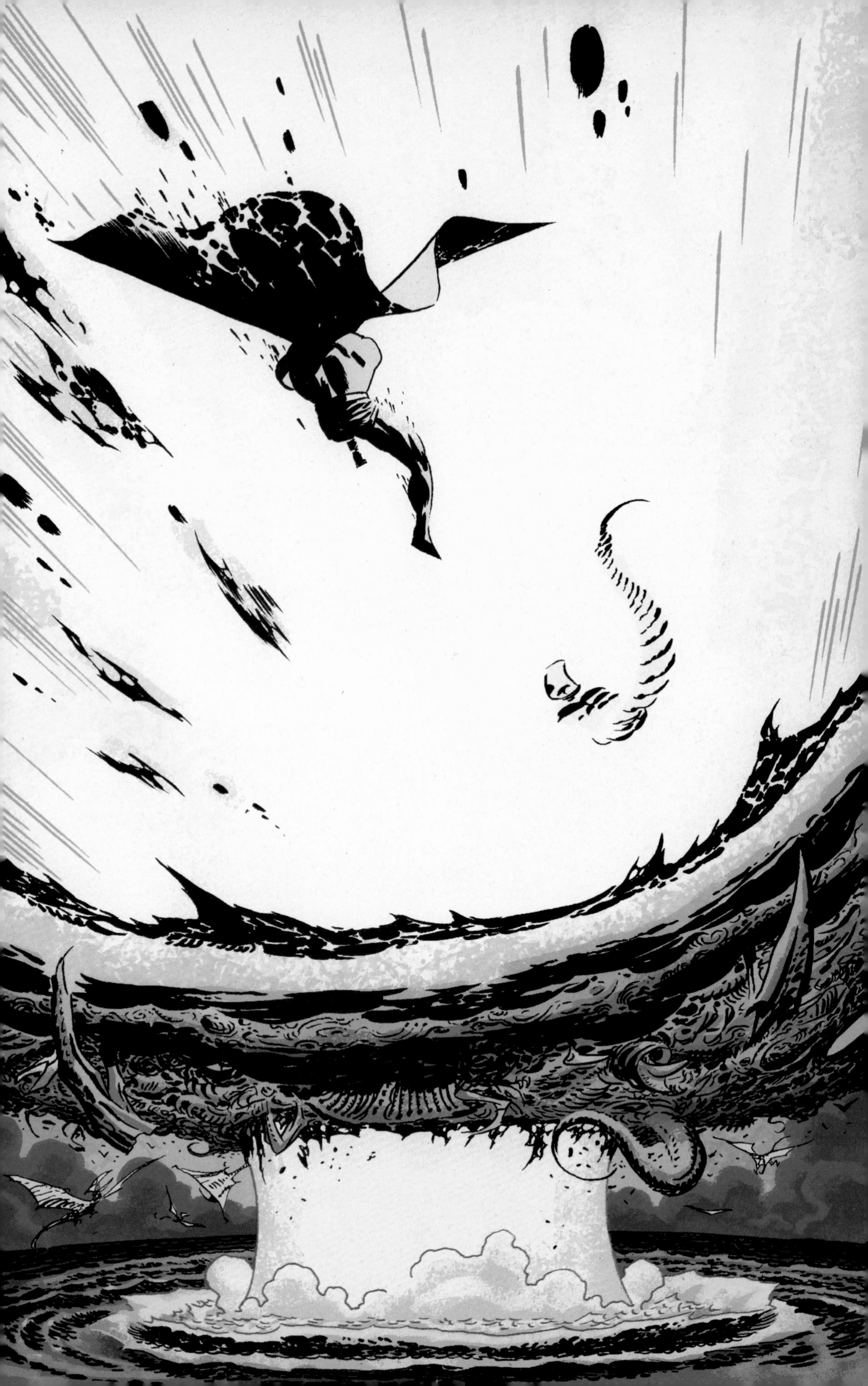

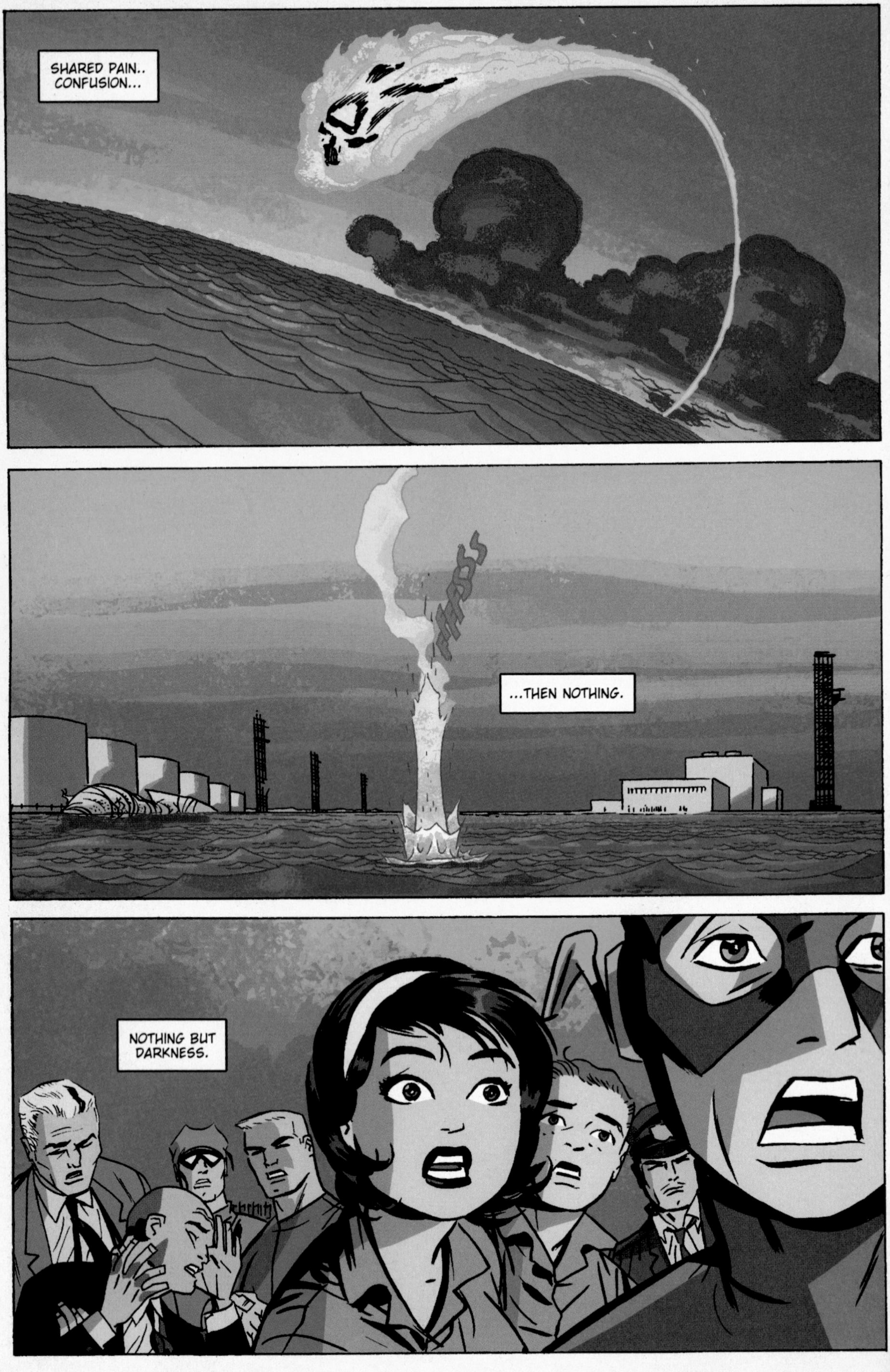
SHARED PAIN..
CONFUSION...
...THEN NOTHING.
NOTHING BUT DARKNESS.

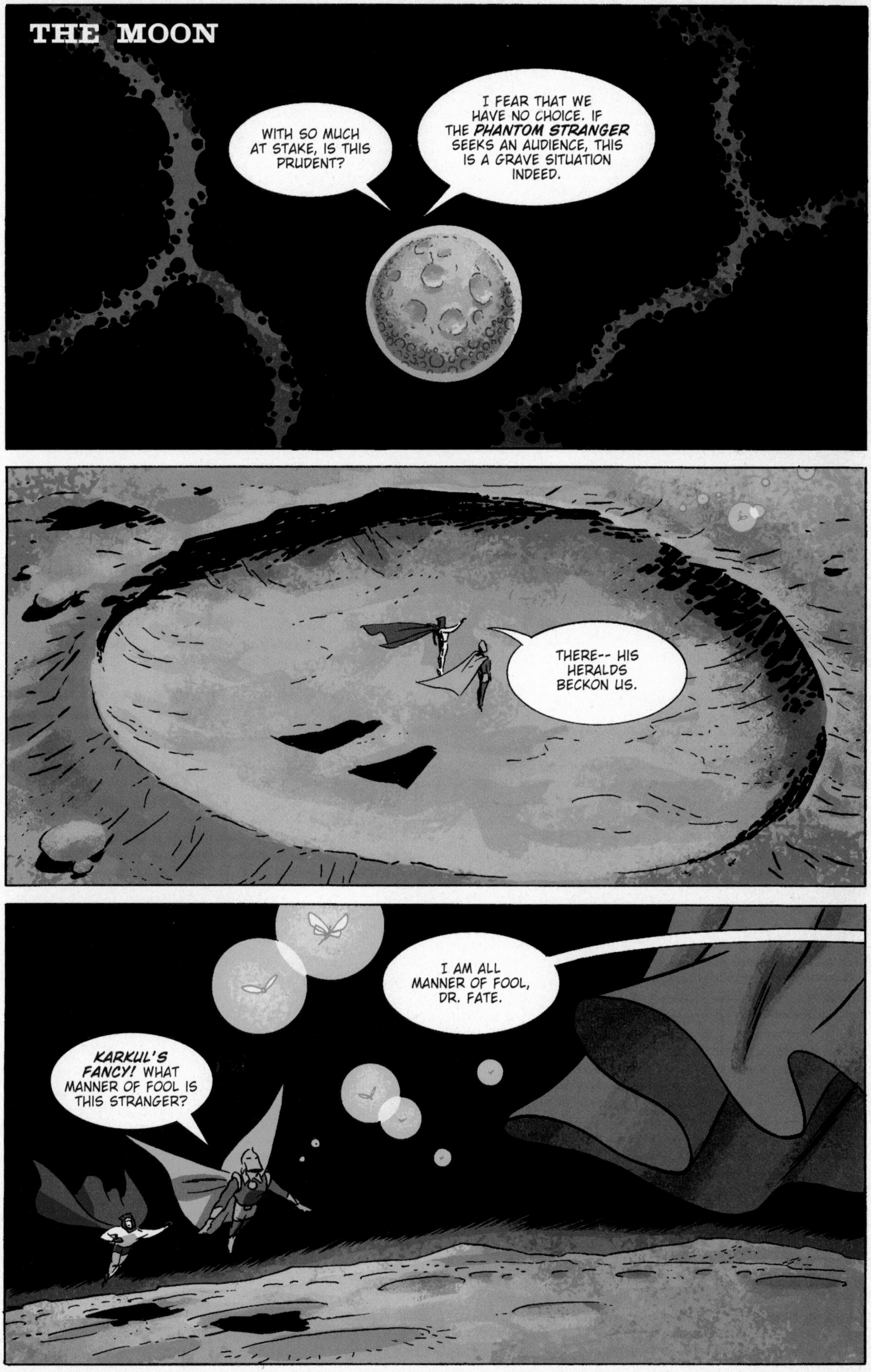
THE MOON
WITH SO MUCH AT STAKE, IS THIS PRUDENT?
I FEAR THAT WE HAVE NO CHOICE. IF THE PHANTOM STRANGER SEEKS AN AUDIENCE, THIS IS A GRAVE SITUATION INDEED.
THERE-- HIS HERALDS BECKON US.
KARKUL'S FANCY! WHAT MANNER OF FOOL IS THIS STRANGER?
I AM ALL MANNER OF FOOL, DR. FATE.

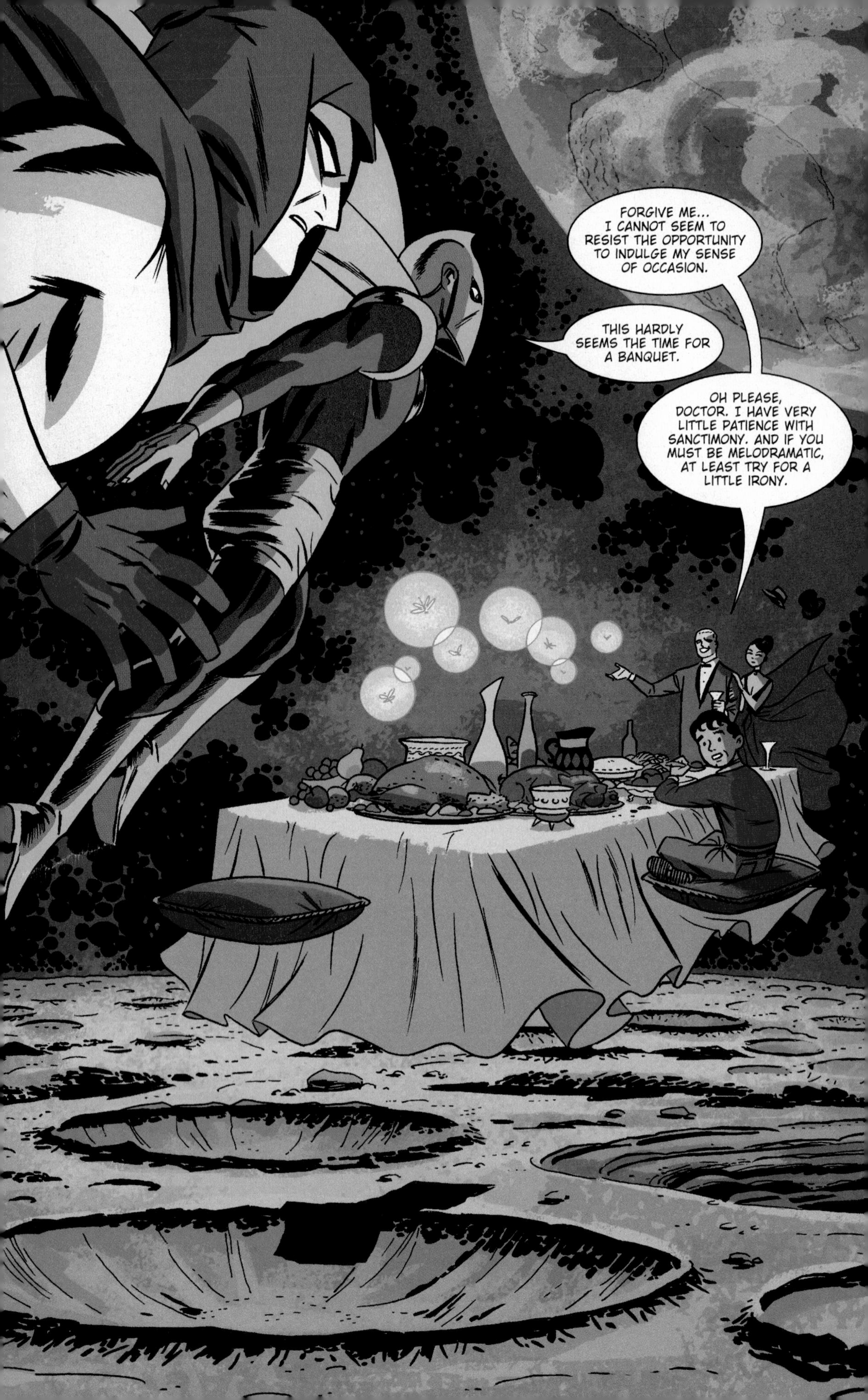
FORGIVE ME... I CANNOT SEEM TO RESIST THE OPPORTUNITY TO INDULGE MY SENSE OF OCCASION.
THIS HARDLY SEEMS THE TIME FOR A BANQUET.
OH PLEASE, DOCTOR. I HAVE VERY LITTLE PATIENCE WITH SANCTIMONY. AND IF YOU MUST BE MELODRAMATIC, AT LEAST TRY FOR A LITTLE IRONY.

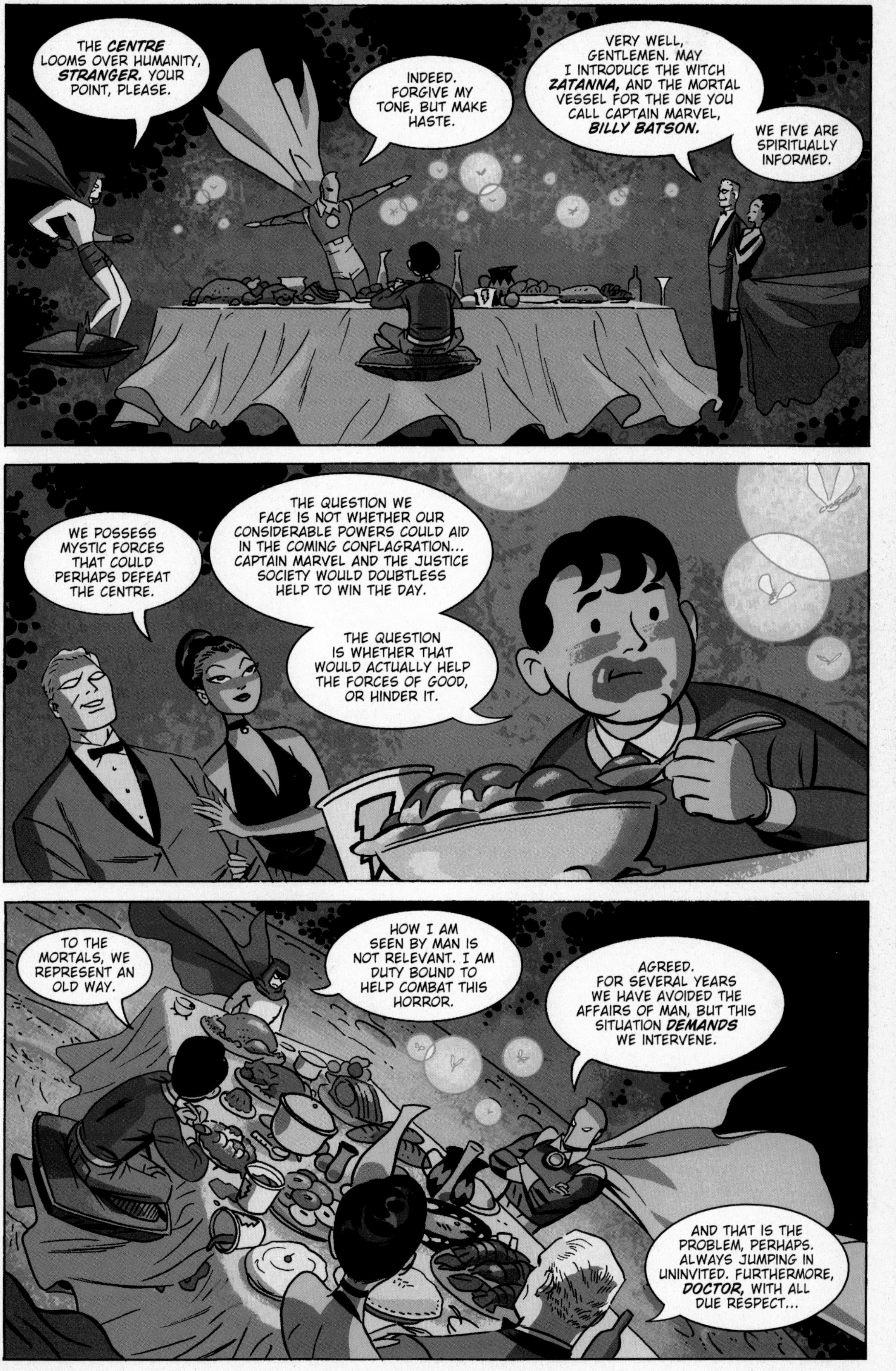

THE CENTRE LOOMS OVER HUMANITY, STRANGER. YOUR POINT, PLEASE.
INDEED. FORGIVE MY TONE, BUT MAKE HASTE.
VERY WELL, GENTLEMEN. MAY I INTRODUCE THE WITCH ZATANNA, AND THE MORTAL VESSEL FOR THE ONE YOU CALL CAPTAIN MARVEL, BILLY BATSON.
WE FIVE ARE SPIRITUALLY INFORMED.
WE POSSESS MYSTIC FORCES THAT COULD PERHAPS DEFEAT THE CENTRE.
THE QUESTION WE FACE IS NOT WHETHER OUR CONSIDERABLE POWERS COULD AID IN THE COMING CONFLAGRATION... CAPTAIN MARVEL AND THE JUSTICE SOCIETY WOULD DOUBTLESS HELP TO WIN THE DAY.
THE QUESTION IS WHETHER THAT WOULD ACTUALLY HELP THE FORCES OF GOOD, OR HINDER IT.
TO THE MORTALS, WE REPRESENT AN OLD WAY.
HOW I AM SEEN BY MAN IS NOT RELEVANT. I AM DUTY BOUND TO HELP COMBAT THIS HORROR.
AGREED. FOR SEVERAL YEARS WE HAVE AVOIDED THE AFFAIRS OF MAN, BUT THIS SITUATION DEMANDS WE INTERVENE.
AND THAT IS THE PROBLEM, PERHAPS. ALWAYS JUMPING IN UNINVITED. FURTHERMORE, DOCTOR, WITH ALL DUE RESPECT...

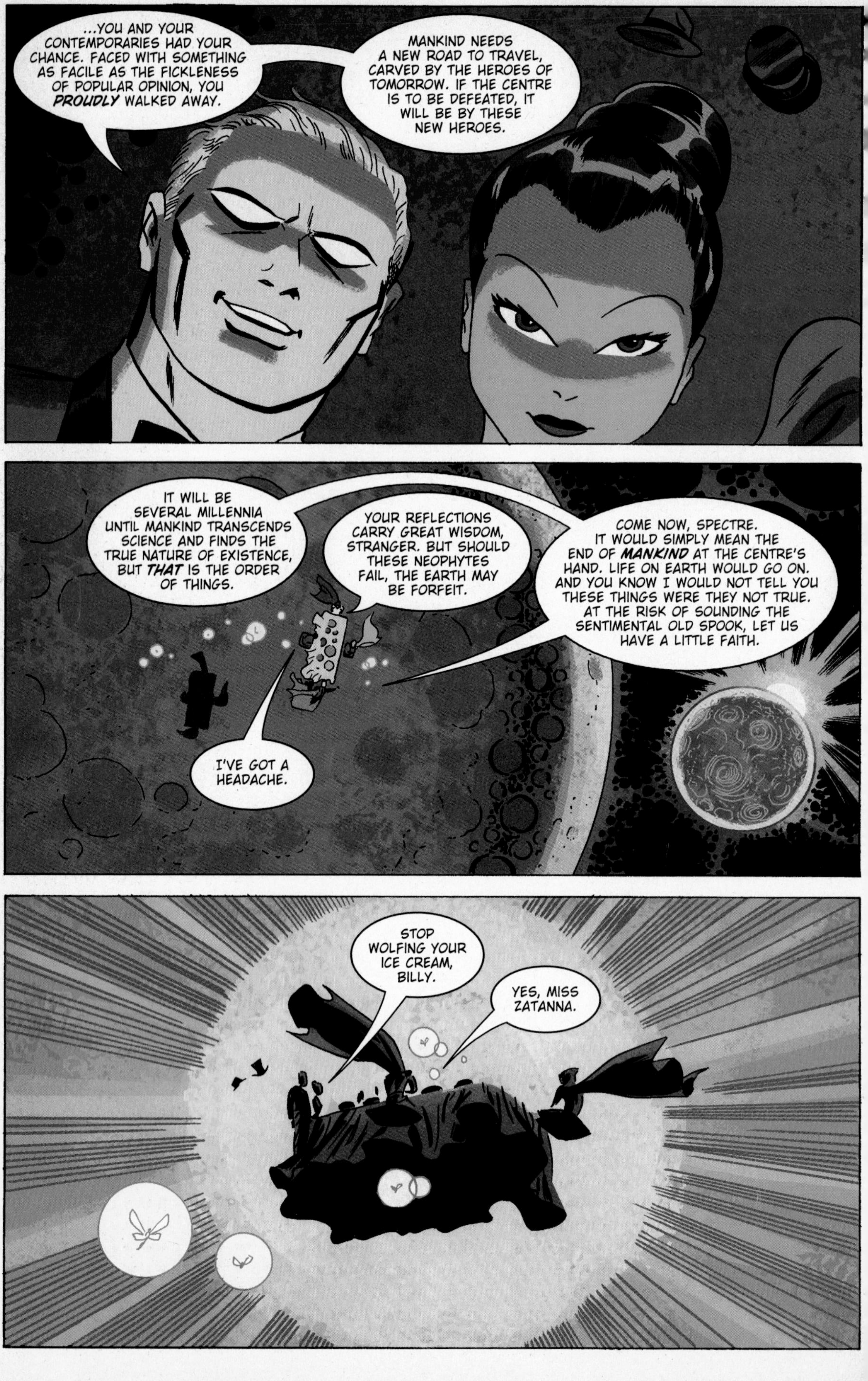
...YOU AND YOUR CONTEMPORARIES HAD YOUR CHANCE. FACED WITH SOMETHING AS FACILE AS THE FICKLENESS OF POPULAR OPINION, YOU PROUDLY WALKED AWAY.
MANKIND NEEDS A NEW ROAD TO TRAVEL, CARVED BY THE HEROES OF TOMORROW. IF THE CENTRE IS TO BE DEFEATED, IT WILL BE BY THESE NEW HEROES.
IT WILL BE SEVERAL MILLENNIA UNTIL MANKIND TRANSCENDS SCIENCE AND FINDS THE TRUE NATURE OF EXISTENCE, BUT THAT IS THE ORDER OF THINGS.
YOUR REFLECTIONS CARRY GREAT WISDOM, STRANGER. BUT SHOULD THESE NEOPHYTES FAIL, THE EARTH MAY BE FORFEIT.
COME NOW, SPECTRE. IT WOULD SIMPLY MEAN THE END OF MANKIND AT THE CENTRE'S HAND. LIFE ON EARTH WOULD GO ON. AND YOU KNOW I WOULD NOT TELL YOU THESE THINGS WERE THEY NOT TRUE. AT THE RISK OF SOUNDING THE SENTIMENTAL OLD SPOOK, LET US HAVE A LITTLE FAITH.
I'VE GOT A HEADACHE.
STOP WOLFING YOUR ICE CREAM, BILLY.
YES, MISS ZATANNA.

CHAPTER FIFTEEN
SHALL EARTH ENDURE?

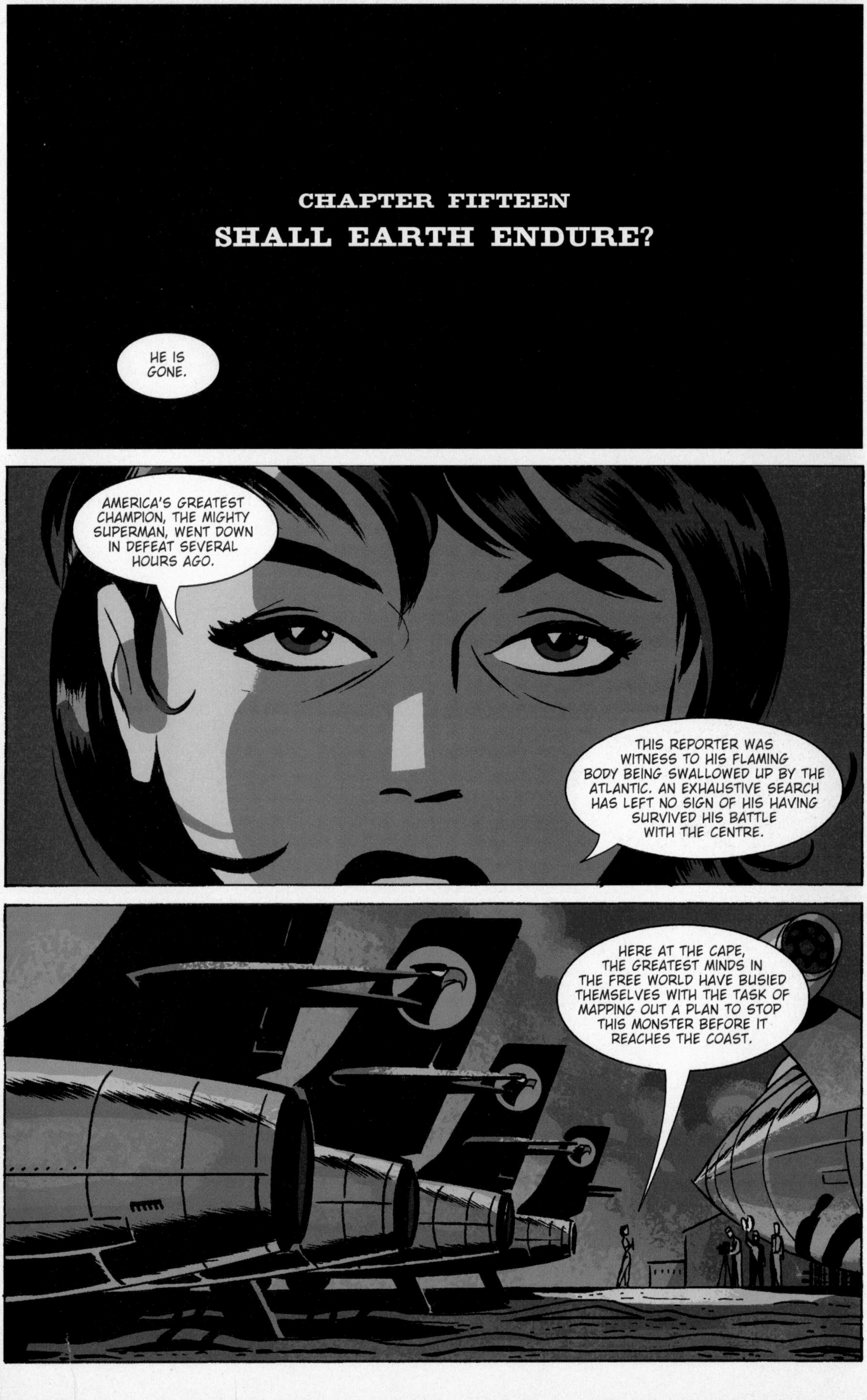
HE IS GONE.
AMERICA'S GREATEST CHAMPION, THE MIGHTY SUPERMAN, WENT DOWN IN DEFEAT SEVERAL HOURS AGO.
THIS REPORTER WAS WITNESS TO HIS FLAMING BODY BEING SWALLOWED UP BY THE ATLANTIC. AN EXHAUSTIVE SEARCH HAS LEFT NO SIGN OF HIS HAVING SURVIVED HIS BATTLE WITH THE CENTRE.
HERE AT THE CAPE, THE GREATEST MINDS IN THE FREE WORLD HAVE BUSIED THEMSELVES WITH THE TASK OF MAPPING OUT A PLAN TO STOP THIS MONSTER BEFORE IT REACHES THE COAST.

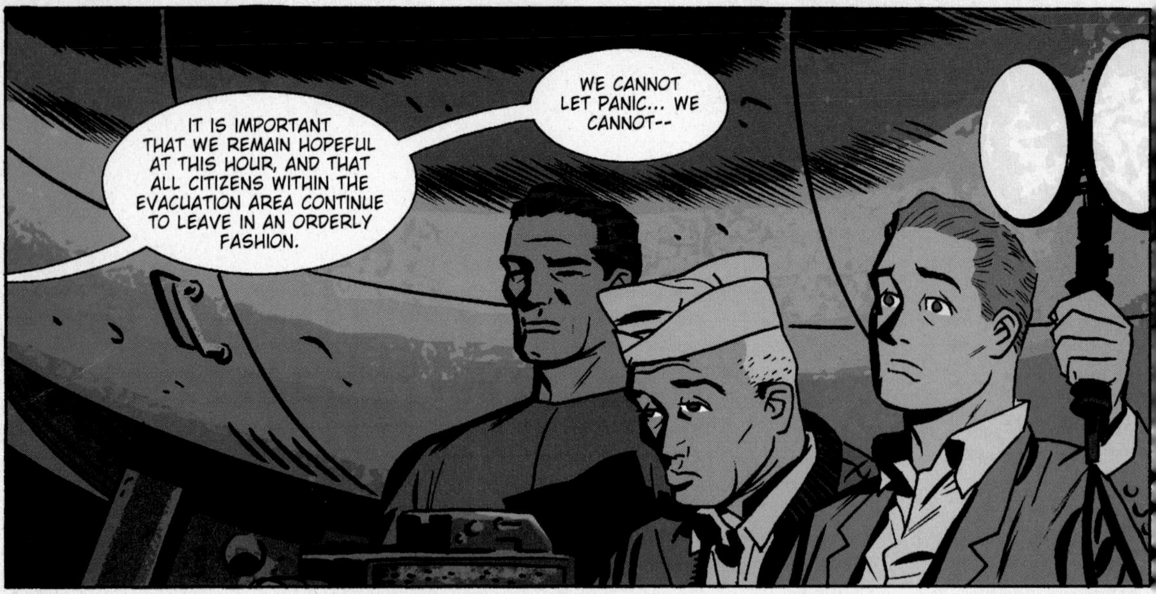
IT IS IMPORTANT THAT WE REMAIN HOPEFUL AT THIS HOUR, AND THAT ALL CITIZENS WITHIN THE EVACUATION AREA CONTINUE TO LEAVE IN AN ORDERLY FASHION.
WE CANNOT LET PANIC... WE CANNOT--

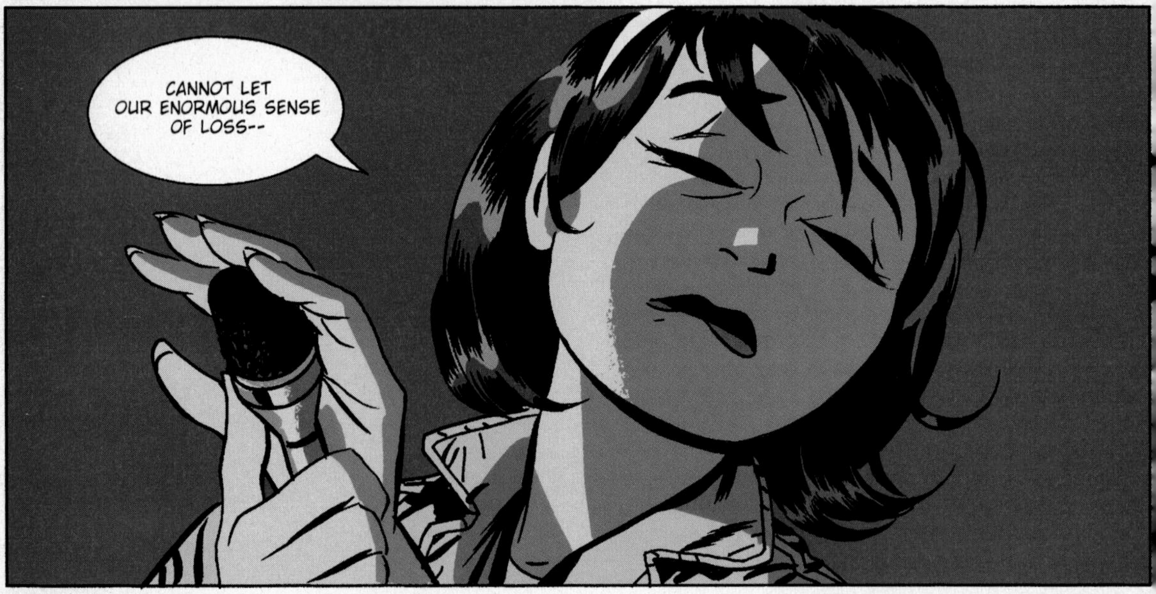
CANNOT LET OUR ENORMOUS SENSE OF LOSS--

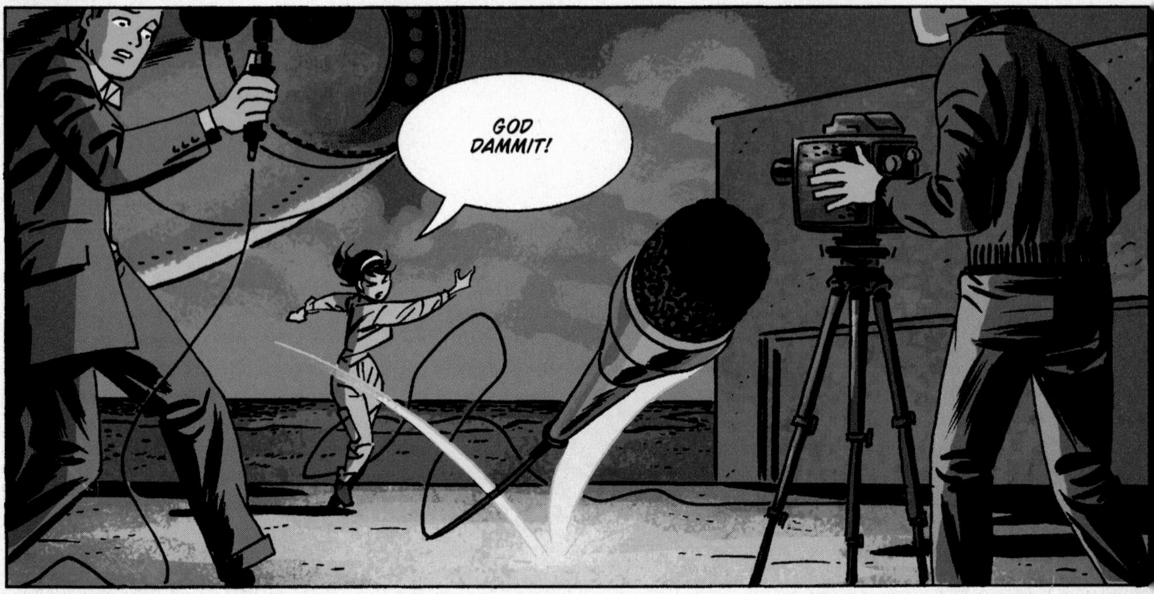
GOD DAMMIT!

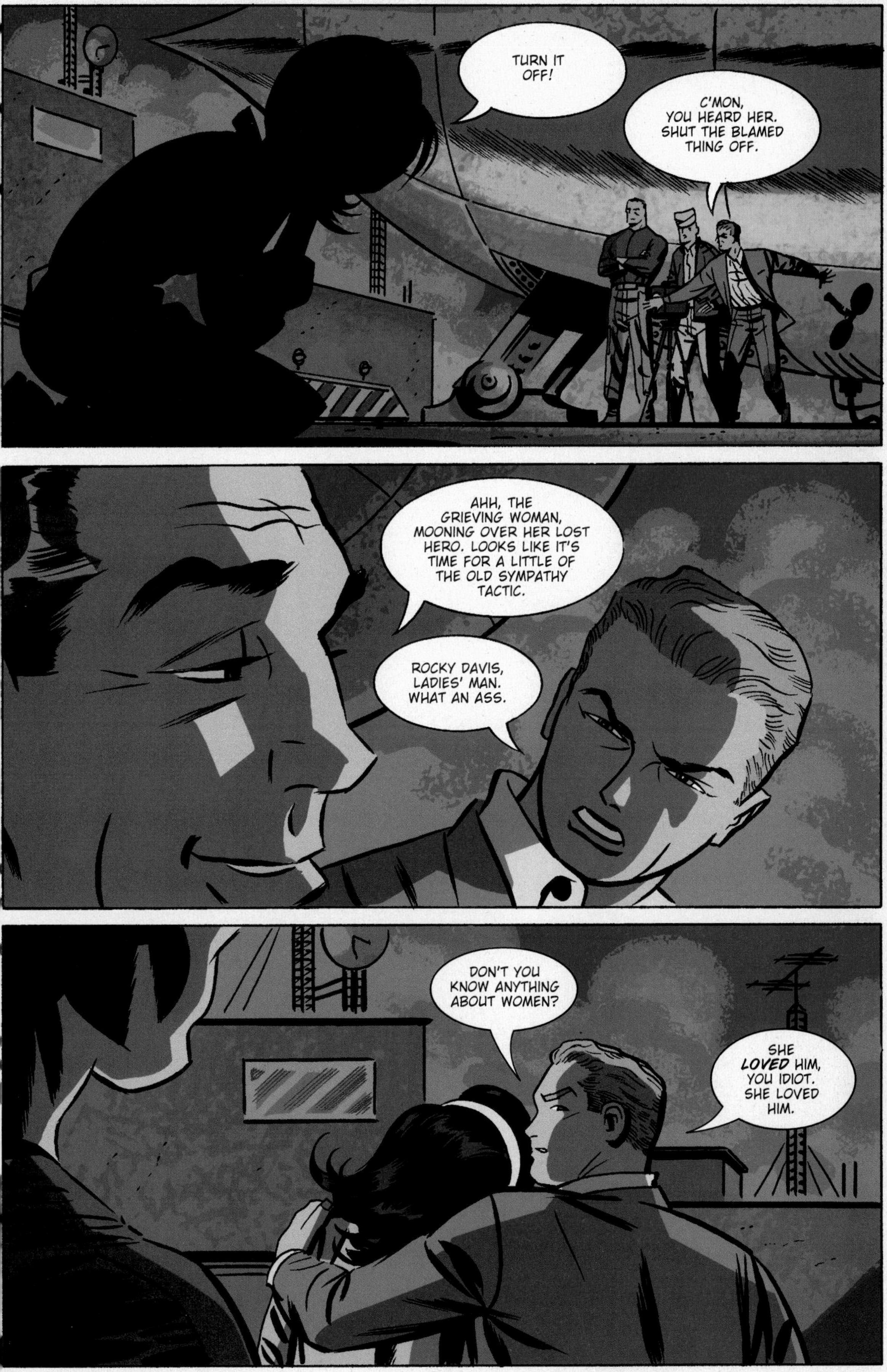
TURN IT OFF!
C'MON, YOU HEARD HER. SHUT THE BLAMED THING OFF.
AHH, THE GRIEVING WOMAN, MOONING OVER HER LOST HERO. LOOKS LIKE IT'S TIME FOR A LITTLE OF THE OLD SYMPATHY TACTIC.
ROCKY DAVIS, LADIES' MAN. WHAT AN ASS.
DON'T YOU KNOW ANYTHING ABOUT WOMEN?
SHE *LOVED* HIM, YOU IDIOT. SHE LOVED HIM.

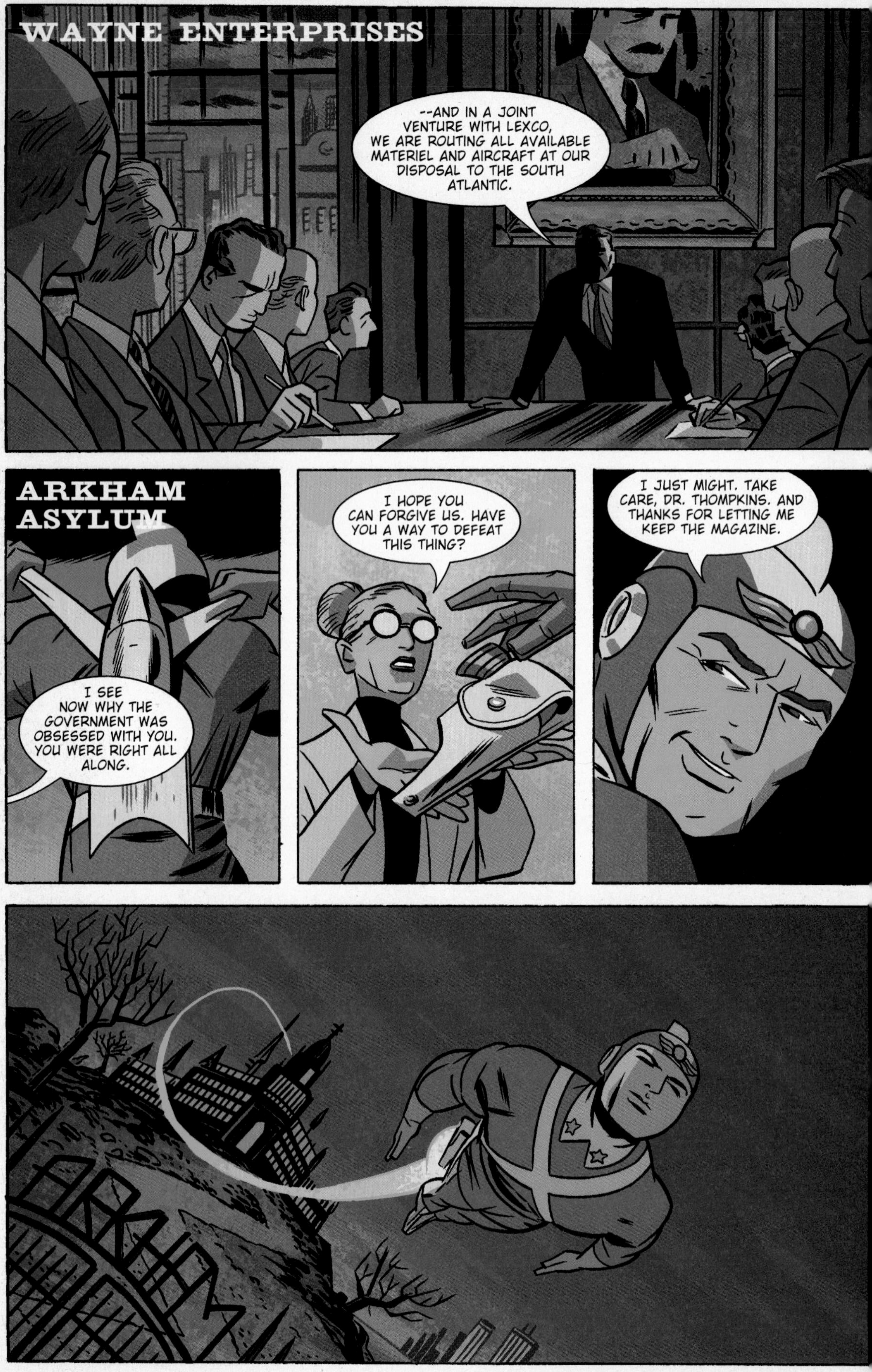
WAYNE ENTERPRISES
--AND IN A JOINT VENTURE WITH LEXCO, WE ARE ROUTING ALL AVAILABLE MATERIEL AND AIRCRAFT AT OUR DISPOSAL TO THE SOUTH ATLANTIC.
ARKHAM ASYLUM
I SEE NOW WHY THE GOVERNMENT WAS OBSESSED WITH YOU. YOU WERE RIGHT ALL ALONG.
I HOPE YOU CAN FORGIVE US. HAVE YOU A WAY TO DEFEAT THIS THING?
I JUST MIGHT. TAKE CARE, DR. THOMPKINS. AND THANKS FOR LETTING ME KEEP THE MAGAZINE.

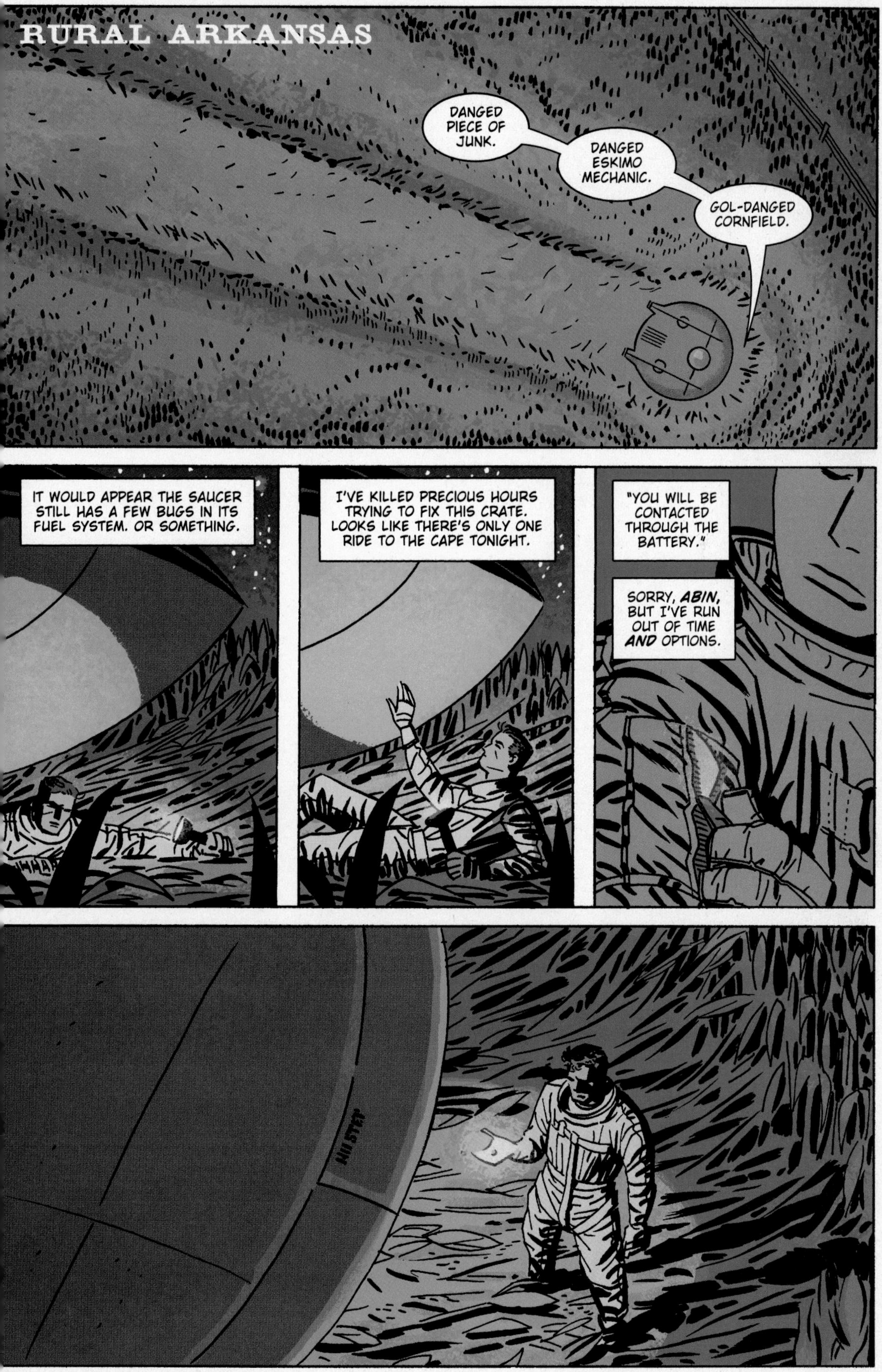
RURAL ARKANSAS
DANGED PIECE OF JUNK.
DANGED ESKIMO MECHANIC.
GOL-DANGED CORNFIELD.
IT WOULD APPEAR THE SAUCER STILL HAS A FEW BUGS IN ITS FUEL SYSTEM. OR SOMETHING.
I'VE KILLED PRECIOUS HOURS TRYING TO FIX THIS CRATE. LOOKS LIKE THERE'S ONLY ONE RIDE TO THE CAPE TONIGHT.
"YOU WILL BE CONTACTED THROUGH THE BATTERY."
SORRY, ABIN, BUT I'VE RUN OUT OF TIME AND OPTIONS.

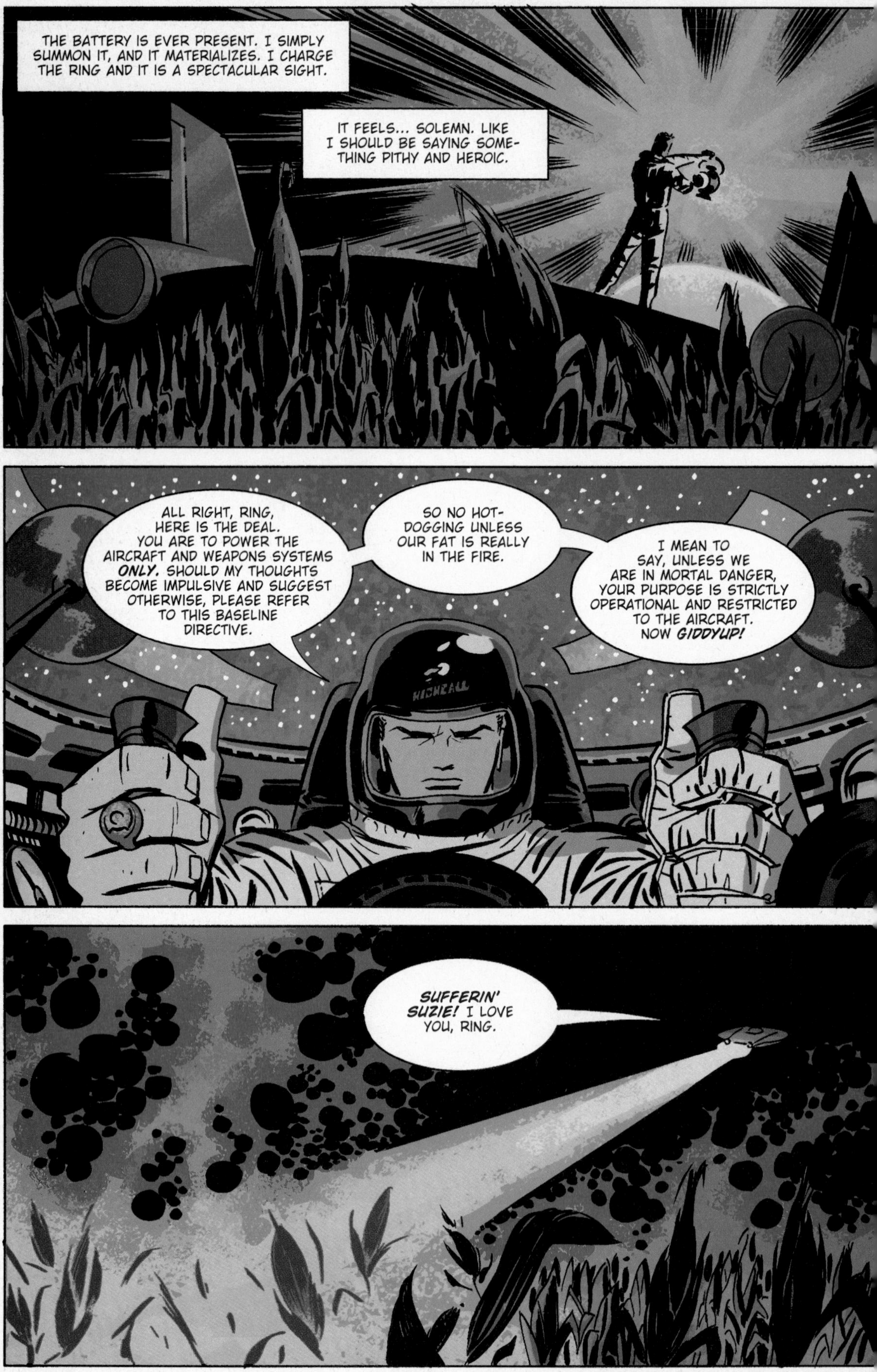
THE BATTERY IS EVER PRESENT. I SIMPLY SUMMON IT, AND IT MATERIALIZES. I CHARGE THE RING AND IT IS A SPECTACULAR SIGHT.
IT FEELS... SOLEMN. LIKE I SHOULD BE SAYING SOMETHING PITHY AND HEROIC.
ALL RIGHT, RING, HERE IS THE DEAL. YOU ARE TO POWER THE AIRCRAFT AND WEAPONS SYSTEMS ***ONLY.*** SHOULD MY THOUGHTS BECOME IMPULSIVE AND SUGGEST OTHERWISE, PLEASE REFER TO THIS BASELINE DIRECTIVE.
SO NO HOT-DOGGING UNLESS OUR FAT IS REALLY IN THE FIRE.
I MEAN TO SAY, UNLESS WE ARE IN MORTAL DANGER, YOUR PURPOSE IS STRICTLY OPERATIONAL AND RESTRICTED TO THE AIRCRAFT. NOW ***GIDDYUP!***
SUFFERIN' SUZIE! I LOVE YOU, RING.

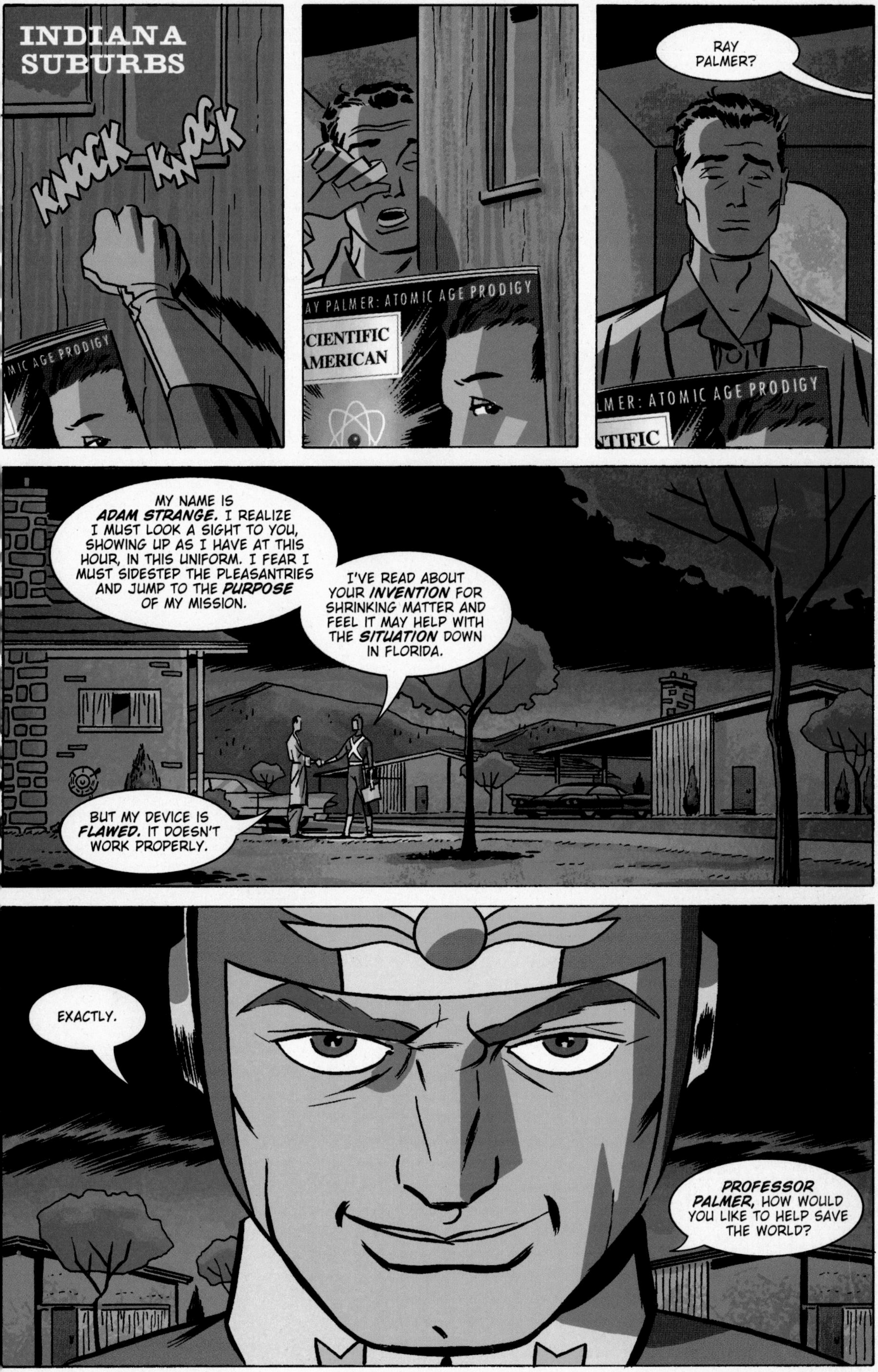

INDIANA SUBURBS
KNOCK KNOCK
MIC AGE PRODIGY
AY PALMER: ATOMIC AGE PRODIGY
SCIENTIFIC AMERICAN
RAY PALMER?
LMER: ATOMIC AGE PRODIGY
MY NAME IS ADAM STRANGE. I REALIZE I MUST LOOK A SIGHT TO YOU, SHOWING UP AS I HAVE AT THIS HOUR, IN THIS UNIFORM. I FEAR I MUST SIDESTEP THE PLEASANTRIES AND JUMP TO THE PURPOSE OF MY MISSION.
I'VE READ ABOUT YOUR INVENTION FOR SHRINKING MATTER AND FEEL IT MAY HELP WITH THE SITUATION DOWN IN FLORIDA.
BUT MY DEVICE IS FLAWED. IT DOESN'T WORK PROPERLY.
EXACTLY.
PROFESSOR PALMER, HOW WOULD YOU LIKE TO HELP SAVE THE WORLD?

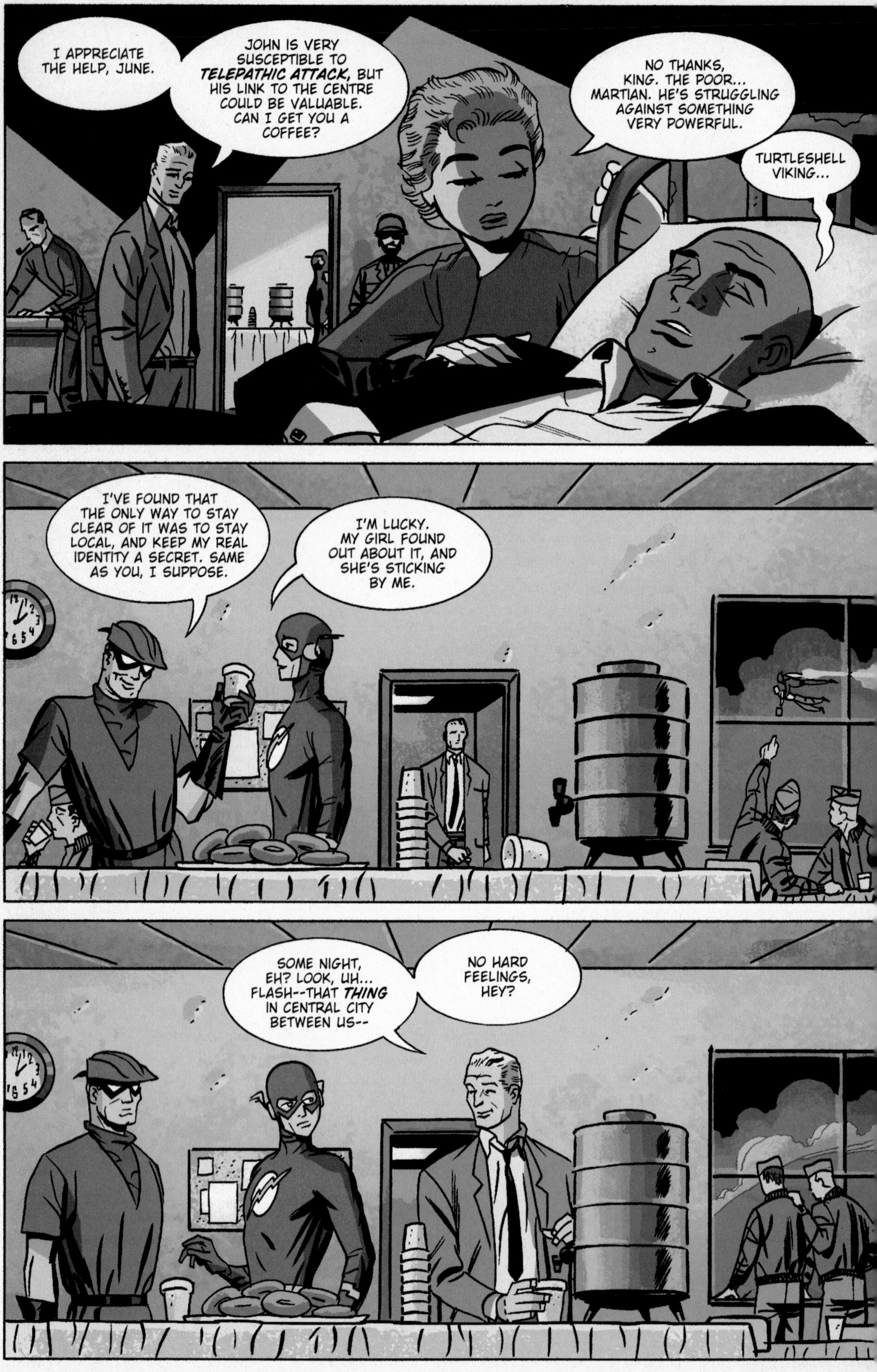
I APPRECIATE THE HELP, JUNE.
JOHN IS VERY SUSCEPTIBLE TO *TELEPATHIC ATTACK*, BUT HIS LINK TO THE CENTRE COULD BE VALUABLE. CAN I GET YOU A COFFEE?
NO THANKS, KING. THE POOR... MARTIAN. HE'S STRUGGLING AGAINST SOMETHING VERY POWERFUL.
TURTLESHELL VIKING...
I'VE FOUND THAT THE ONLY WAY TO STAY CLEAR OF IT WAS TO STAY LOCAL, AND KEEP MY REAL IDENTITY A SECRET. SAME AS YOU, I SUPPOSE.
I'M LUCKY. MY GIRL FOUND OUT ABOUT IT, AND SHE'S STICKING BY ME.
SOME NIGHT, EH? LOOK, UH... FLASH--THAT *THING* IN CENTRAL CITY BETWEEN US--
NO HARD FEELINGS, HEY?

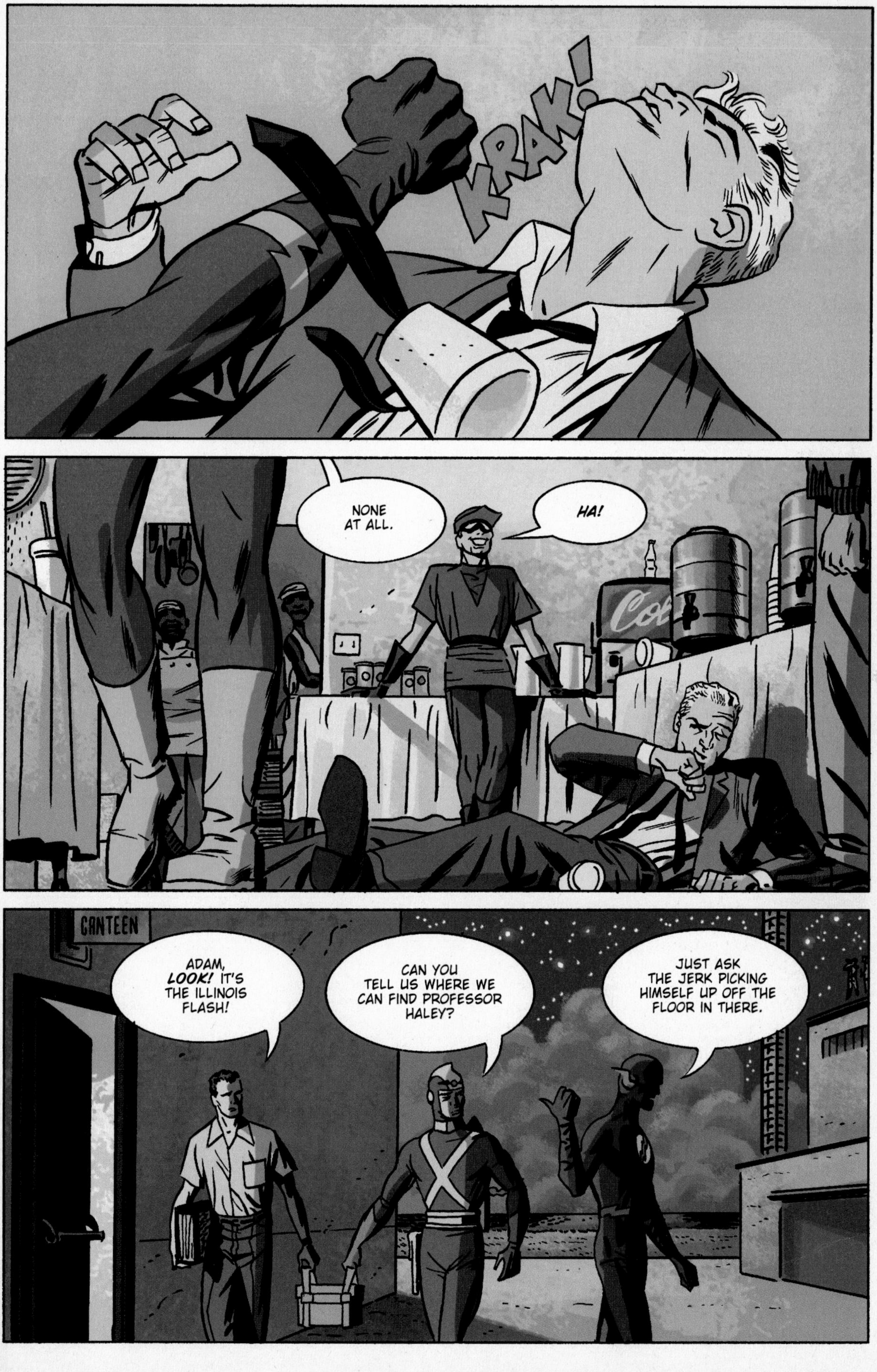
KRAK!
NONE AT ALL.
HA!
CANTEEN
ADAM, LOOK! IT'S THE ILLINOIS FLASH!
CAN YOU TELL US WHERE WE CAN FIND PROFESSOR HALEY?
JUST ASK THE JERK PICKING HIMSELF UP OFF THE FLOOR IN THERE.

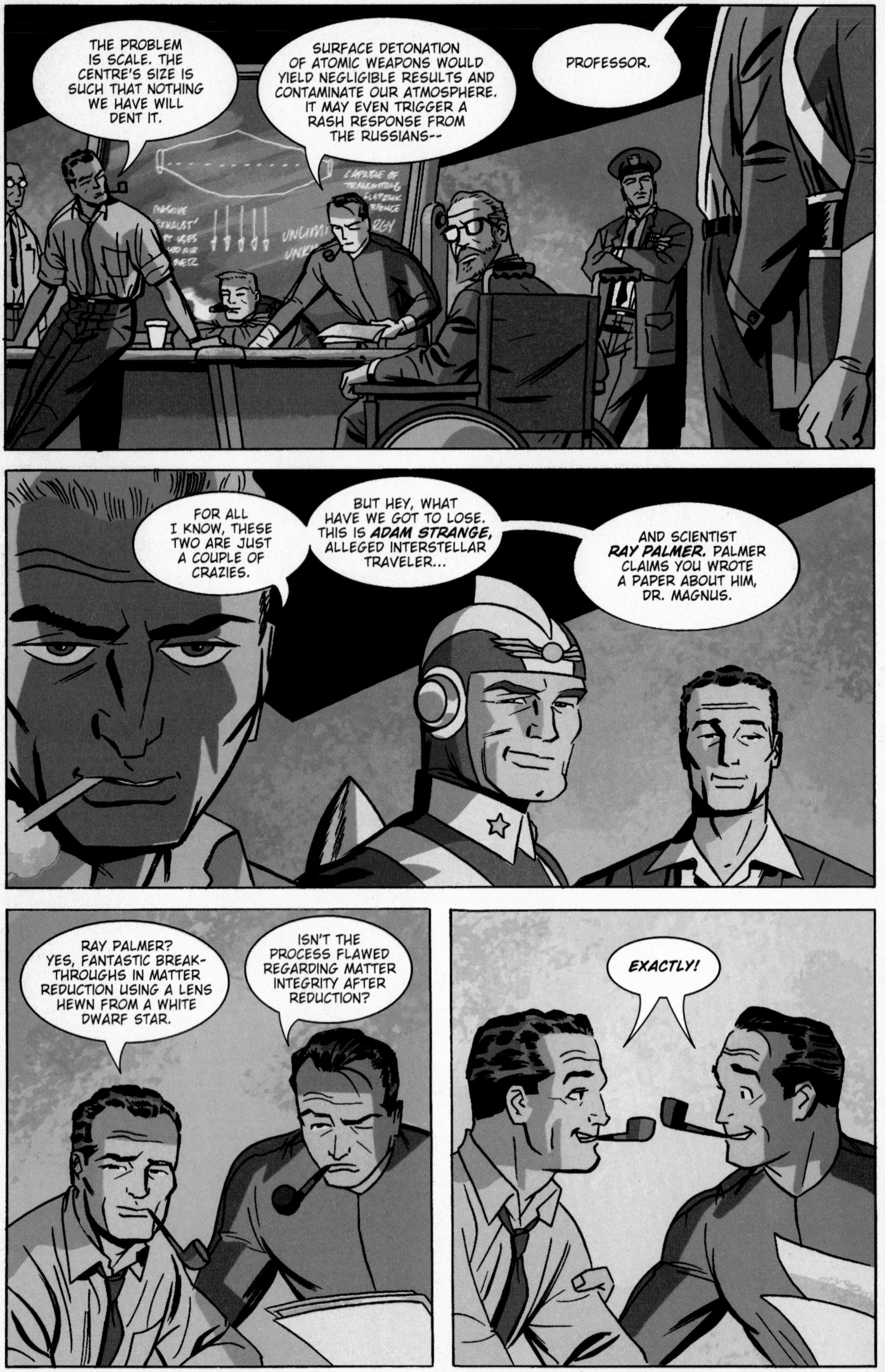
THE PROBLEM IS SCALE. THE CENTRE'S SIZE IS SUCH THAT NOTHING WE HAVE WILL DENT IT.
SURFACE DETONATION OF ATOMIC WEAPONS WOULD YIELD NEGLIGIBLE RESULTS AND CONTAMINATE OUR ATMOSPHERE. IT MAY EVEN TRIGGER A RASH RESPONSE FROM THE RUSSIANS--
PROFESSOR.
FOR ALL I KNOW, THESE TWO ARE JUST A COUPLE OF CRAZIES.
BUT HEY, WHAT HAVE WE GOT TO LOSE. THIS IS ***ADAM STRANGE,*** ALLEGED INTERSTELLAR TRAVELER...
AND SCIENTIST ***RAY PALMER.*** PALMER CLAIMS YOU WROTE A PAPER ABOUT HIM, DR. MAGNUS.
RAY PALMER? YES, FANTASTIC BREAK-THROUGHS IN MATTER REDUCTION USING A LENS HEWN FROM A WHITE DWARF STAR.
ISN'T THE PROCESS FLAWED REGARDING MATTER INTEGRITY AFTER REDUCTION?
EXACTLY!

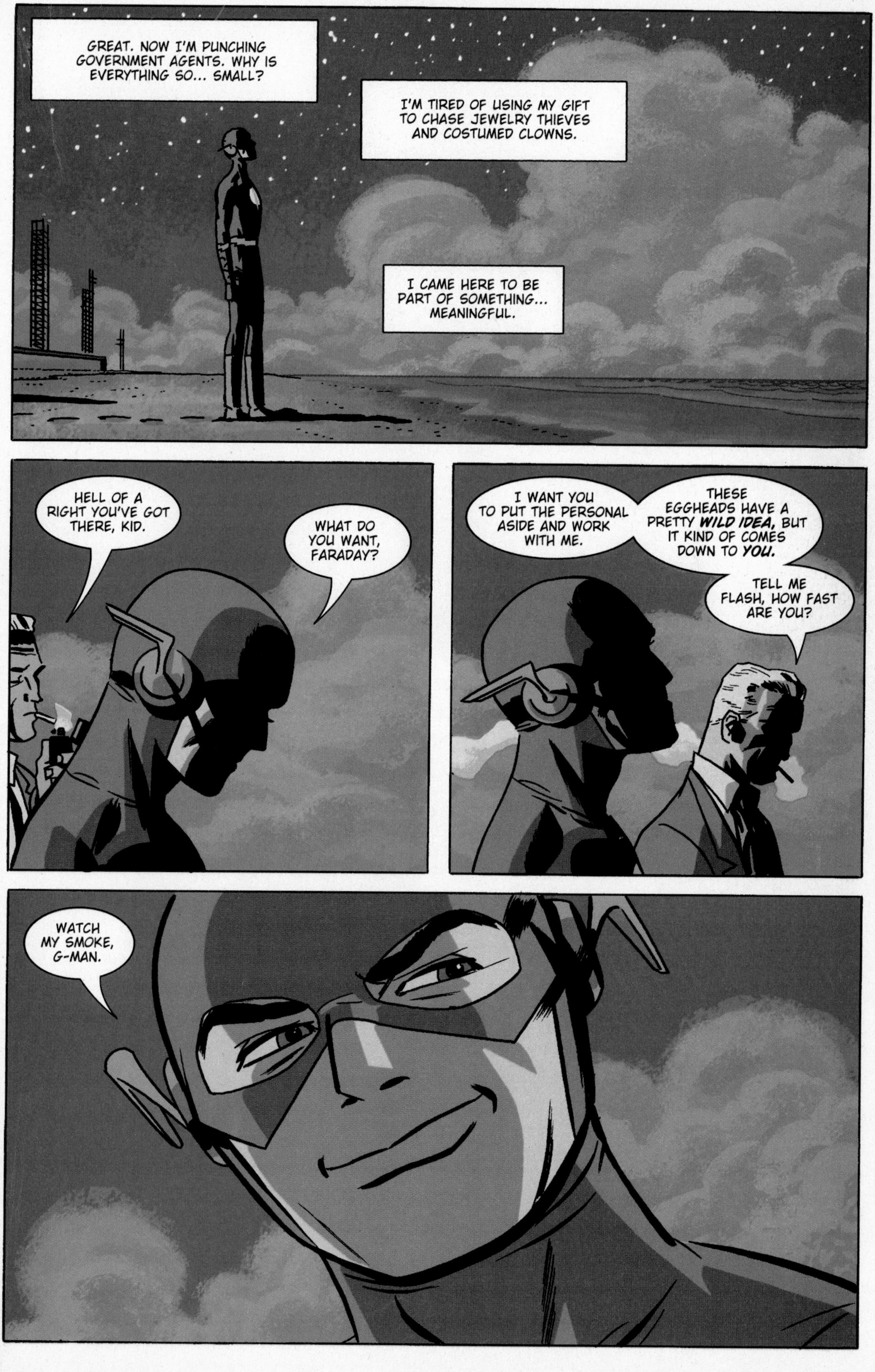
GREAT. NOW I'M PUNCHING GOVERNMENT AGENTS. WHY IS EVERYTHING SO... SMALL?
I'M TIRED OF USING MY GIFT TO CHASE JEWELRY THIEVES AND COSTUMED CLOWNS.
I CAME HERE TO BE PART OF SOMETHING... MEANINGFUL.
HELL OF A RIGHT YOU'VE GOT THERE, KID.
WHAT DO YOU WANT, FARADAY?
I WANT YOU TO PUT THE PERSONAL ASIDE AND WORK WITH ME.
THESE EGGHEADS HAVE A PRETTY ***WILD IDEA,*** BUT IT KIND OF COMES DOWN TO ***YOU.***
TELL ME FLASH, HOW FAST ARE YOU?
WATCH MY SMOKE, G-MAN.

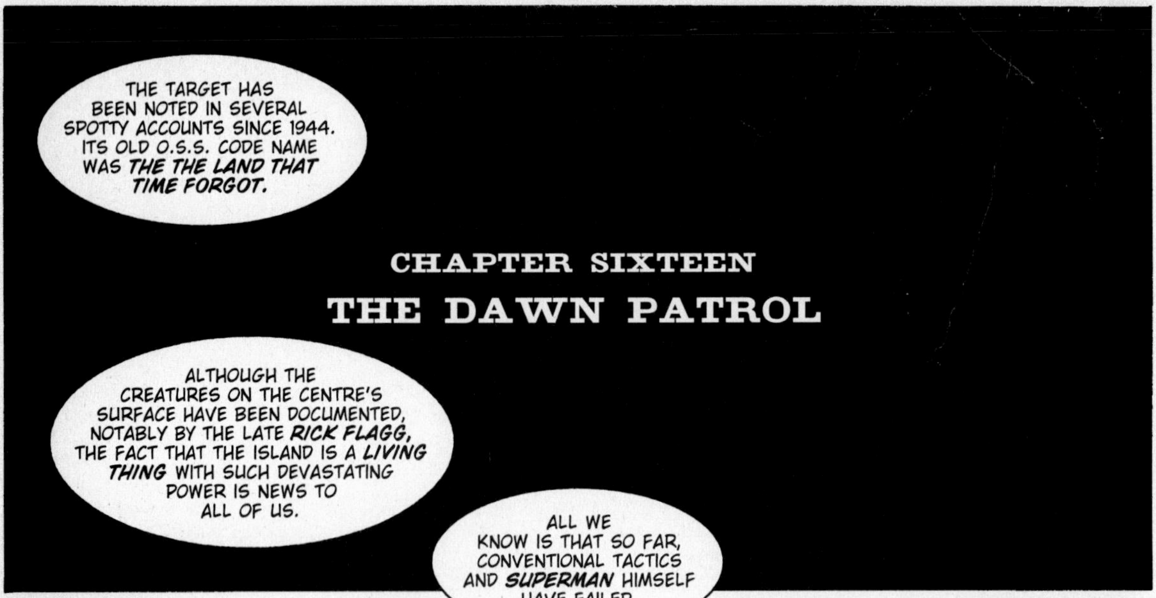
THE TARGET HAS BEEN NOTED IN SEVERAL SPOTTY ACCOUNTS SINCE 1944. ITS OLD O.S.S. CODE NAME WAS *THE THE LAND THAT TIME FORGOT.*
CHAPTER SIXTEEN
THE DAWN PATROL
ALTHOUGH THE CREATURES ON THE CENTRE'S SURFACE HAVE BEEN DOCUMENTED, NOTABLY BY THE LATE *RICK FLAGG,* THE FACT THAT THE ISLAND IS A *LIVING THING* WITH SUCH DEVASTATING POWER IS NEWS TO ALL OF US.
ALL WE KNOW IS THAT SO FAR, CONVENTIONAL TACTICS AND *SUPERMAN* HIMSELF HAVE FAILED.

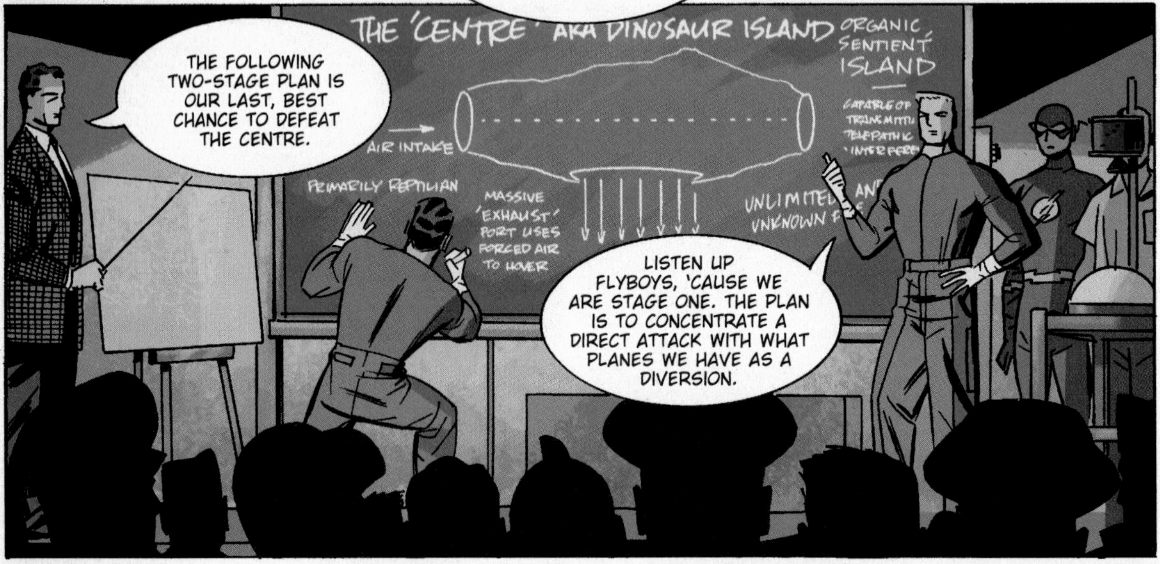
THE 'CENTRE' AKA DINOSAUR ISLAND
ORGANIC, SENTIENT ISLAND
AIR INTAKE
PRIMARILY REPTILIAN
MASSIVE 'EXHAUST' PORT USES FORCED AIR TO HOVER
THE FOLLOWING TWO-STAGE PLAN IS OUR LAST, BEST CHANCE TO DEFEAT THE CENTRE.
LISTEN UP FLYBOYS, 'CAUSE WE ARE STAGE ONE. THE PLAN IS TO CONCENTRATE A DIRECT ATTACK WITH WHAT PLANES WE HAVE AS A DIVERSION.

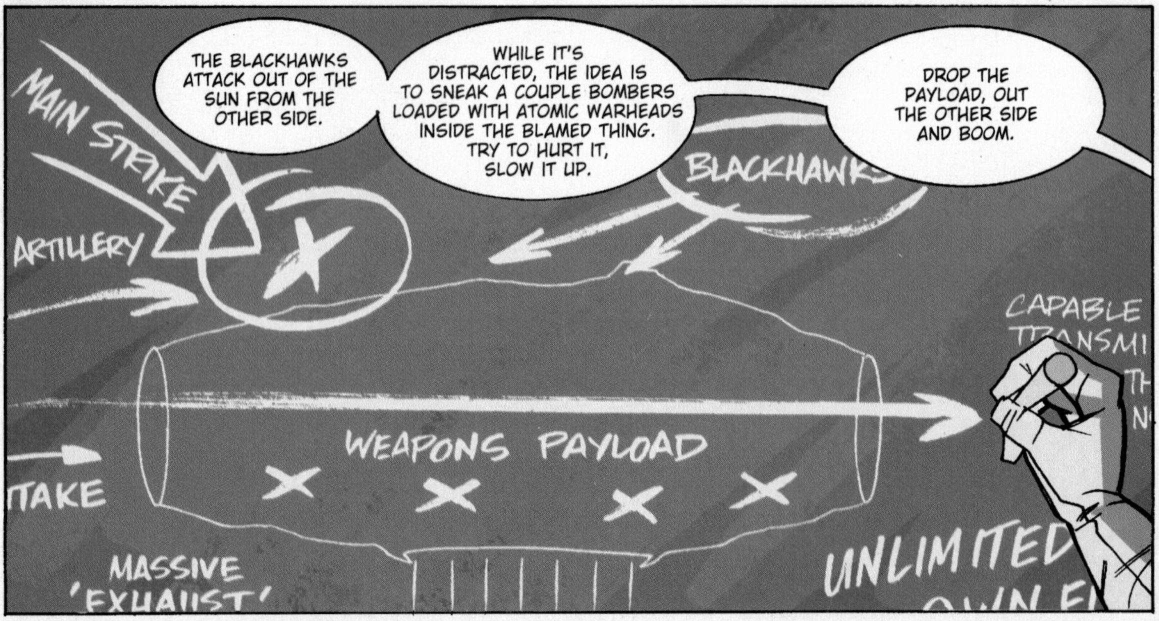
THE BLACKHAWKS ATTACK OUT OF THE SUN FROM THE OTHER SIDE.
WHILE IT'S DISTRACTED, THE IDEA IS TO SNEAK A COUPLE BOMBERS LOADED WITH ATOMIC WARHEADS INSIDE THE BLAMED THING. TRY TO HURT IT, SLOW IT UP.
DROP THE PAYLOAD, OUT THE OTHER SIDE AND BOOM.
MAIN STRIKE
ARTILLERY
WEAPONS PAYLOAD
CAPABLE
MASSIVE

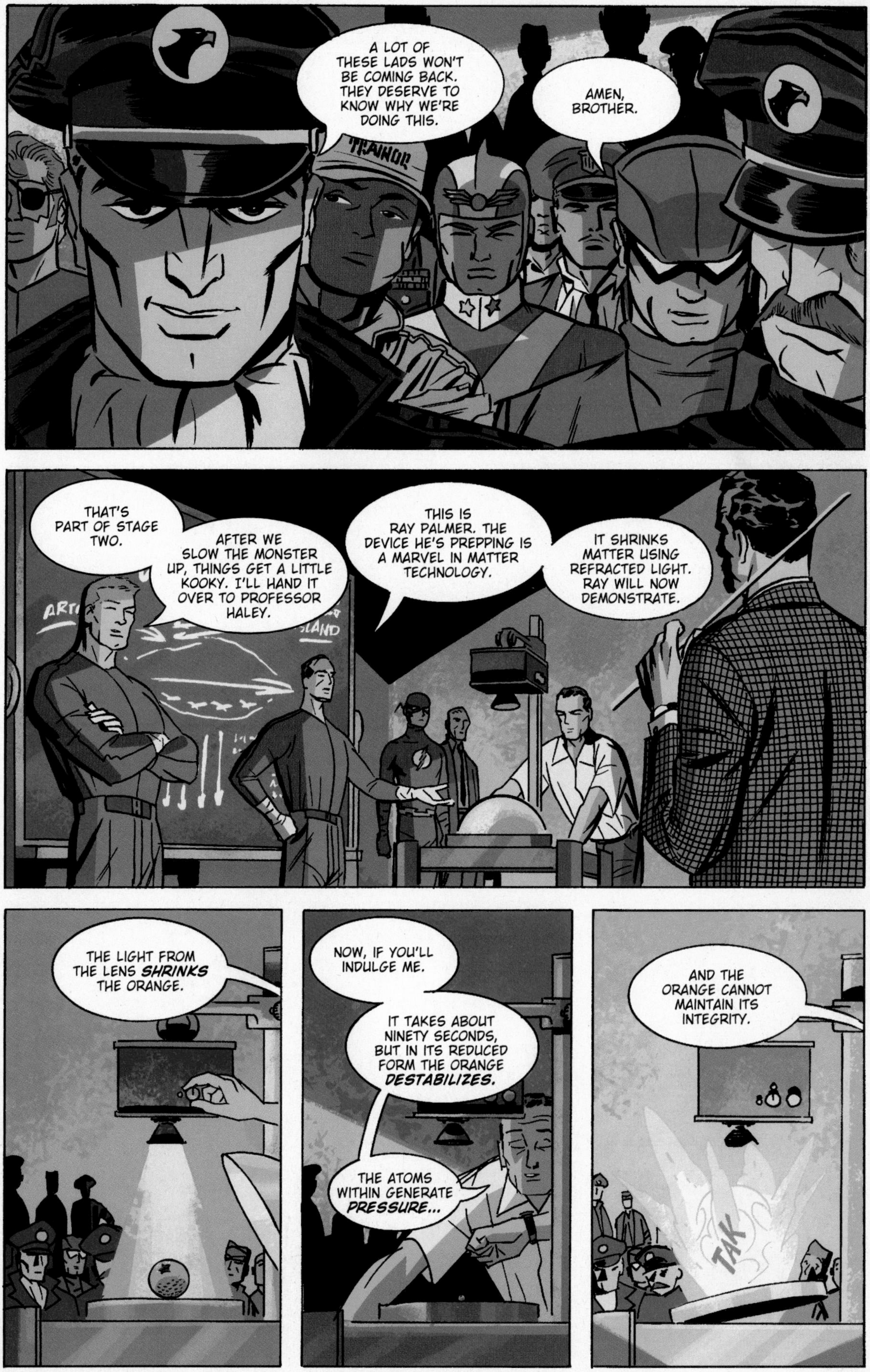
A LOT OF THESE LADS WON'T BE COMING BACK. THEY DESERVE TO KNOW WHY WE'RE DOING THIS.
AMEN, BROTHER.
THAT'S PART OF STAGE TWO.
AFTER WE SLOW THE MONSTER UP, THINGS GET A LITTLE KOOKY. I'LL HAND IT OVER TO PROFESSOR HALEY.
THIS IS RAY PALMER. THE DEVICE HE'S PREPPING IS A MARVEL IN MATTER TECHNOLOGY.
IT SHRINKS MATTER USING REFRACTED LIGHT. RAY WILL NOW DEMONSTRATE.
THE LIGHT FROM THE LENS ***SHRINKS*** THE ORANGE.
NOW, IF YOU'LL INDULGE ME.
IT TAKES ABOUT NINETY SECONDS, BUT IN ITS REDUCED FORM THE ORANGE ***DESTABILIZES.***
THE ATOMS WITHIN GENERATE ***PRESSURE...***
AND THE ORANGE CANNOT MAINTAIN ITS INTEGRITY.
TAK

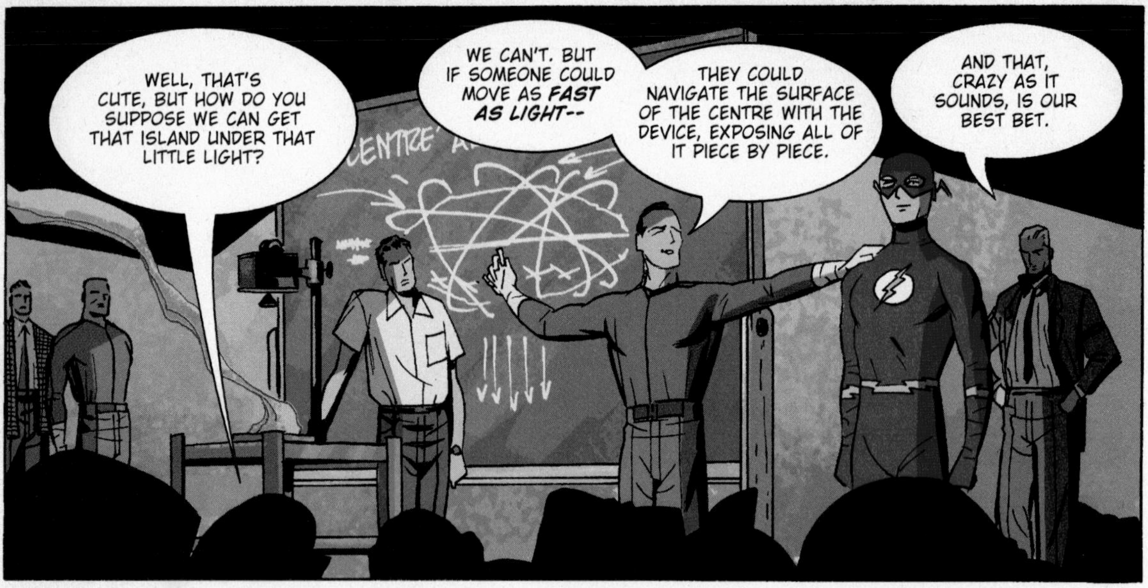
WELL, THAT'S CUTE, BUT HOW DO YOU SUPPOSE WE CAN GET THAT ISLAND UNDER THAT LITTLE LIGHT?
WE CAN'T. BUT IF SOMEONE COULD MOVE AS FAST AS LIGHT--
THEY COULD NAVIGATE THE SURFACE OF THE CENTRE WITH THE DEVICE, EXPOSING ALL OF IT PIECE BY PIECE.
AND THAT, CRAZY AS IT SOUNDS, IS OUR BEST BET.

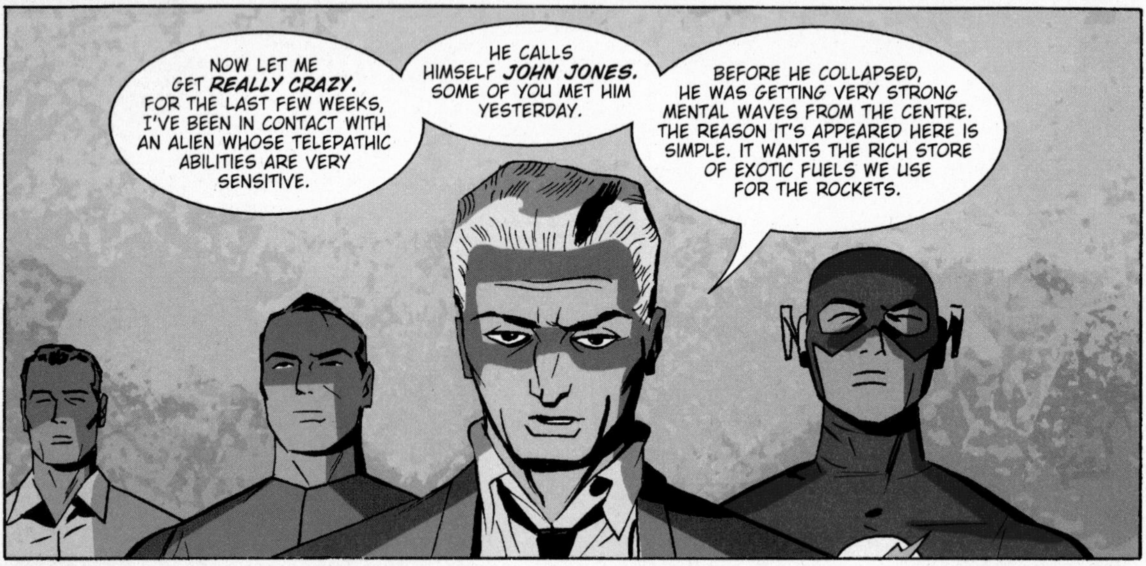
NOW LET ME GET REALLY CRAZY. FOR THE LAST FEW WEEKS, I'VE BEEN IN CONTACT WITH AN ALIEN WHOSE TELEPATHIC ABILITIES ARE VERY SENSITIVE.
HE CALLS HIMSELF JOHN JONES. SOME OF YOU MET HIM YESTERDAY.
BEFORE HE COLLAPSED, HE WAS GETTING VERY STRONG MENTAL WAVES FROM THE CENTRE. THE REASON IT'S APPEARED HERE IS SIMPLE. IT WANTS THE RICH STORE OF EXOTIC FUELS WE USE FOR THE ROCKETS.

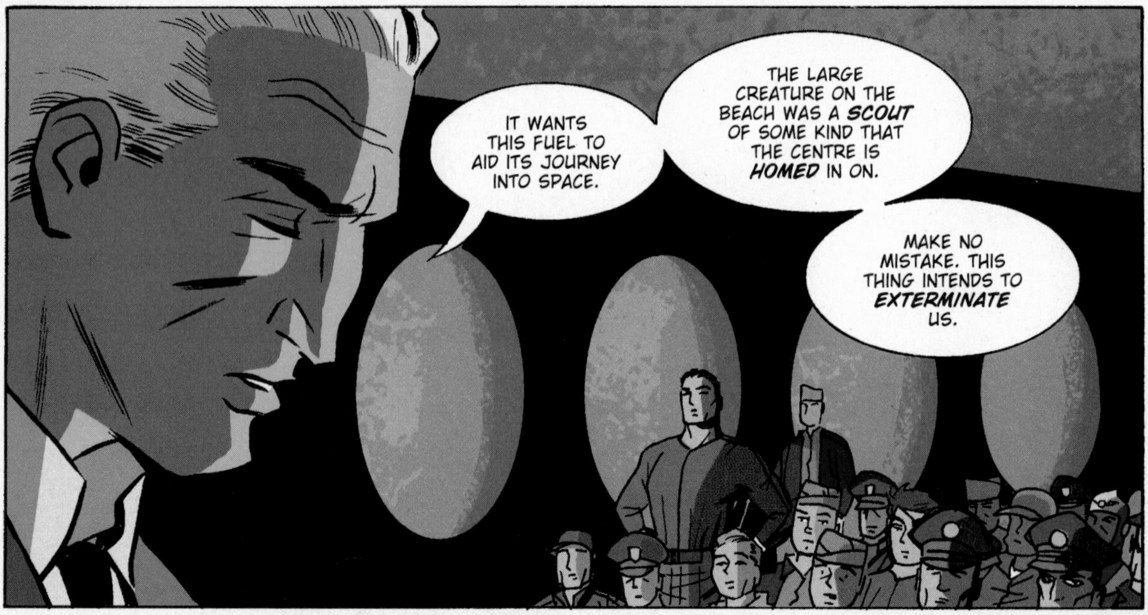
IT WANTS THIS FUEL TO AID ITS JOURNEY INTO SPACE.
THE LARGE CREATURE ON THE BEACH WAS A SCOUT OF SOME KIND THAT THE CENTRE IS HOMED IN ON.
MAKE NO MISTAKE. THIS THING INTENDS TO EXTERMINATE US.

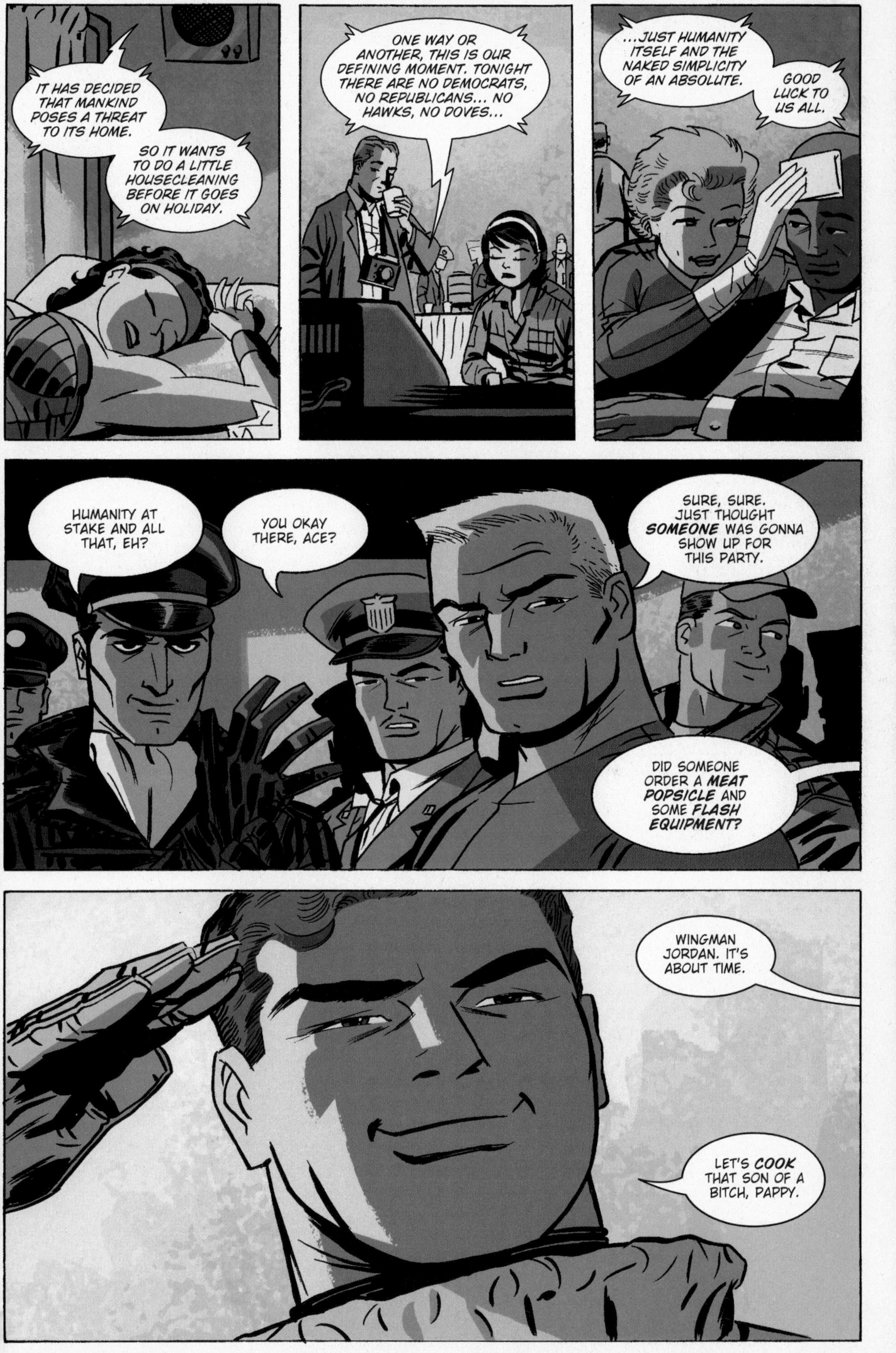
IT HAS DECIDED THAT MANKIND POSES A THREAT TO ITS HOME.
SO IT WANTS TO DO A LITTLE HOUSECLEANING BEFORE IT GOES ON HOLIDAY.
ONE WAY OR ANOTHER, THIS IS OUR DEFINING MOMENT. TONIGHT THERE ARE NO DEMOCRATS, NO REPUBLICANS... NO HAWKS, NO DOVES...
...JUST HUMANITY ITSELF AND THE NAKED SIMPLICITY OF AN ABSOLUTE.
GOOD LUCK TO US ALL.
HUMANITY AT STAKE AND ALL THAT, EH?
YOU OKAY THERE, ACE?
SURE, SURE. JUST THOUGHT SOMEONE WAS GONNA SHOW UP FOR THIS PARTY.
DID SOMEONE ORDER A MEAT POPSICLE AND SOME FLASH EQUIPMENT?
WINGMAN JORDAN. IT'S ABOUT TIME.
LET'S COOK THAT SON OF A BITCH, PAPPY.

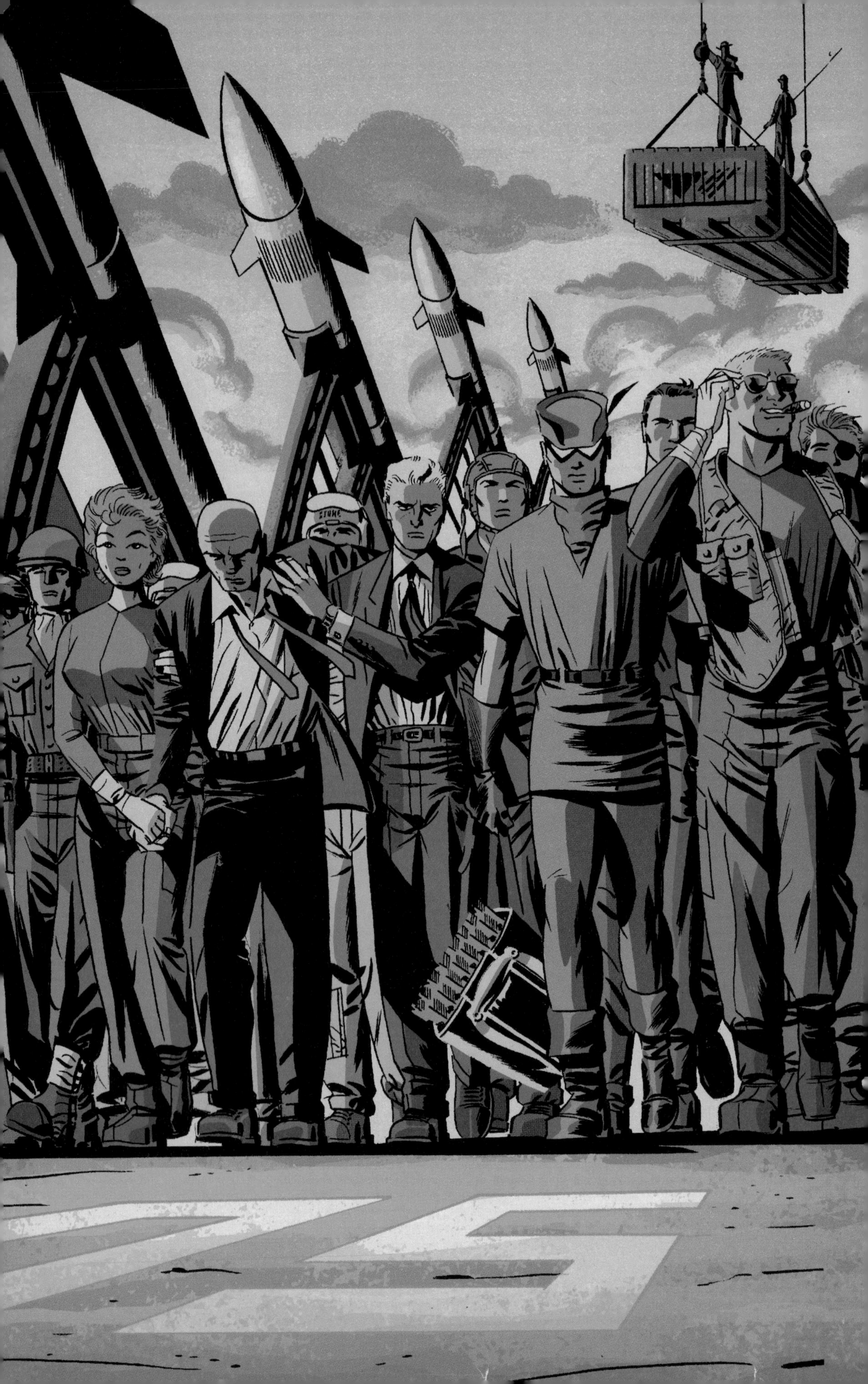

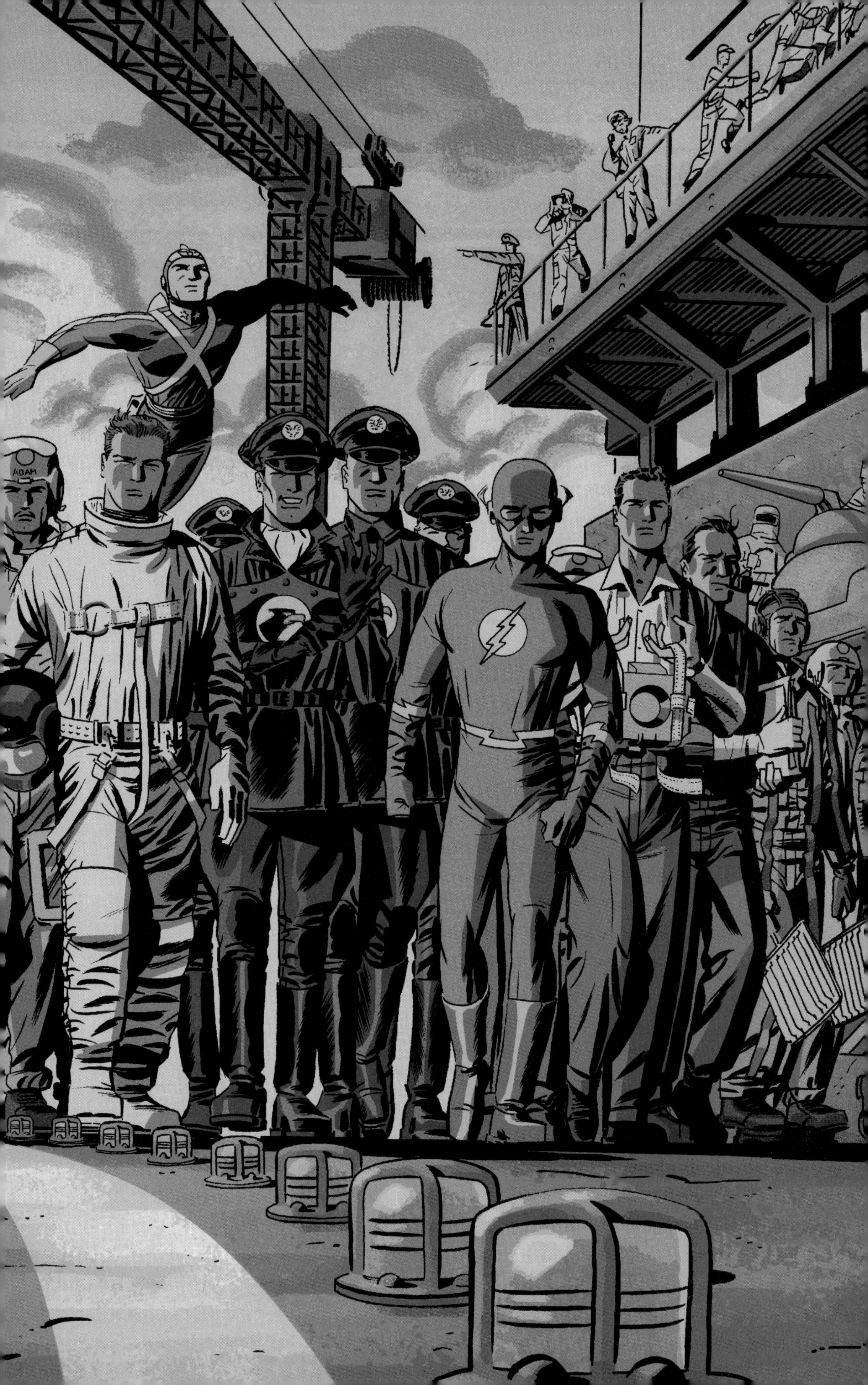
ADAM

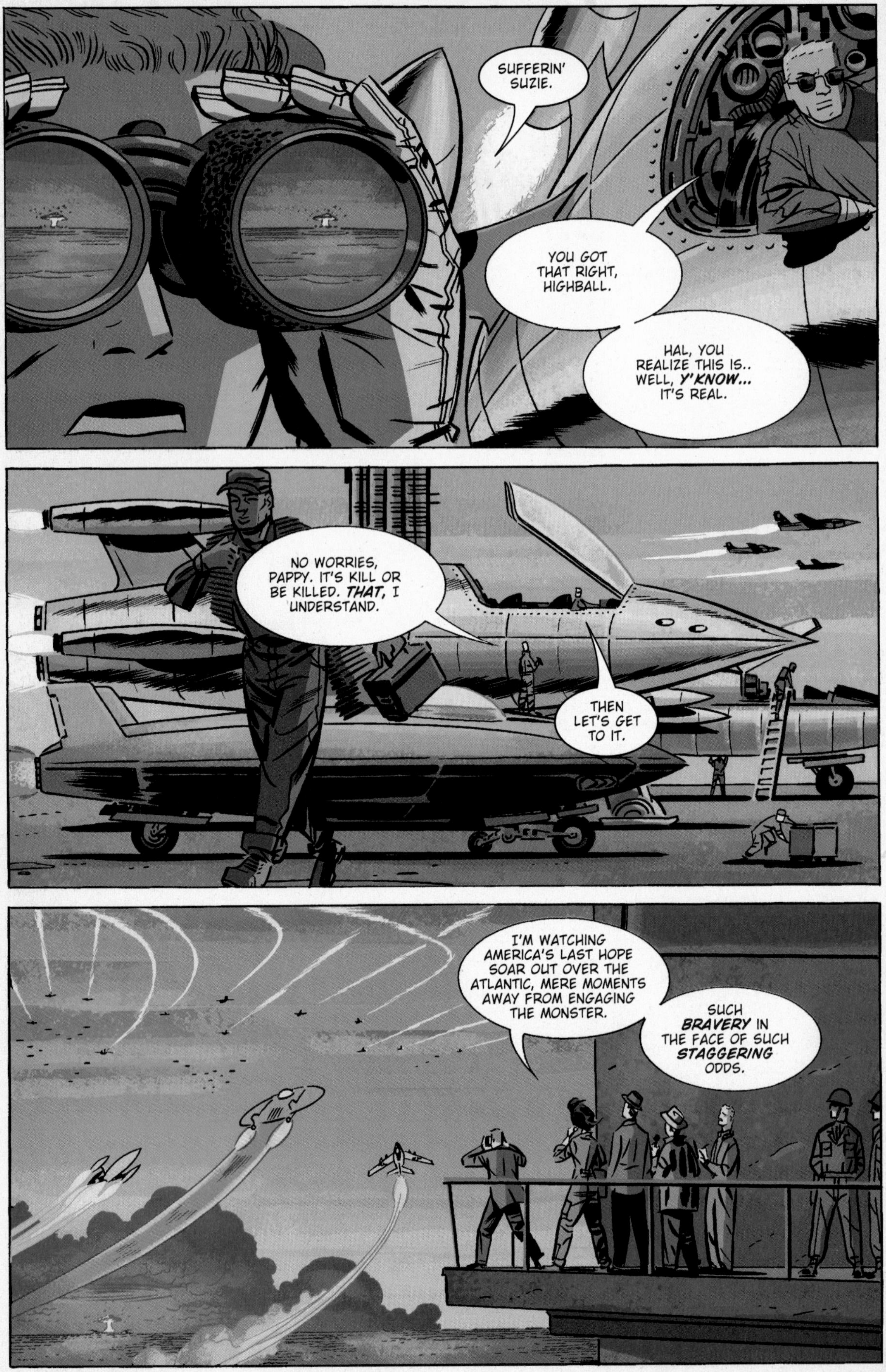
SUFFERIN' SUZIE.
YOU GOT THAT RIGHT, HIGHBALL.
HAL, YOU REALIZE THIS IS.. WELL, Y'KNOW... IT'S REAL.
NO WORRIES, PAPPY. IT'S KILL OR BE KILLED. THAT, I UNDERSTAND.
THEN LET'S GET TO IT.
I'M WATCHING AMERICA'S LAST HOPE SOAR OUT OVER THE ATLANTIC, MERE MOMENTS AWAY FROM ENGAGING THE MONSTER.
SUCH BRAVERY IN THE FACE OF SUCH STAGGERING ODDS.

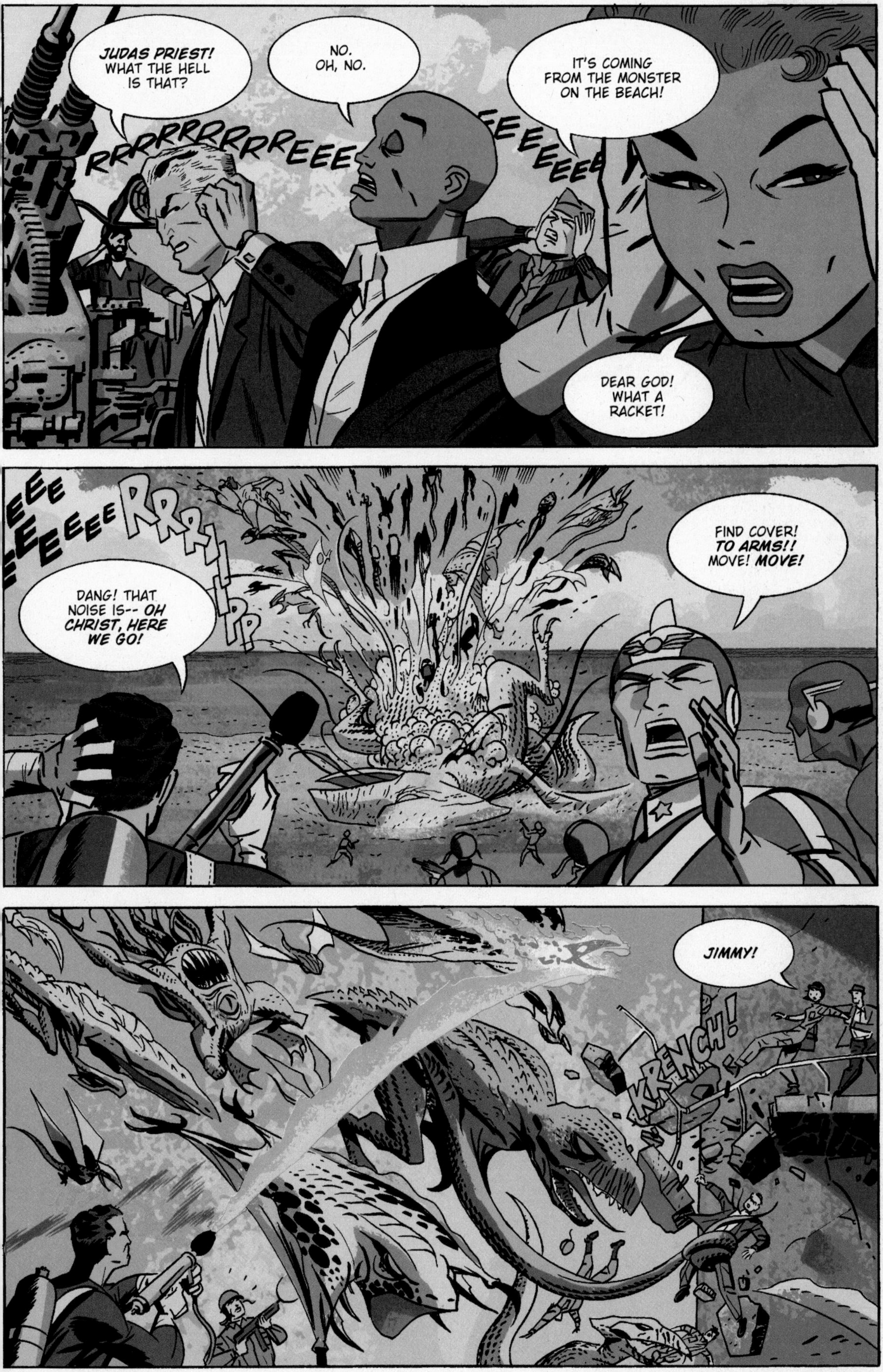

JUDAS PRIEST! WHAT THE HELL IS THAT?
NO. OH, NO.
IT'S COMING FROM THE MONSTER ON THE BEACH!
DEAR GOD! WHAT A RACKET!
DANG! THAT NOISE IS-- OH CHRIST, HERE WE GO!
FIND COVER! TO ARMS!! MOVE! MOVE!
JIMMY!
KRENCH!

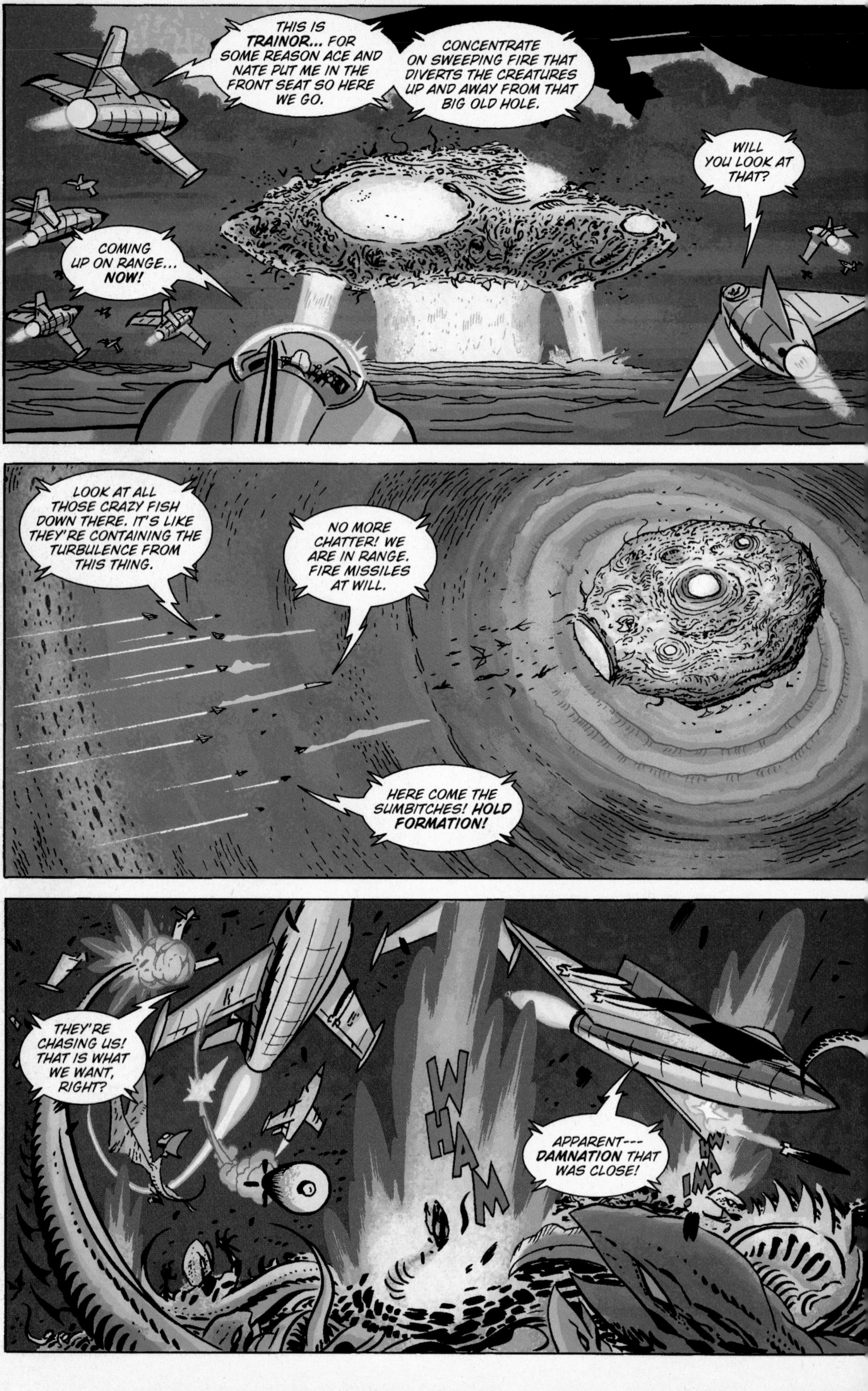

THIS IS **TRAINOR...** FOR SOME REASON ACE AND NATE PUT ME IN THE FRONT SEAT SO HERE WE GO.
CONCENTRATE ON SWEEPING FIRE THAT DIVERTS THE CREATURES UP AND AWAY FROM THAT BIG OLD HOLE.
WILL YOU LOOK AT THAT?
COMING UP ON RANGE... **NOW!**
LOOK AT ALL THOSE CRAZY FISH DOWN THERE. IT'S LIKE THEY'RE CONTAINING THE TURBULENCE FROM THIS THING.
NO MORE CHATTER! WE ARE IN RANGE. FIRE MISSILES AT WILL.
HERE COME THE SUMBITCHES! **HOLD FORMATION!**
THEY'RE CHASING US! THAT IS WHAT WE WANT, RIGHT?
WHAM
APPARENT--- **DAMNATION** THAT WAS CLOSE!

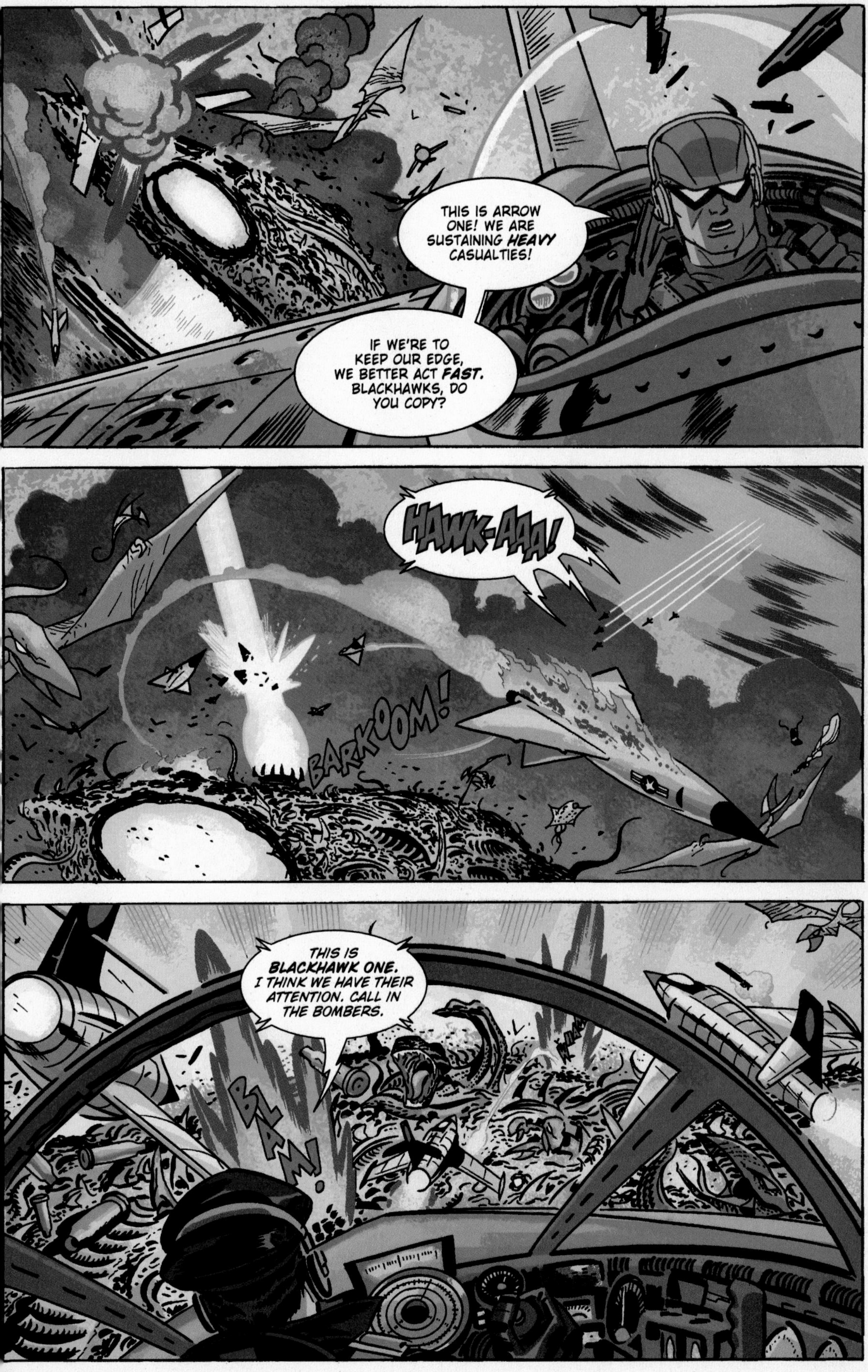
THIS IS ARROW ONE! WE ARE SUSTAINING HEAVY CASUALTIES!
IF WE'RE TO KEEP OUR EDGE, WE BETTER ACT FAST. BLACKHAWKS, DO YOU COPY?
HAWK-AAA!
BARKOOM!
THIS IS BLACKHAWK ONE. I THINK WE HAVE THEIR ATTENTION. CALL IN THE BOMBERS.
BLAM!

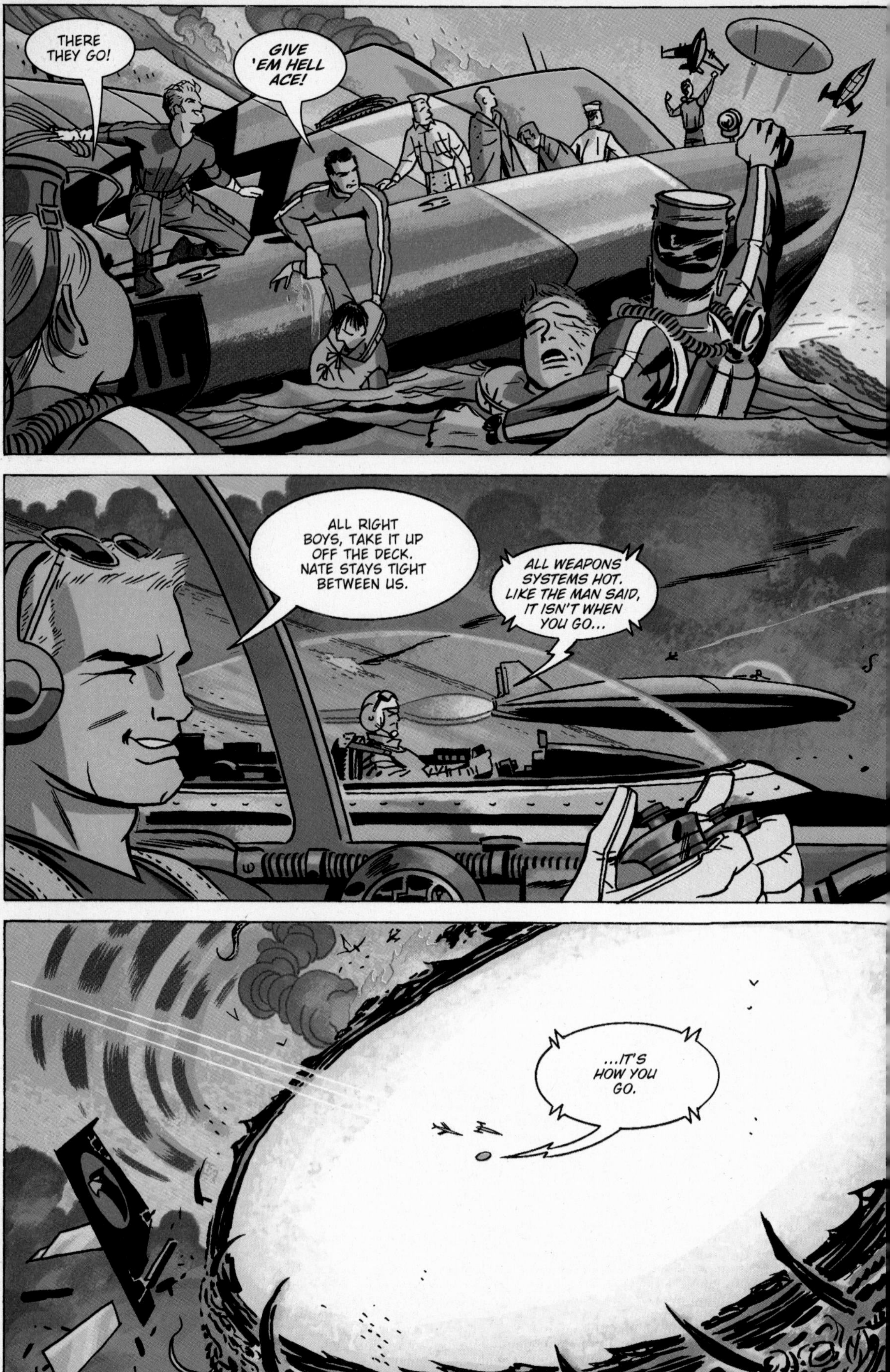

THERE THEY GO!
GIVE 'EM HELL ACE!
ALL RIGHT BOYS, TAKE IT UP OFF THE DECK. NATE STAYS TIGHT BETWEEN US.
ALL WEAPONS SYSTEMS HOT. LIKE THE MAN SAID, IT ISN'T WHEN YOU GO...
...IT'S HOW YOU GO.

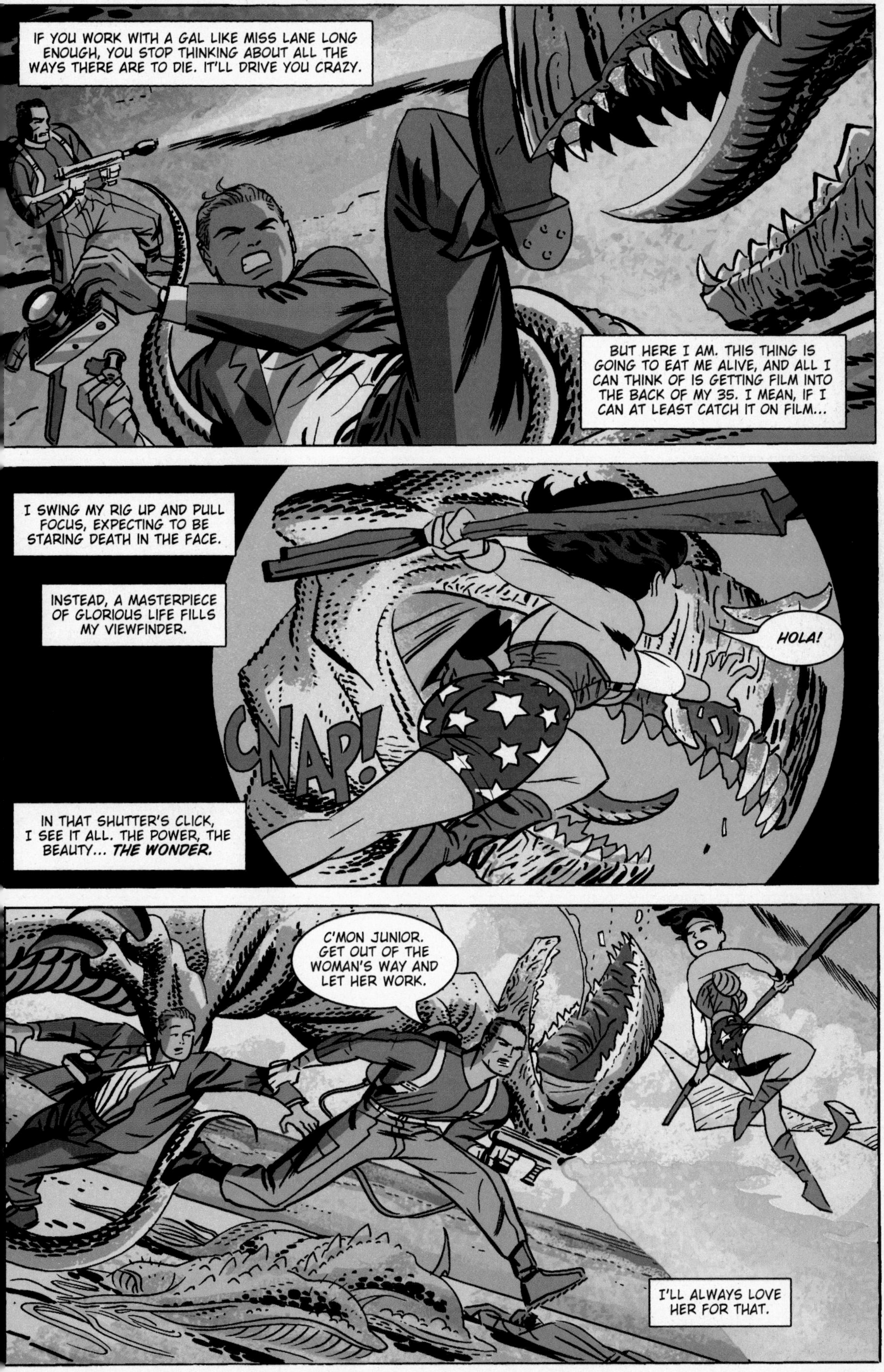
IF YOU WORK WITH A GAL LIKE MISS LANE LONG ENOUGH, YOU STOP THINKING ABOUT ALL THE WAYS THERE ARE TO DIE. IT'LL DRIVE YOU CRAZY.
BUT HERE I AM. THIS THING IS GOING TO EAT ME ALIVE, AND ALL I CAN THINK OF IS GETTING FILM INTO THE BACK OF MY 35. I MEAN, IF I CAN AT LEAST CATCH IT ON FILM...
I SWING MY RIG UP AND PULL FOCUS, EXPECTING TO BE STARING DEATH IN THE FACE.
INSTEAD, A MASTERPIECE OF GLORIOUS LIFE FILLS MY VIEWFINDER.
HOLA!
CNAP!
IN THAT SHUTTER'S CLICK, I SEE IT ALL. THE POWER, THE BEAUTY... THE WONDER.
C'MON JUNIOR. GET OUT OF THE WOMAN'S WAY AND LET HER WORK.
I'LL ALWAYS LOVE HER FOR THAT.

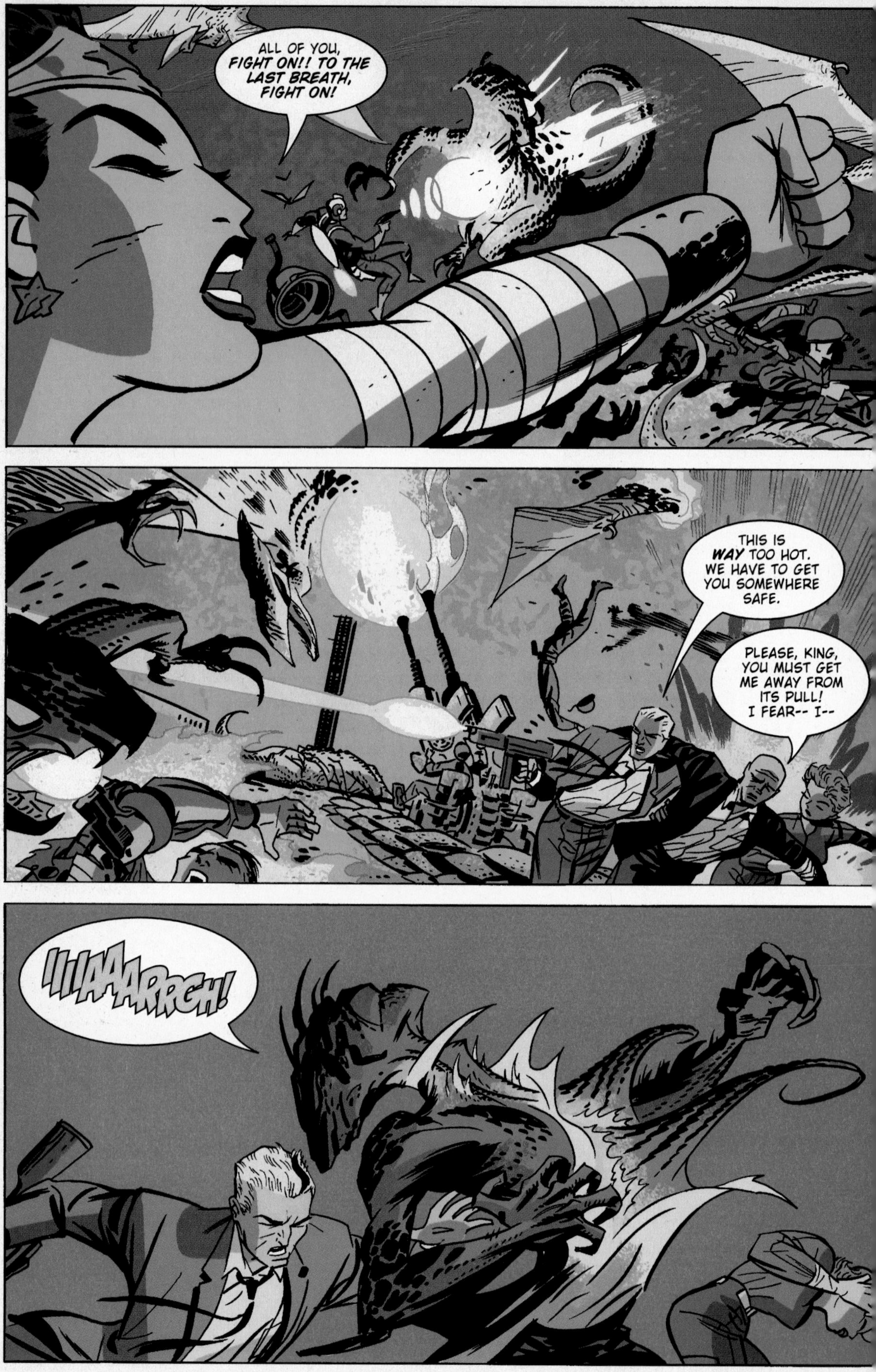
ALL OF YOU, FIGHT ON!! TO THE LAST BREATH, FIGHT ON!
THIS IS WAY TOO HOT. WE HAVE TO GET YOU SOMEWHERE SAFE.
PLEASE, KING, YOU MUST GET ME AWAY FROM ITS PULL! I FEAR-- I--
IIIIAAARRRGH!

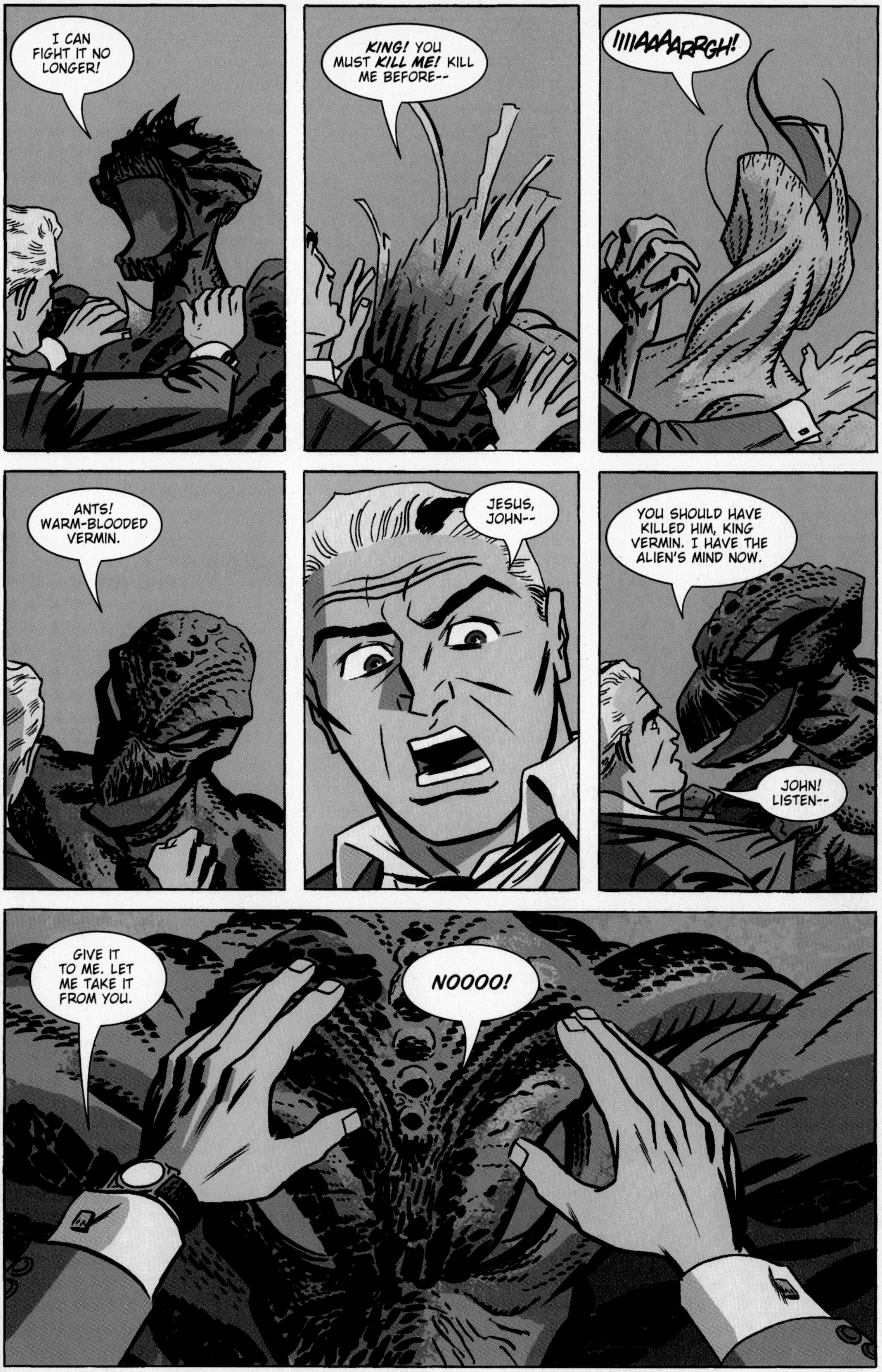
I CAN FIGHT IT NO LONGER!
KING! YOU MUST KILL ME! KILL ME BEFORE--
IIIIAAAARRGH!
ANTS! WARM-BLOODED VERMIN.
JESUS, JOHN--
YOU SHOULD HAVE KILLED HIM, KING VERMIN. I HAVE THE ALIEN'S MIND NOW.
JOHN! LISTEN--
GIVE IT TO ME. LET ME TAKE IT FROM YOU.
NOOOO!

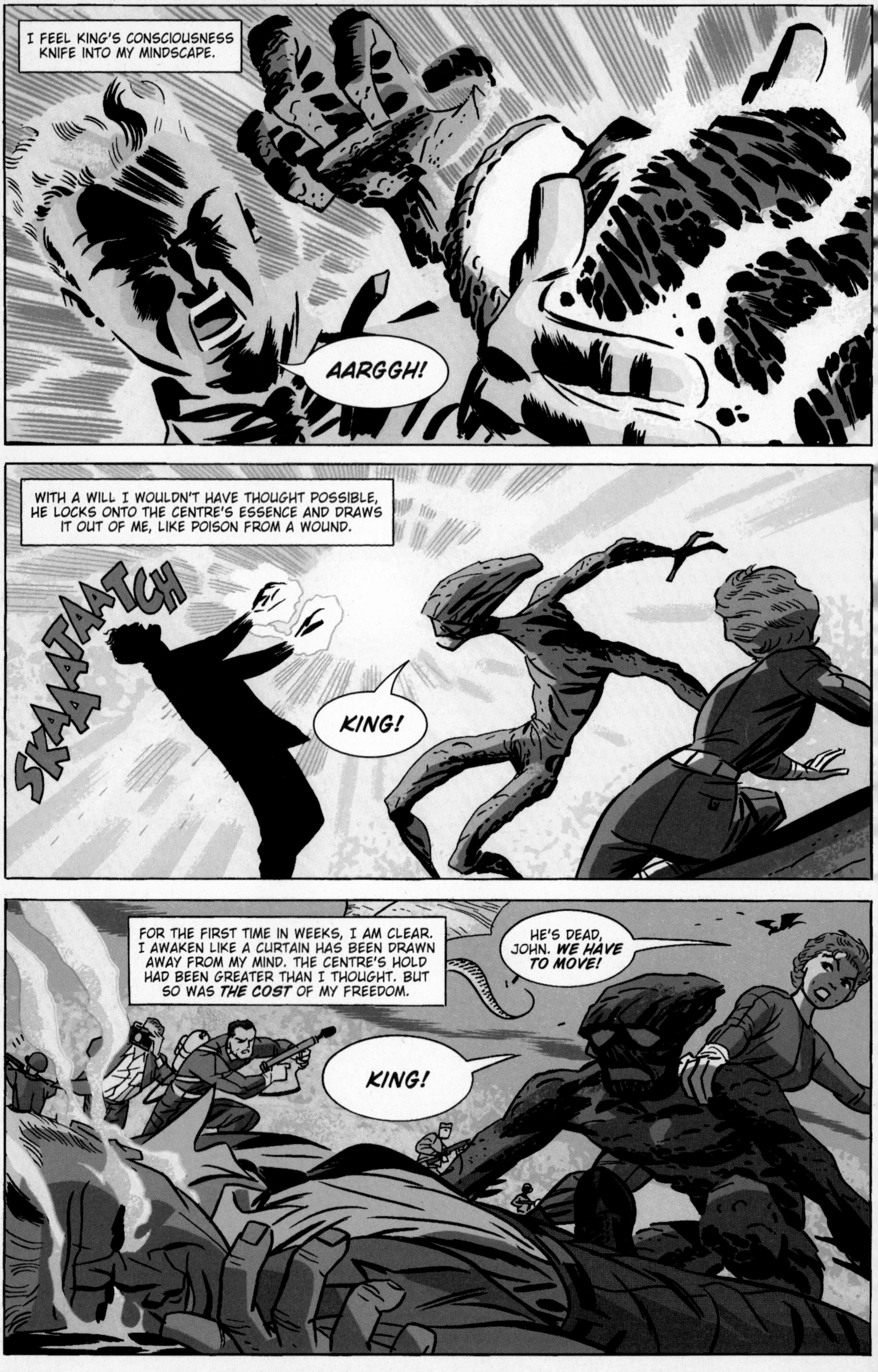

I FEEL KING'S CONSCIOUSNESS KNIFE INTO MY MINDSCAPE.
AARGGH!
WITH A WILL I WOULDN'T HAVE THOUGHT POSSIBLE, HE LOCKS ONTO THE CENTRE'S ESSENCE AND DRAWS IT OUT OF ME, LIKE POISON FROM A WOUND.
SKAAAJAATCH
KING!
FOR THE FIRST TIME IN WEEKS, I AM CLEAR. I AWAKEN LIKE A CURTAIN HAS BEEN DRAWN AWAY FROM MY MIND. THE CENTRE'S HOLD HAD BEEN GREATER THAN I THOUGHT. BUT SO WAS THE COST OF MY FREEDOM.
HE'S DEAD, JOHN. WE HAVE TO MOVE!
KING!

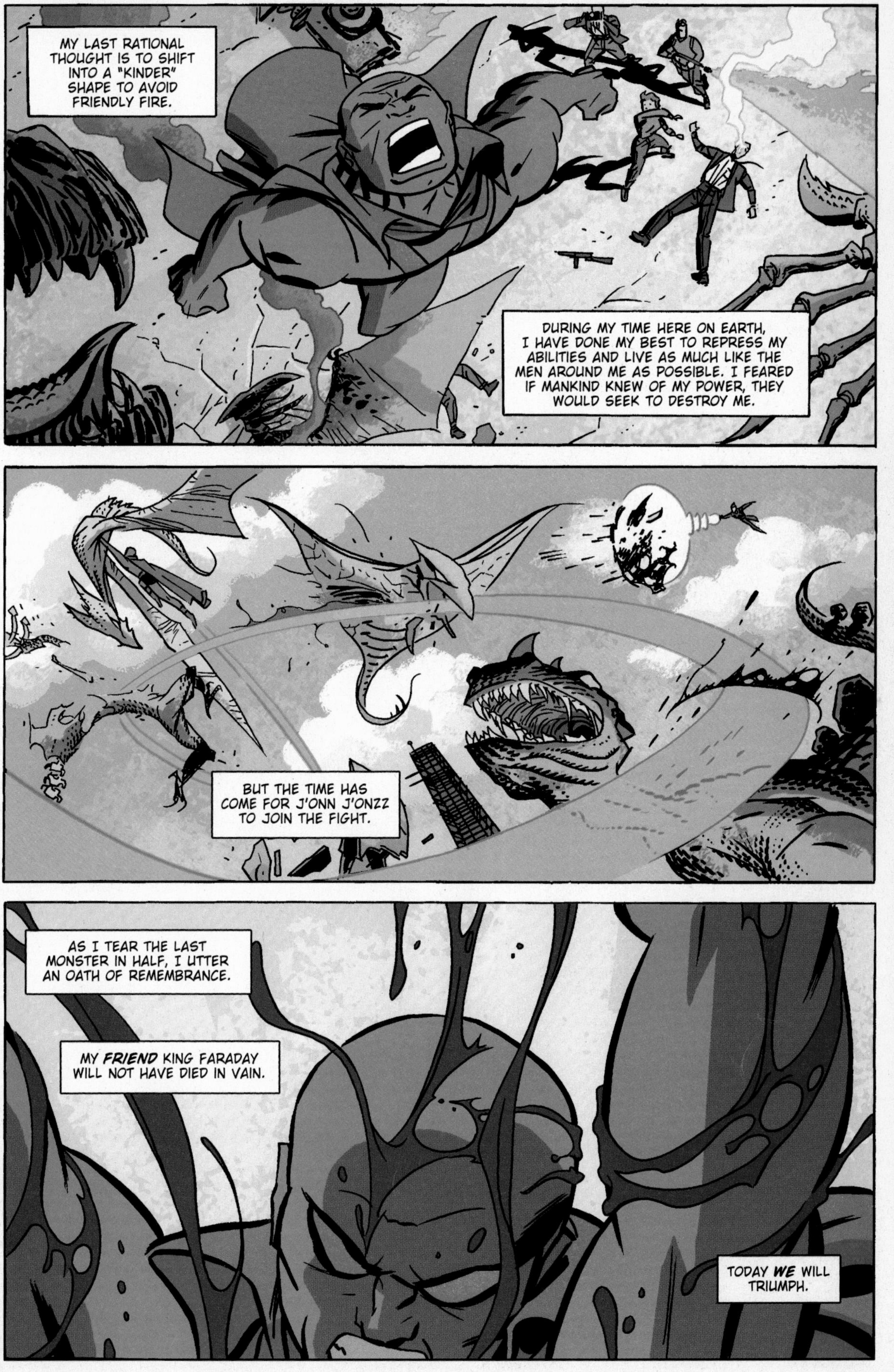
MY LAST RATIONAL THOUGHT IS TO SHIFT INTO A "KINDER" SHAPE TO AVOID FRIENDLY FIRE.
DURING MY TIME HERE ON EARTH, I HAVE DONE MY BEST TO REPRESS MY ABILITIES AND LIVE AS MUCH LIKE THE MEN AROUND ME AS POSSIBLE. I FEARED IF MANKIND KNEW OF MY POWER, THEY WOULD SEEK TO DESTROY ME.
BUT THE TIME HAS COME FOR J'ONN J'ONZZ TO JOIN THE FIGHT.
AS I TEAR THE LAST MONSTER IN HALF, I UTTER AN OATH OF REMEMBRANCE.
MY FRIEND KING FARADAY WILL NOT HAVE DIED IN VAIN.
TODAY WE WILL TRIUMPH.

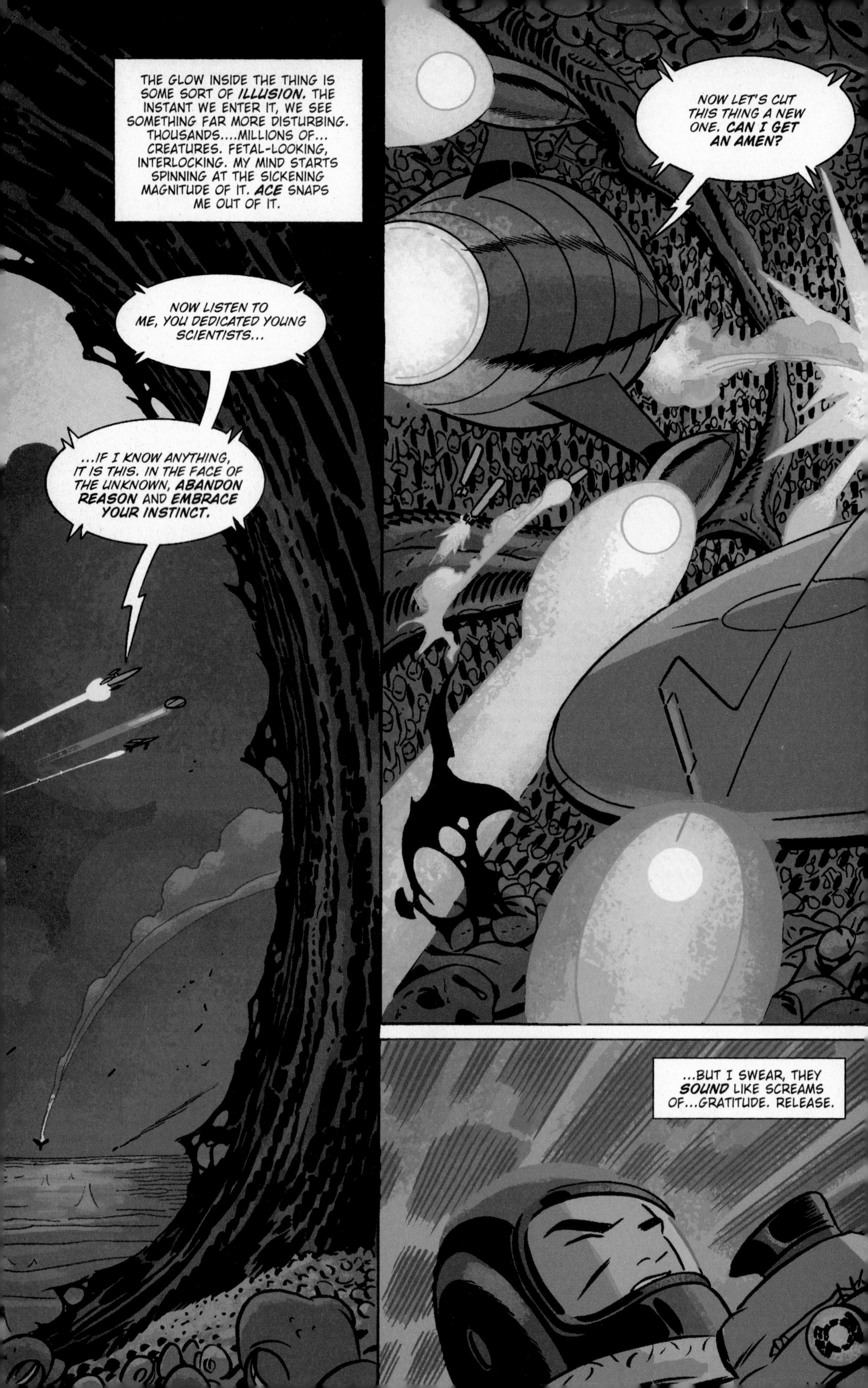
THE GLOW INSIDE THE THING IS SOME SORT OF ILLUSION. THE INSTANT WE ENTER IT, WE SEE SOMETHING FAR MORE DISTURBING. THOUSANDS....MILLIONS OF... CREATURES. FETAL-LOOKING, INTERLOCKING. MY MIND STARTS SPINNING AT THE SICKENING MAGNITUDE OF IT. ACE SNAPS ME OUT OF IT.
NOW LISTEN TO ME, YOU DEDICATED YOUNG SCIENTISTS...
...IF I KNOW ANYTHING, IT IS THIS. IN THE FACE OF THE UNKNOWN, ABANDON REASON AND EMBRACE YOUR INSTINCT.
NOW LET'S CUT THIS THING A NEW ONE. CAN I GET AN AMEN?
...BUT I SWEAR, THEY SOUND LIKE SCREAMS OF...GRATITUDE. RELEASE.

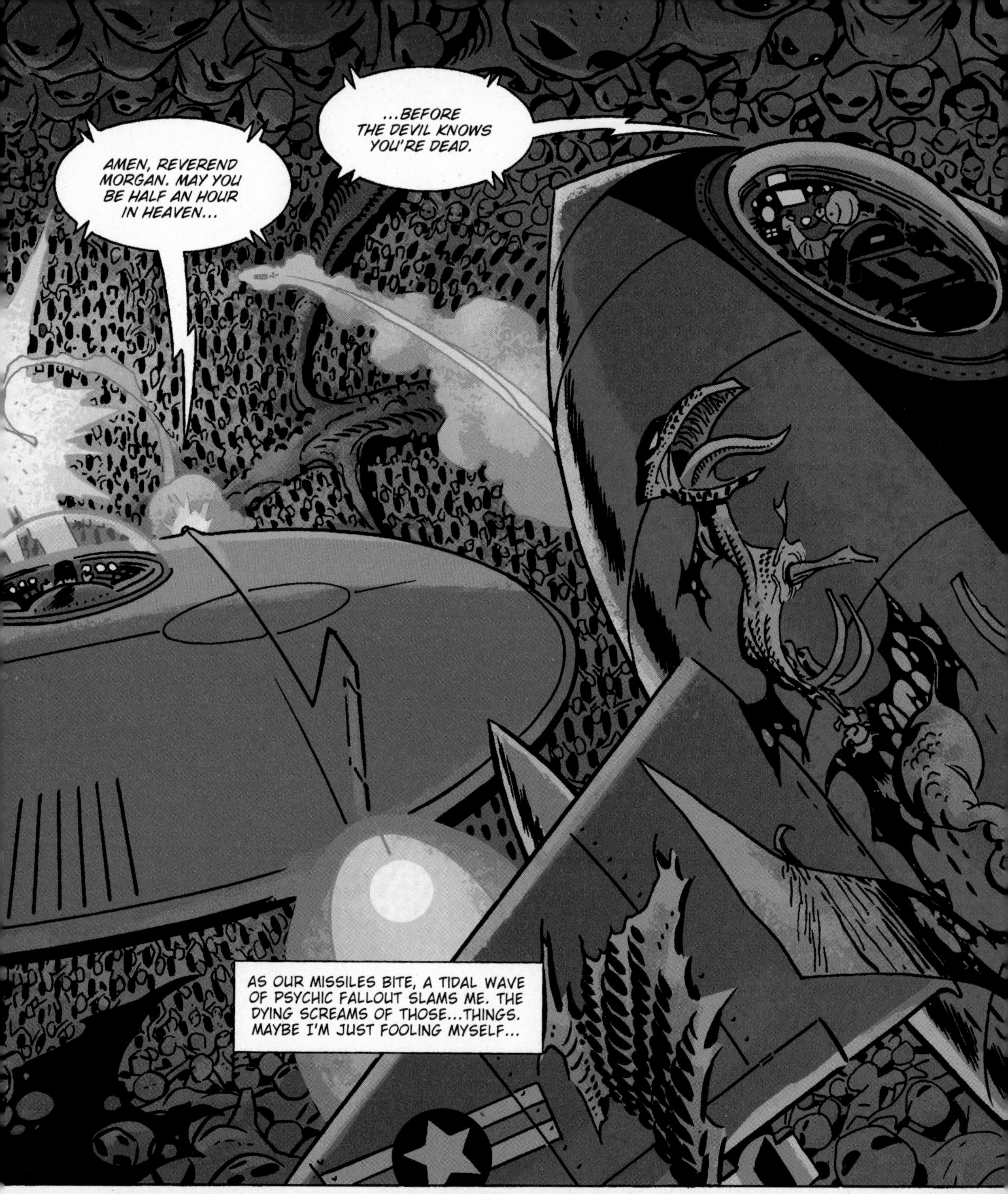
AMEN, REVEREND MORGAN. MAY YOU BE HALF AN HOUR IN HEAVEN...
...BEFORE THE DEVIL KNOWS YOU'RE DEAD.
AS OUR MISSILES BITE, A TIDAL WAVE OF PSYCHIC FALLOUT SLAMS ME. THE DYING SCREAMS OF THOSE...THINGS. MAYBE I'M JUST FOOLING MYSELF...

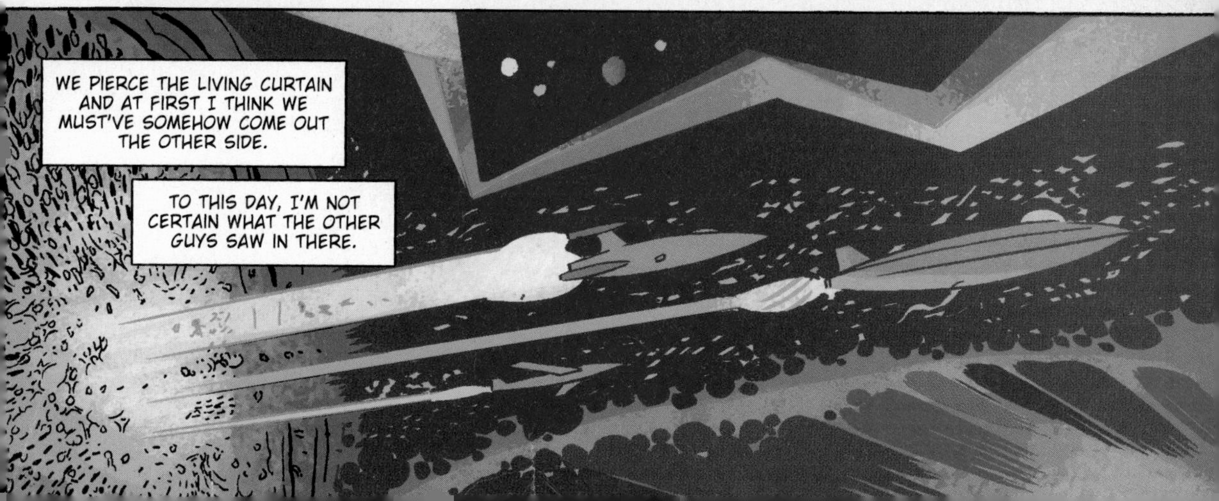
WE PIERCE THE LIVING CURTAIN AND AT FIRST I THINK WE MUST'VE SOMEHOW COME OUT THE OTHER SIDE.
TO THIS DAY, I'M NOT CERTAIN WHAT THE OTHER GUYS SAW IN THERE.

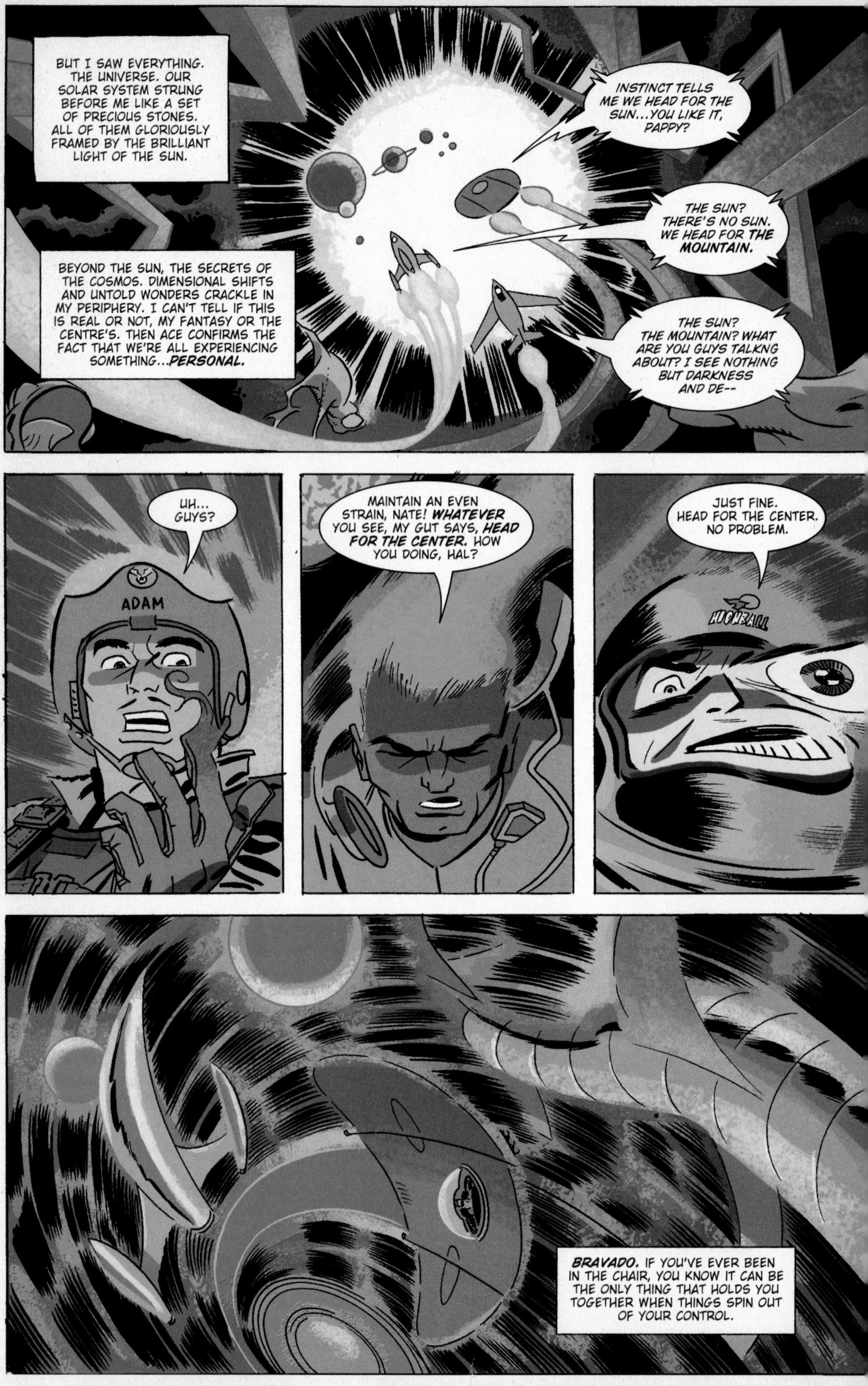
BUT I SAW EVERYTHING. THE UNIVERSE. OUR SOLAR SYSTEM STRUNG BEFORE ME LIKE A SET OF PRECIOUS STONES. ALL OF THEM GLORIOUSLY FRAMED BY THE BRILLIANT LIGHT OF THE SUN.
INSTINCT TELLS ME WE HEAD FOR THE SUN...YOU LIKE IT, PAPPY?
THE SUN? THERE'S NO SUN. WE HEAD FOR **THE MOUNTAIN.**
BEYOND THE SUN, THE SECRETS OF THE COSMOS. DIMENSIONAL SHIFTS AND UNTOLD WONDERS CRACKLE IN MY PERIPHERY. I CAN'T TELL IF THIS IS REAL OR NOT, MY FANTASY OR THE CENTRE'S. THEN ACE CONFIRMS THE FACT THAT WE'RE ALL EXPERIENCING SOMETHING...**PERSONAL.**
THE SUN? THE MOUNTAIN? WHAT ARE YOU GUYS TALKNG ABOUT? I SEE NOTHING BUT DARKNESS AND DE--
UH... GUYS?
ADAM
MAINTAIN AN EVEN STRAIN, NATE! **WHATEVER** YOU SEE, MY GUT SAYS, **HEAD FOR THE CENTER.** HOW YOU DOING, HAL?
JUST FINE. HEAD FOR THE CENTER. NO PROBLEM.
BRAVADO. IF YOU'VE EVER BEEN IN THE CHAIR, YOU KNOW IT CAN BE THE ONLY THING THAT HOLDS YOU TOGETHER WHEN THINGS SPIN OUT OF YOUR CONTROL.

CHAPTER SEVENTEEN
THE PURE RUGGED

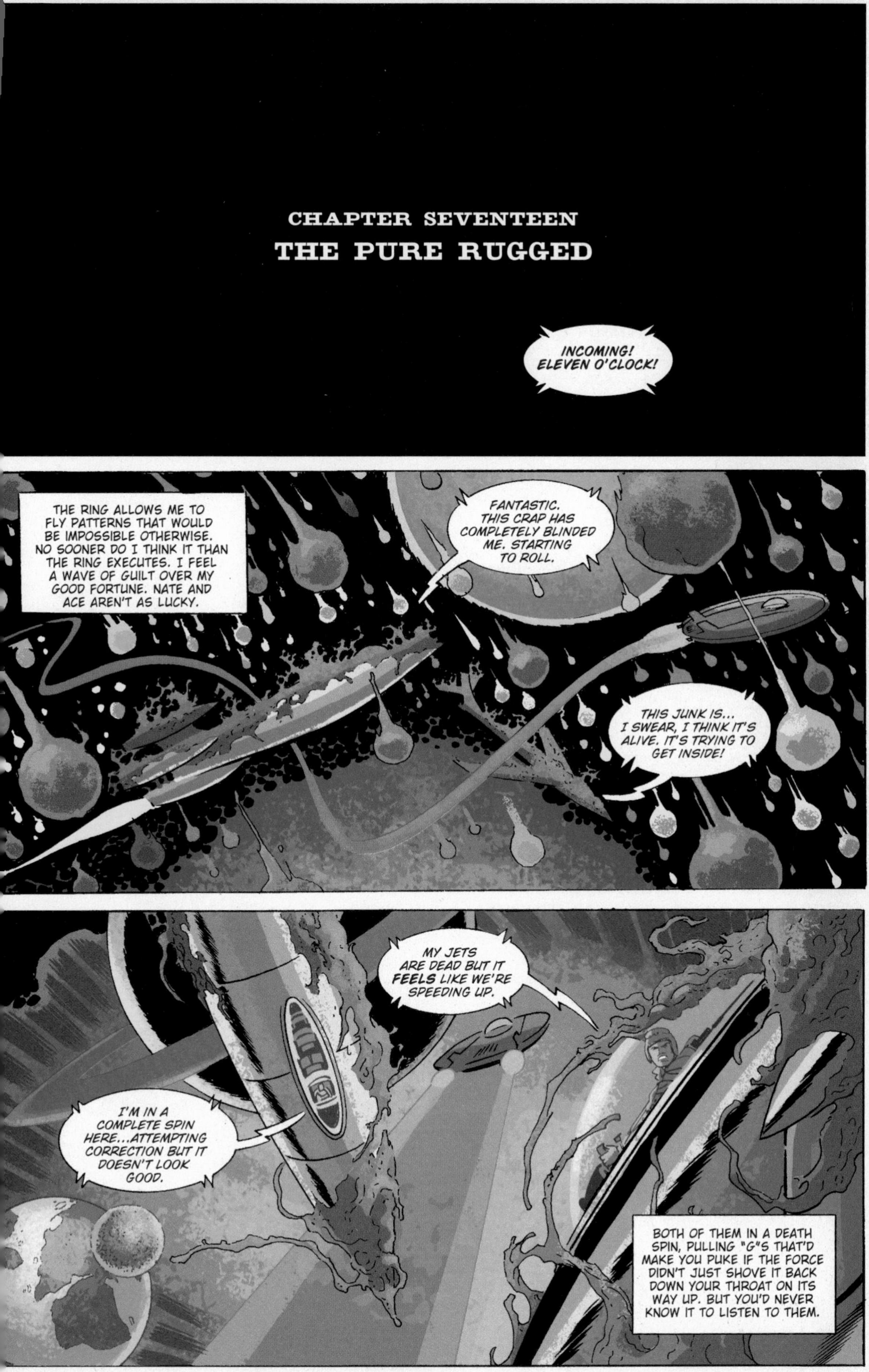
INCOMING! ELEVEN O'CLOCK!
THE RING ALLOWS ME TO FLY PATTERNS THAT WOULD BE IMPOSSIBLE OTHERWISE. NO SOONER DO I THINK IT THAN THE RING EXECUTES. I FEEL A WAVE OF GUILT OVER MY GOOD FORTUNE. NATE AND ACE AREN'T AS LUCKY.
FANTASTIC. THIS CRAP HAS COMPLETELY BLINDED ME. STARTING TO ROLL.
THIS JUNK IS... I SWEAR, I THINK IT'S ALIVE. IT'S TRYING TO GET INSIDE!
MY JETS ARE DEAD BUT IT FEELS LIKE WE'RE SPEEDING UP.
I'M IN A COMPLETE SPIN HERE...ATTEMPTING CORRECTION BUT IT DOESN'T LOOK GOOD.
BOTH OF THEM IN A DEATH SPIN, PULLING "G"S THAT'D MAKE YOU PUKE IF THE FORCE DIDN'T JUST SHOVE IT BACK DOWN YOUR THROAT ON ITS WAY UP. BUT YOU'D NEVER KNOW IT TO LISTEN TO THEM.

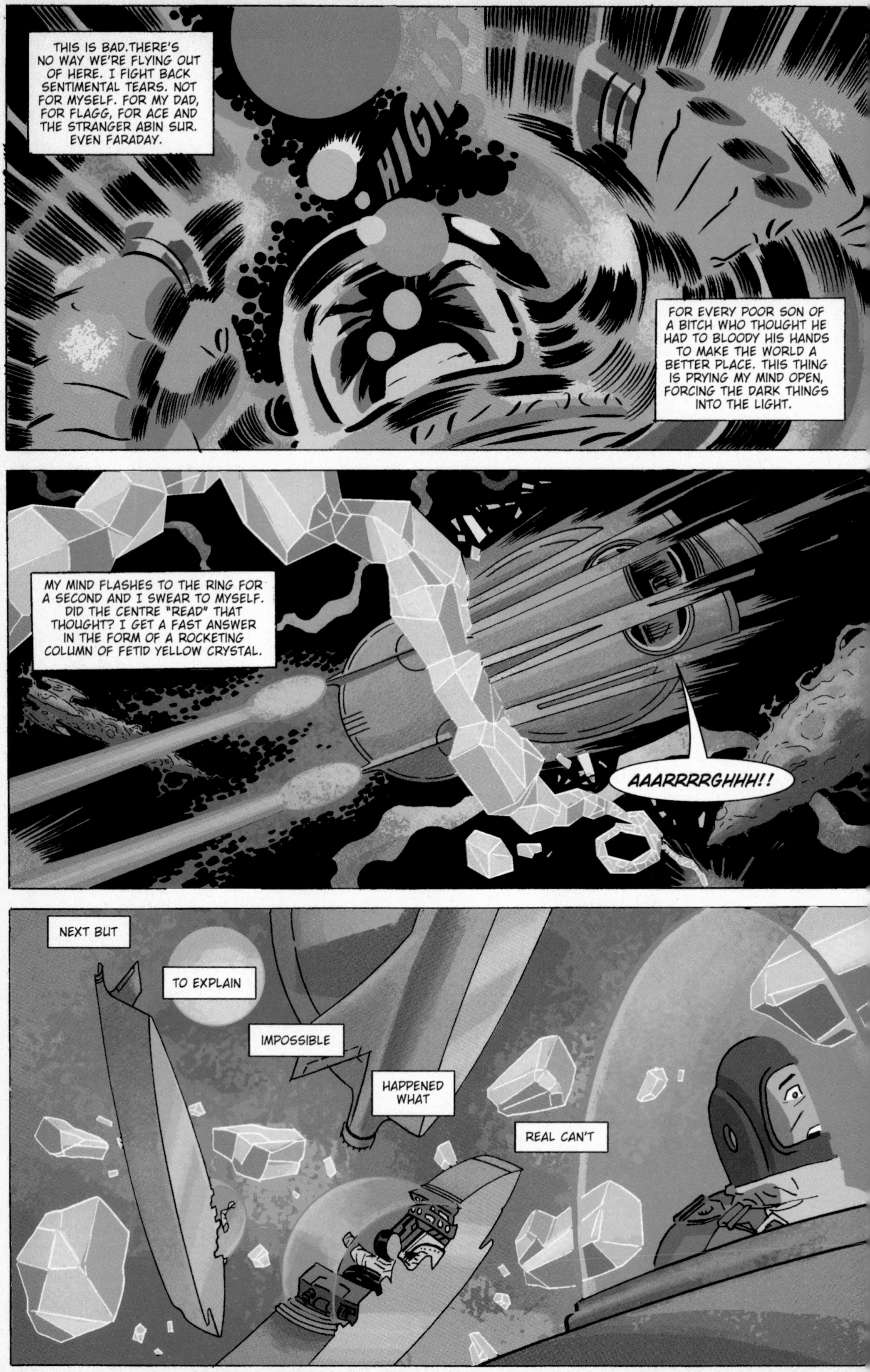
THIS IS BAD.THERE'S NO WAY WE'RE FLYING OUT OF HERE. I FIGHT BACK SENTIMENTAL TEARS. NOT FOR MYSELF. FOR MY DAD, FOR FLAGG, FOR ACE AND THE STRANGER ABIN SUR. EVEN FARADAY.
HIGH
FOR EVERY POOR SON OF A BITCH WHO THOUGHT HE HAD TO BLOODY HIS HANDS TO MAKE THE WORLD A BETTER PLACE. THIS THING IS PRYING MY MIND OPEN, FORCING THE DARK THINGS INTO THE LIGHT.
MY MIND FLASHES TO THE RING FOR A SECOND AND I SWEAR TO MYSELF. DID THE CENTRE "READ" THAT THOUGHT? I GET A FAST ANSWER IN THE FORM OF A ROCKETING COLUMN OF FETID YELLOW CRYSTAL.
AAARRRRGHHH!!
NEXT BUT
TO EXPLAIN
IMPOSSIBLE
HAPPENED WHAT
REAL CAN'T

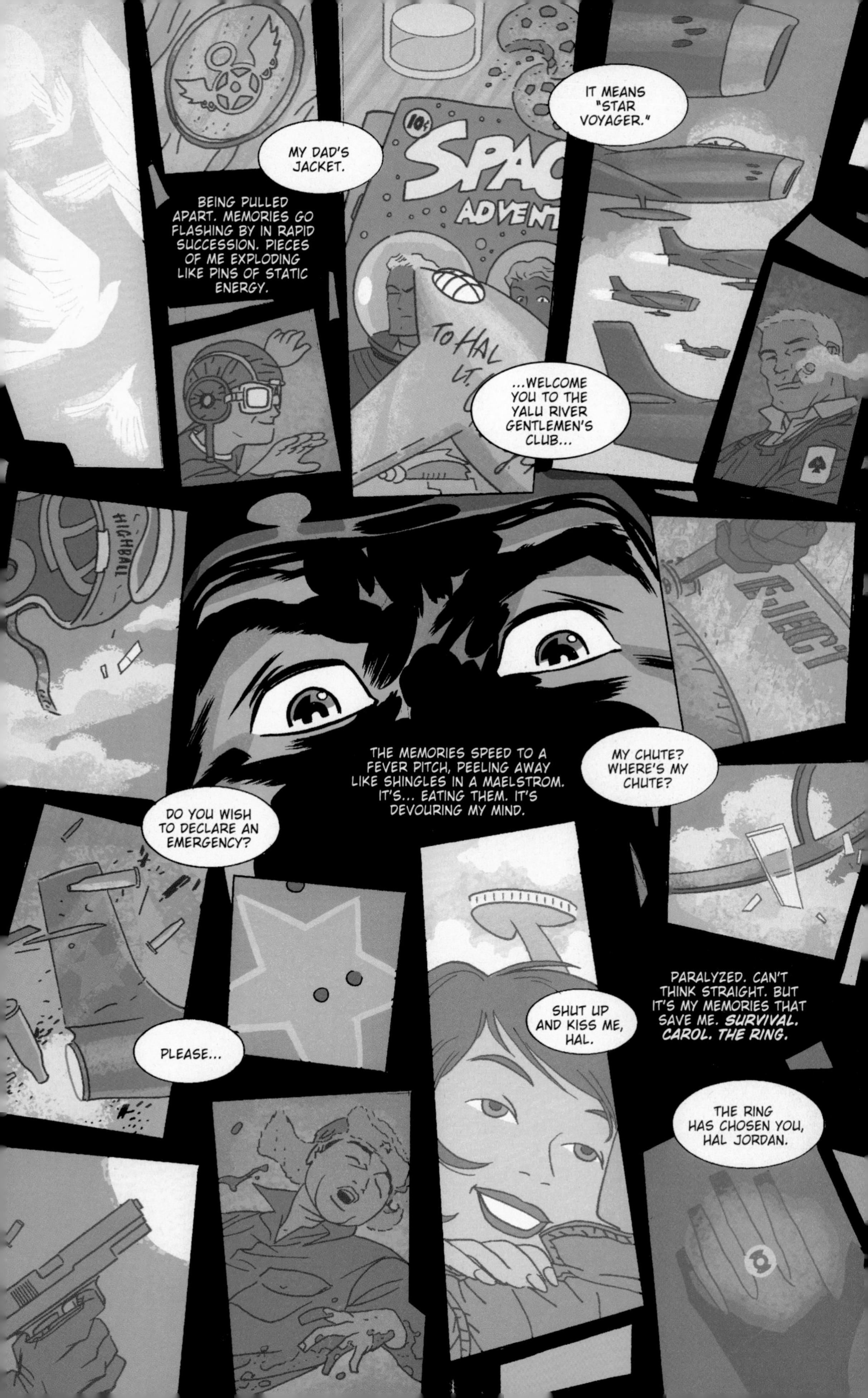
MY DAD'S JACKET.
BEING PULLED APART. MEMORIES GO FLASHING BY IN RAPID SUCCESSION. PIECES OF ME EXPLODING LIKE PINS OF STATIC ENERGY.
10¢
SPAC
ADVENT
TO HAL
IT MEANS "STAR VOYAGER."
...WELCOME YOU TO THE YALU RIVER GENTLEMEN'S CLUB...
HIGHBALL
EJECT
THE MEMORIES SPEED TO A FEVER PITCH, PEELING AWAY LIKE SHINGLES IN A MAELSTROM. IT'S... EATING THEM. IT'S DEVOURING MY MIND.
MY CHUTE? WHERE'S MY CHUTE?
DO YOU WISH TO DECLARE AN EMERGENCY?
PARALYZED. CAN'T THINK STRAIGHT. BUT IT'S MY MEMORIES THAT SAVE ME. ***SURVIVAL. CAROL. THE RING.***
SHUT UP AND KISS ME, HAL.
PLEASE...
THE RING HAS CHOSEN YOU, HAL JORDAN.

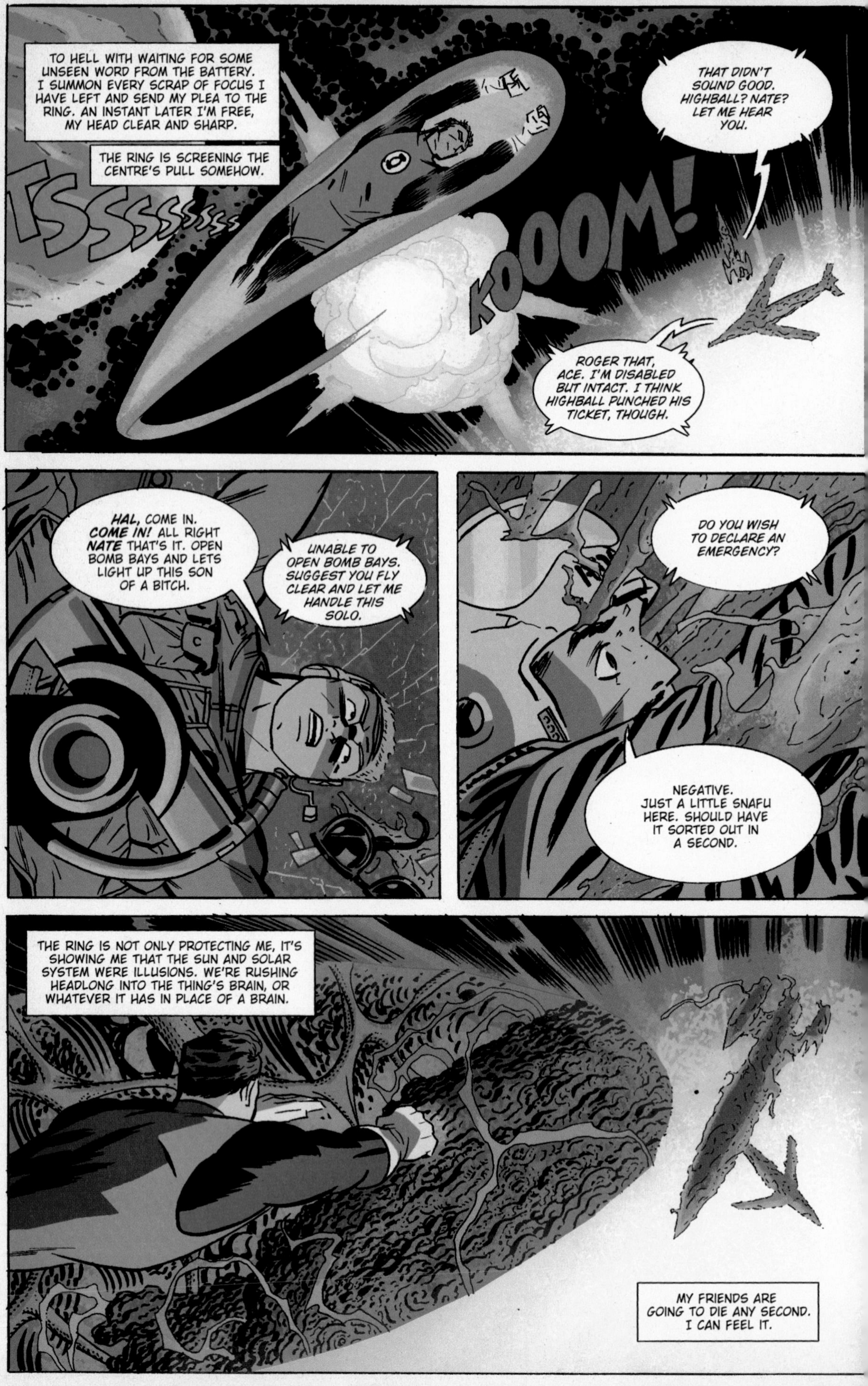
TO HELL WITH WAITING FOR SOME UNSEEN WORD FROM THE BATTERY. I SUMMON EVERY SCRAP OF FOCUS I HAVE LEFT AND SEND MY PLEA TO THE RING. AN INSTANT LATER I'M FREE, MY HEAD CLEAR AND SHARP.
THE RING IS SCREENING THE CENTRE'S PULL SOMEHOW.
TSSSSSSSSS
KOOOM!
THAT DIDN'T SOUND GOOD. HIGHBALL? NATE? LET ME HEAR YOU.
ROGER THAT, ACE. I'M DISABLED BUT INTACT. I THINK HIGHBALL PUNCHED HIS TICKET, THOUGH.
HAL, COME IN. COME IN! ALL RIGHT NATE THAT'S IT. OPEN BOMB BAYS AND LETS LIGHT UP THIS SON OF A BITCH.
UNABLE TO OPEN BOMB BAYS. SUGGEST YOU FLY CLEAR AND LET ME HANDLE THIS SOLO.
DO YOU WISH TO DECLARE AN EMERGENCY?
NEGATIVE. JUST A LITTLE SNAFU HERE. SHOULD HAVE IT SORTED OUT IN A SECOND.
THE RING IS NOT ONLY PROTECTING ME, IT'S SHOWING ME THAT THE SUN AND SOLAR SYSTEM WERE ILLUSIONS. WE'RE RUSHING HEADLONG INTO THE THING'S BRAIN, OR WHATEVER IT HAS IN PLACE OF A BRAIN.
MY FRIENDS ARE GOING TO DIE ANY SECOND. I CAN FEEL IT.

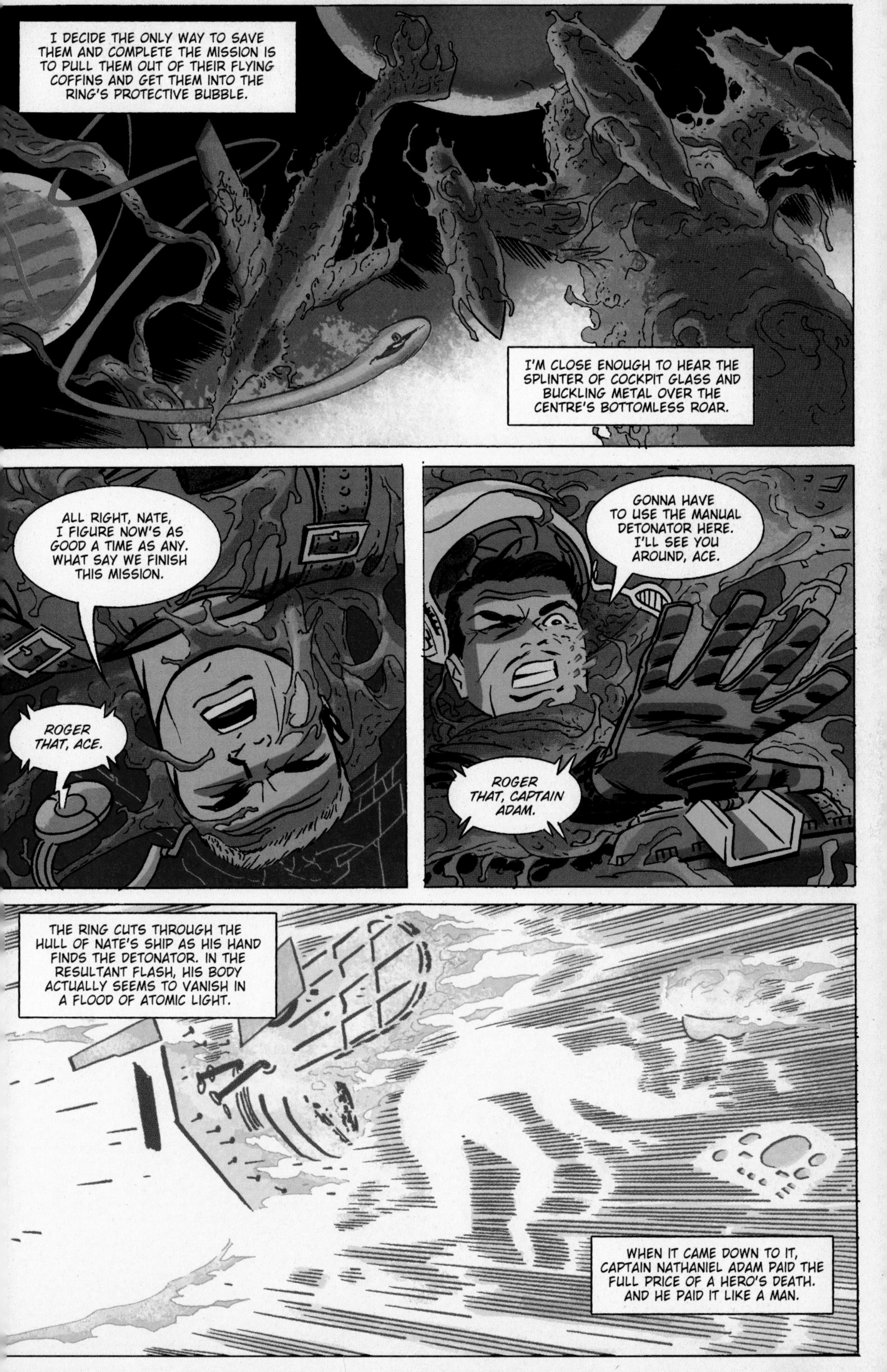
I DECIDE THE ONLY WAY TO SAVE THEM AND COMPLETE THE MISSION IS TO PULL THEM OUT OF THEIR FLYING COFFINS AND GET THEM INTO THE RING'S PROTECTIVE BUBBLE.
I'M CLOSE ENOUGH TO HEAR THE SPLINTER OF COCKPIT GLASS AND BUCKLING METAL OVER THE CENTRE'S BOTTOMLESS ROAR.
ALL RIGHT, NATE, I FIGURE NOW'S AS GOOD A TIME AS ANY. WHAT SAY WE FINISH THIS MISSION.
ROGER THAT, ACE.
GONNA HAVE TO USE THE MANUAL DETONATOR HERE. I'LL SEE YOU AROUND, ACE.
ROGER THAT, CAPTAIN ADAM.
THE RING CUTS THROUGH THE HULL OF NATE'S SHIP AS HIS HAND FINDS THE DETONATOR. IN THE RESULTANT FLASH, HIS BODY ACTUALLY SEEMS TO VANISH IN A FLOOD OF ATOMIC LIGHT.
WHEN IT CAME DOWN TO IT, CAPTAIN NATHANIEL ADAM PAID THE FULL PRICE OF A HERO'S DEATH. AND HE PAID IT LIKE A MAN.

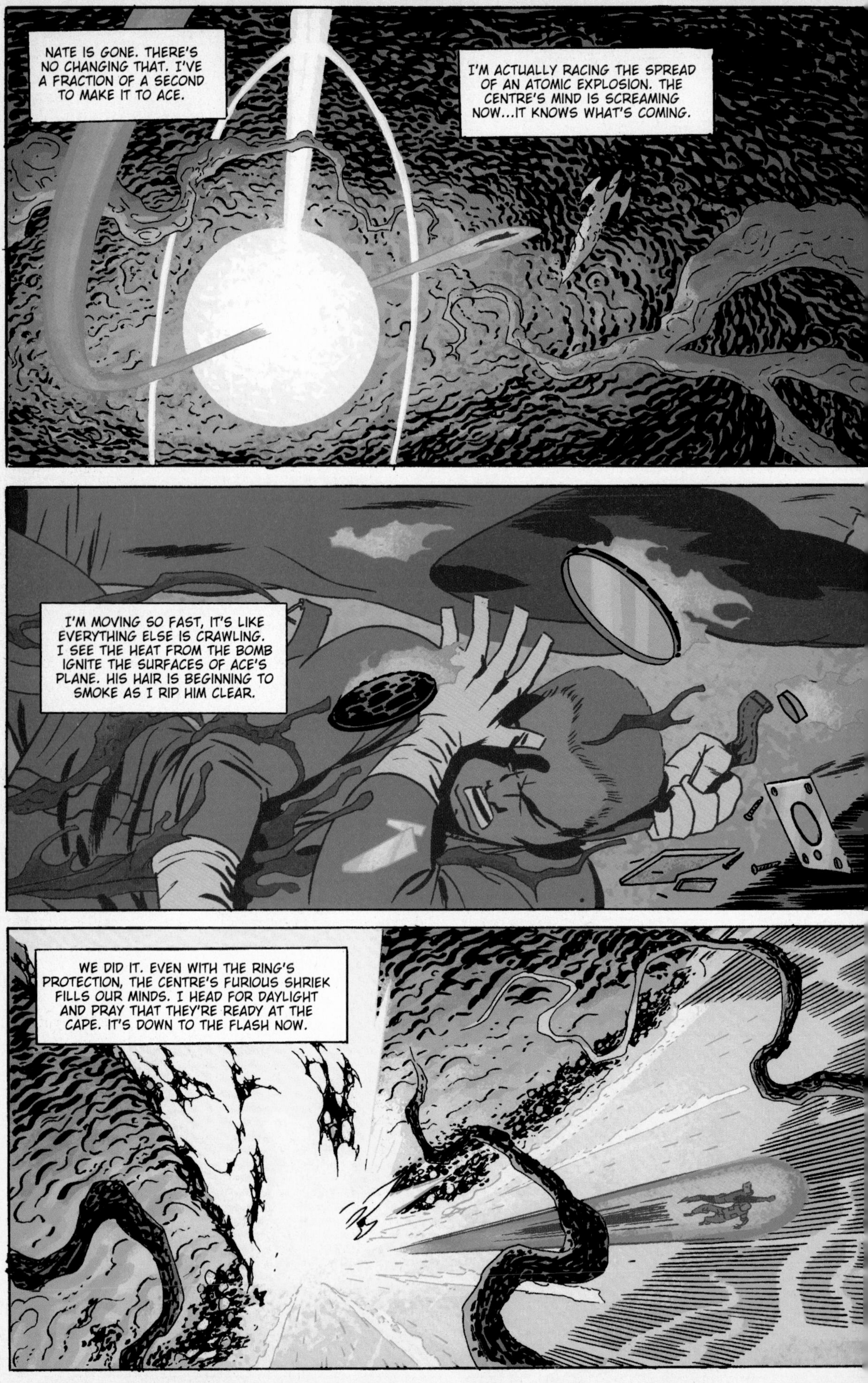
NATE IS GONE. THERE'S NO CHANGING THAT. I'VE A FRACTION OF A SECOND TO MAKE IT TO ACE.
I'M ACTUALLY RACING THE SPREAD OF AN ATOMIC EXPLOSION. THE CENTRE'S MIND IS SCREAMING NOW...IT KNOWS WHAT'S COMING.
I'M MOVING SO FAST, IT'S LIKE EVERYTHING ELSE IS CRAWLING. I SEE THE HEAT FROM THE BOMB IGNITE THE SURFACES OF ACE'S PLANE. HIS HAIR IS BEGINNING TO SMOKE AS I RIP HIM CLEAR.
WE DID IT. EVEN WITH THE RING'S PROTECTION, THE CENTRE'S FURIOUS SHRIEK FILLS OUR MINDS. I HEAD FOR DAYLIGHT AND PRAY THAT THEY'RE READY AT THE CAPE. IT'S DOWN TO THE FLASH NOW.

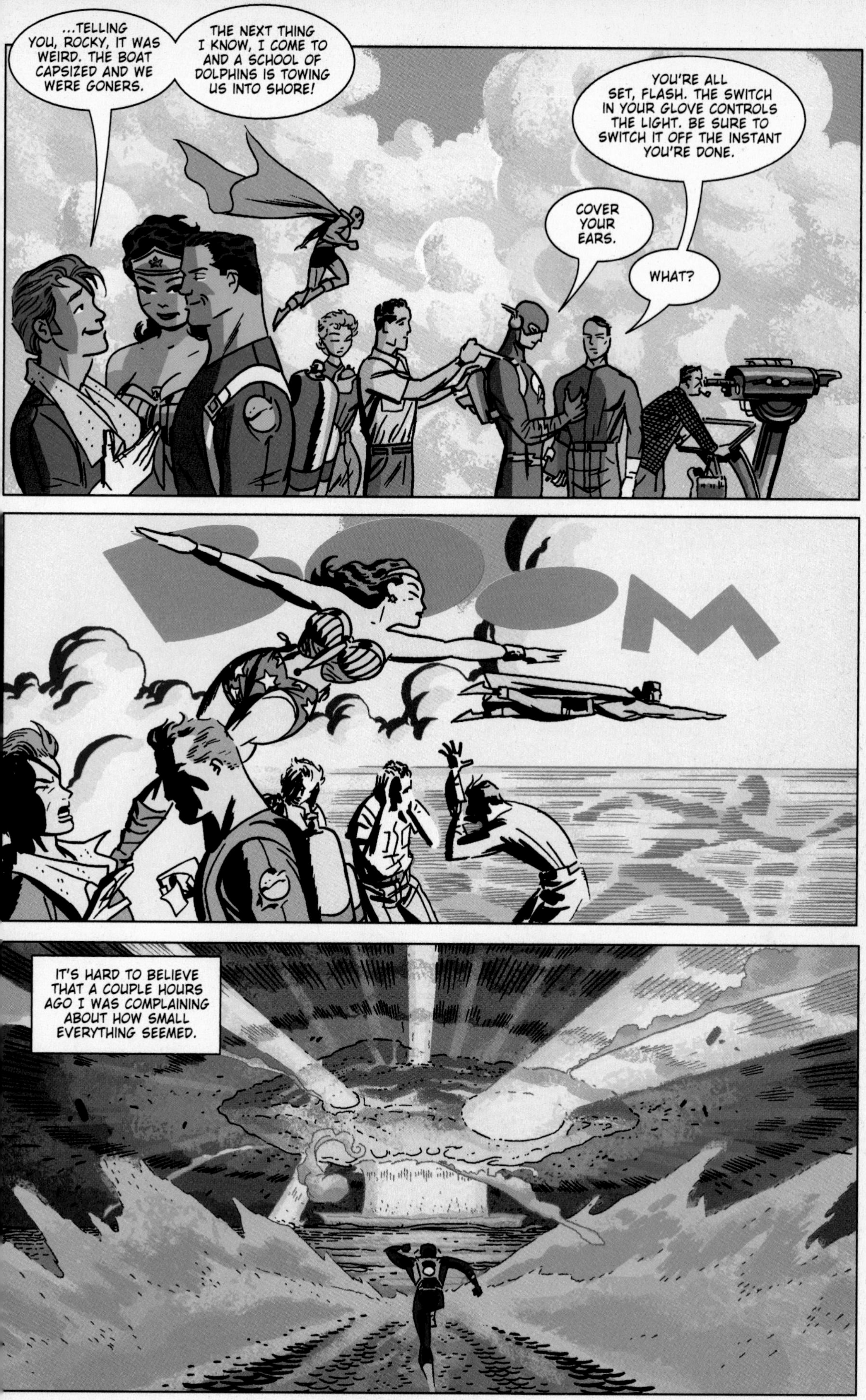
...TELLING YOU, ROCKY, IT WAS WEIRD. THE BOAT CAPSIZED AND WE WERE GONERS.
THE NEXT THING I KNOW, I COME TO AND A SCHOOL OF DOLPHINS IS TOWING US INTO SHORE!
YOU'RE ALL SET, FLASH. THE SWITCH IN YOUR GLOVE CONTROLS THE LIGHT. BE SURE TO SWITCH IT OFF THE INSTANT YOU'RE DONE.
COVER YOUR EARS.
WHAT?
BOOM
IT'S HARD TO BELIEVE THAT A COUPLE HOURS AGO I WAS COMPLAINING ABOUT HOW SMALL EVERYTHING SEEMED.

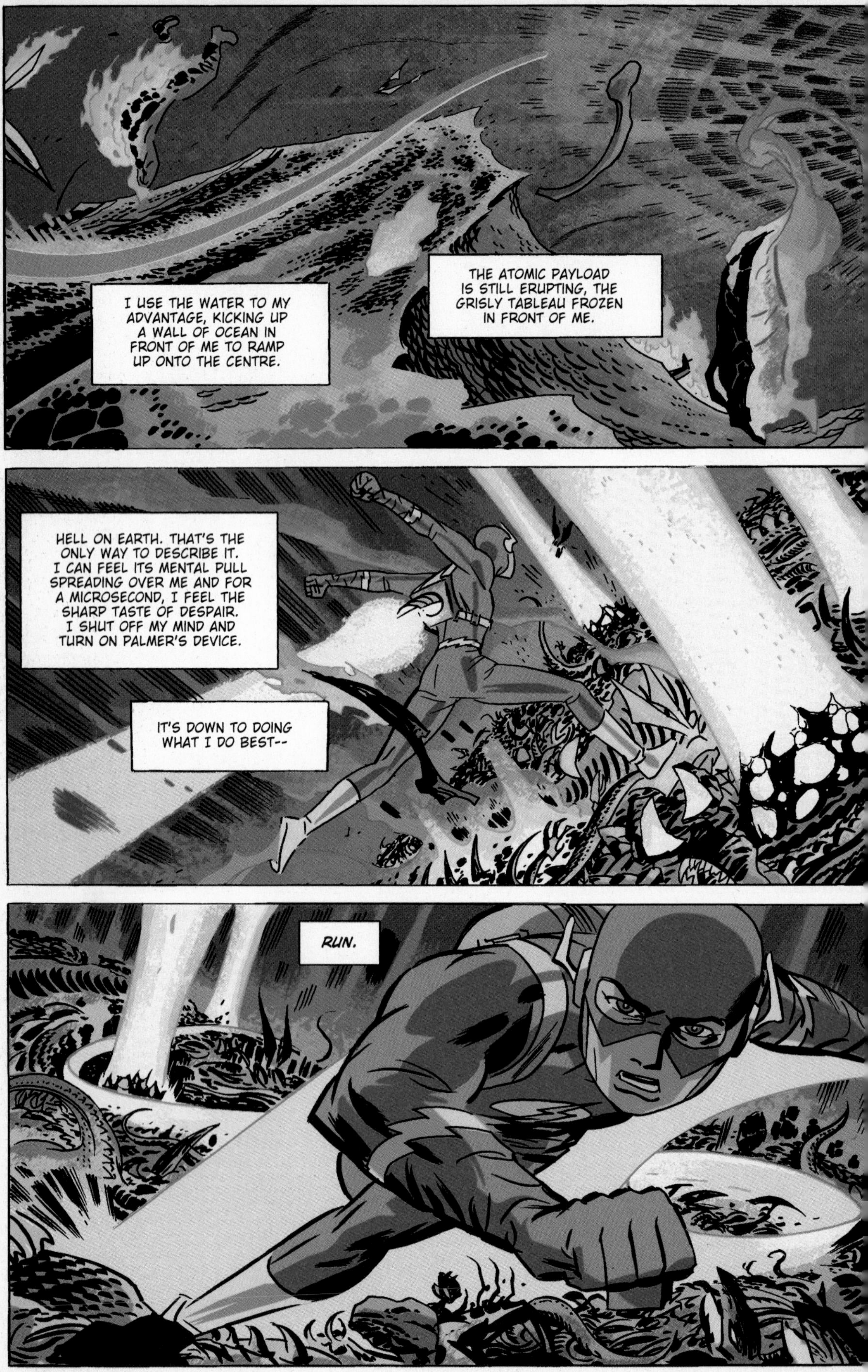
I USE THE WATER TO MY ADVANTAGE, KICKING UP A WALL OF OCEAN IN FRONT OF ME TO RAMP UP ONTO THE CENTRE.
THE ATOMIC PAYLOAD IS STILL ERUPTING, THE GRISLY TABLEAU FROZEN IN FRONT OF ME.
HELL ON EARTH. THAT'S THE ONLY WAY TO DESCRIBE IT. I CAN FEEL ITS MENTAL PULL SPREADING OVER ME AND FOR A MICROSECOND, I FEEL THE SHARP TASTE OF DESPAIR. I SHUT OFF MY MIND AND TURN ON PALMER'S DEVICE.
IT'S DOWN TO DOING WHAT I DO BEST--
RUN.

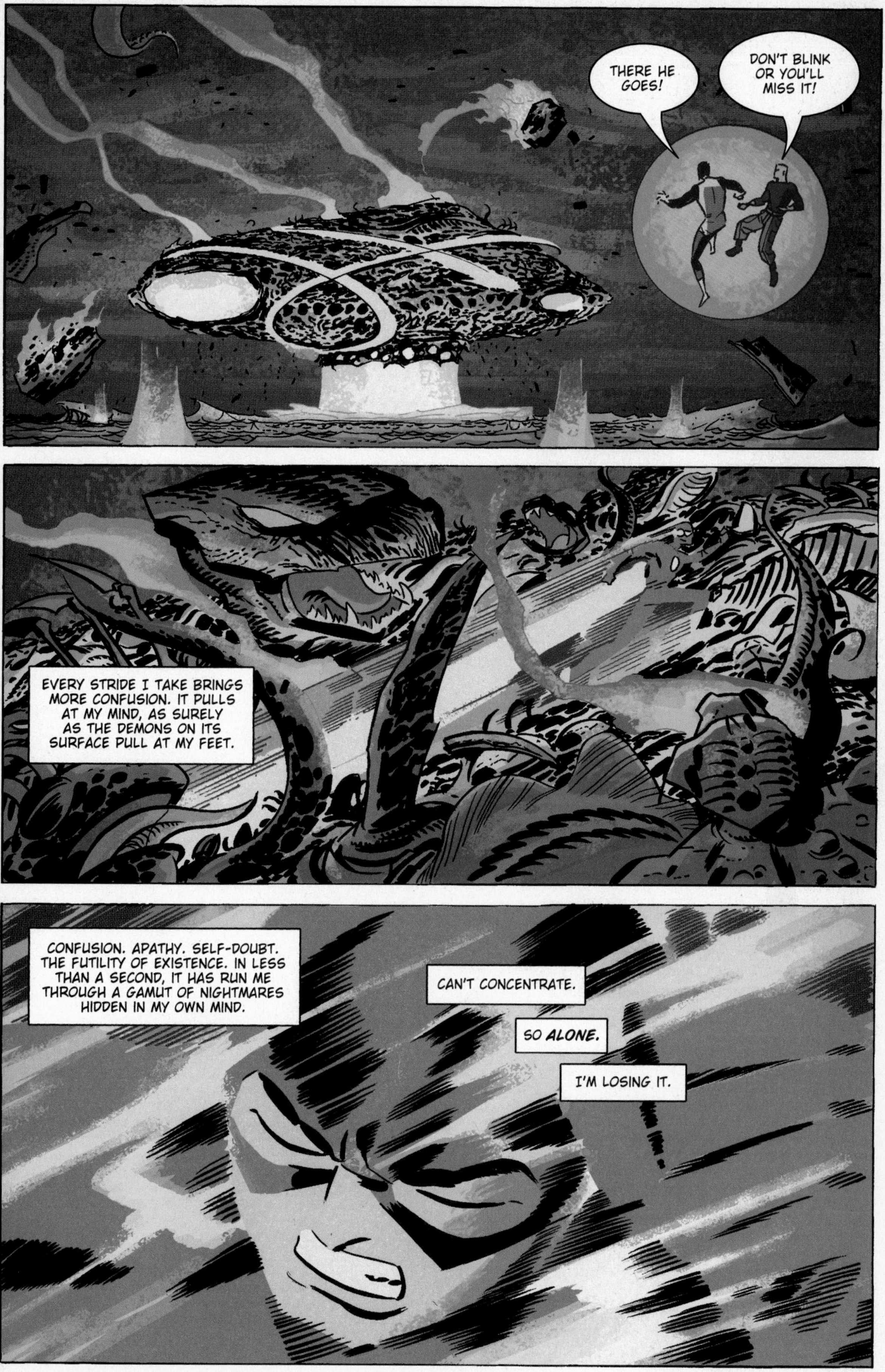
THERE HE GOES!
DON'T BLINK OR YOU'LL MISS IT!
EVERY STRIDE I TAKE BRINGS MORE CONFUSION. IT PULLS AT MY MIND, AS SURELY AS THE DEMONS ON ITS SURFACE PULL AT MY FEET.
CONFUSION. APATHY. SELF-DOUBT. THE FUTILITY OF EXISTENCE. IN LESS THAN A SECOND, IT HAS RUN ME THROUGH A GAMUT OF NIGHTMARES HIDDEN IN MY OWN MIND.
CAN'T CONCENTRATE.
SO *ALONE.*
I'M LOSING IT.

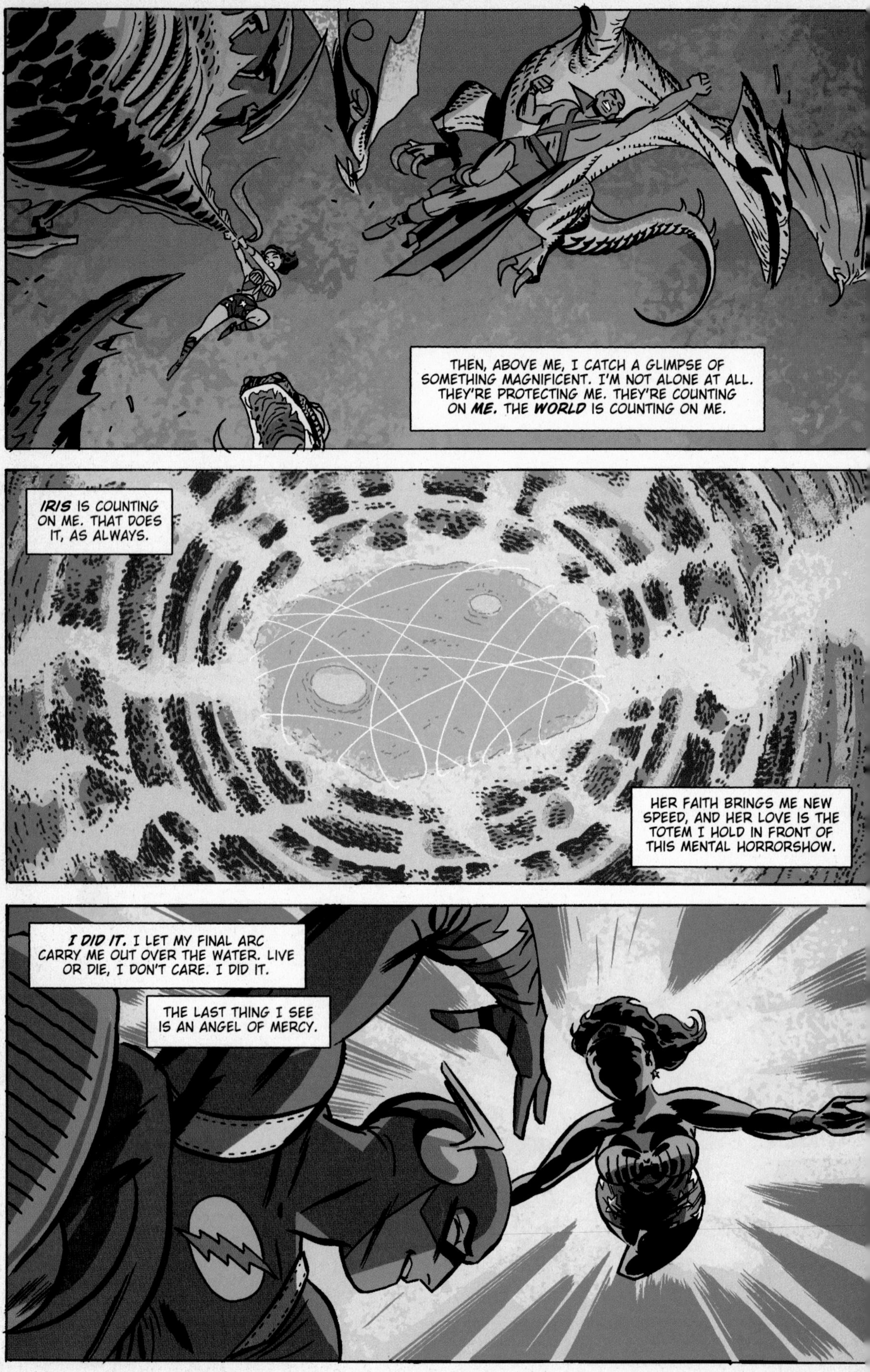
THEN, ABOVE ME, I CATCH A GLIMPSE OF SOMETHING MAGNIFICENT. I'M NOT ALONE AT ALL. THEY'RE PROTECTING ME. THEY'RE COUNTING ON ME. THE WORLD IS COUNTING ON ME.
IRIS IS COUNTING ON ME. THAT DOES IT, AS ALWAYS.
HER FAITH BRINGS ME NEW SPEED, AND HER LOVE IS THE TOTEM I HOLD IN FRONT OF THIS MENTAL HORRORSHOW.
I DID IT. I LET MY FINAL ARC CARRY ME OUT OVER THE WATER. LIVE OR DIE, I DON'T CARE. I DID IT.
THE LAST THING I SEE IS AN ANGEL OF MERCY.

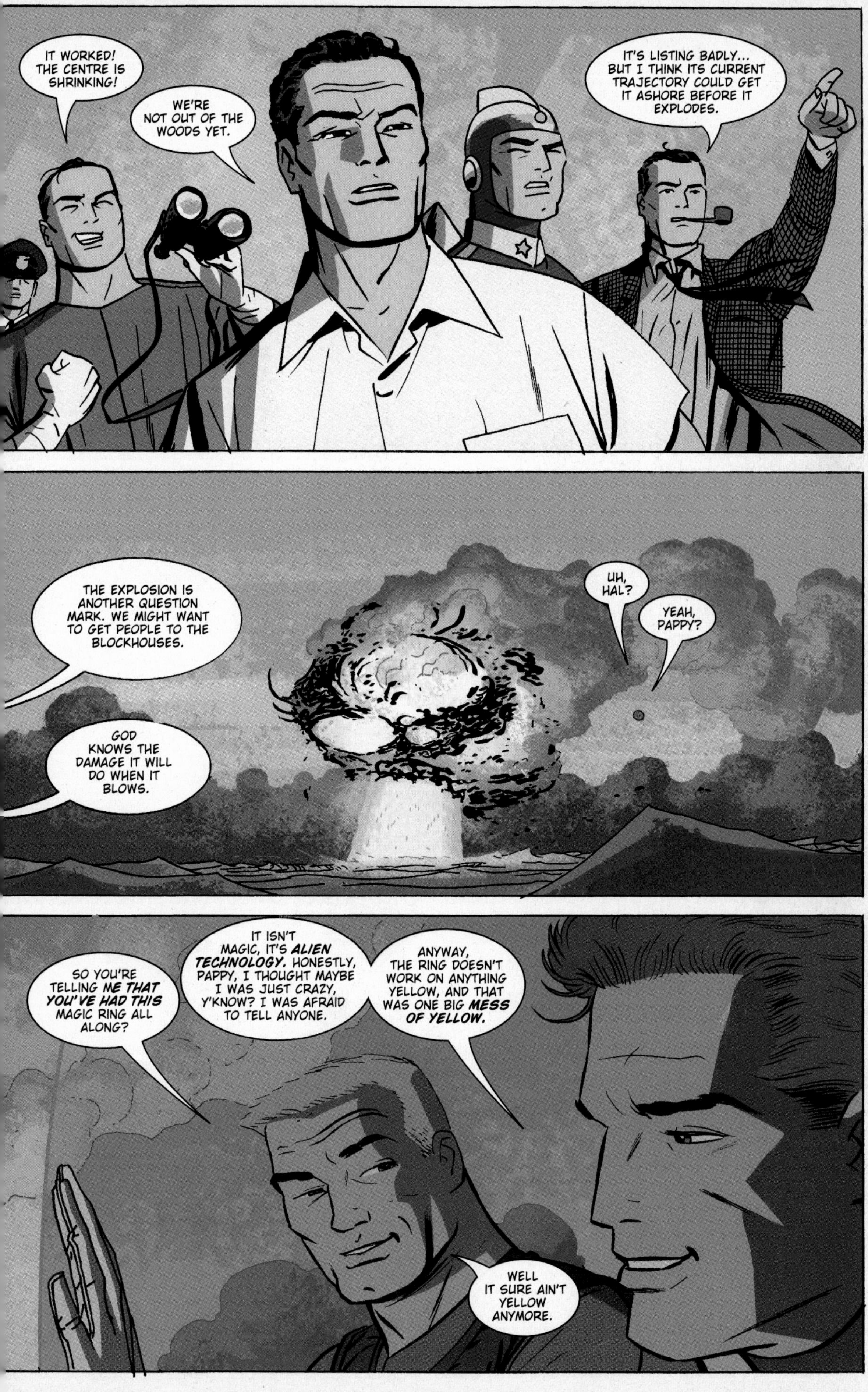
IT WORKED! THE CENTRE IS SHRINKING!
WE'RE NOT OUT OF THE WOODS YET.
IT'S LISTING BADLY... BUT I THINK ITS CURRENT TRAJECTORY COULD GET IT ASHORE BEFORE IT EXPLODES.
THE EXPLOSION IS ANOTHER QUESTION MARK. WE MIGHT WANT TO GET PEOPLE TO THE BLOCKHOUSES.
GOD KNOWS THE DAMAGE IT WILL DO WHEN IT BLOWS.
UH, HAL?
YEAH, PAPPY?
SO YOU'RE TELLING ME THAT YOU'VE HAD THIS MAGIC RING ALL ALONG?
IT ISN'T MAGIC, IT'S ALIEN TECHNOLOGY. HONESTLY, PAPPY, I THOUGHT MAYBE I WAS JUST CRAZY, Y'KNOW? I WAS AFRAID TO TELL ANYONE.
ANYWAY, THE RING DOESN'T WORK ON ANYTHING YELLOW, AND THAT WAS ONE BIG MESS OF YELLOW.
WELL IT SURE AIN'T YELLOW ANYMORE.

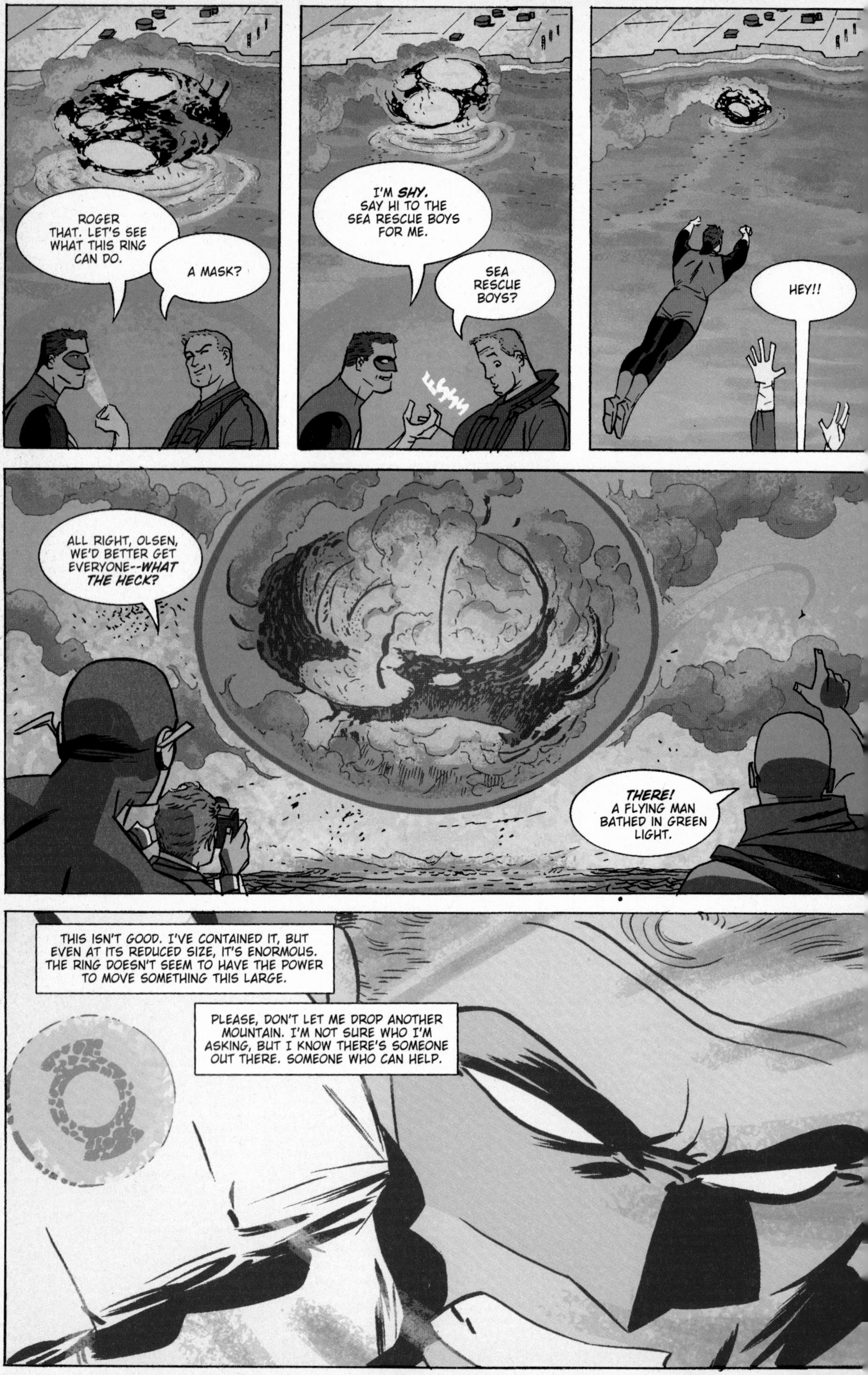
ROGER THAT. LET'S SEE WHAT THIS RING CAN DO.
A MASK?
I'M SHY. SAY HI TO THE SEA RESCUE BOYS FOR ME.
SEA RESCUE BOYS?
HEY!!
ALL RIGHT, OLSEN, WE'D BETTER GET EVERYONE--WHAT THE HECK?
THERE! A FLYING MAN BATHED IN GREEN LIGHT.
THIS ISN'T GOOD. I'VE CONTAINED IT, BUT EVEN AT ITS REDUCED SIZE, IT'S ENORMOUS. THE RING DOESN'T SEEM TO HAVE THE POWER TO MOVE SOMETHING THIS LARGE.
PLEASE, DON'T LET ME DROP ANOTHER MOUNTAIN. I'M NOT SURE WHO I'M ASKING, BUT I KNOW THERE'S SOMEONE OUT THERE. SOMEONE WHO CAN HELP.

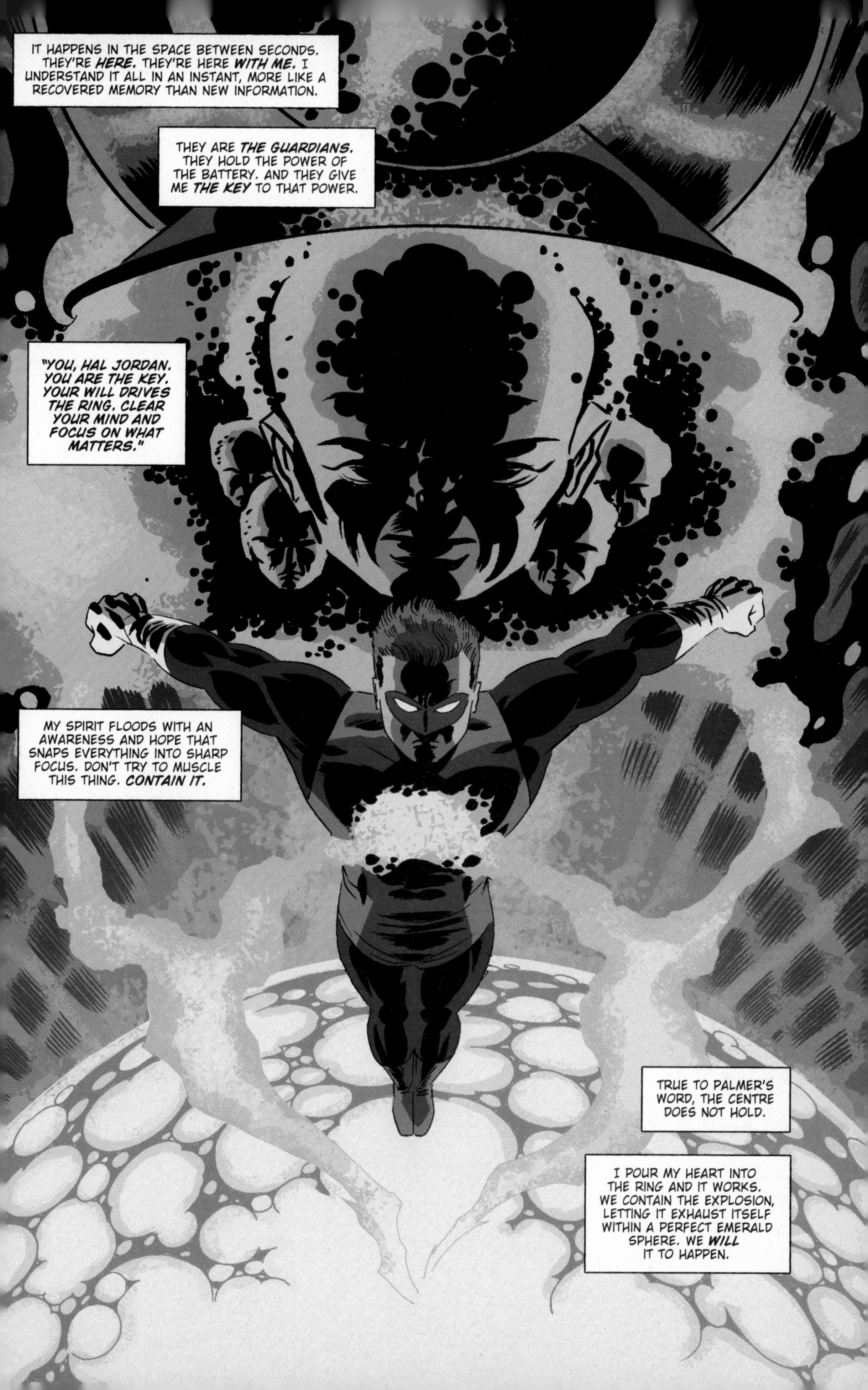
IT HAPPENS IN THE SPACE BETWEEN SECONDS. THEY'RE HERE. THEY'RE HERE WITH ME. I UNDERSTAND IT ALL IN AN INSTANT, MORE LIKE A RECOVERED MEMORY THAN NEW INFORMATION.
THEY ARE THE GUARDIANS. THEY HOLD THE POWER OF THE BATTERY. AND THEY GIVE ME THE KEY TO THAT POWER.
"YOU, HAL JORDAN. YOU ARE THE KEY. YOUR WILL DRIVES THE RING. CLEAR YOUR MIND AND FOCUS ON WHAT MATTERS."
MY SPIRIT FLOODS WITH AN AWARENESS AND HOPE THAT SNAPS EVERYTHING INTO SHARP FOCUS. DON'T TRY TO MUSCLE THIS THING. CONTAIN IT.
TRUE TO PALMER'S WORD, THE CENTRE DOES NOT HOLD.
I POUR MY HEART INTO THE RING AND IT WORKS. WE CONTAIN THE EXPLOSION, LETTING IT EXHAUST ITSELF WITHIN A PERFECT EMERALD SPHERE. WE WILL IT TO HAPPEN.

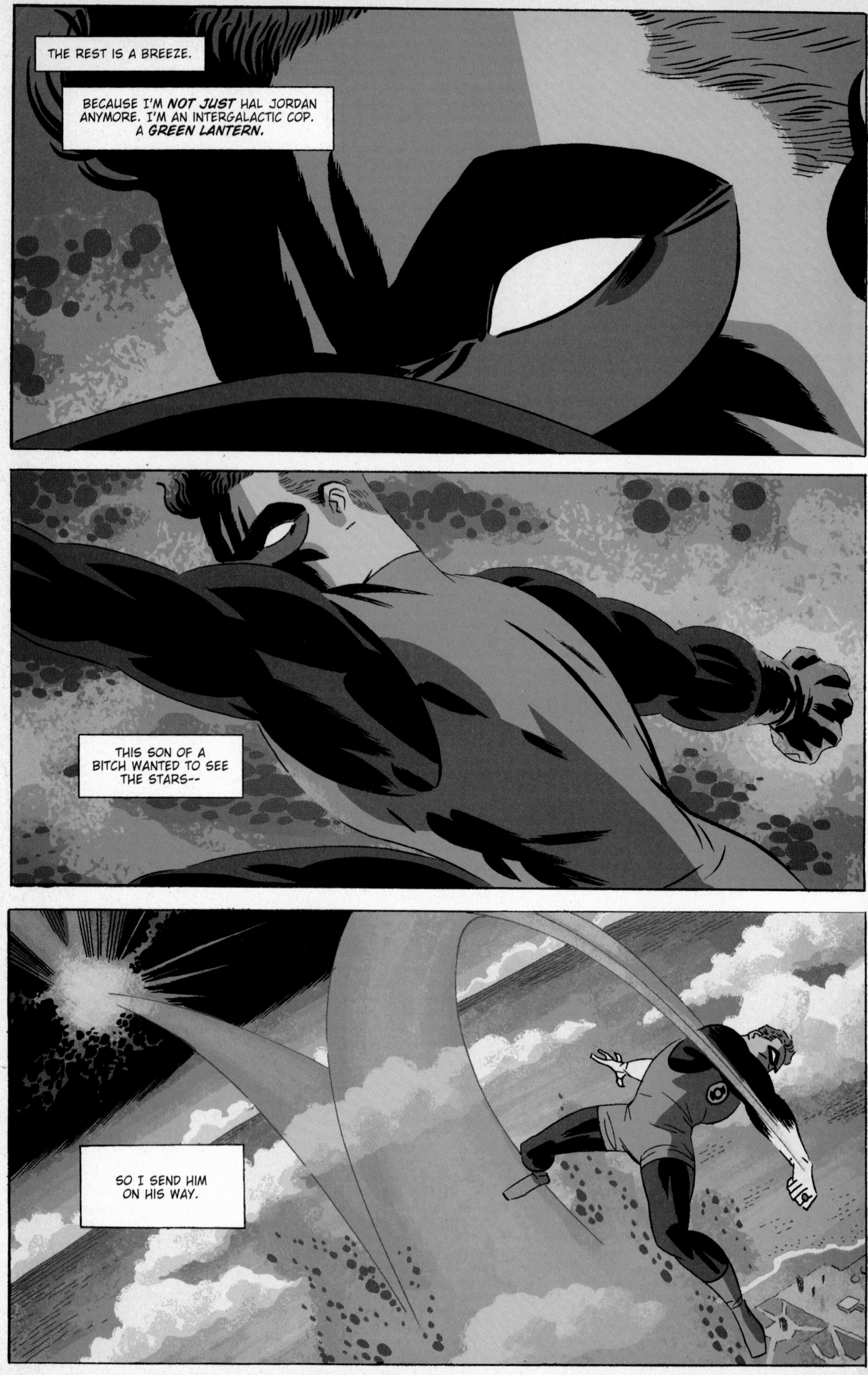

THE REST IS A BREEZE.
BECAUSE I'M **NOT JUST** HAL JORDAN ANYMORE. I'M AN INTERGALACTIC COP. A **GREEN LANTERN.**
THIS SON OF A BITCH WANTED TO SEE THE STARS--
SO I SEND HIM ON HIS WAY.

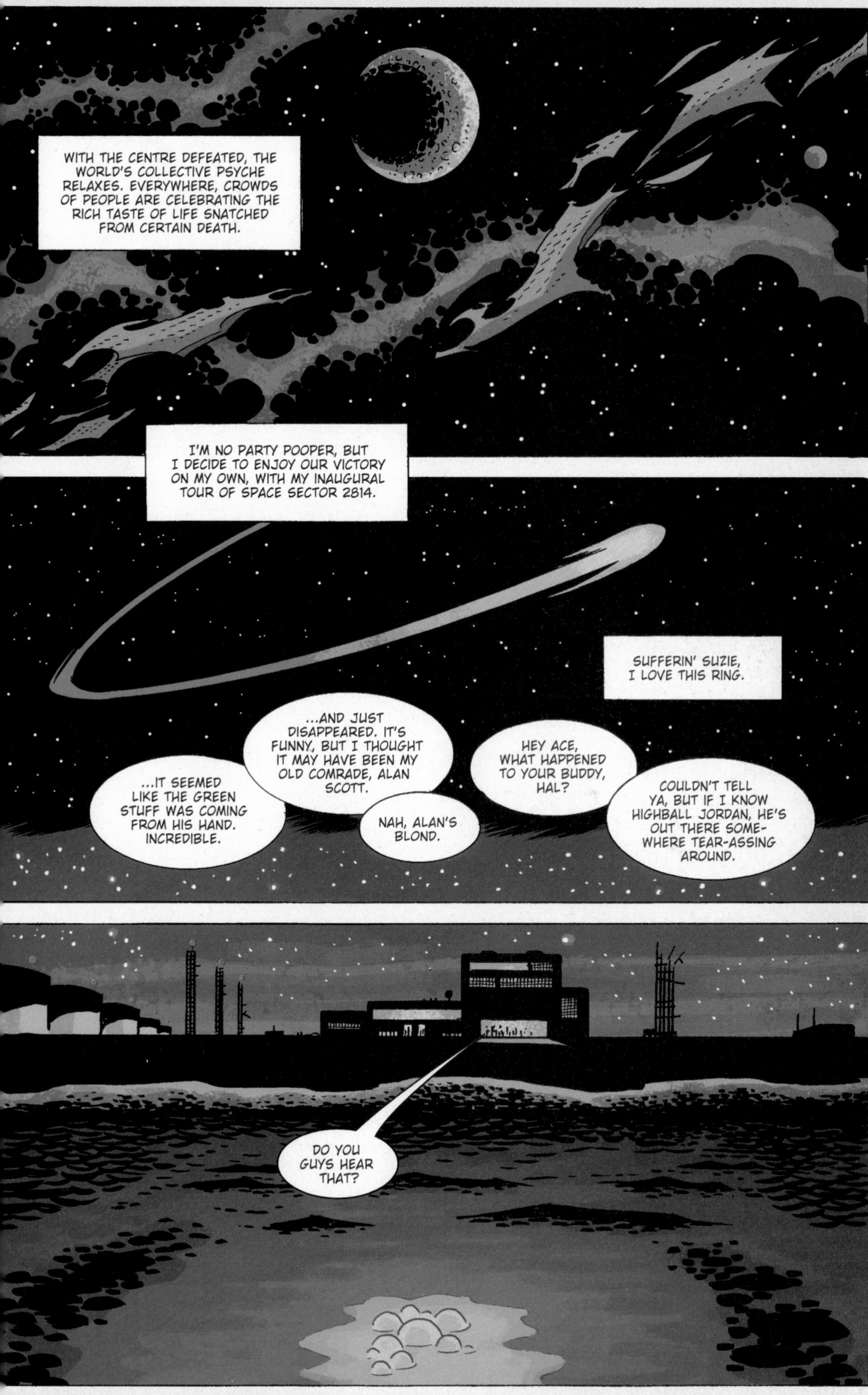
WITH THE CENTRE DEFEATED, THE WORLD'S COLLECTIVE PSYCHE RELAXES. EVERYWHERE, CROWDS OF PEOPLE ARE CELEBRATING THE RICH TASTE OF LIFE SNATCHED FROM CERTAIN DEATH.
I'M NO PARTY POOPER, BUT I DECIDE TO ENJOY OUR VICTORY ON MY OWN, WITH MY INAUGURAL TOUR OF SPACE SECTOR 2814.
SUFFERIN' SUZIE, I LOVE THIS RING.
...IT SEEMED LIKE THE GREEN STUFF WAS COMING FROM HIS HAND. INCREDIBLE.
...AND JUST DISAPPEARED. IT'S FUNNY, BUT I THOUGHT IT MAY HAVE BEEN MY OLD COMRADE, ALAN SCOTT.
NAH, ALAN'S BLOND.
HEY ACE, WHAT HAPPENED TO YOUR BUDDY, HAL?
COULDN'T TELL YA, BUT IF I KNOW HIGHBALL JORDAN, HE'S OUT THERE SOME-WHERE TEAR-ASSING AROUND.
DO YOU GUYS HEAR THAT?

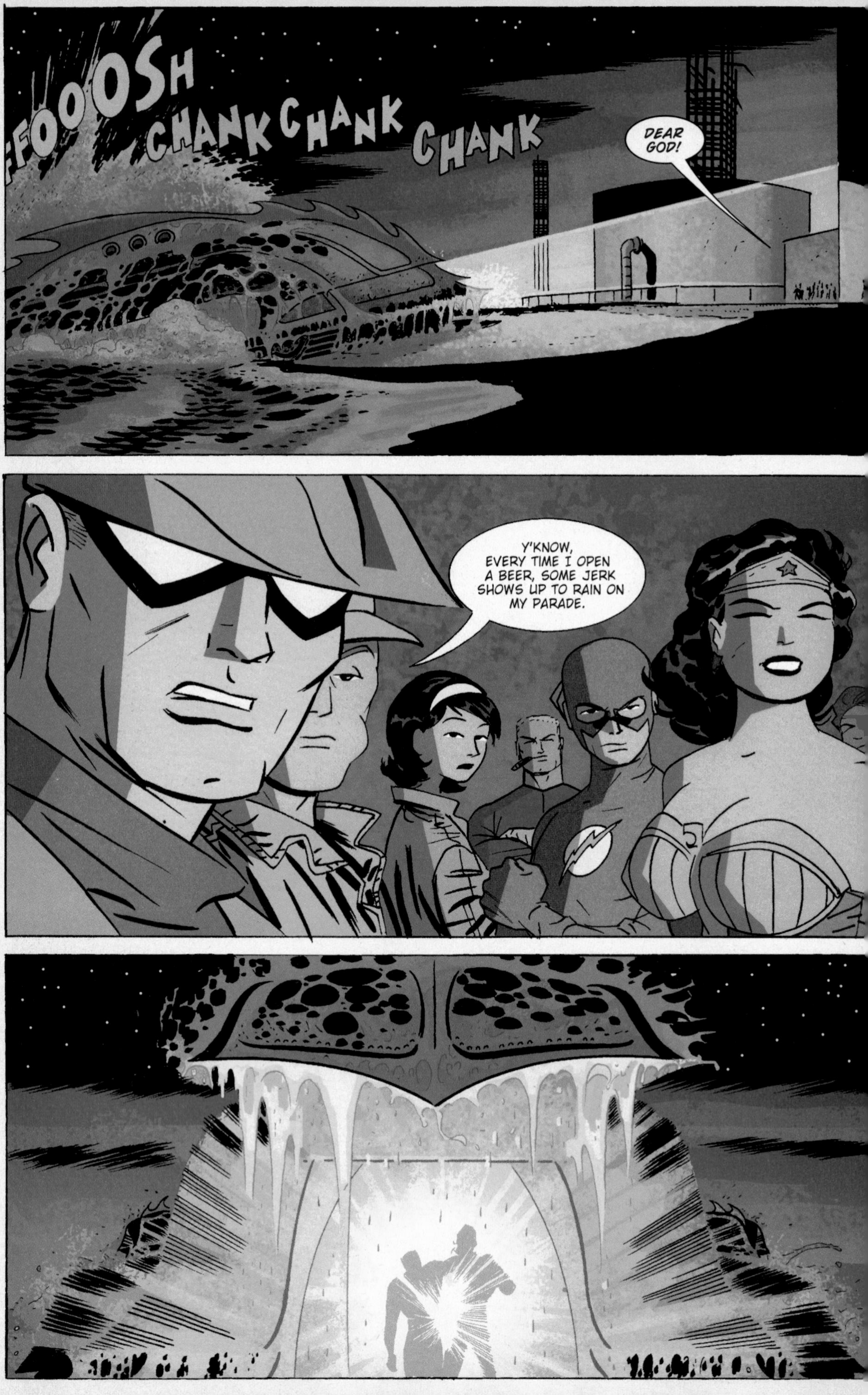
FOOOSH
CHANK CHANK
CHANK
DEAR GOD!
Y'KNOW, EVERY TIME I OPEN A BEER, SOME JERK SHOWS UP TO RAIN ON MY PARADE.

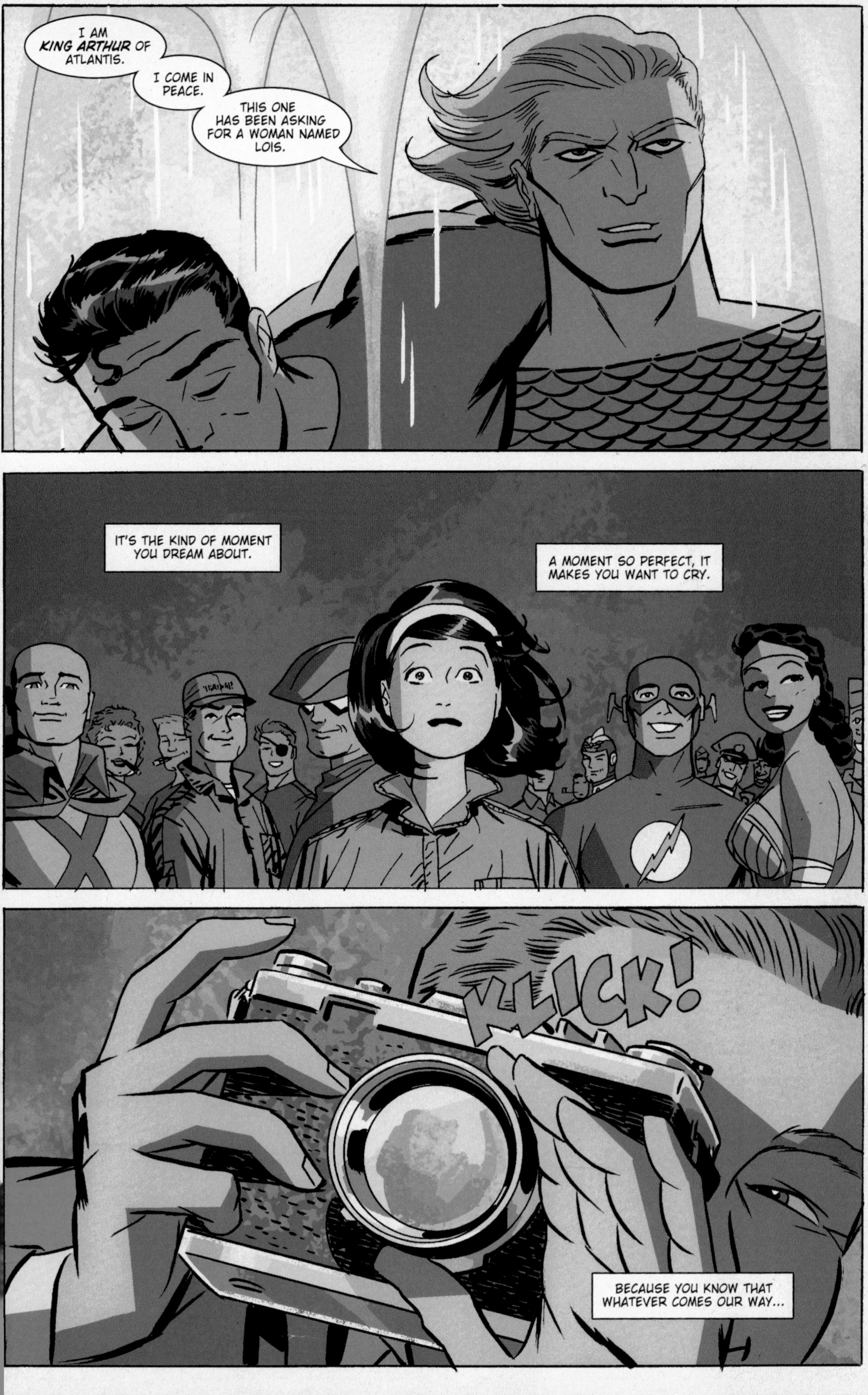
I AM KING ARTHUR OF ATLANTIS.
I COME IN PEACE.
THIS ONE HAS BEEN ASKING FOR A WOMAN NAMED LOIS.
IT'S THE KIND OF MOMENT YOU DREAM ABOUT.
A MOMENT SO PERFECT, IT MAKES YOU WANT TO CRY.
KLICK!
BECAUSE YOU KNOW THAT WHATEVER COMES OUR WAY...

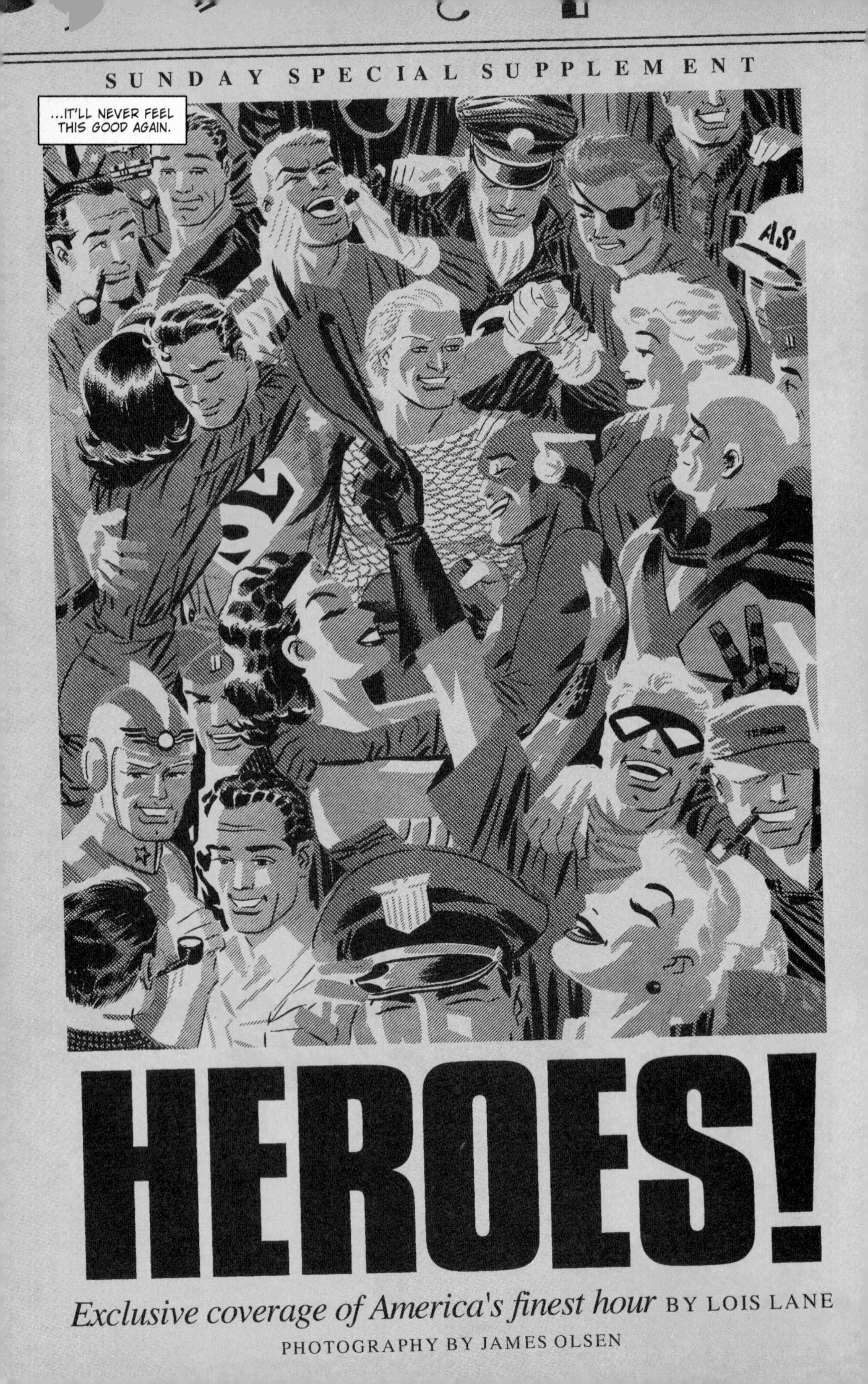
SUNDAY SPECIAL SUPPLEMENT
...IT'LL NEVER FEEL THIS GOOD AGAIN.
AS
HEROES!
Exclusive coverage of America's finest hour BY LOIS LANE
PHOTOGRAPHY BY JAMES OLSEN

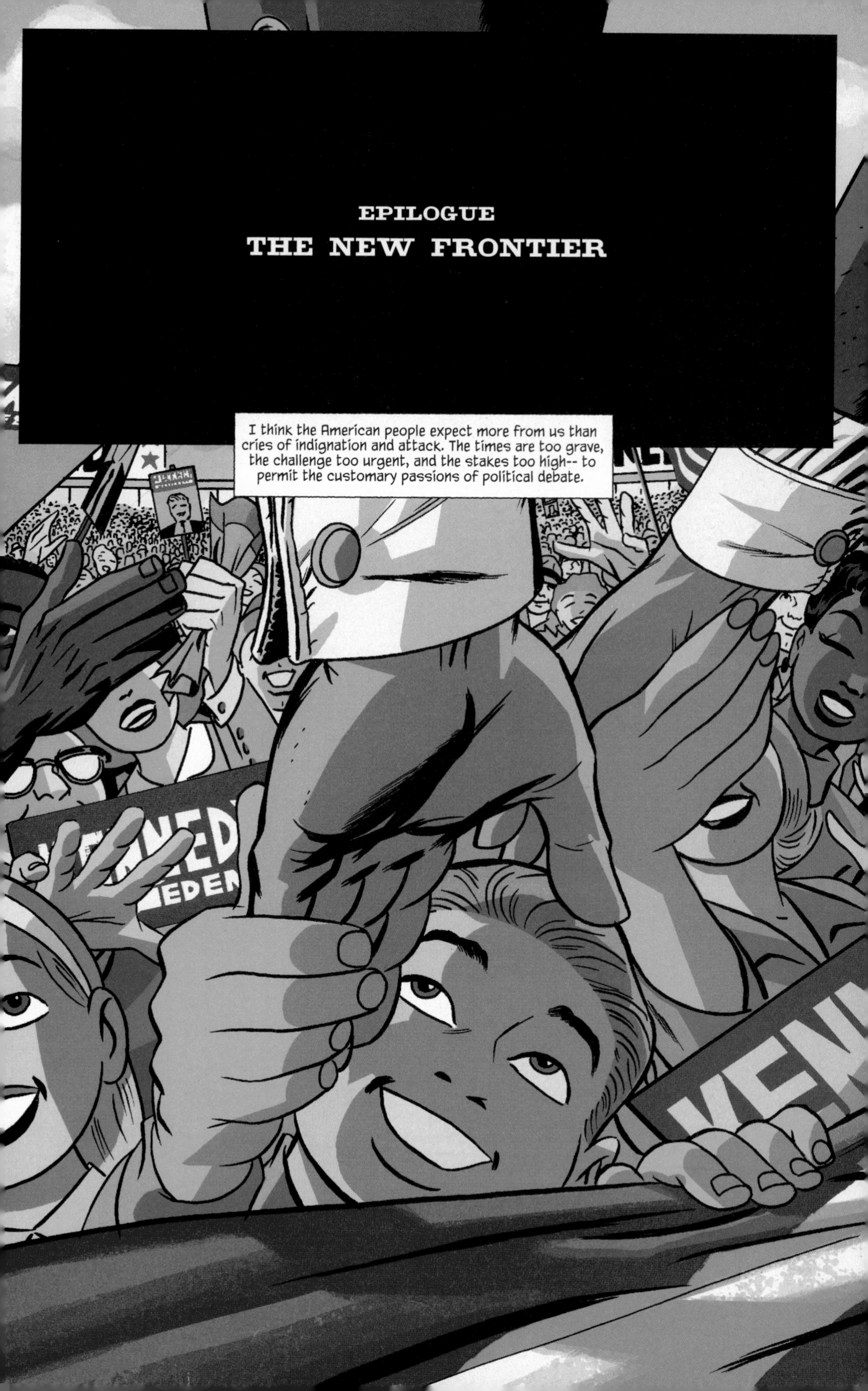
EPILOGUE
THE NEW FRONTIER
I think the American people expect more from us than cries of indignation and attack. The times are too grave, the challenge too urgent, and the stakes too high-- to permit the customary passions of political debate.

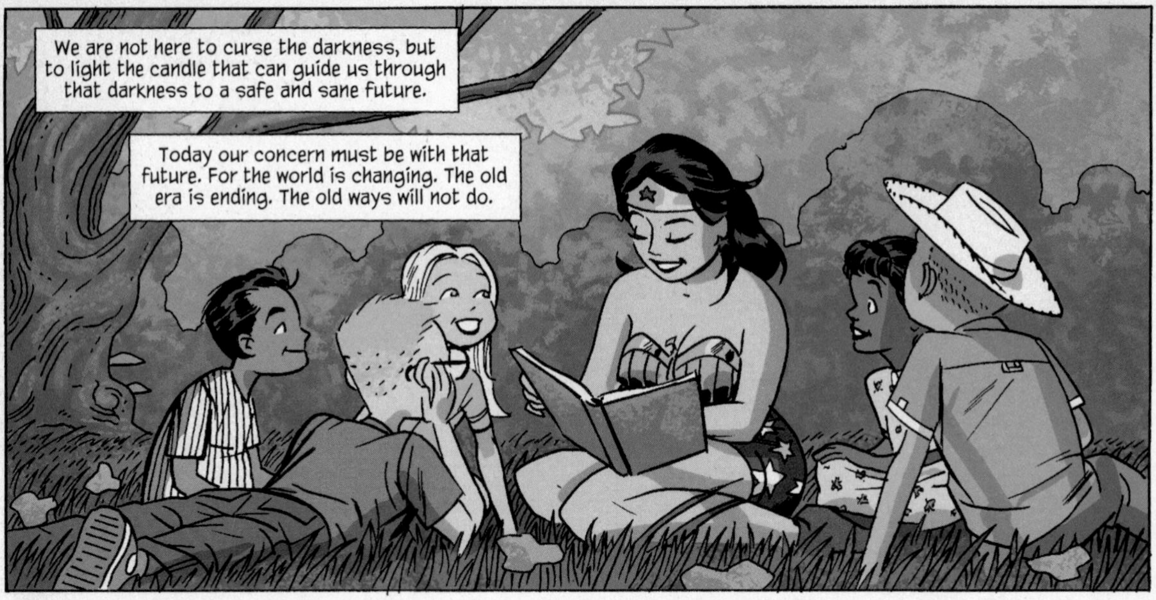
We are not here to curse the darkness, but to light the candle that can guide us through that darkness to a safe and sane future.
Today our concern must be with that future. For the world is changing. The old era is ending. The old ways will not do.

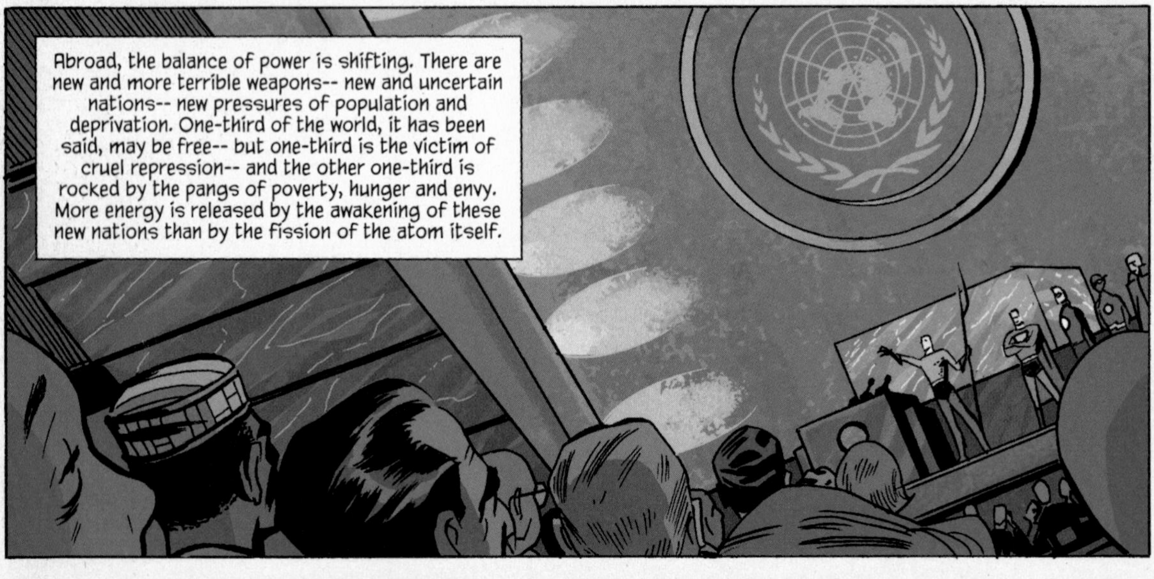
Abroad, the balance of power is shifting. There are new and more terrible weapons-- new and uncertain nations-- new pressures of population and deprivation. One-third of the world, it has been said, may be free-- but one-third is the victim of cruel repression-- and the other one-third is rocked by the pangs of poverty, hunger and envy. More energy is released by the awakening of these new nations than by the fission of the atom itself.

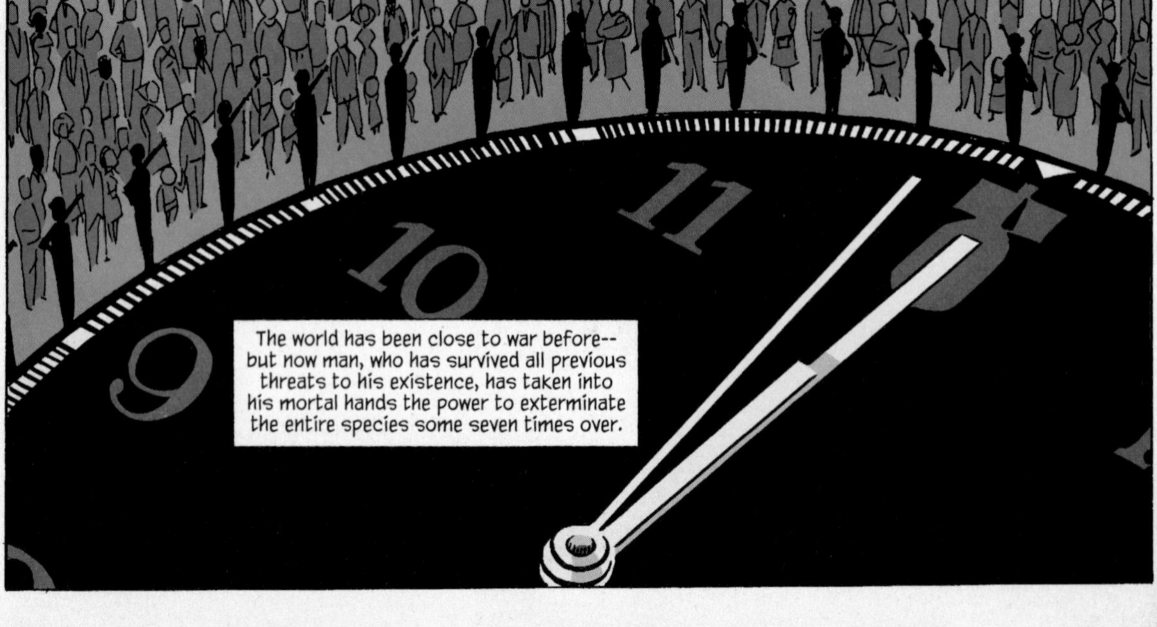
The world has been close to war before-- but now man, who has survived all previous threats to his existence, has taken into his mortal hands the power to exterminate the entire species some seven times over.

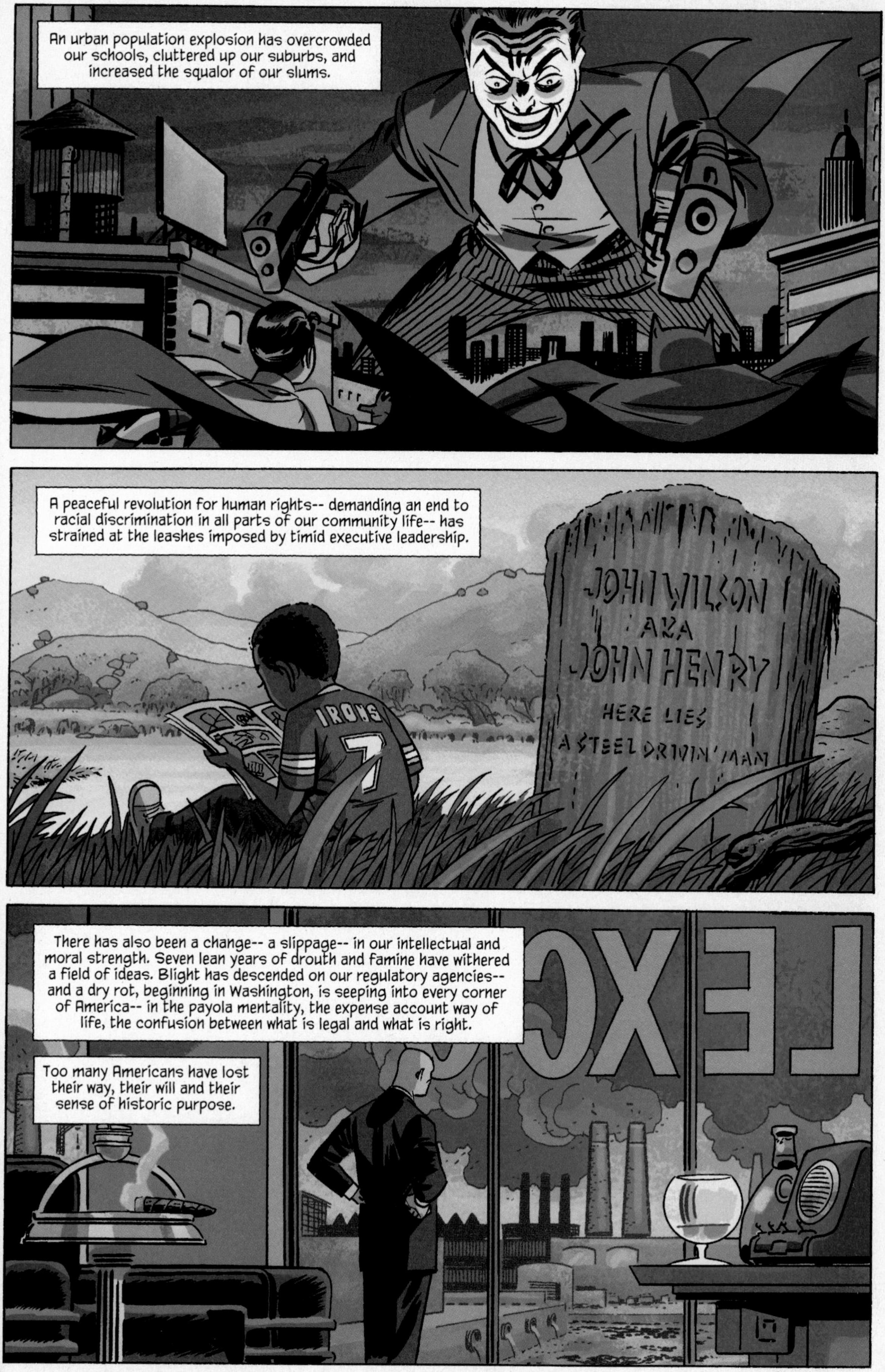
An urban population explosion has overcrowded our schools, cluttered up our suburbs, and increased the squalor of our slums.
A peaceful revolution for human rights-- demanding an end to racial discrimination in all parts of our community life-- has strained at the leashes imposed by timid executive leadership.
JOHN WILSON
AKA
JOHN HENRY
HERE LIES
A STEEL DRIVIN' MAN
IRONS
7
There has also been a change-- a slippage-- in our intellectual and moral strength. Seven lean years of drouth and famine have withered a field of ideas. Blight has descended on our regulatory agencies-- and a dry rot, beginning in Washington, is seeping into every corner of America-- in the payola mentality, the expense account way of life, the confusion between what is legal and what is right.
Too many Americans have lost their way, their will and their sense of historic purpose.

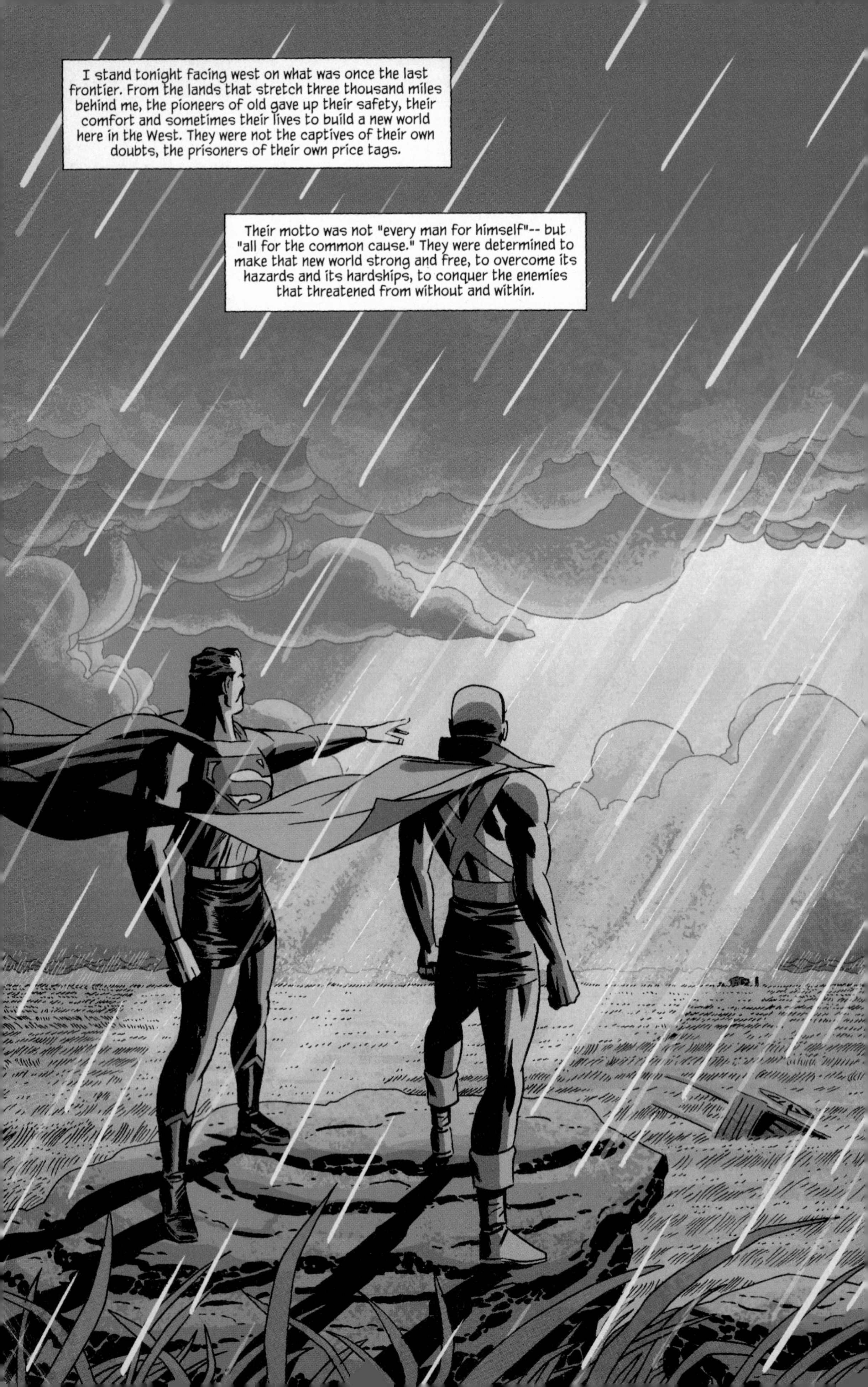
I stand tonight facing west on what was once the last frontier. From the lands that stretch three thousand miles behind me, the pioneers of old gave up their safety, their comfort and sometimes their lives to build a new world here in the West. They were not the captives of their own doubts, the prisoners of their own price tags.
Their motto was not "every man for himself"-- but "all for the common cause." They were determined to make that new world strong and free, to overcome its hazards and its hardships, to conquer the enemies that threatened from without and within.

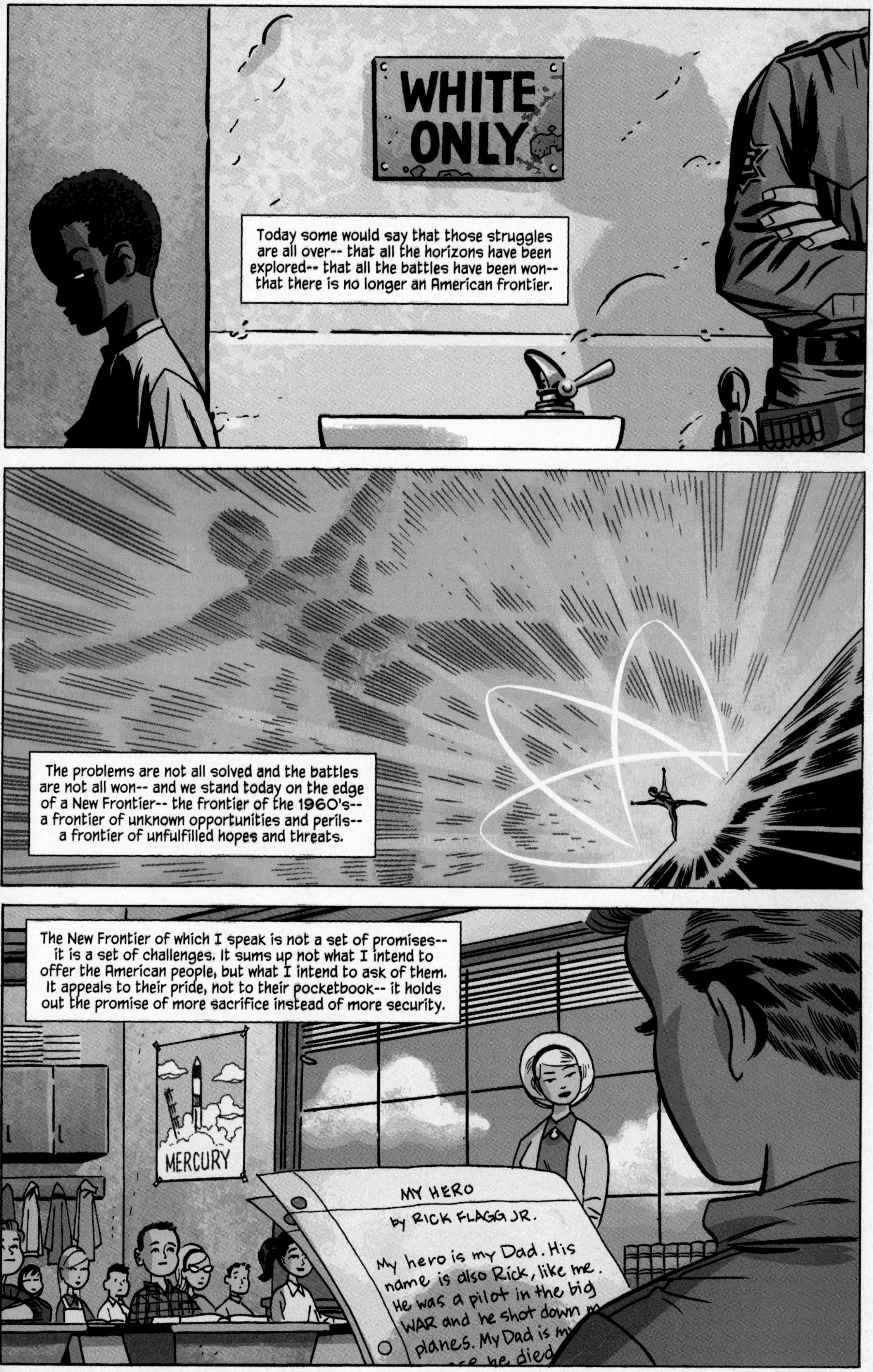
WHITE ONLY
Today some would say that those struggles are all over-- that all the horizons have been explored-- that all the battles have been won-- that there is no longer an American frontier.
The problems are not all solved and the battles are not all won-- and we stand today on the edge of a New Frontier-- the frontier of the 1960's-- a frontier of unknown opportunities and perils-- a frontier of unfulfilled hopes and threats.
The New Frontier of which I speak is not a set of promises-- it is a set of challenges. It sums up not what I intend to offer the American people, but what I intend to ask of them. It appeals to their pride, not to their pocketbook-- it holds out the promise of more sacrifice instead of more security.
MERCURY
MY HERO
by RICK FLAGG JR.
My hero is my Dad. His name is also Rick, like me. He was a pilot in the big WAR and he shot down
planes. My Dad is

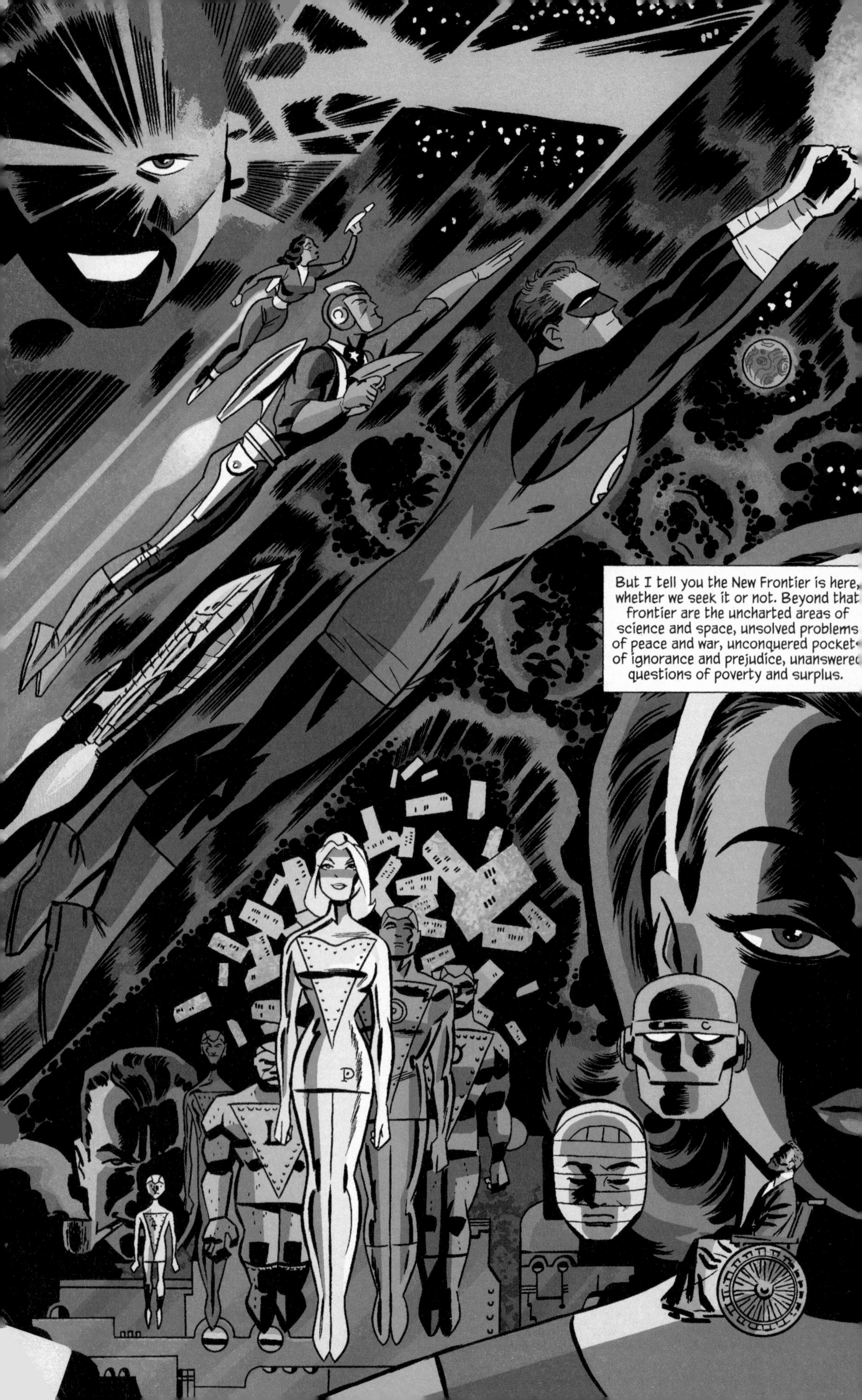
But I tell you the New Frontier is here, whether we seek it or not. Beyond that frontier are the uncharted areas of science and space, unsolved problems of peace and war, unconquered pockets of ignorance and prejudice, unanswered questions of poverty and surplus.

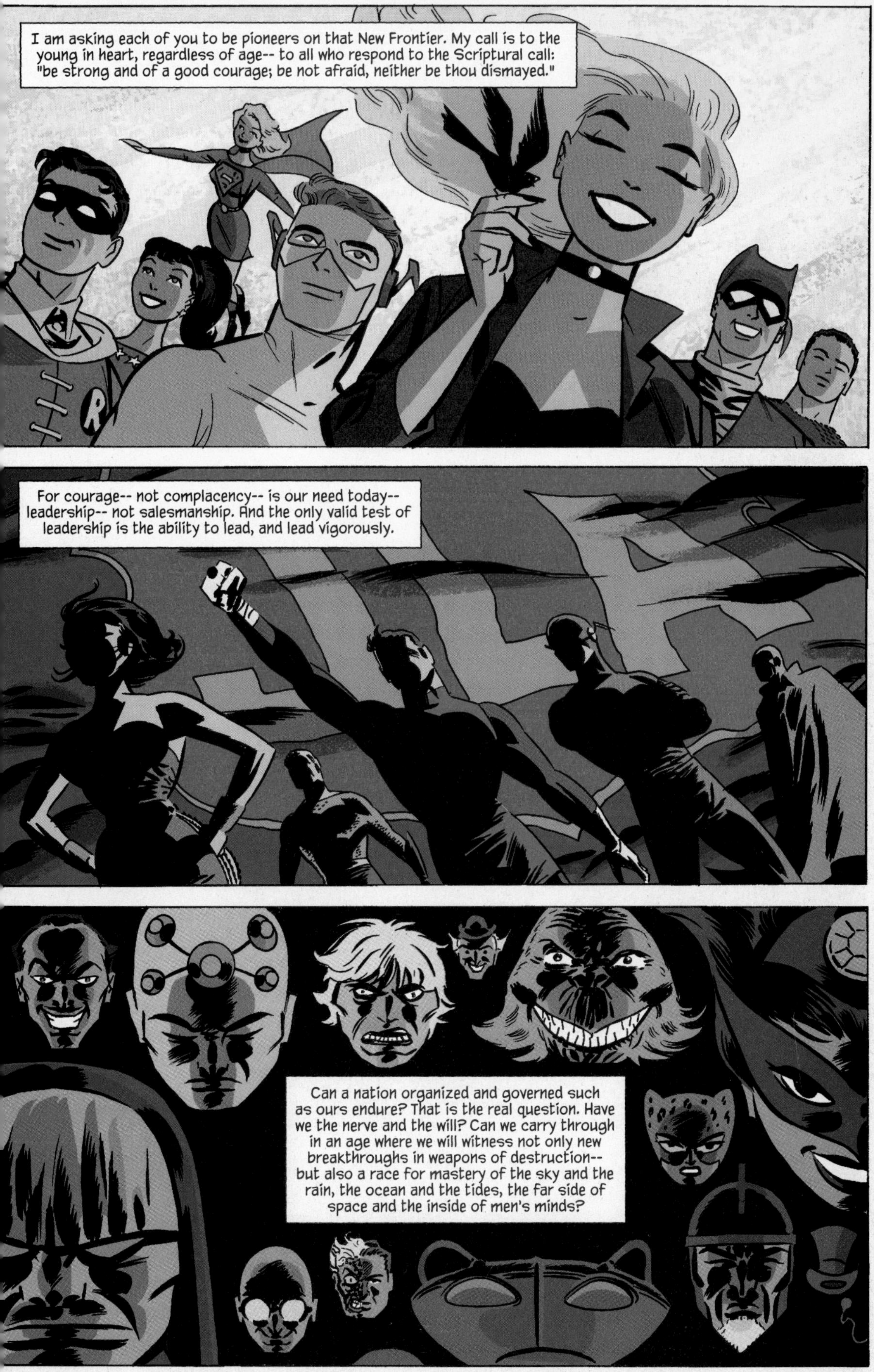
I am asking each of you to be pioneers on that New Frontier. My call is to the young in heart, regardless of age-- to all who respond to the Scriptural call: "be strong and of a good courage; be not afraid, neither be thou dismayed."
For courage-- not complacency-- is our need today-- leadership-- not salesmanship. And the only valid test of leadership is the ability to lead, and lead vigorously.
Can a nation organized and governed such as ours endure? That is the real question. Have we the nerve and the will? Can we carry through in an age where we will witness not only new breakthroughs in weapons of destruction-- but also a race for mastery of the sky and the rain, the ocean and the tides, the far side of space and the inside of men's minds?

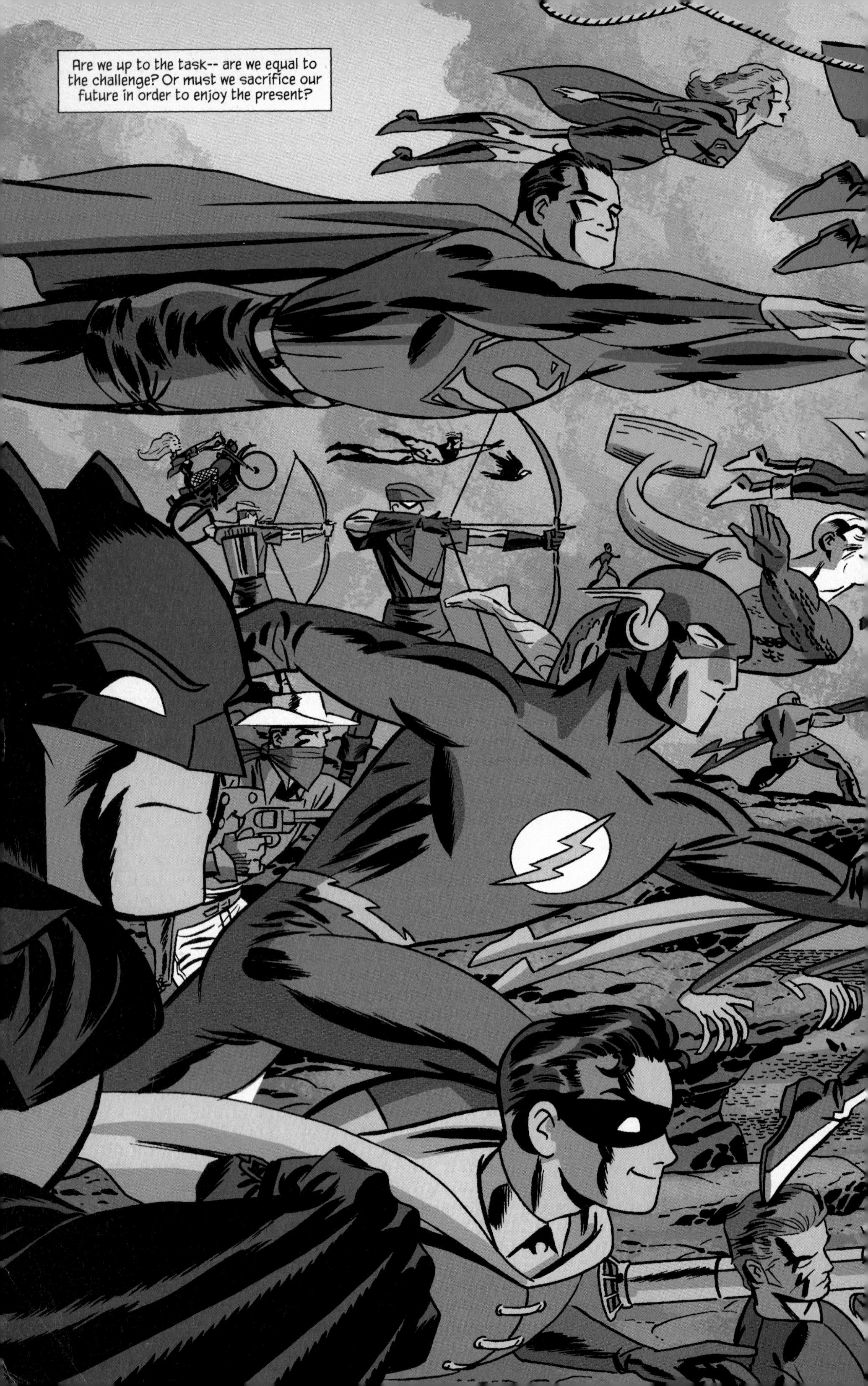
Are we up to the task-- are we equal to the challenge? Or must we sacrifice our future in order to enjoy the present?

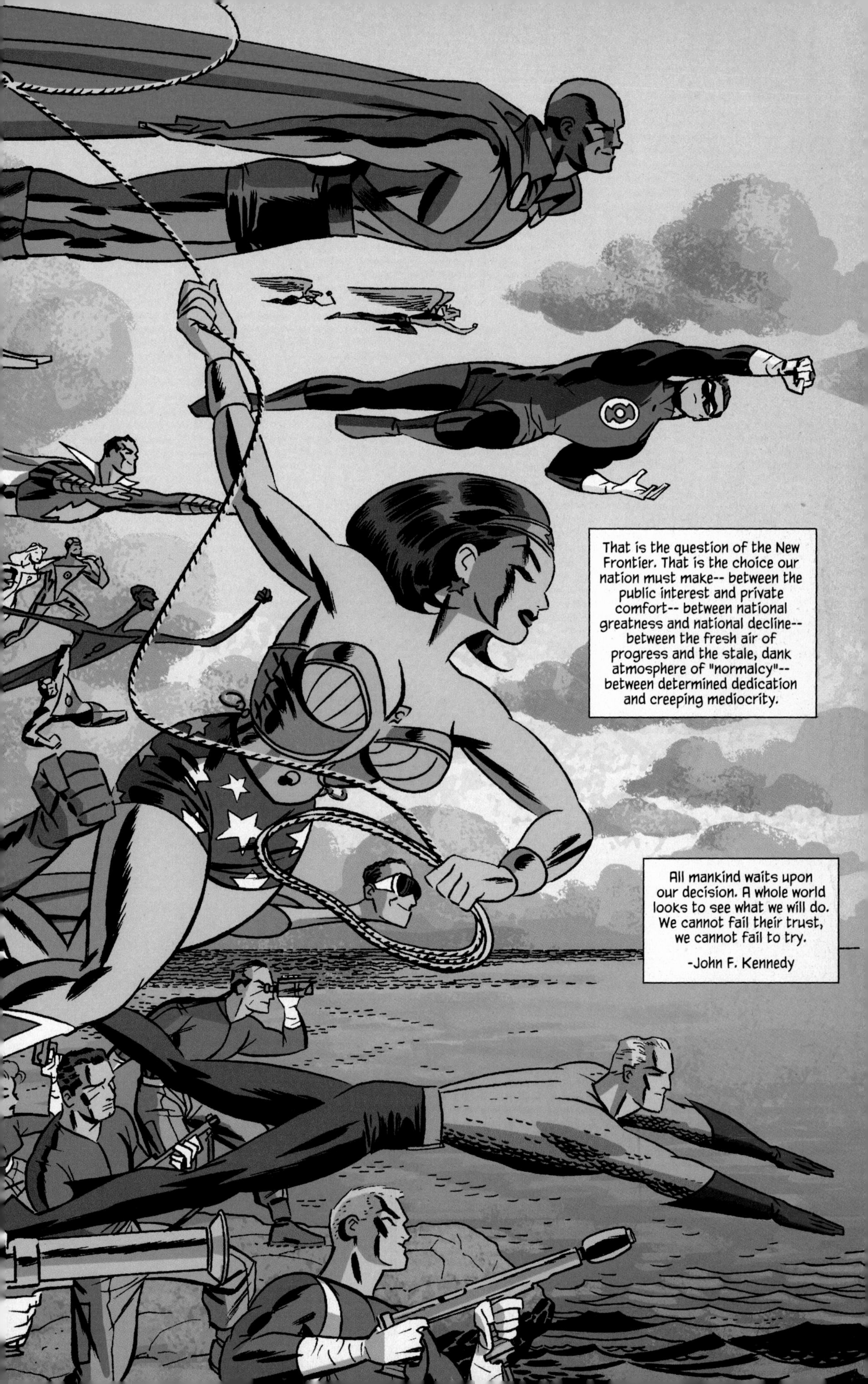
That is the question of the New Frontier. That is the choice our nation must make-- between the public interest and private comfort-- between national greatness and national decline-- between the fresh air of progress and the stale, dank atmosphere of "normalcy"-- between determined dedication and creeping mediocrity.
All mankind waits upon our decision. A whole world looks to see what we will do. We cannot fail their trust, we cannot fail to try.
-John F. Kennedy

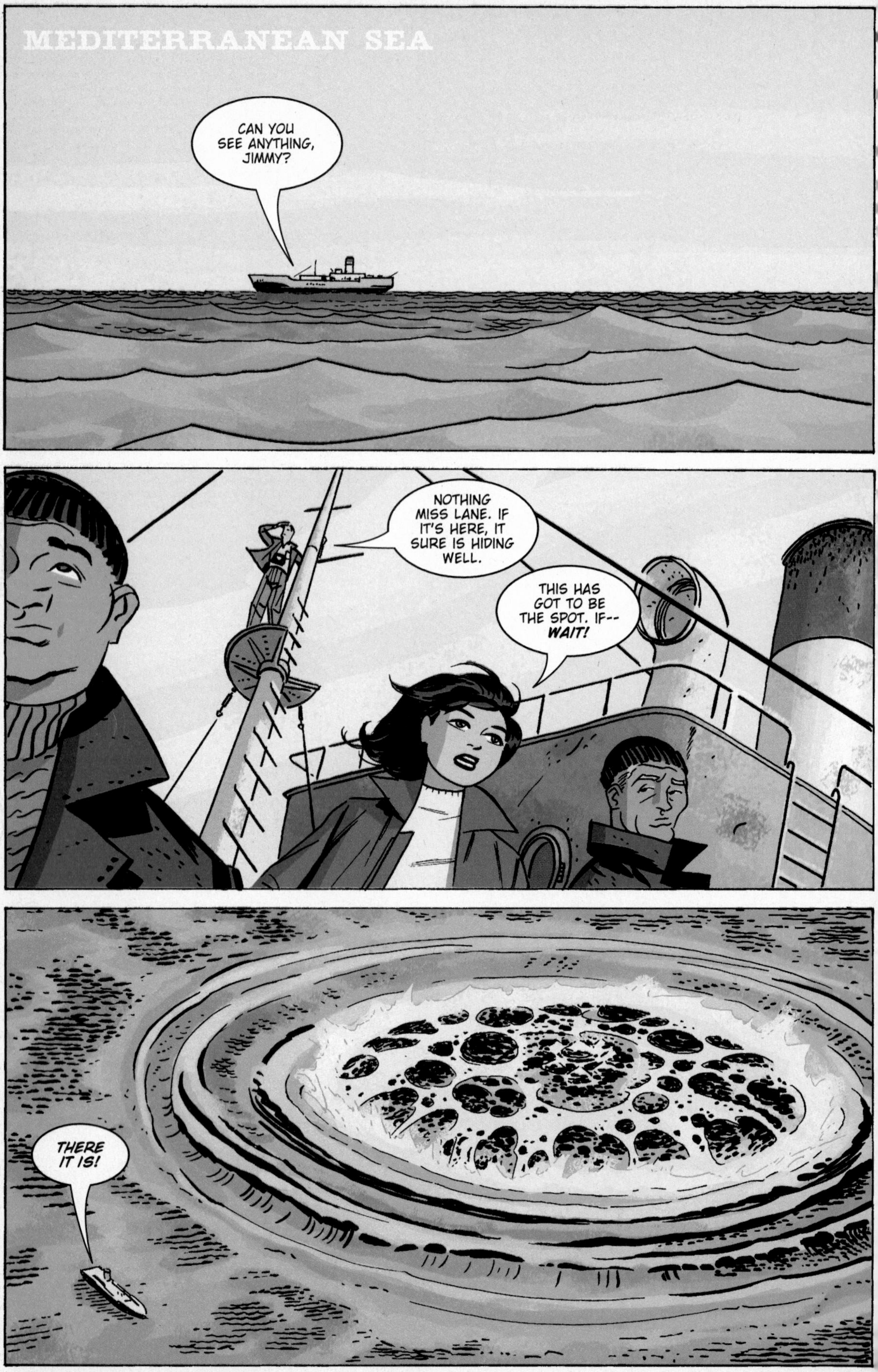
MEDITERRANEAN SEA
CAN YOU SEE ANYTHING, JIMMY?
NOTHING MISS LANE. IF IT'S HERE, IT SURE IS HIDING WELL.
THIS HAS GOT TO BE THE SPOT. IF-- WAIT!
THERE IT IS!

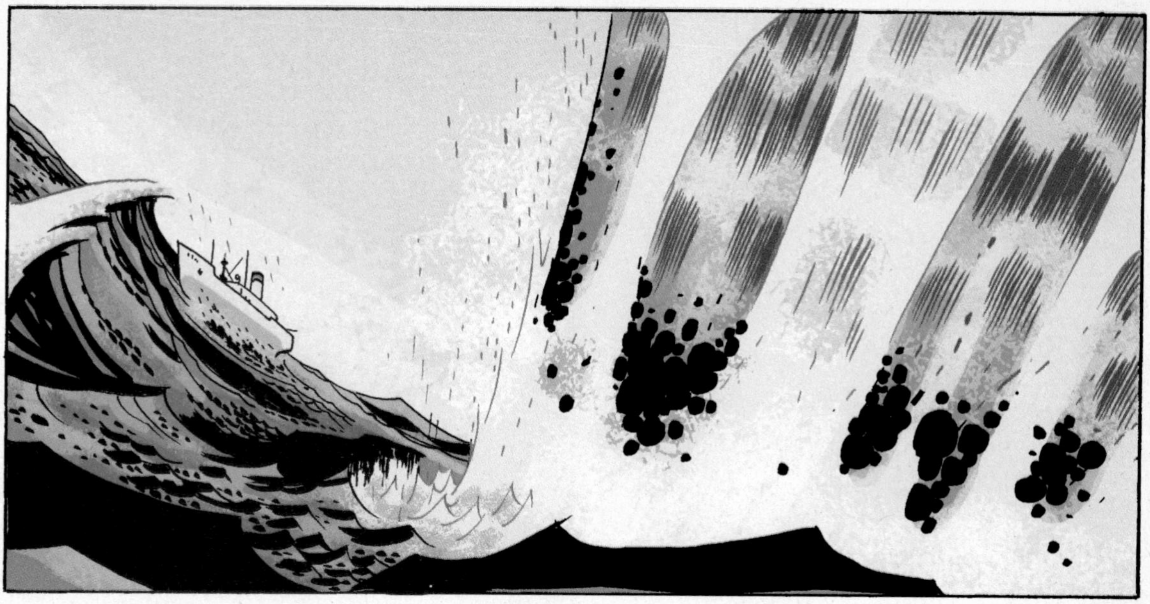

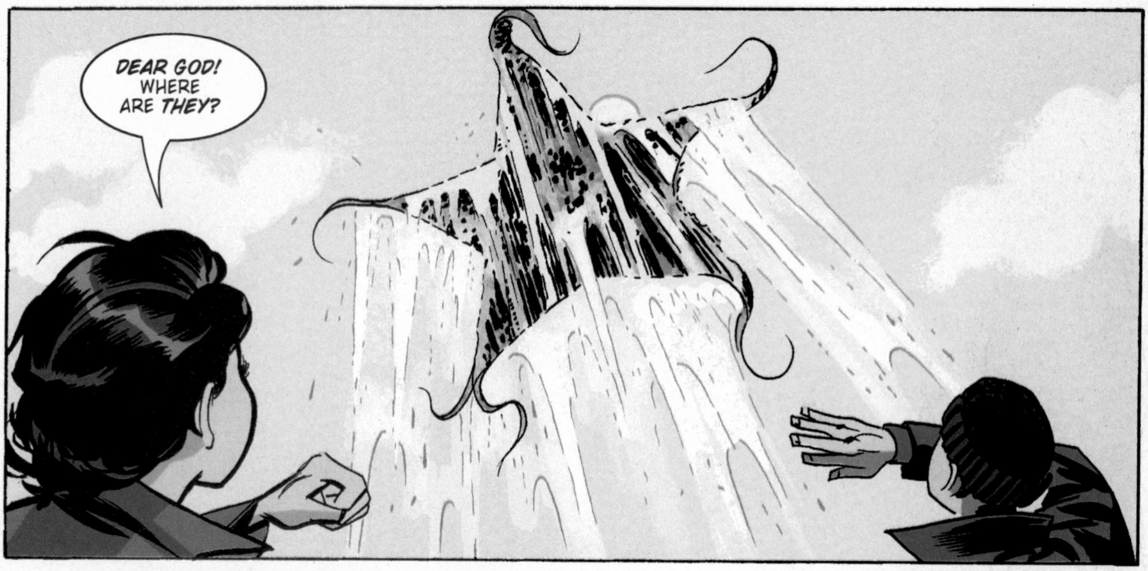
DEAR GOD! WHERE ARE THEY?

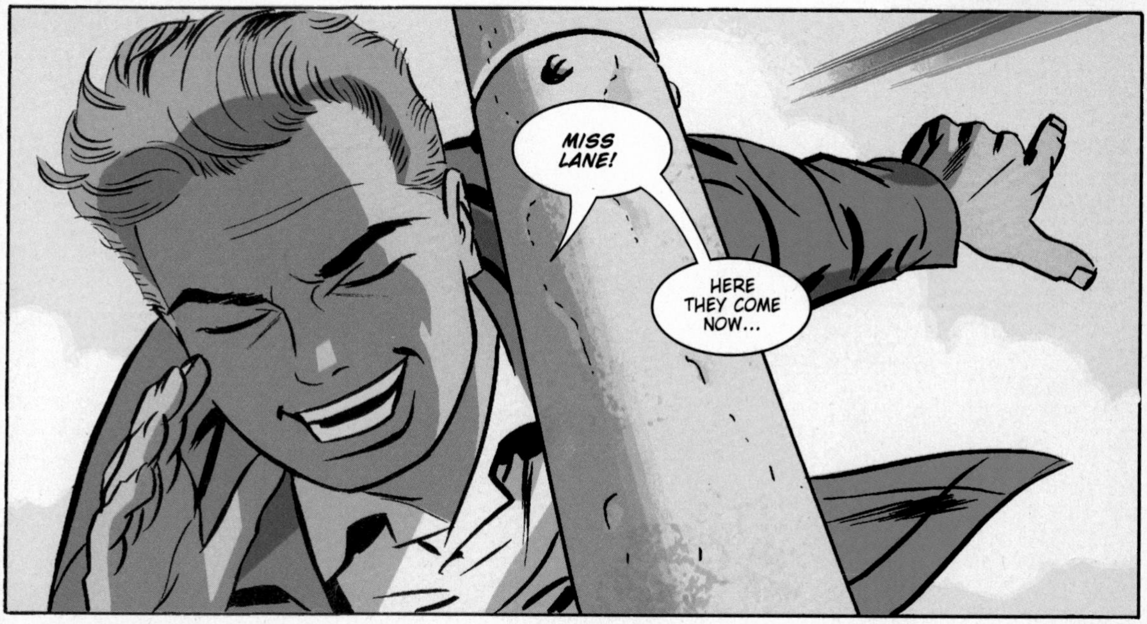
MISS LANE!
HERE THEY COME NOW...

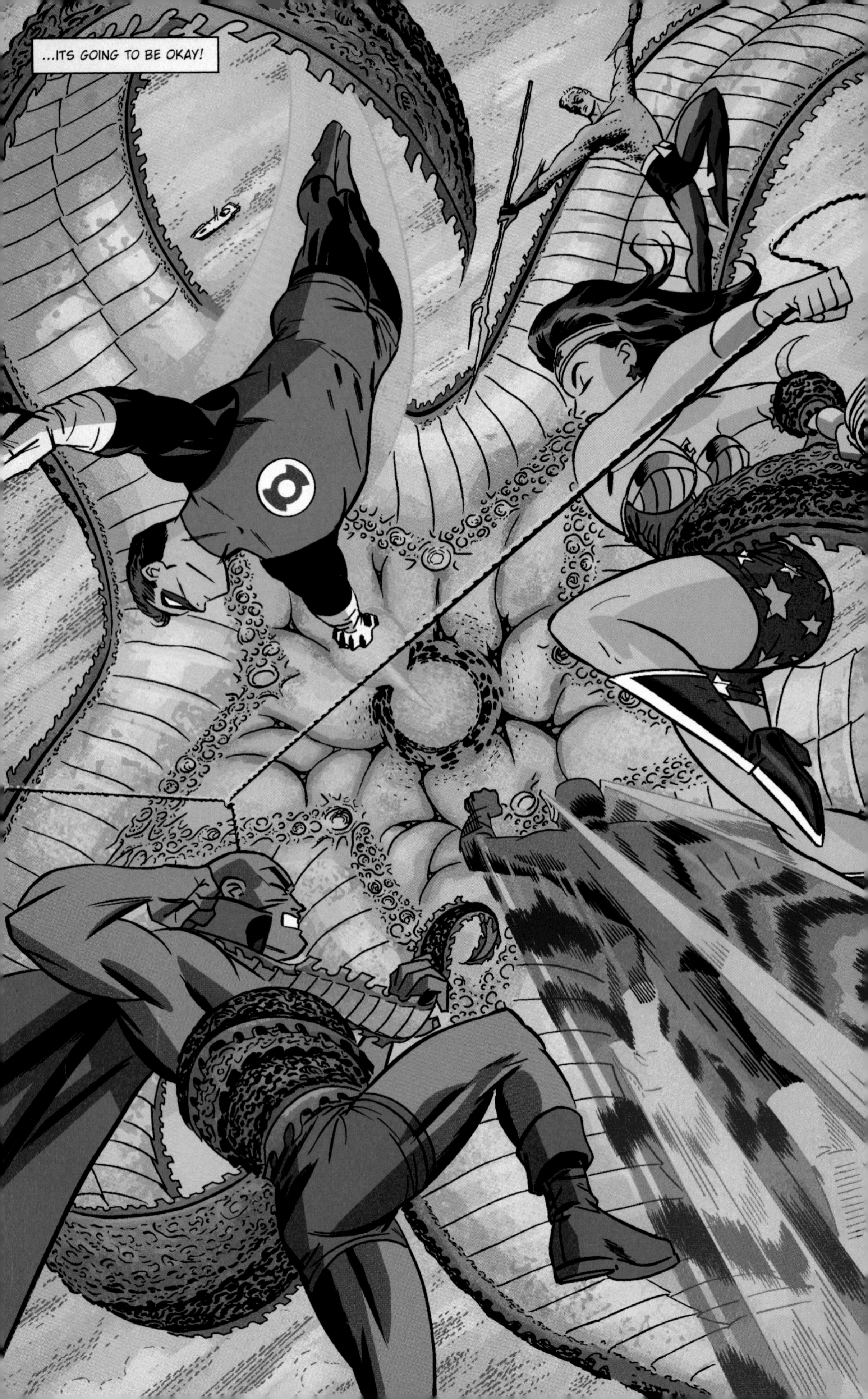
...ITS GOING TO BE OKAY!

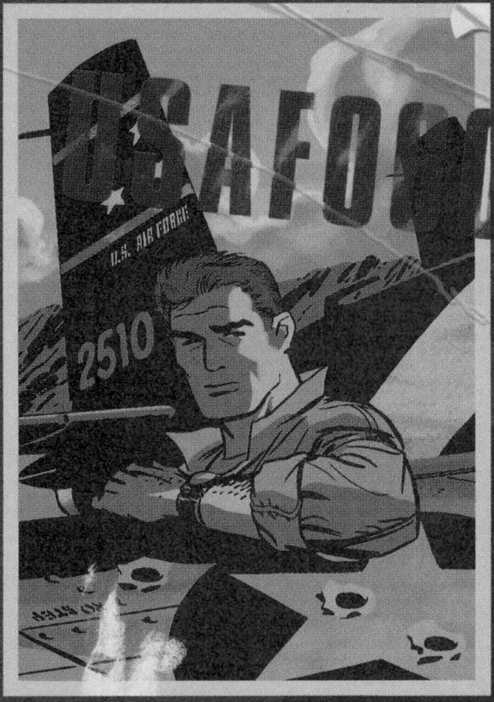
U.S. AIR FORCE
2510

COVER GALLERY

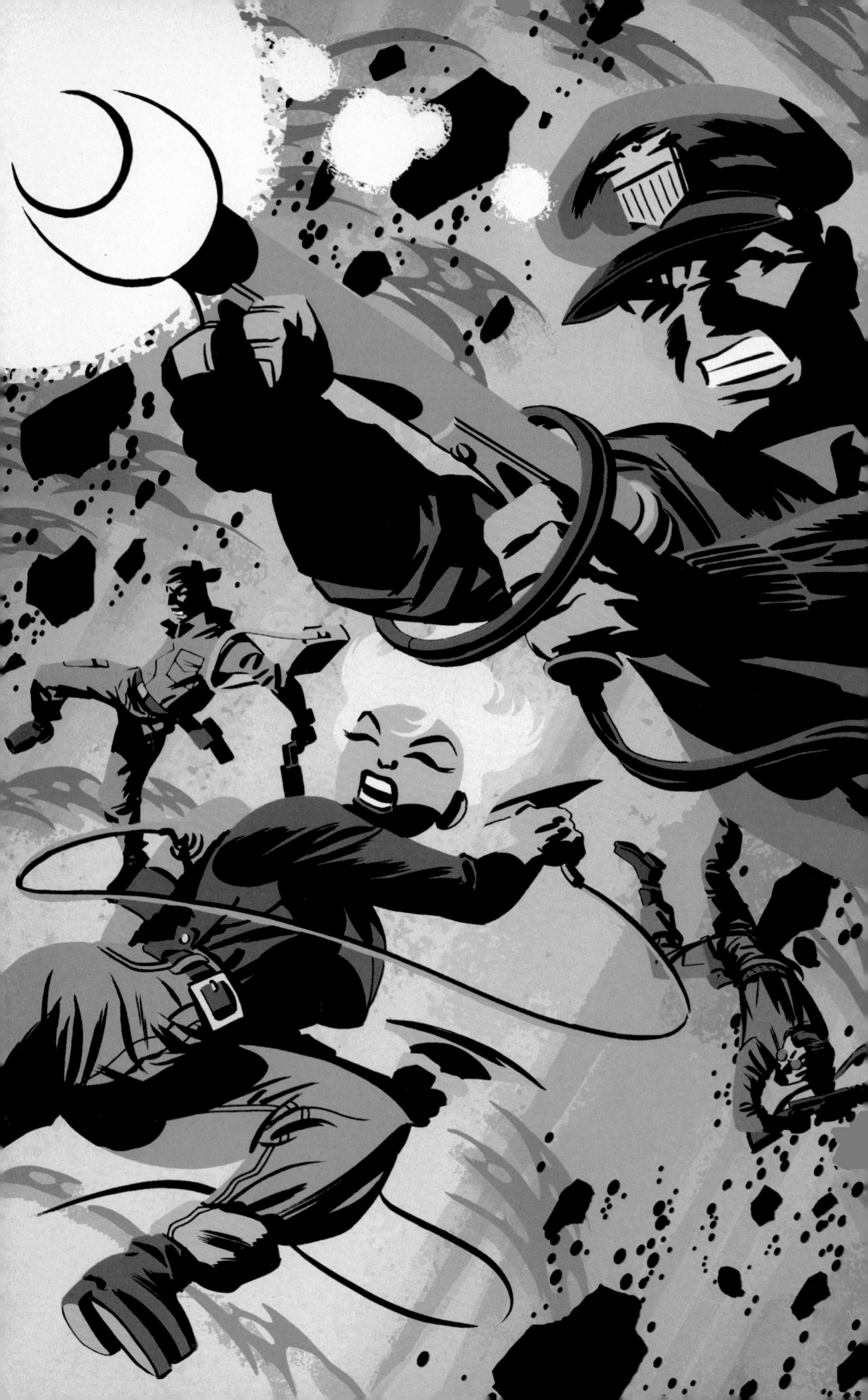

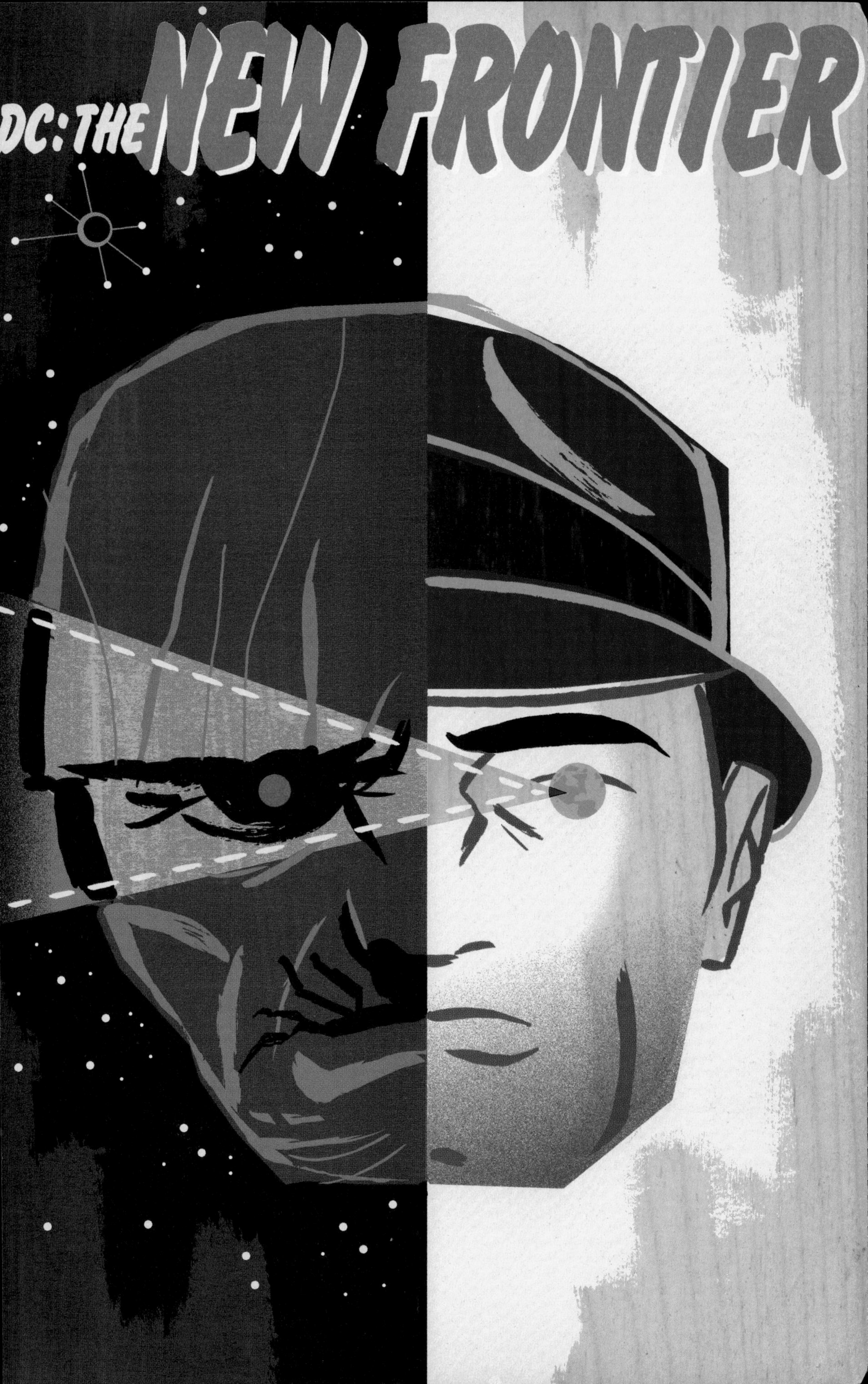
DC: THE NEW FRONTIER

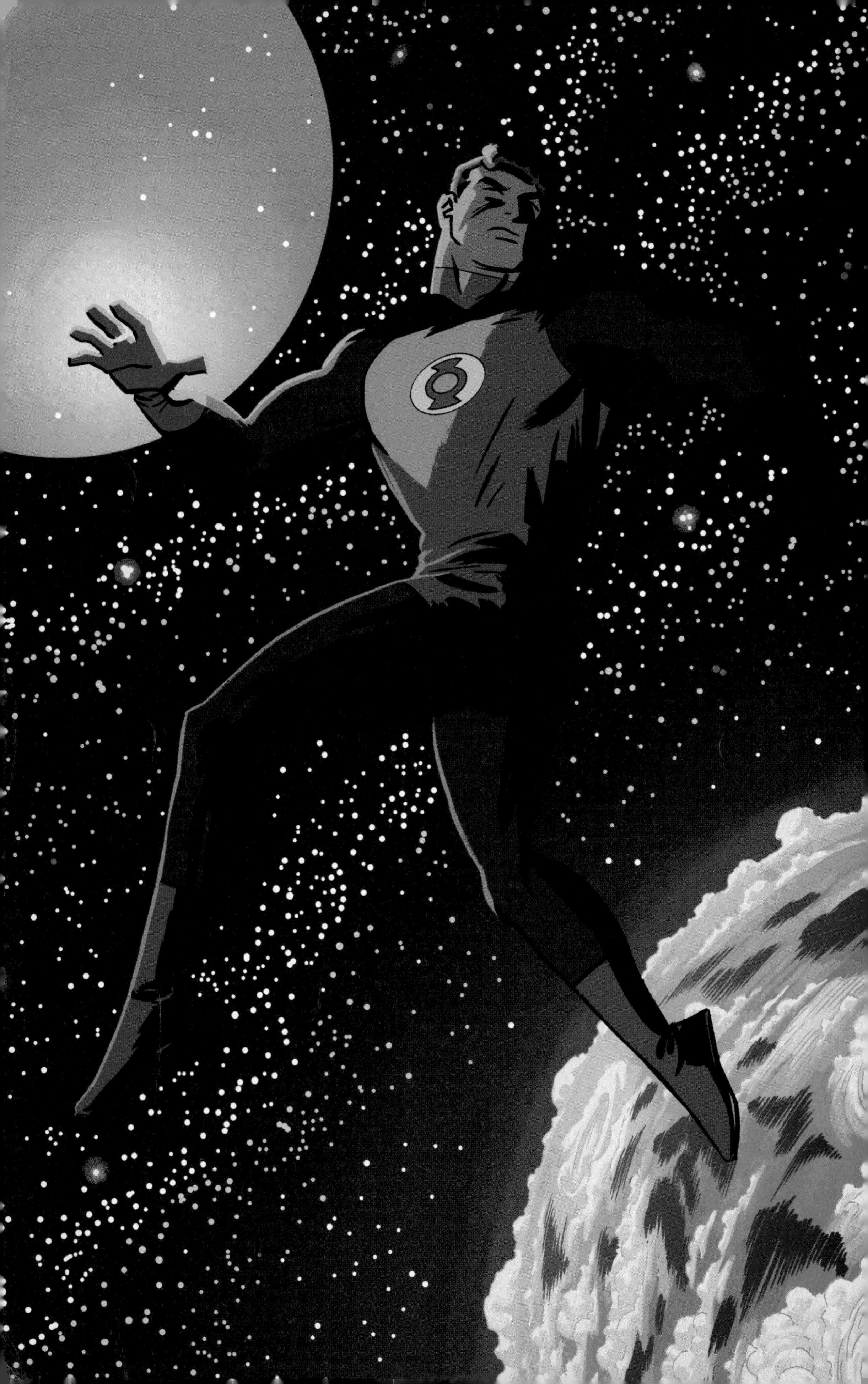

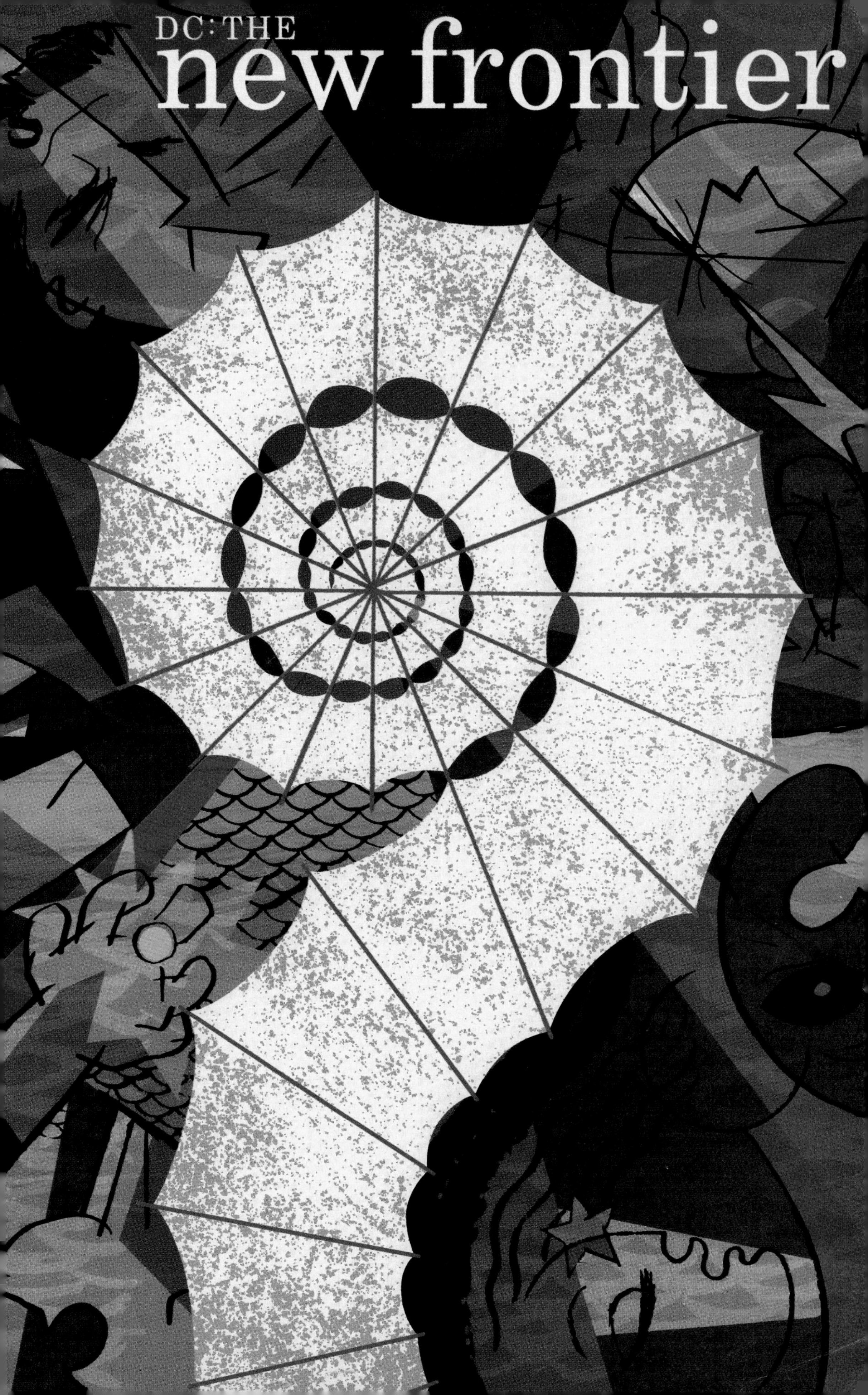
DC: THE
new frontier

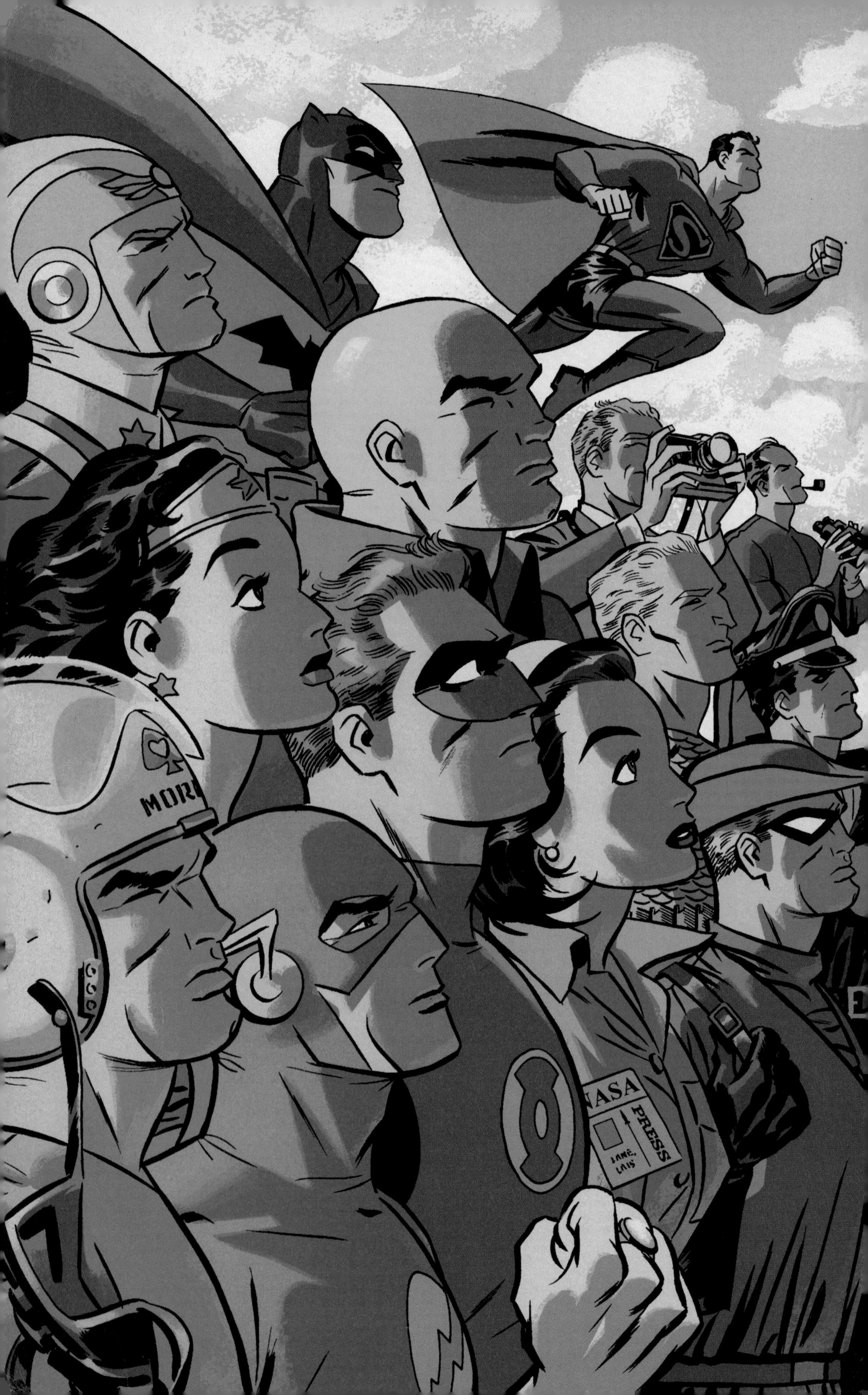
NASA
PRESS

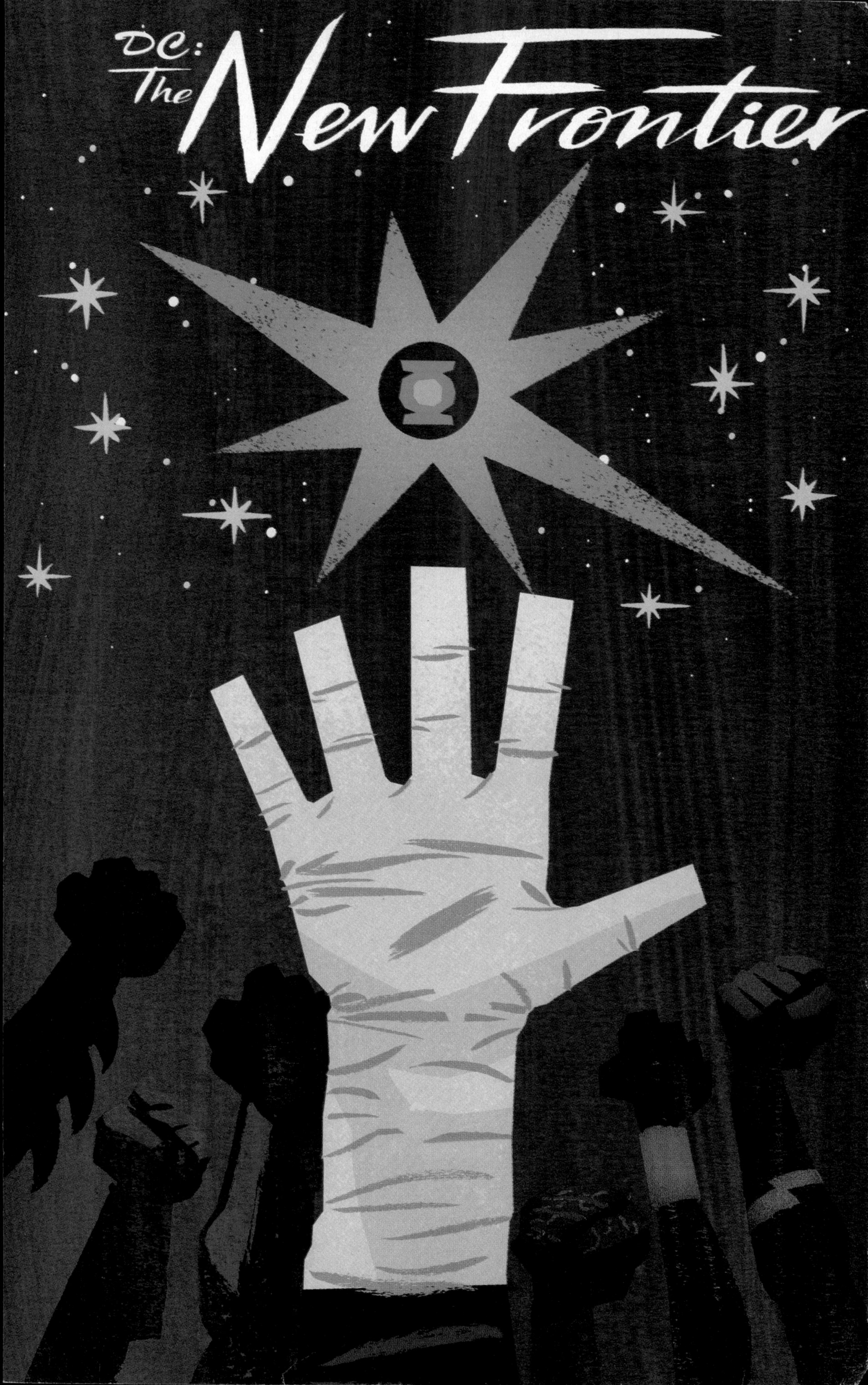
DC:
The
New Frontier

AFTERWORD

It occurs to me as I attempt to type this obligatory comment on such a large and fresh piece of work that it is probably a little soon for any kind of objective analysis of the work itself.

As a matter of course, I prefer to avoid explaining what a piece like this "means." Depending on your "in" to the story, it could be seen as a love letter to a bygone era, or an allegorical reflection of contemporary concerns. Big shoot-'em-up with a giant monster or character-driven historical melodrama. The choice, as always, should belong with the reader.

Whether NEW FRONTIER heralds a return to the heroic ideal or is simply a reminder that it existed remains to be seen. I'd like to abandon the rather cramped quarters of industry discussion or literary self-analysis and try to explain the spirit of this book through a quick story.

Dave Thomas was the genial Buffalo television personality that portrayed WKBW's Astronaut host of their weekday morning kid's show, *Rocketship* 7. Set in an imaginary rocketship, the lively 90 minute show featured skits, news and tips for kids, the obligatory visits from magicians and zookeepers and glorious uncut Warner Bros. cartoons. On Fridays, *Rocketship* 7 had a weekly feature called Draw Along With the Scope-View.

This was the late sixties and the world was astro-crazed. *Rocketship* 7 did its low budget best to put across to its young viewers that this was really unfolding on a hi-tech space vehicle. Devices like the Scope-View went a long way towards convincing us. The Scope-View was essentially an old school wall-mounted bluescreen for viewing clips and photos, but on Fridays, they would have a fairly talented artist sit behind the screen, and on a very thin piece of paper, he would draw a picture with a thick marker. The illusion was perfect. From the front, The Scope-View seemed to be drawing the picture like some futuristic…machine or something!

The challenge was to draw along with the Scope-View and try to do your best. Those Friday mornings I would perch in my chair, pencil at the ready, in a world where anything was possible. A world of magic televisions in space, sunny mornings full of promise, and my drawing.

And before anyone gets up to leave before speech 12,367 about how those were better days, relax. It wasn't the times, or the place, or the cultural comforts of the era. It was something you can find anywhere, at any time. It was the earnest faith of youth.

Inevitably, I grew older and one day realized the Scope-View was an elaborate scam, a parlor trick that only a kid would fall for. It didn't cause me to write in to the station and demand more realistic drawing lessons involving more serious themes. I didn't run around trying to tell people that the Scope-View had artistic merit that only a select few were sensitive enough to divine. I simply sought out more detailed and realistic instruction. My youngest brother is several years my junior. When he began to sit on Fridays, pencil in hand, I felt no need to ridicule the Scope-View or change it to fit my more "adult" taste. I wanted him to take that little scrap of magic forward with him, as I had.

The Scope-View wasn't real. It was an imaginative fiction that was better than real, constructed to help you, in some small way, to develop your own youthful imagination, just like Astronaut Dave was there to help us learn the Golden Rule.

Which brings us around to super-heroes. Specifically, the Justice League. The world will always have dark corners, and black and white comes in thousands of shades of grey, but here are seven people, good and true, come what may. They have the power to enslave the world, but work tirelessly to keep it free. They don't succumb to envy, greed or jealousy, and their sense of purpose is driven by an unshakable faith in mankind's basic good. They are, in the best sense of the word, childlike. It is the very essence of the term Super-hero. An imaginative fiction that is better than real, constructed to help you, in some small way, to develop your own youthful imagination and value system.

I'm 42 now, and I suppose that I believe that the magic of this specific genre is based on the notion that seven powerful people can work together to make the world a better place. That they will do the right thing no matter what the personal cost, no matter how "grim and gritty" the world around them becomes. They are the heroic ideal. That is the spirit driving the characters in the New Frontier.

Like my beloved Scope-View, I suppose only a child could buy into such a ridiculous premise. But once it's in your heart, you can't help but take that little scrap of magic forward with you.

Darwyn Cooke
Toronto, 2005

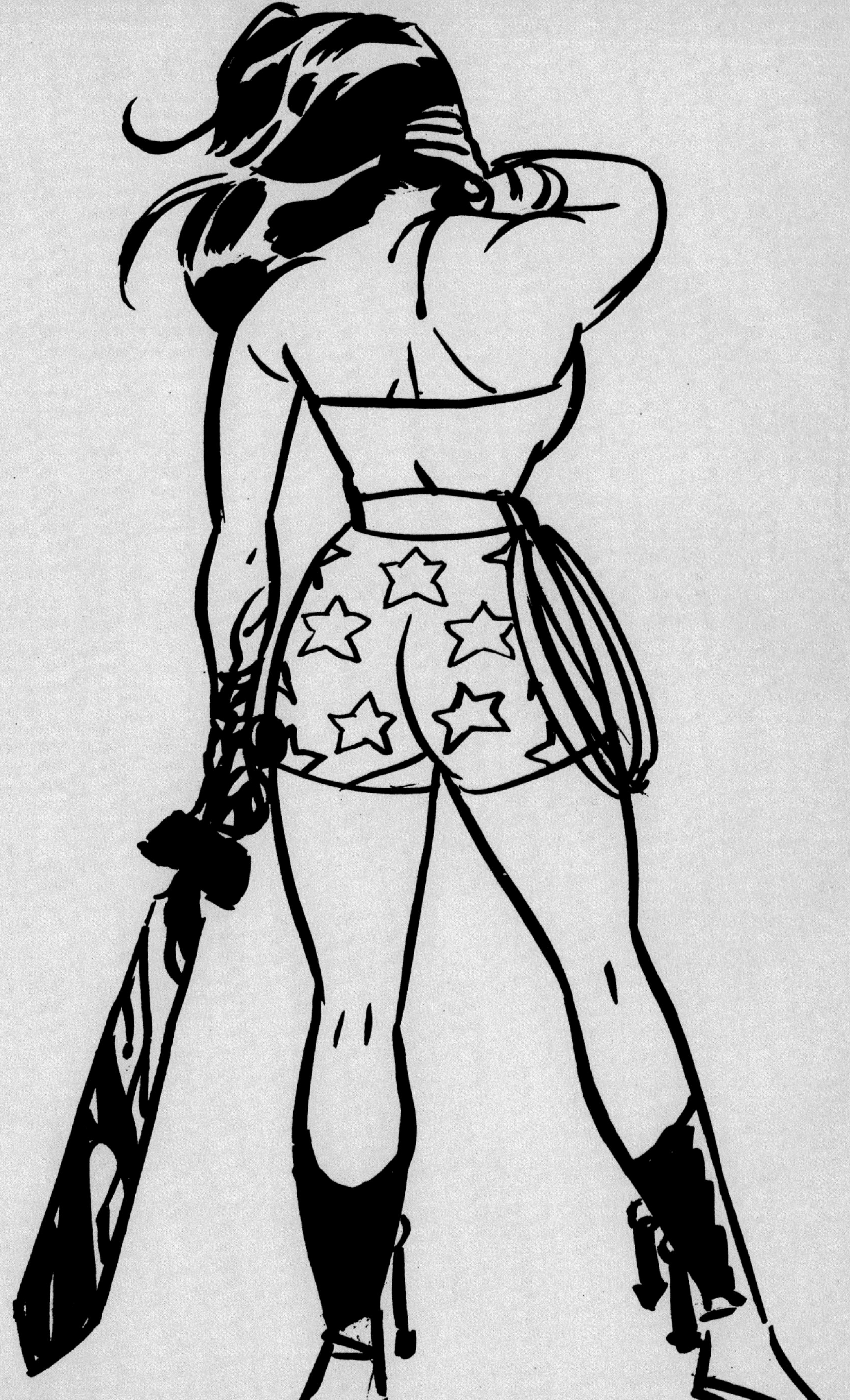

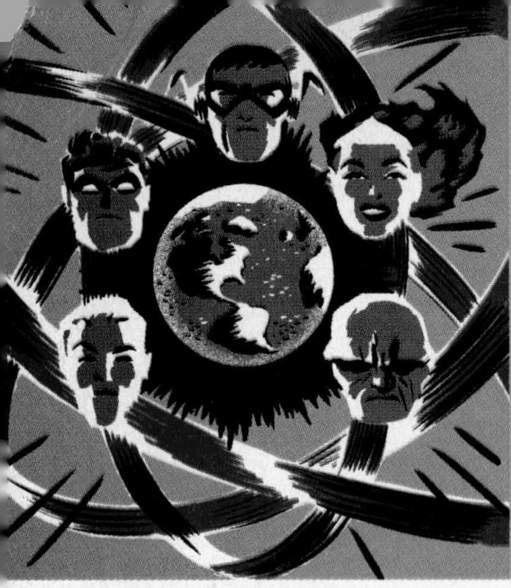

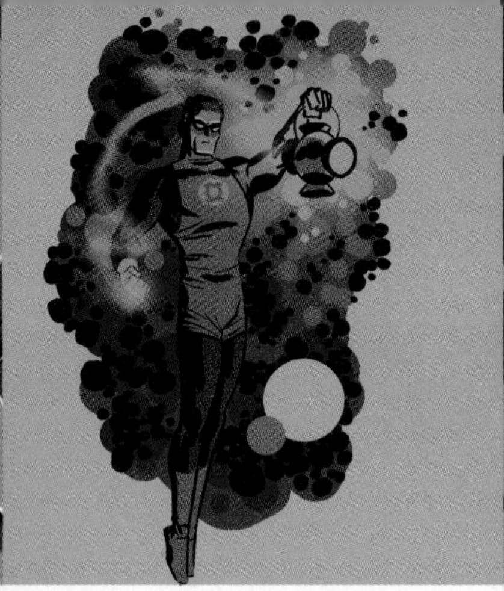

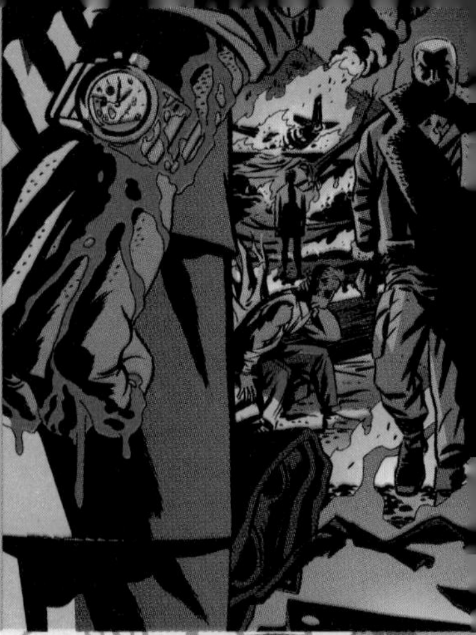

UNPUBLISHED

Various cover concepts and development art created between 1999 and 2004.

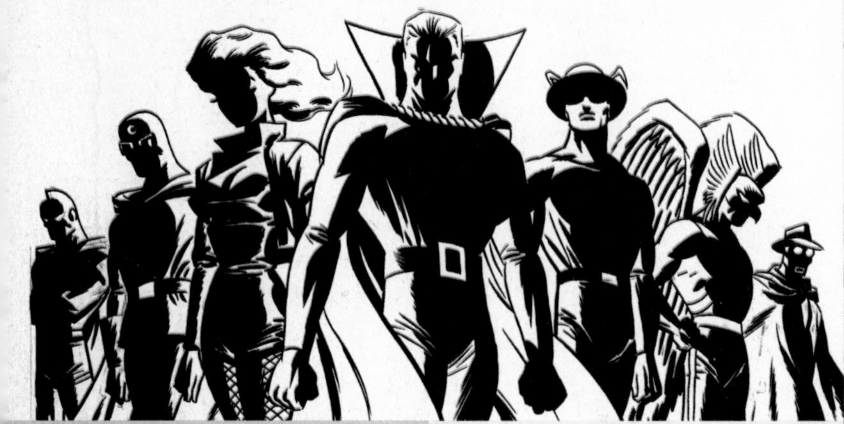

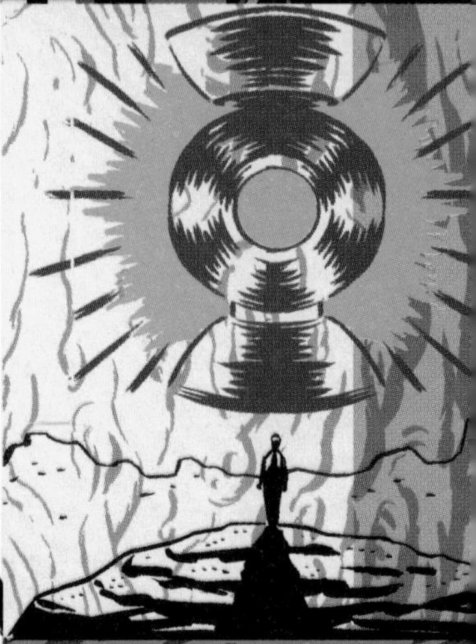

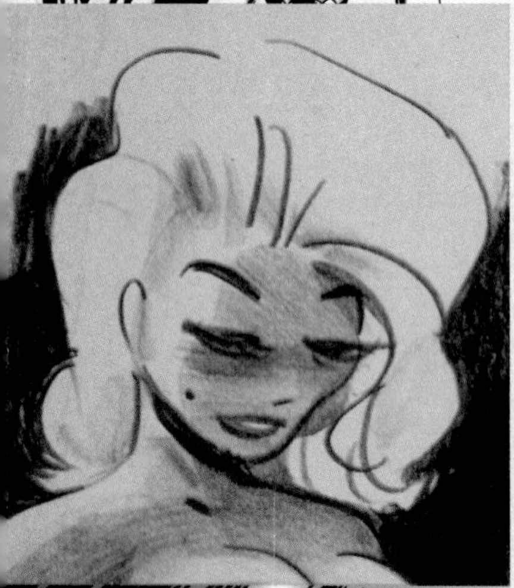

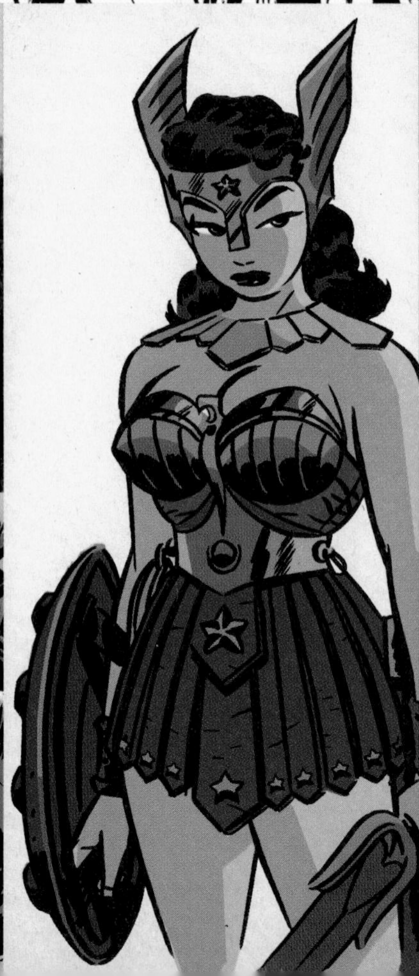

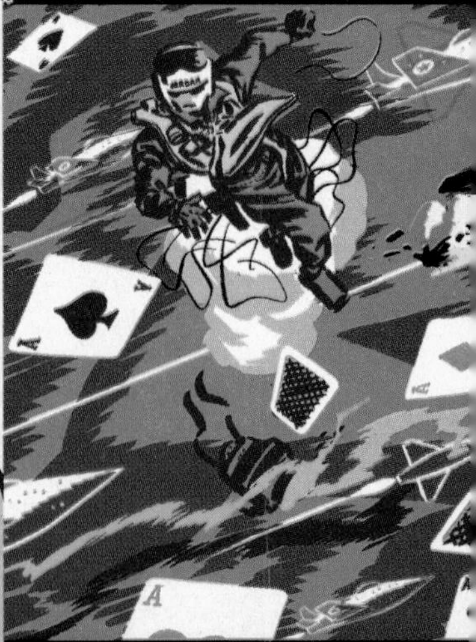

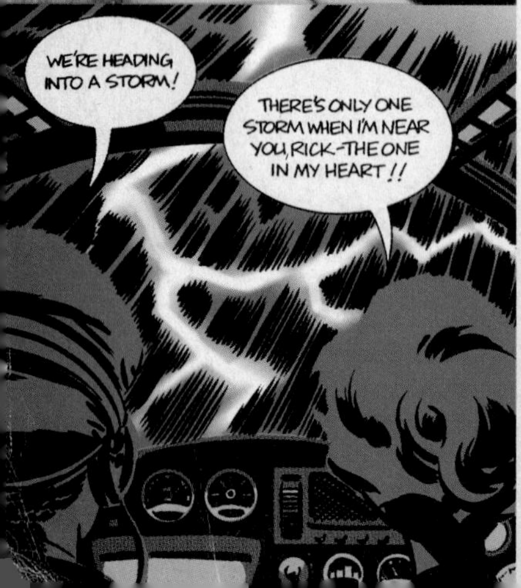
WE'RE HEADING INTO A STORM!
THERE'S ONLY ONE STORM WHEN I'M NEAR YOU, RICK-THE ONE IN MY HEART!!

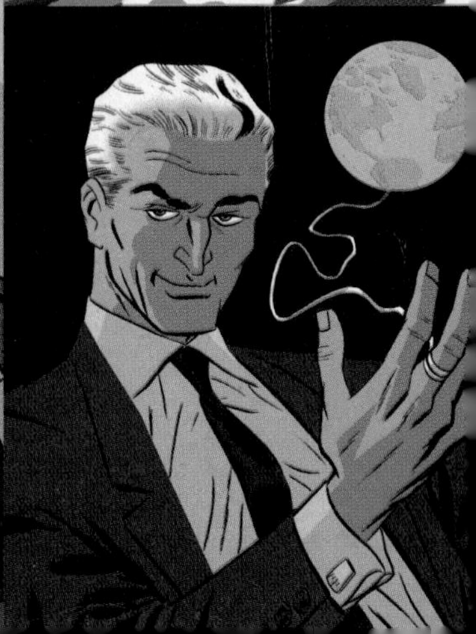

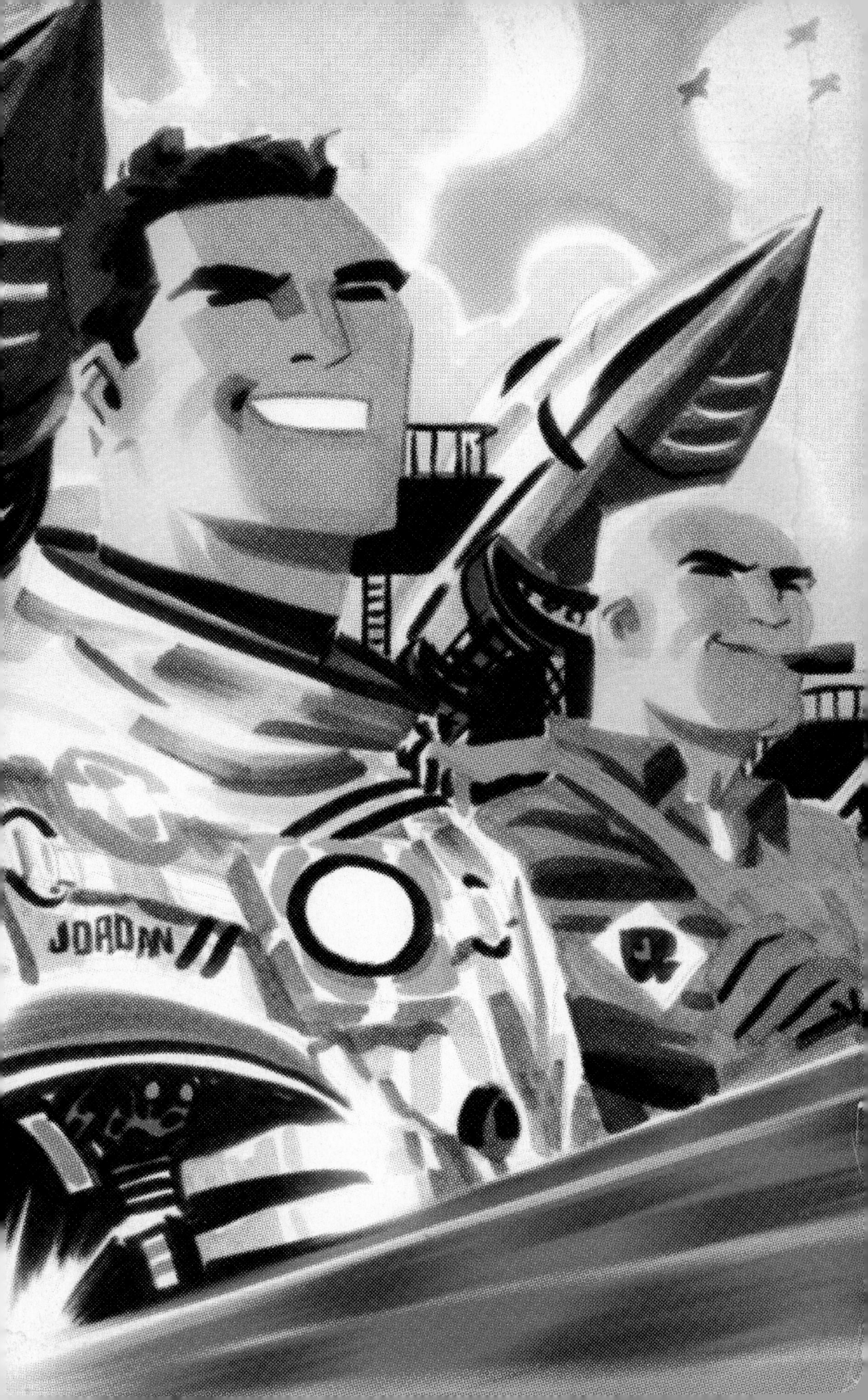

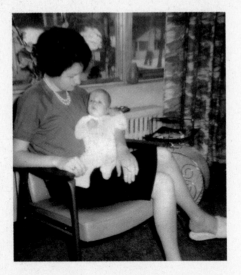

ACKNOWLEDGMENTS

It would take months to compile a list of everyone who contributed to the genesis of NEW FRONTIER. Perhaps in a future edition. For now, a tip of the helmet to acknowledge the efforts of my assistant on NEW FRONTIER, Christopher Stone, and the inking assist of my dear friend J. Bone. My heartfelt thanks also go out to my partners on NEW FRONTIER, letterer Jared Fletcher, colour artist Dave Stewart and my friend Mark Chiarello, editor extraordinaire. They are the industry's best, and I am forever in their debt.

Above all others, I would like to thank my Mom. Her love, determination and strength set a powerful example for me, and gave me the spirit to climb this mountain.